Yuto Tsukuda

...rd that in the French ...dition of the *Michelin* ...another Japanese chef ...received their second star. This chef is only the second Japanese chef in all of France to manage that feat. Quite amazing. I can only imagine how much effort and grit it must have taken. My hat is off to you, Chef.

Shun Saeki

It's been a while since I last had a ferret pic here. They're as friendly as always.

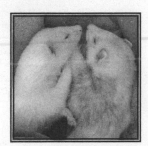

About the authors

Yuto Tsukuda won the 34th Jump Juniketsu Newcomers' Manga Award for his one-shot story *Kiba ni Naru*. He made his *Weekly Shonen Jump* debut in 2010 with the series *Shonen Shikku*. His follow-up series, *Food Wars!: Shokugeki no Soma*, is his first English-language release.

Shun Saeki made his *Jump NEXT!* debut in 2011 with the one-shot story *Kimi to Watashi no Renai Soudan*. *Food Wars!: Shokugeki no Soma* is his first *Shonen Jump* series.

Food Wars!

SHOKUGEKI NO SOMA

Volume 24
Shonen Jump Advanced Manga Edition
Story by Yuto Tsukuda, Art by Shun Saeki
Contributor Yuki Morisaki

Translation: Adrienne Beck
Touch-Up Art & Lettering: James Gaubatz, Mara Coman
Design: Alice Lewis
Editor: Jennifer LeBlanc

SHOKUGEKI NO SOMA © 2012 by Yuto Tsukuda, Shun Saeki
All rights reserved.
First published in Japan in 2012 by SHUEISHA Inc., Tokyo.
English translation rights arranged by SHUEISHA Inc.

The stories, characters and incidents mentioned in this publication
are entirely fictional.

Printed in the U.S.A.

Published by VIZ Media, LLC
P.O. Box 77010
San Francisco, CA 94107

10 9 8 7 6 5 4 3 2 1
First printing, June 2018

viz.com   shonenjump.com

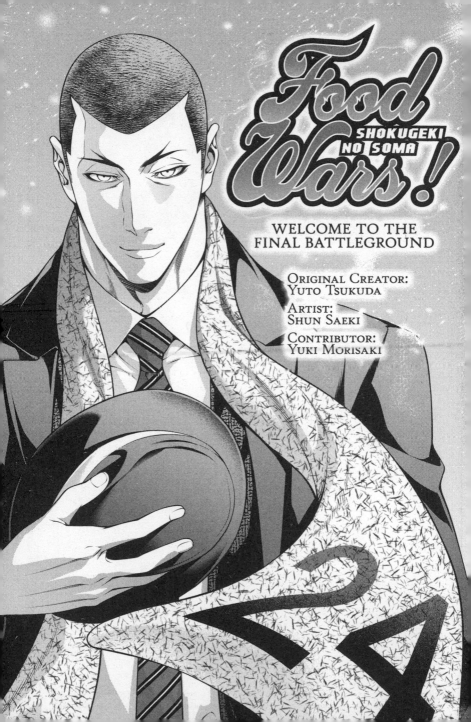

Food Wars!

SHOKUGEKI NO SOMA

WELCOME TO THE FINAL BATTLEGROUND

ORIGINAL CREATOR:
Yuto Tsukuda

ARTIST:
Shun Saeki

CONTRIBUTOR:
Yuki Morisaki

CHARACTERS

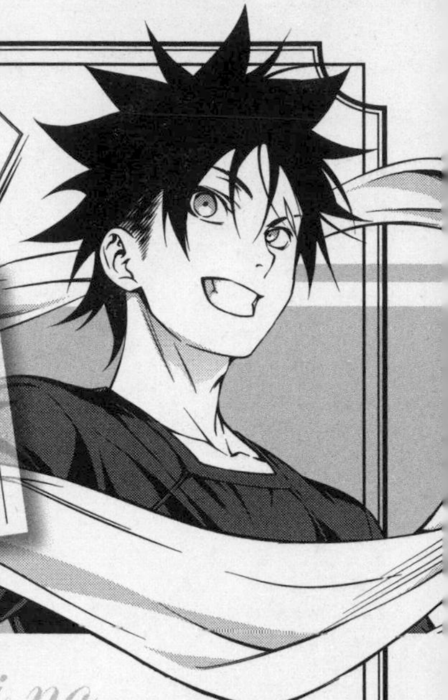

SOMA YUKIHIRA First Year High School

Helping out at his family's restaurant since he was little, Soma trained as a chef with the goal of someday surpassing his father. Out of junior high, he's suddenly sent off to culinary school. He's skilled, but sometimes invents questionable new recipes.

Shokugeki no SOMA

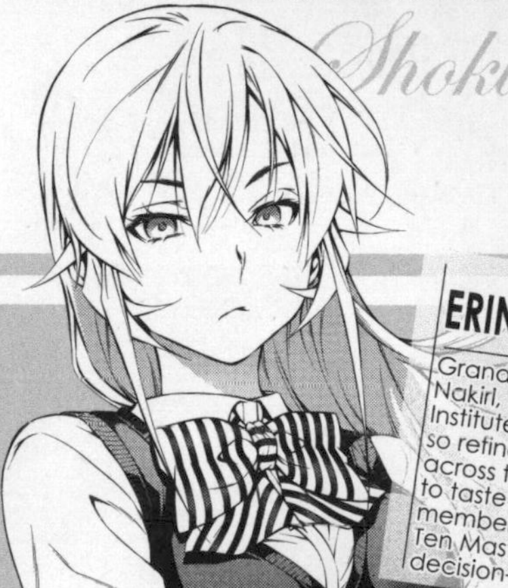

ERINA NAKIRI First Year High School

Granddaughter of Senzaemon Nakiri, former dean of the Totsuki Institute, she has a sense of taste so refined, famous restaurants across the nation come to her to taste test their dishes. She is a member of Totsuki's Council of Ten Masters, the institute's highest decision-making student body.

STORY

Soma grew up helping to cook at his family's restaurant, Yukihira. But one day his father enrolls him in Japan's premier culinary school, the Totsuki Institute. Having met other students as skilled as he is and with similar goals, Soma has grown a little as a chef.

During stage three of the advancement exams, Soma faces off against new Council of Ten ninth seat Akira Hayama in a bear-meat shokugeki. Hayama, who only agreed to join Central as a way to save the Shiomi Seminar, makes Southern-fried bear, earning rave reviews from the three judges. Burning with a desire for payback over his loss in the Fall Classic, Soma pours everything he has into his dish, a bear menchi-katsu hamburger steak. Will he emerge the victor? And what of the other resistance members' battles with the council?

Shokugeki no SOMA

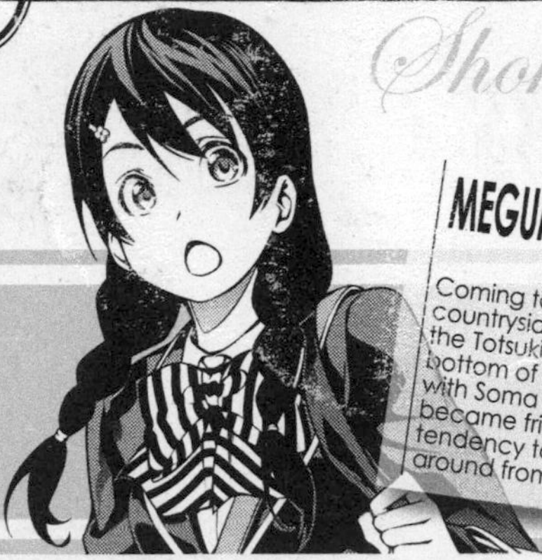

MEGUMI TADOKORO First Year High School

Coming to the big city from the countryside, Megumi made it into the Totsuki Institute at the very bottom of the rankings. Partnered with Soma in their first class, the two became friends. However, he has a tendency to inadvertently yank her around from time to time.

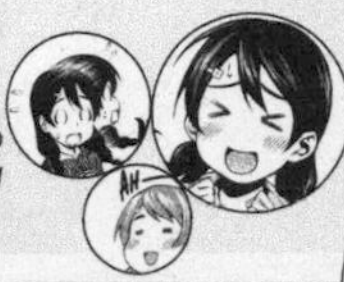
AH

TAKUMI ALDINI First Year High School

Working at his family's trattoria in Italy from a young age, he transferred into the Totsuki Institute in junior high. Isami is his younger twin brother.

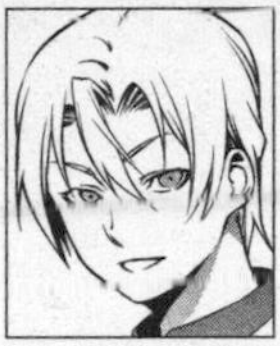

AKIRA HAYAMA First Year High School

With his inhumanly sharp sense of smell, he's a master of manipulating fragrance. He joined Central to save the Shiomi Seminar but was redeemed after losing to Soma.

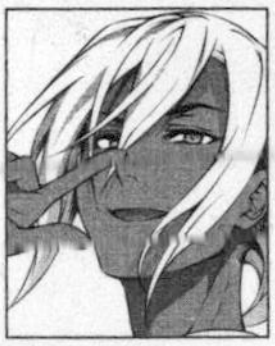

JOICHIRO YUKIHIRA

Soma's father, he owns and runs Yukihira Family Restaurant. A former Totsuki student, he was once the second seat on the Council of Ten.

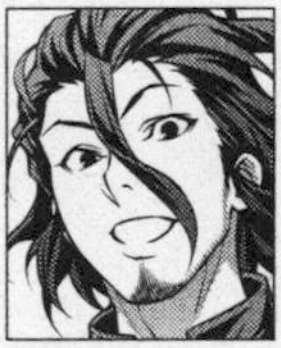

GIN DOJIMA

Head chef and company director of Totsuki Resort Hotels, he is Joichiro's old classmate and a former first seat on the Council of Ten.

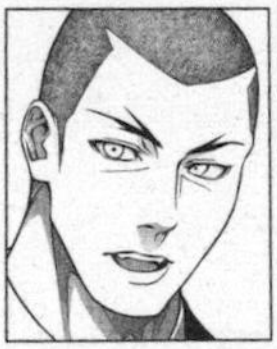

EISHI TSUKASA Third Year High School

The current first seat on Totsuki's Council of Ten. He comes off as meek and weak-willed at first, but he has absolute confidence in his skills as a chef.

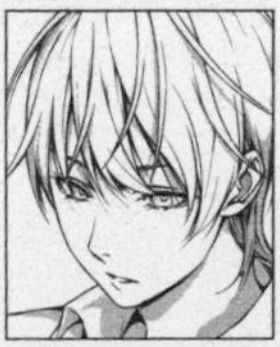

AZAMI NAKIRI

Erina's father, he convinced over half the Council of Ten to back him in staging a coup to take control of the institute, forcing former dean Senzaemon Nakiri into retirement.

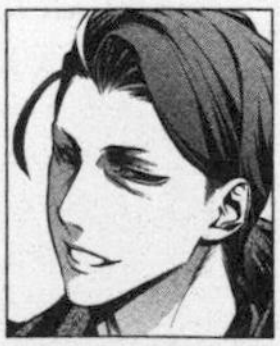

Food Wars! Shokugeki no Soma 24

Table of Contents

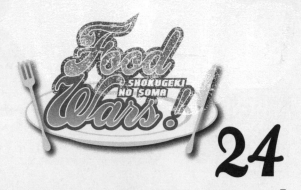

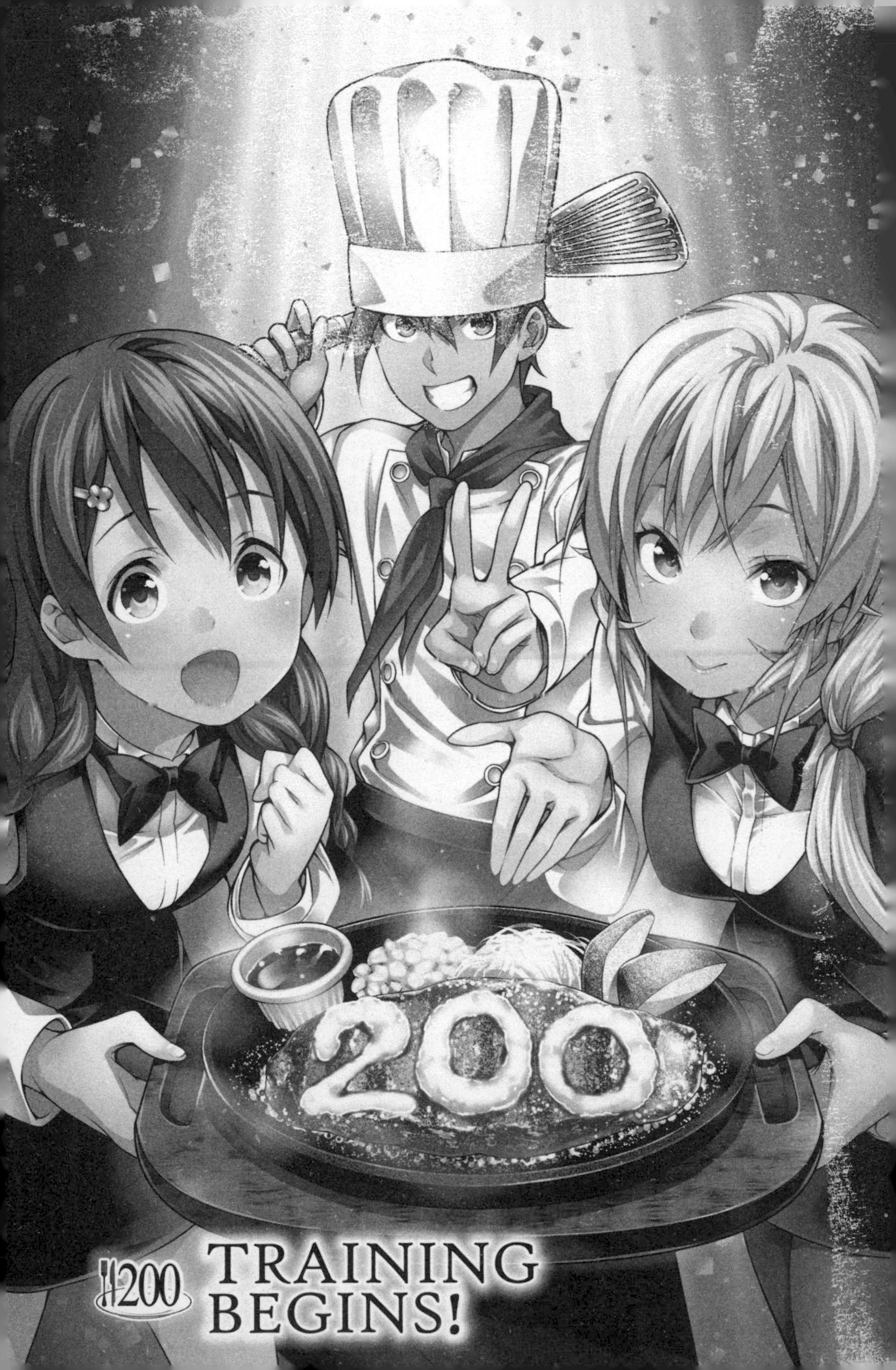
200

200 TRAINING BEGINS!

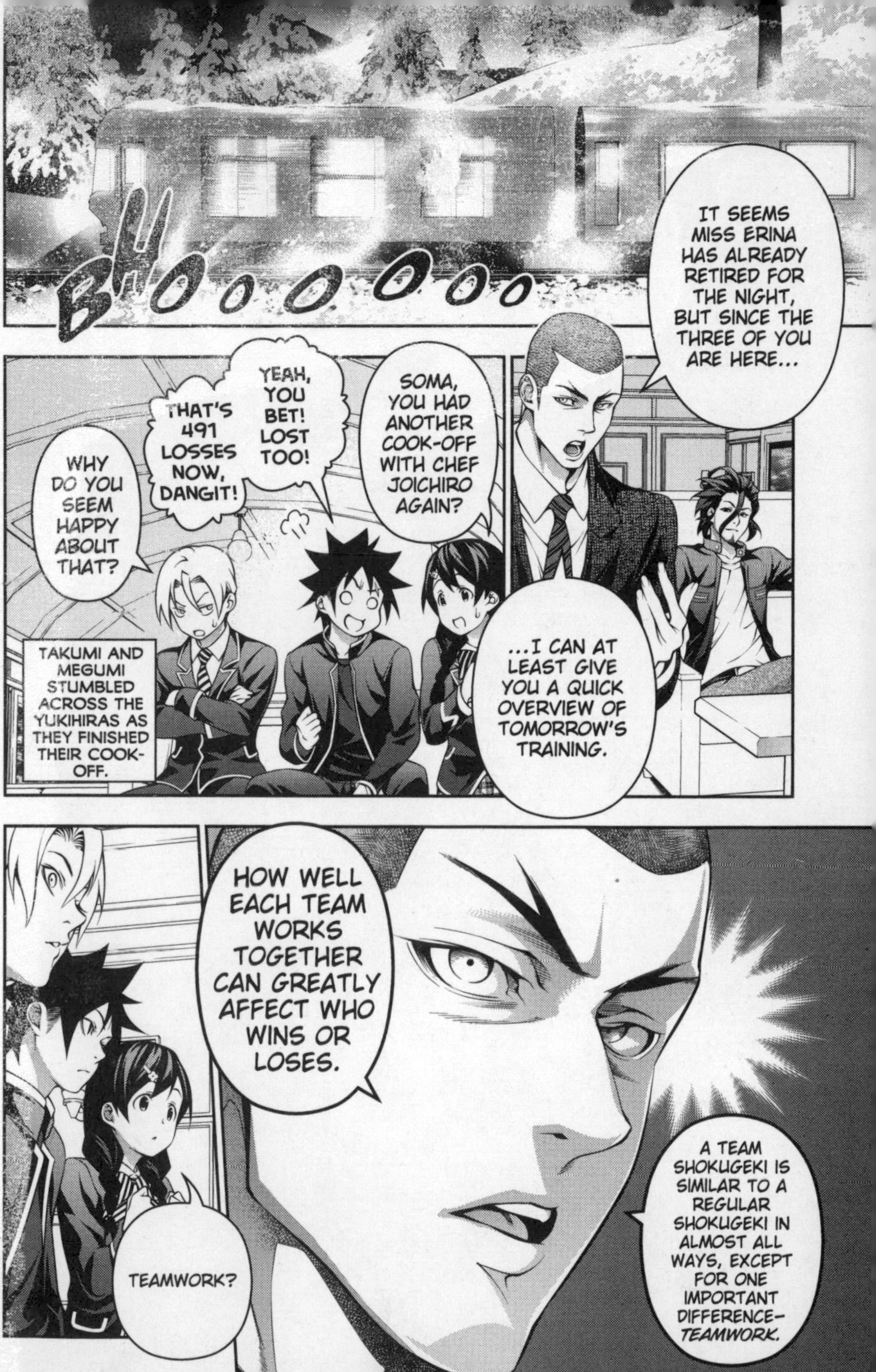
BHOOOOOOO
IT SEEMS MISS ERINA HAS ALREADY RETIRED FOR THE NIGHT, BUT SINCE THE THREE OF YOU ARE HERE...
...I CAN AT LEAST GIVE YOU A QUICK OVERVIEW OF TOMORROW'S TRAINING.
SOMA, YOU HAD ANOTHER COOK-OFF WITH CHEF JOICHIRO AGAIN?
YEAH, YOU BET! LOST TOO!
THAT'S 491 LOSSES NOW, DANGIT!
WHY DO YOU SEEM HAPPY ABOUT THAT?
TAKUMI AND MEGUMI STUMBLED ACROSS THE YUKIHIRAS AS THEY FINISHED THEIR COOK-OFF.
A TEAM SHOKUGEKI IS SIMILAR TO A REGULAR SHOKUGEKI IN ALMOST ALL WAYS, EXCEPT FOR ONE IMPORTANT DIFFERENCE—*TEAMWORK.*
TEAMWORK?
HOW WELL EACH TEAM WORKS TOGETHER CAN GREATLY AFFECT WHO WINS OR LOSES.

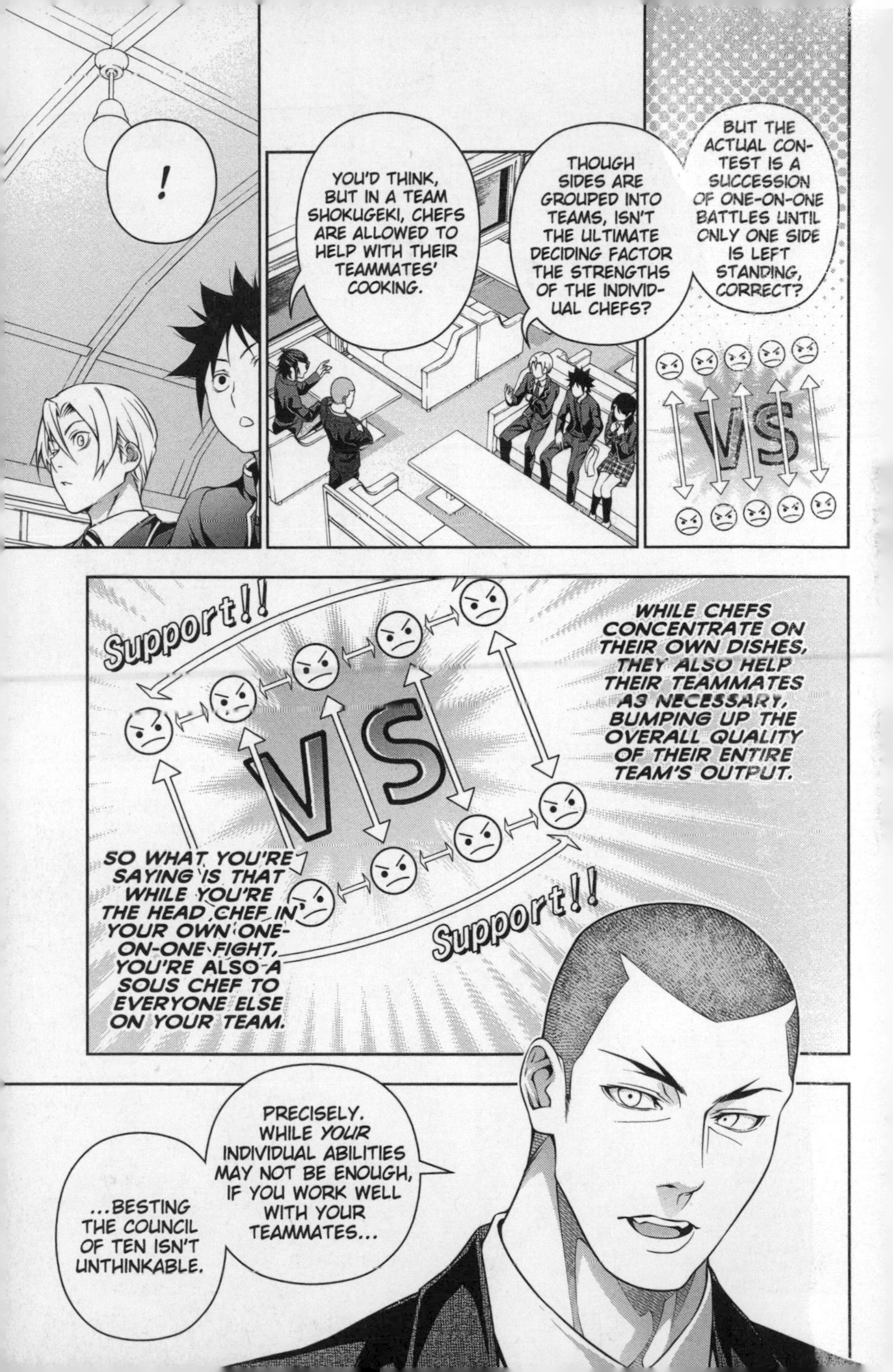
!
THOUGH SIDES ARE GROUPED INTO TEAMS, ISN'T THE ULTIMATE DECIDING FACTOR THE STRENGTHS OF THE INDIVIDUAL CHEFS?
BUT THE ACTUAL CONTEST IS A SUCCESSION OF ONE-ON-ONE BATTLES UNTIL ONLY ONE SIDE IS LEFT STANDING, CORRECT?
VS
YOU'D THINK, BUT IN A TEAM SHOKUGEKI, CHEFS ARE ALLOWED TO HELP WITH THEIR TEAMMATES' COOKING.
WHILE CHEFS CONCENTRATE ON THEIR OWN DISHES, THEY ALSO HELP THEIR TEAMMATES AS NECESSARY, BUMPING UP THE OVERALL QUALITY OF THEIR ENTIRE TEAM'S OUTPUT.
Support!!
VS
Support!!
SO WHAT YOU'RE SAYING IS THAT WHILE YOU'RE THE HEAD CHEF IN YOUR OWN ONE-ON-ONE FIGHT, YOU'RE ALSO A SOUS CHEF TO EVERYONE ELSE ON YOUR TEAM.
PRECISELY. WHILE *YOUR* INDIVIDUAL ABILITIES MAY NOT BE ENOUGH, IF YOU WORK WELL WITH YOUR TEAMMATES...
...BESTING THE COUNCIL OF TEN ISN'T UNTHINKABLE.

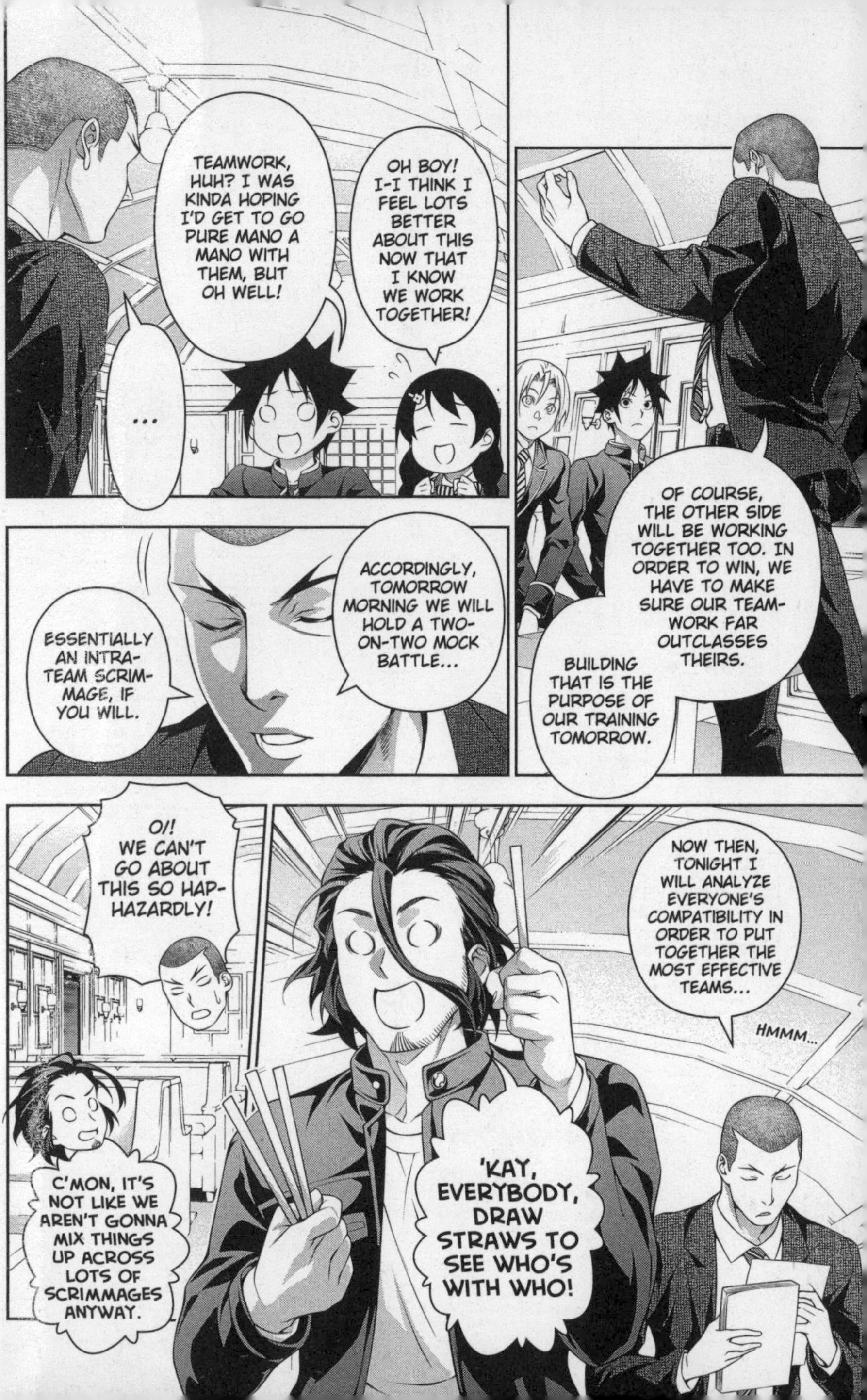
TEAMWORK, HUH? I WAS KINDA HOPING I'D GET TO GO PURE MANO A MANO WITH THEM, BUT OH WELL!
OH BOY! I-I THINK I FEEL LOTS BETTER ABOUT THIS NOW THAT I KNOW WE WORK TOGETHER!
...
OF COURSE, THE OTHER SIDE WILL BE WORKING TOGETHER TOO. IN ORDER TO WIN, WE HAVE TO MAKE SURE OUR TEAM-WORK FAR OUTCLASSES THEIRS.
BUILDING THAT IS THE PURPOSE OF OUR TRAINING TOMORROW.
ACCORDINGLY, TOMORROW MORNING WE WILL HOLD A TWO-ON-TWO MOCK BATTLE...
ESSENTIALLY AN INTRA-TEAM SCRIM-MAGE, IF YOU WILL.
NOW THEN, TONIGHT I WILL ANALYZE EVERYONE'S COMPATIBILITY IN ORDER TO PUT TOGETHER THE MOST EFFECTIVE TEAMS...
HMMM...
OI! WE CAN'T GO ABOUT THIS SO HAP-HAZARDLY!
'KAY, EVERYBODY, DRAW STRAWS TO SEE WHO'S WITH WHO!
C'MON, IT'S NOT LIKE WE AREN'T GONNA MIX THINGS UP ACROSS LOTS OF SCRIMMAGES ANYWAY.

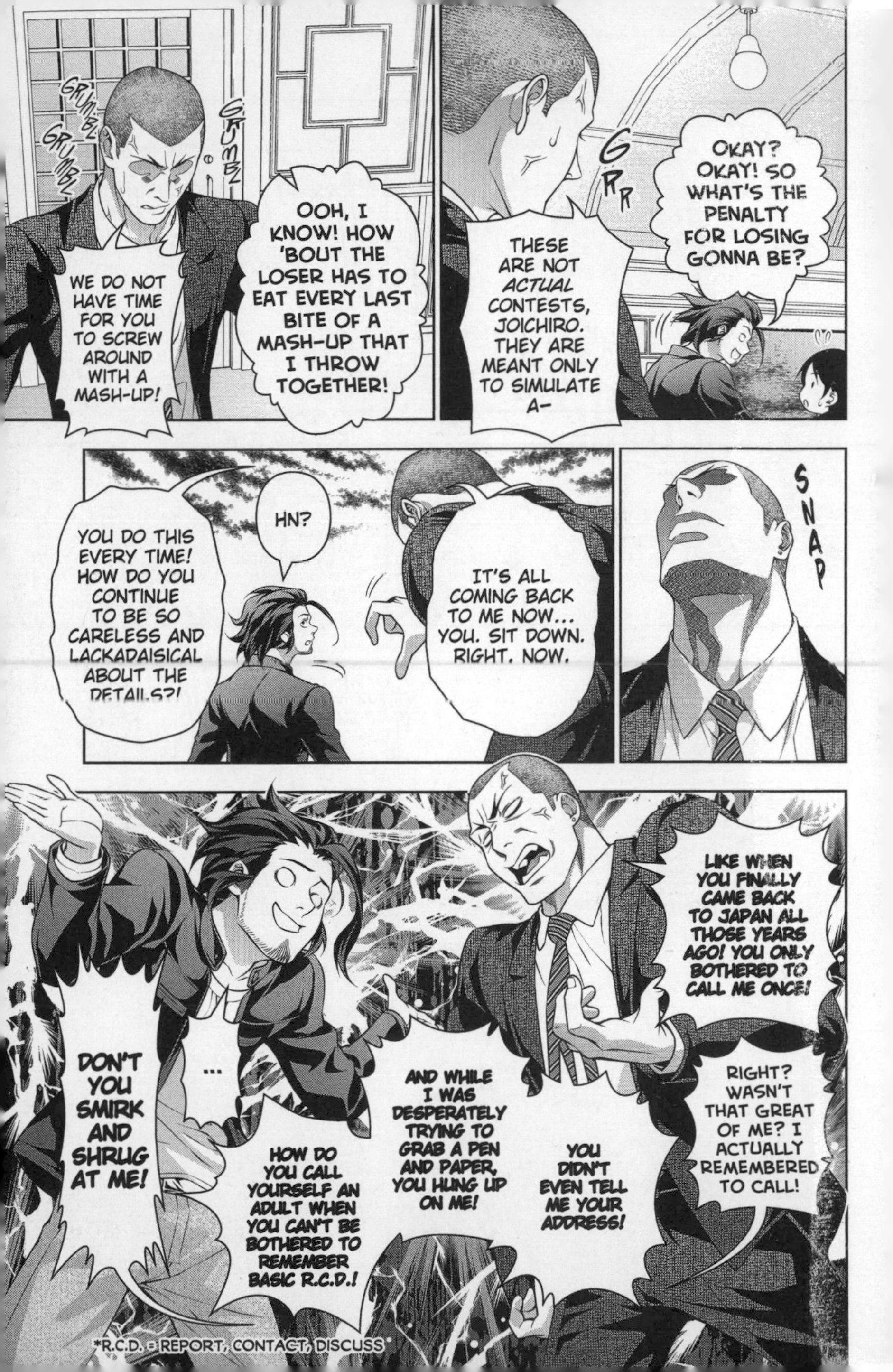
OKAY? OKAY! SO WHAT'S THE PENALTY FOR LOSING GONNA BE?
GRR
THESE ARE NOT *ACTUAL* CONTESTS, JOICHIRO. THEY ARE MEANT ONLY TO SIMULATE A–
OOH, I KNOW! HOW 'BOUT THE LOSER HAS TO EAT EVERY LAST BITE OF A MASH-UP THAT I THROW TOGETHER!
GRUMBL
GRUMBL GRUMBL
WE DO NOT HAVE TIME FOR YOU TO SCREW AROUND WITH A MASH-UP!
SNAP
IT'S ALL COMING BACK TO ME NOW... YOU. SIT DOWN. RIGHT. NOW.
HN?
YOU DO THIS EVERY TIME! HOW DO YOU CONTINUE TO BE SO CARELESS AND LACKADAISICAL ABOUT THE DETAILS?!
LIKE WHEN YOU FINALLY CAME BACK TO JAPAN ALL THOSE YEARS AGO! YOU ONLY BOTHERED TO CALL ME ONCE!
RIGHT? WASN'T THAT GREAT OF ME? I ACTUALLY REMEMBERED TO CALL!
YOU DIDN'T EVEN TELL ME YOUR ADDRESS!
AND WHILE I WAS DESPERATELY TRYING TO GRAB A PEN AND PAPER, YOU HUNG UP ON ME!
HOW DO YOU CALL YOURSELF AN ADULT WHEN YOU CAN'T BE BOTHERED TO REMEMBER BASIC R.C.D.!
...
DON'T YOU SMIRK AND SHRUG AT ME!
*R.C.D. = REPORT, CONTACT, DISCUSS

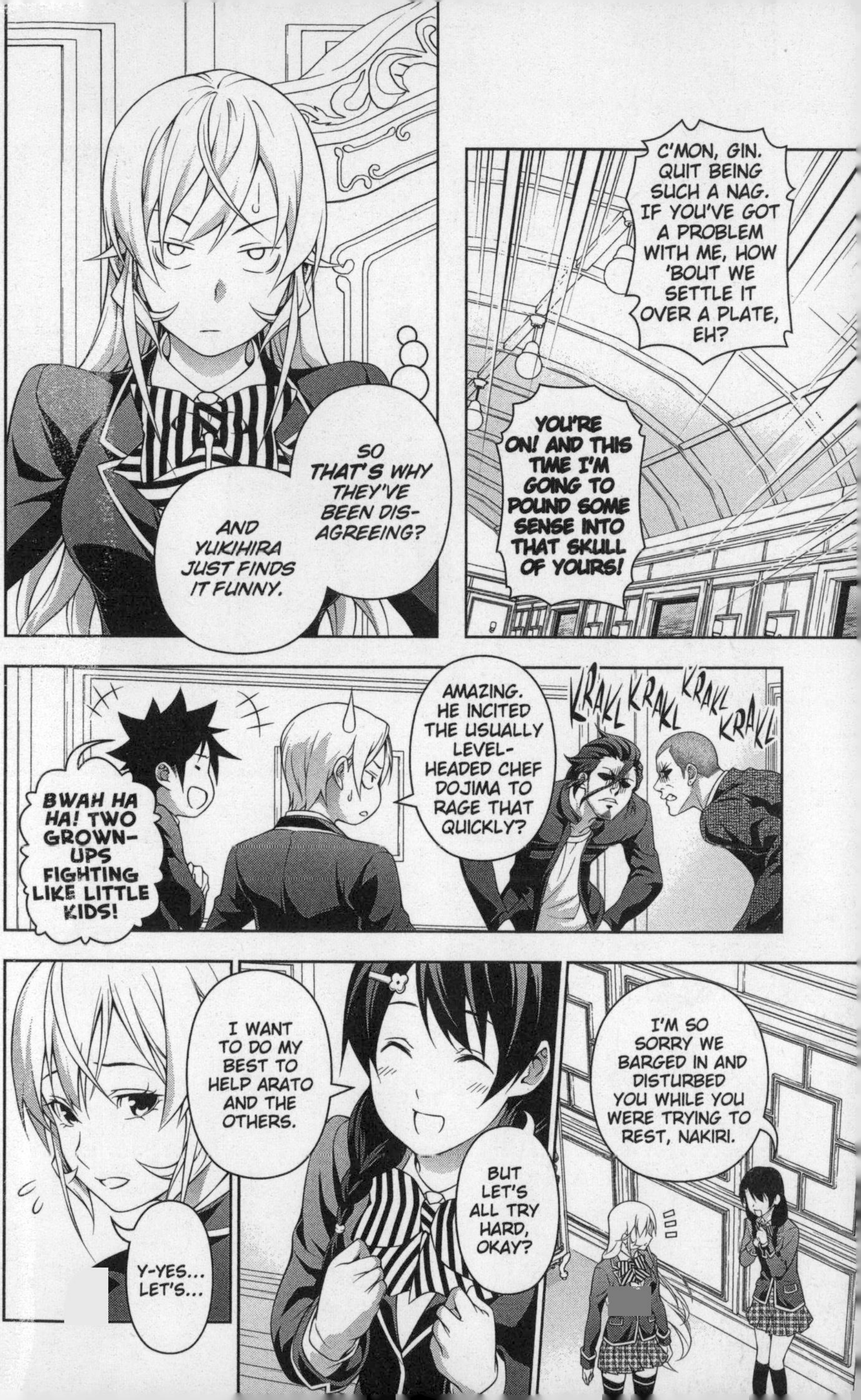
C'MON, GIN. QUIT BEING SUCH A NAG. IF YOU'VE GOT A PROBLEM WITH ME, HOW 'BOUT WE SETTLE IT OVER A PLATE, EH?
YOU'RE ON! AND THIS TIME I'M GOING TO POUND SOME SENSE INTO THAT SKULL OF YOURS!
SO THAT'S WHY THEY'VE BEEN DIS-AGREEING?
AND YUKIHIRA JUST FINDS IT FUNNY.
KRAKL KRAKL KRAKL KRAKL
AMAZING. HE INCITED THE USUALLY LEVEL-HEADED CHEF DOJIMA TO RAGE THAT QUICKLY?
BWAH HA HA! TWO GROWN-UPS FIGHTING LIKE LITTLE KIDS!
I'M SO SORRY WE BARGED IN AND DISTURBED YOU WHILE YOU WERE TRYING TO REST, NAKIRI.
I WANT TO DO MY BEST TO HELP ARATO AND THE OTHERS.
BUT LET'S ALL TRY HARD, OKAY?
Y-YES... LET'S...

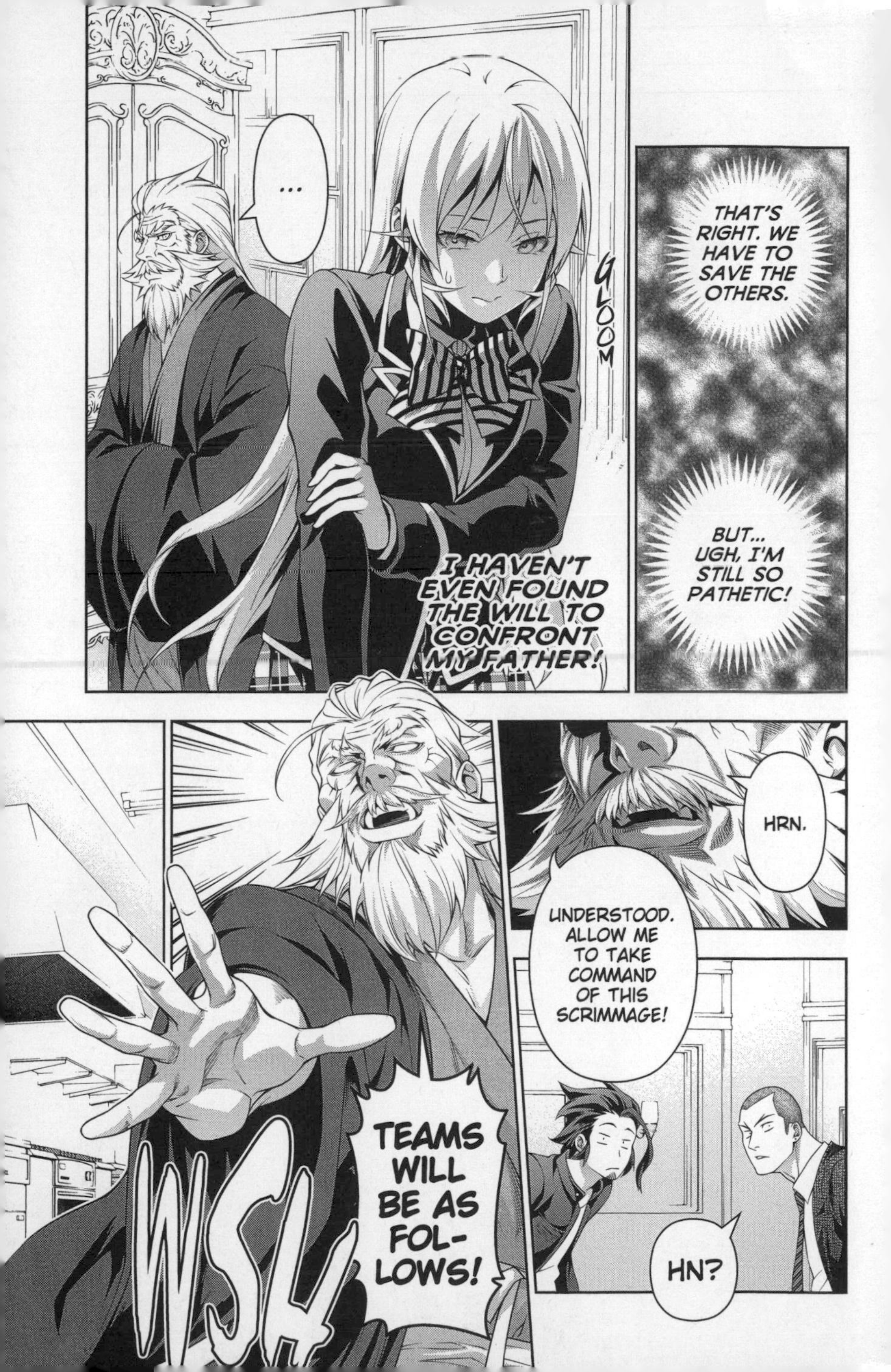

THAT'S RIGHT. WE HAVE TO SAVE THE OTHERS.
BUT... UGH, I'M STILL SO PATHETIC!
...
GLOOM
I HAVEN'T EVEN FOUND THE WILL TO CONFRONT MY FATHER!
HRN.
UNDERSTOOD. ALLOW ME TO TAKE COMMAND OF THIS SCRIMMAGE!
HN?
TEAMS WILL BE AS FOL-LOWS!
WSH

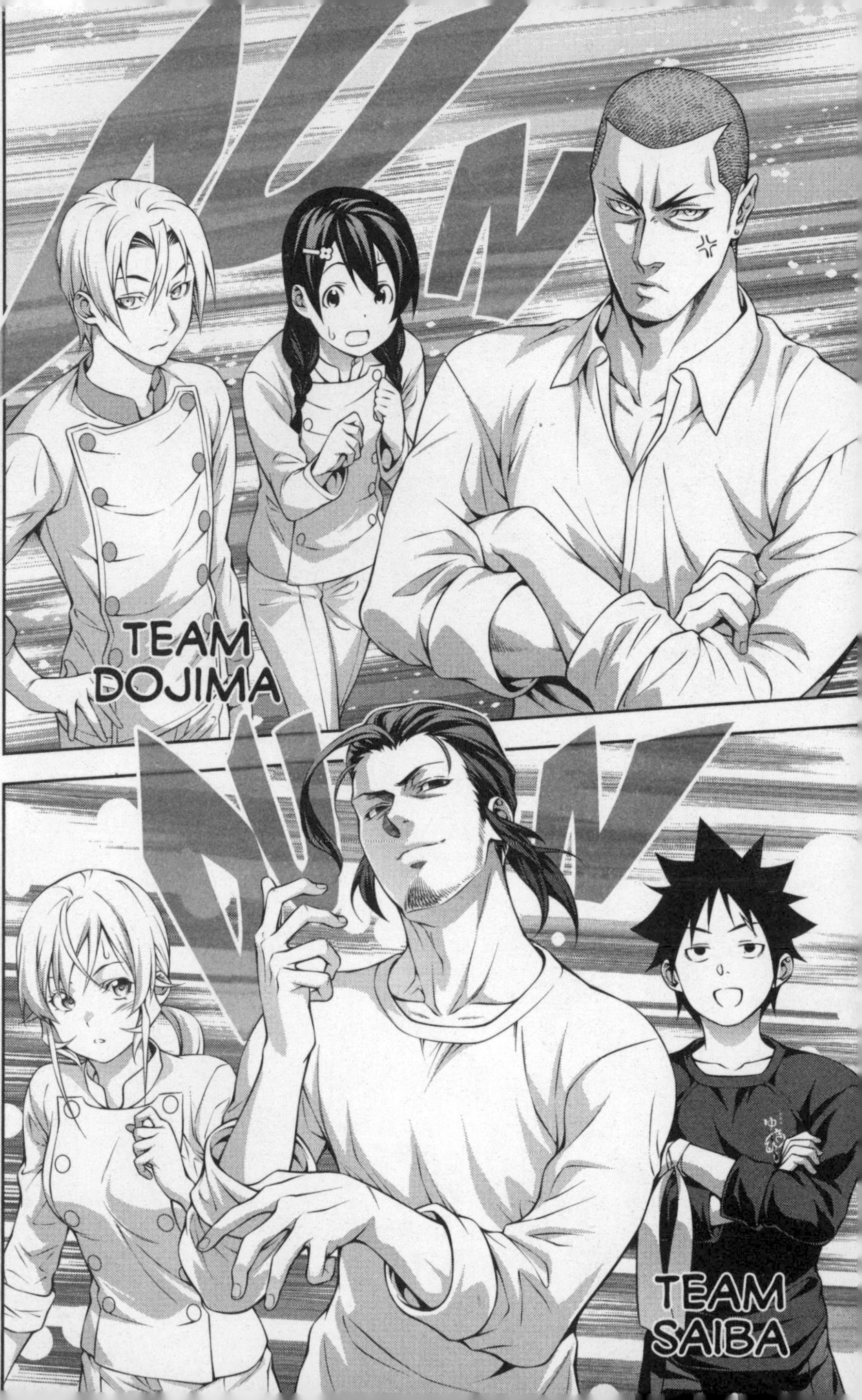
TEAM
DOJIMA
TEAM
SAIBA

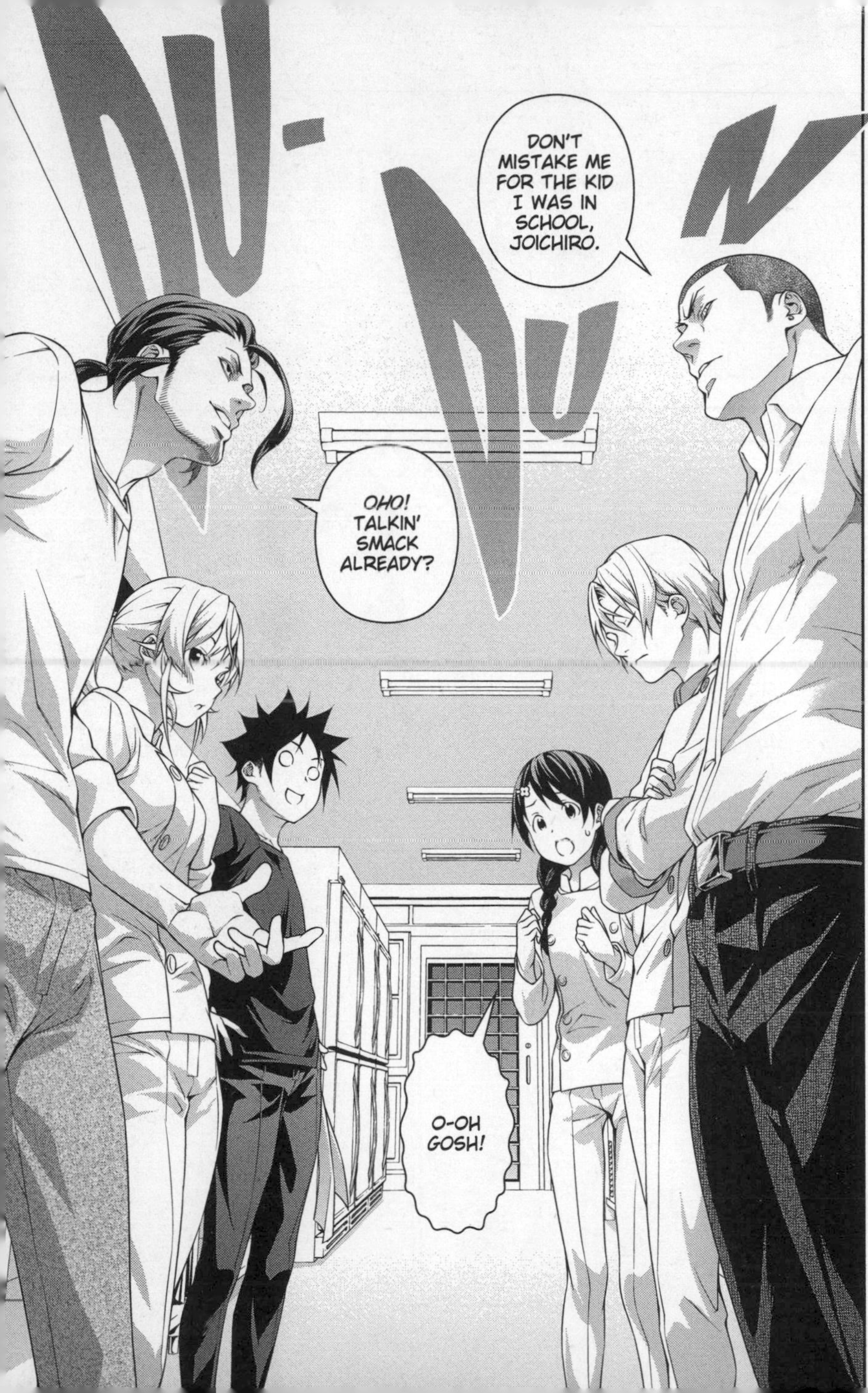
DON'T MISTAKE ME FOR THE KID I WAS IN SCHOOL, JOICHIRO.
DU-DU-N
OHO! TALKIN' SMACK ALREADY?
O-OH GOSH!

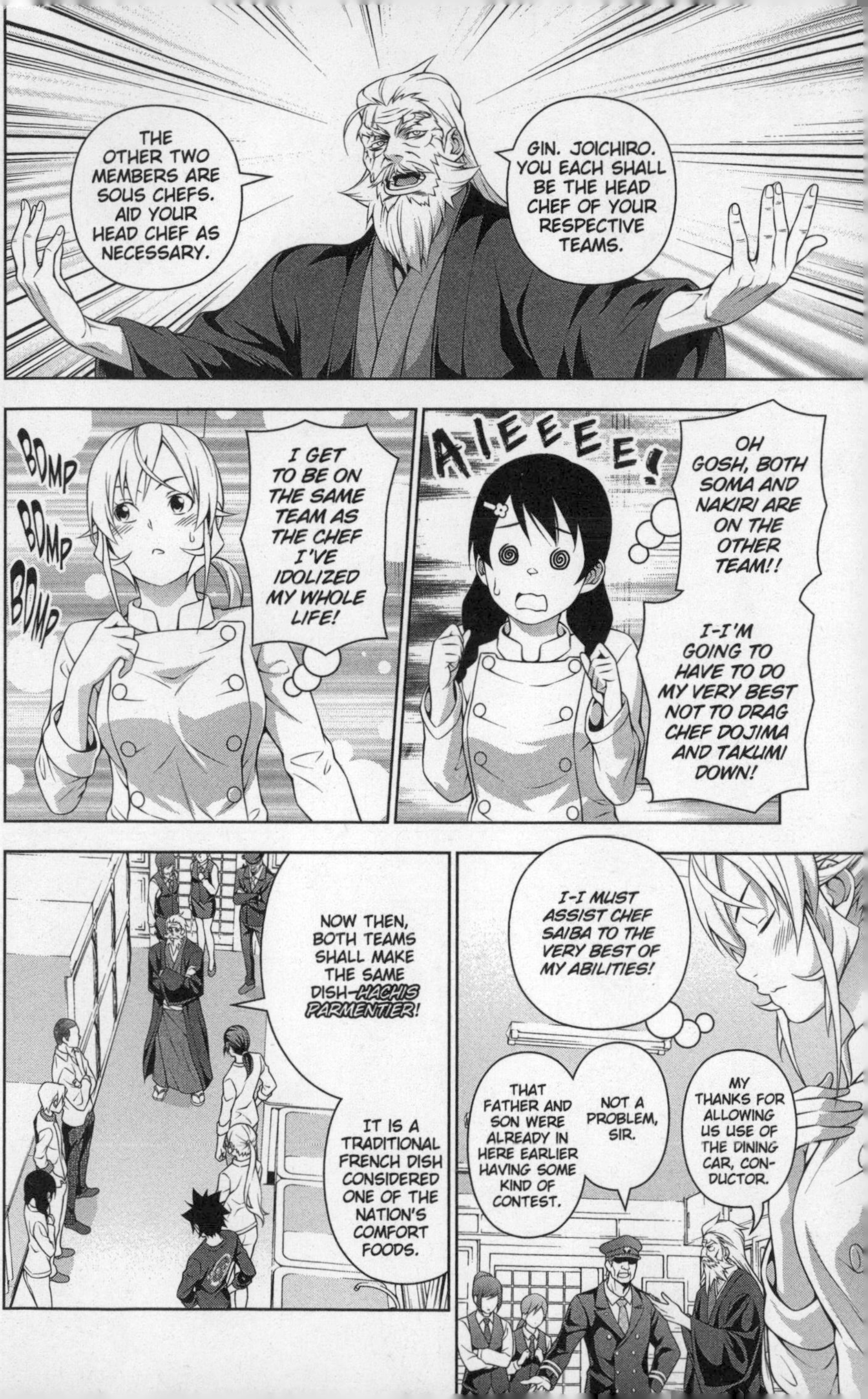
GIN. JOICHIRO. YOU EACH SHALL BE THE HEAD CHEF OF YOUR RESPECTIVE TEAMS.
THE OTHER TWO MEMBERS ARE SOUS CHEFS. AID YOUR HEAD CHEF AS NECESSARY.
AIEEEEE!
OH GOSH, BOTH SOMA AND NAKIRI ARE ON THE OTHER TEAM!!
I-I'M GOING TO HAVE TO DO MY VERY BEST NOT TO DRAG CHEF DOJIMA AND TAKUMI DOWN!
BOMP
BOMP
BOMP
I GET TO BE ON THE SAME TEAM AS THE CHEF I'VE IDOLIZED MY WHOLE LIFE!
I-I MUST ASSIST CHEF SAIBA TO THE VERY BEST OF MY ABILITIES!
MY THANKS FOR ALLOWING US USE OF THE DINING CAR, CONDUCTOR.
NOT A PROBLEM, SIR.
THAT FATHER AND SON WERE ALREADY IN HERE EARLIER HAVING SOME KIND OF CONTEST.
NOW THEN, BOTH TEAMS SHALL MAKE THE SAME DISH—HACHIS PARMENTIER!
IT IS A TRADITIONAL FRENCH DISH CONSIDERED ONE OF THE NATION'S COMFORT FOODS.

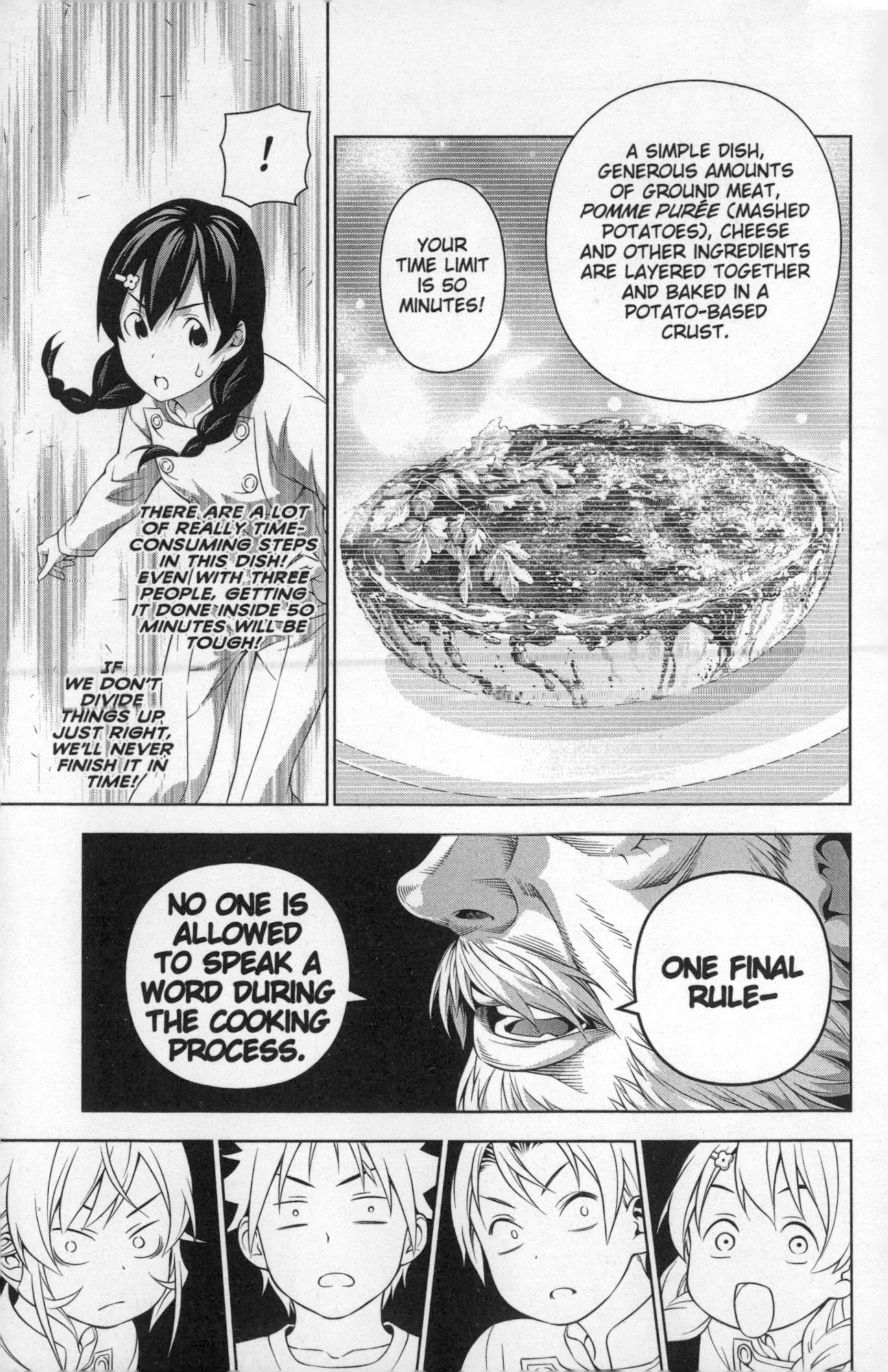
A SIMPLE DISH, GENEROUS AMOUNTS OF GROUND MEAT, *POMME PURÉE* (MASHED POTATOES), CHEESE AND OTHER INGREDIENTS ARE LAYERED TOGETHER AND BAKED IN A POTATO-BASED CRUST.
YOUR TIME LIMIT IS 50 MINUTES!
!
THERE ARE A LOT OF REALLY TIME-CONSUMING STEPS IN THIS DISH! EVEN WITH THREE PEOPLE, GETTING IT DONE INSIDE 50 MINUTES WILL BE TOUGH!
IF WE DON'T DIVIDE THINGS UP JUST RIGHT, WE'LL NEVER FINISH IT IN TIME!
ONE FINAL RULE-
NO ONE IS ALLOWED TO SPEAK A WORD DURING THE COOKING PROCESS.

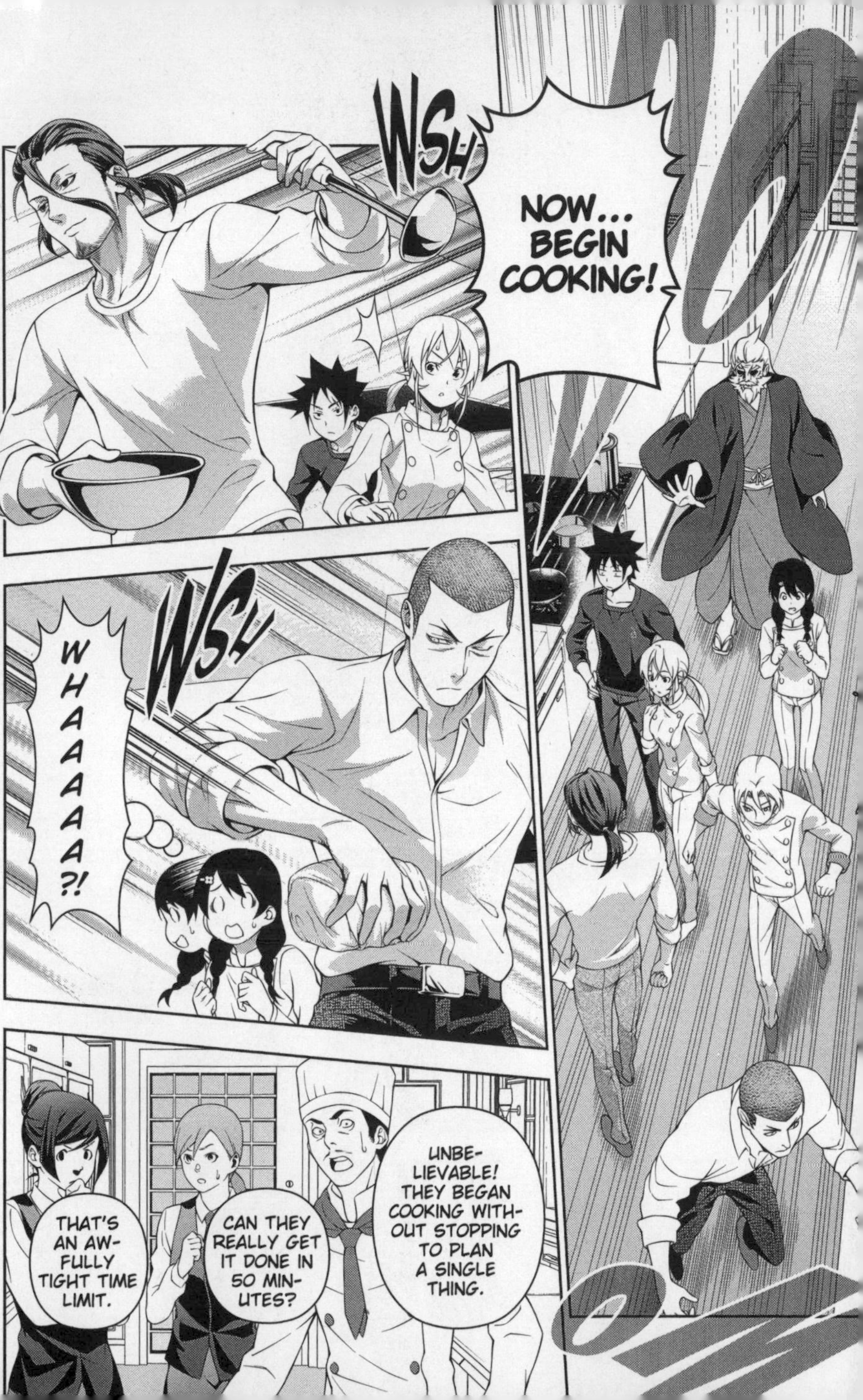
NOW... BEGIN COOKING!
WSH
WSH
WHAAAAAAA?!
UNBE-LIEVABLE! THEY BEGAN COOKING WITH-OUT STOPPING TO PLAN A SINGLE THING.
CAN THEY REALLY GET IT DONE IN 50 MIN-UTES?
THAT'S AN AW-FULLY TIGHT TIME LIMIT.

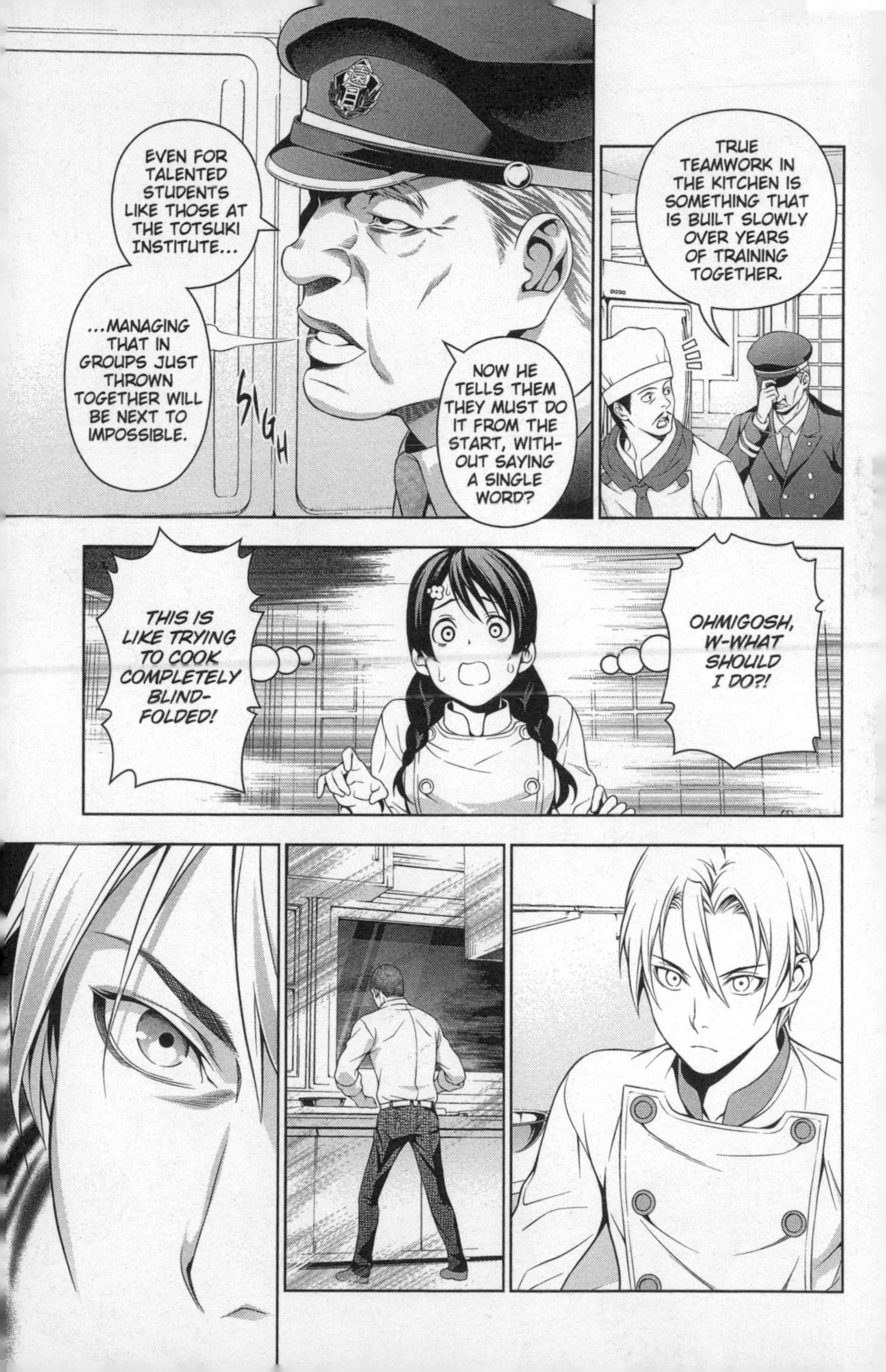
TRUE TEAMWORK IN THE KITCHEN IS SOMETHING THAT IS BUILT SLOWLY OVER YEARS OF TRAINING TOGETHER.
EVEN FOR TALENTED STUDENTS LIKE THOSE AT THE TOTSUKI INSTITUTE...
...MANAGING THAT IN GROUPS JUST THROWN TOGETHER WILL BE NEXT TO IMPOSSIBLE.
SIGH
NOW HE TELLS THEM THEY MUST DO IT FROM THE START, WITHOUT SAYING A SINGLE WORD?
OHMIGOSH, W-WHAT SHOULD I DO?!
THIS IS LIKE TRYING TO COOK COMPLETELY BLINDFOLDED!

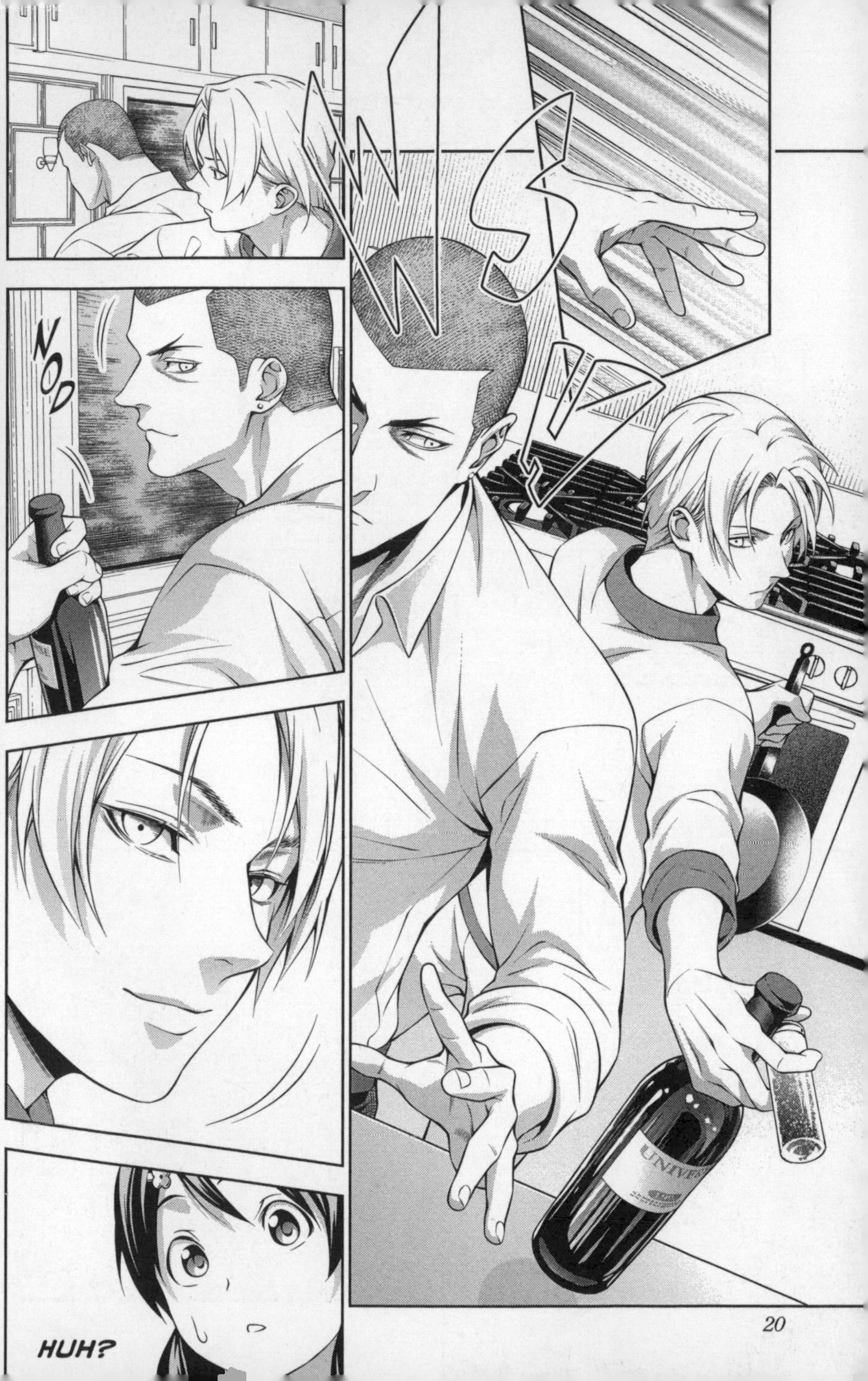
WISH
NOD
HUH?

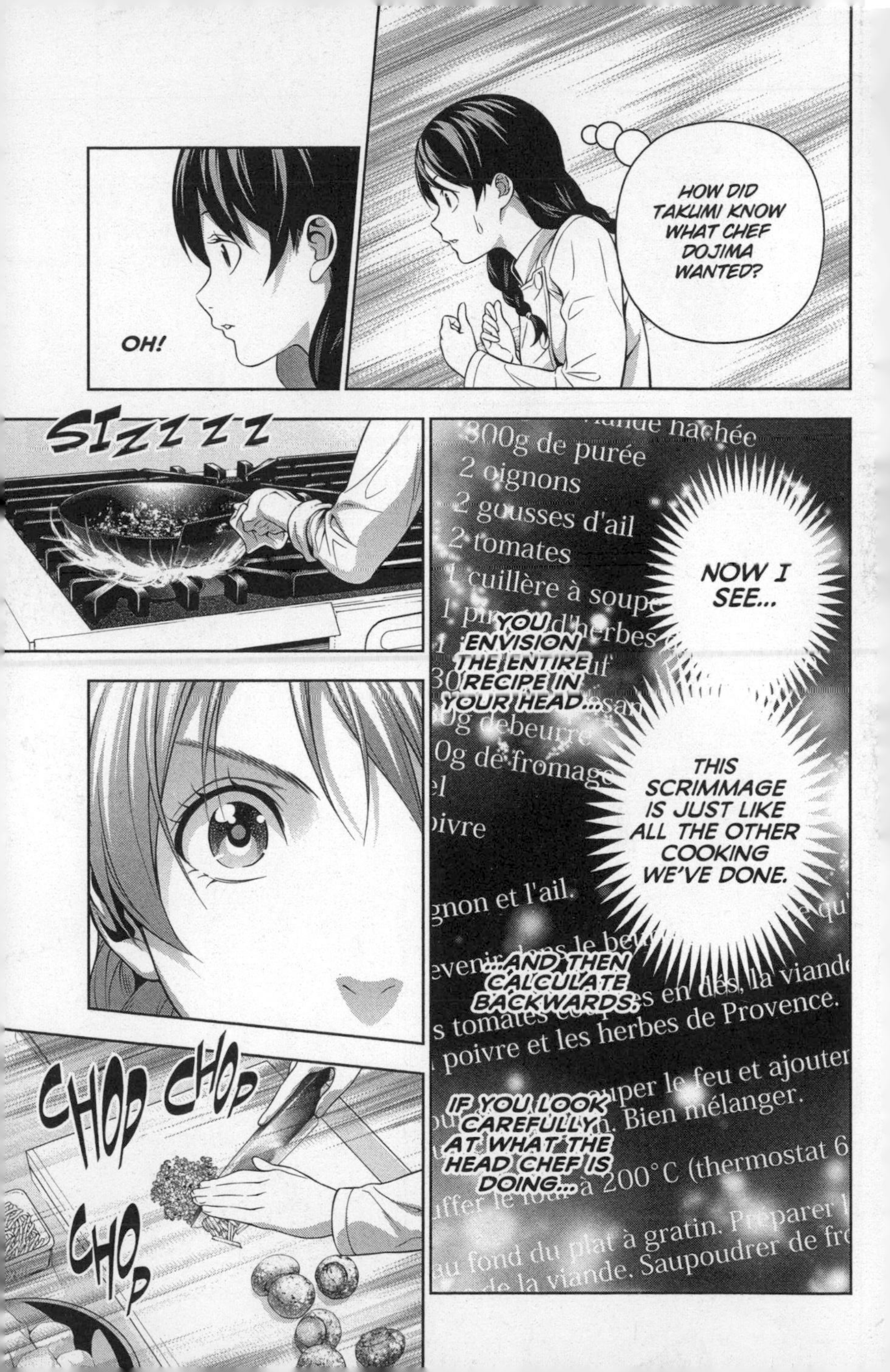
HOW DID TAKUMI KNOW WHAT CHEF DOJIMA WANTED?
OH!
NOW I SEE...
YOU ENVISION THE ENTIRE RECIPE IN YOUR HEAD...
THIS SCRIMMAGE IS JUST LIKE ALL THE OTHER COOKING WE'VE DONE.
...AND THEN CALCULATE BACKWARDS.
IF YOU LOOK CAREFULLY AT WHAT THE HEAD CHEF IS DOING...
300g de purée
2 oignons
2 gousses d'ail
2 tomates
poivre et les herbes de Provence.
Bien mélanger.
SIZZZZZ
CHOP CHOP
CHOP

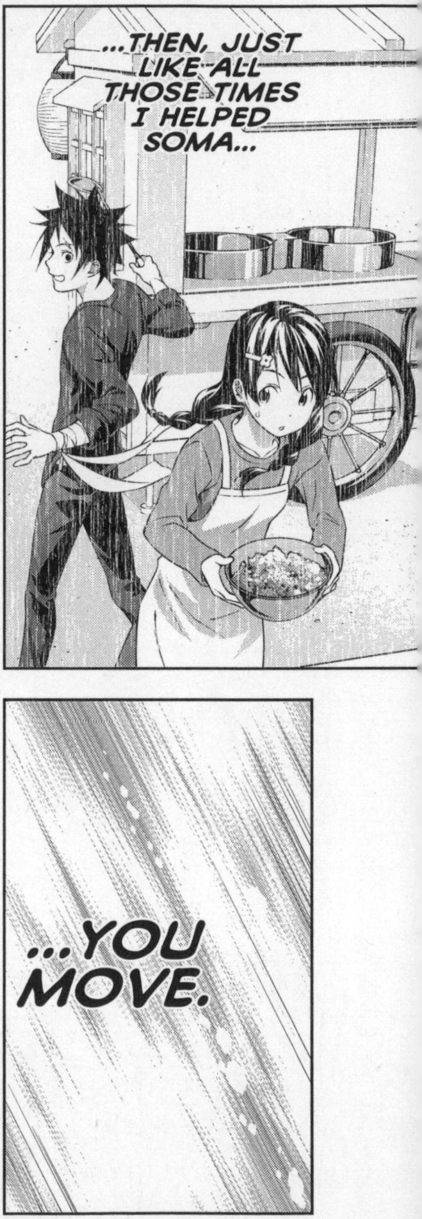
...THEN, JUST LIKE ALL THOSE TIMES I HELPED SOMA...
...YOU MOVE.

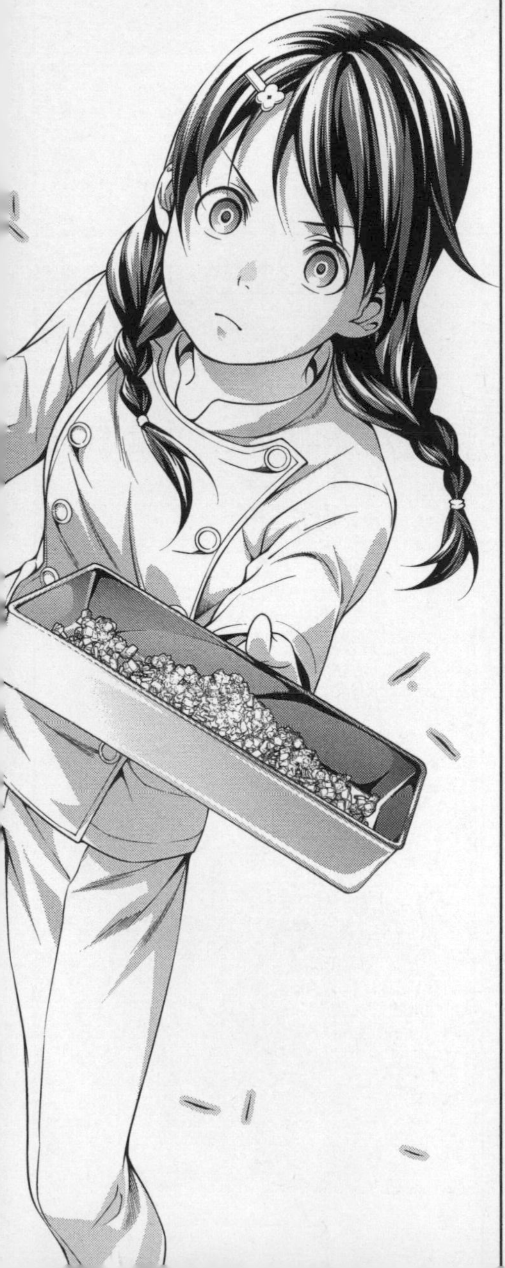

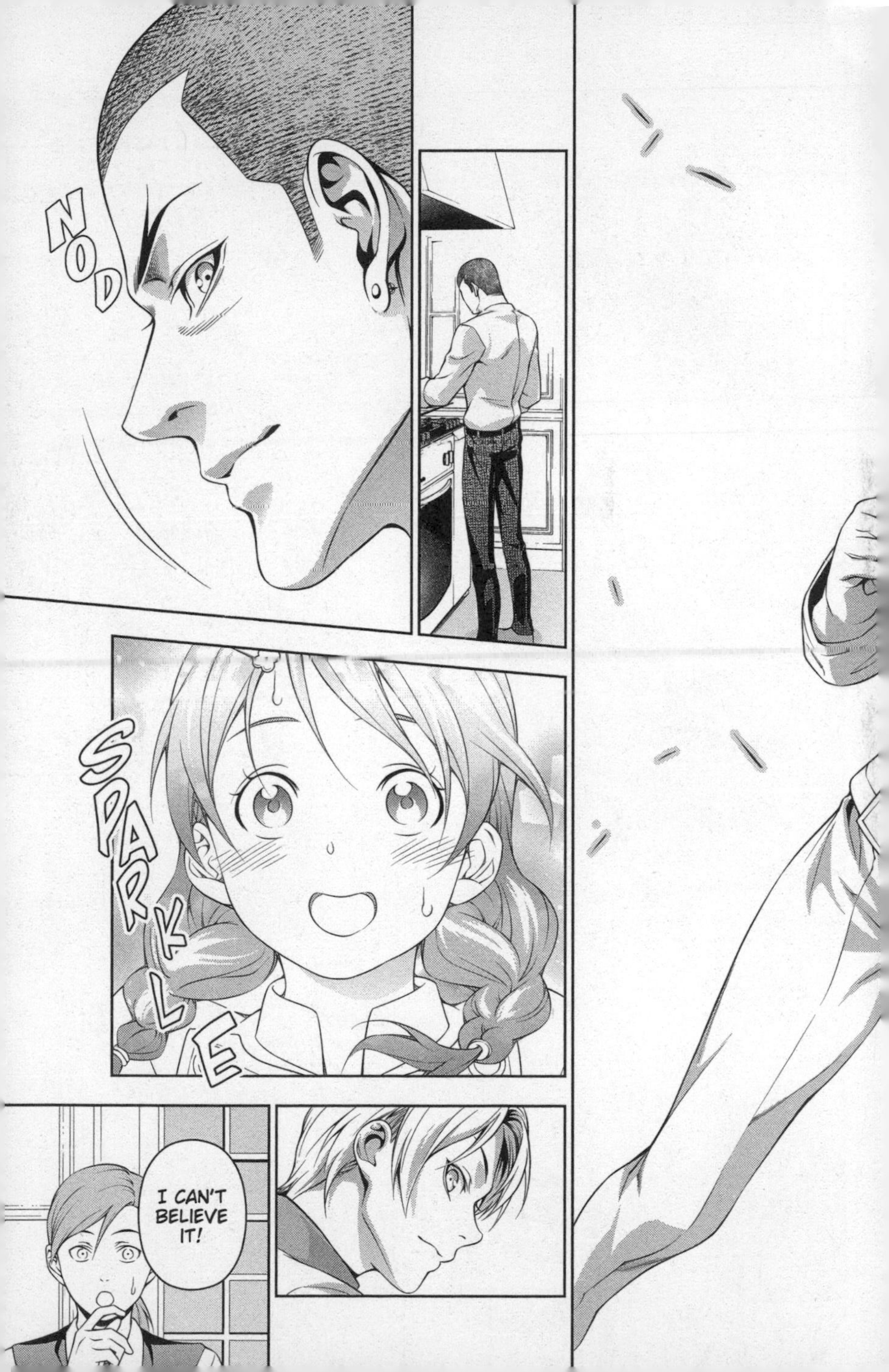
NOD
SPARKLE
I CAN'T BELIEVE IT!

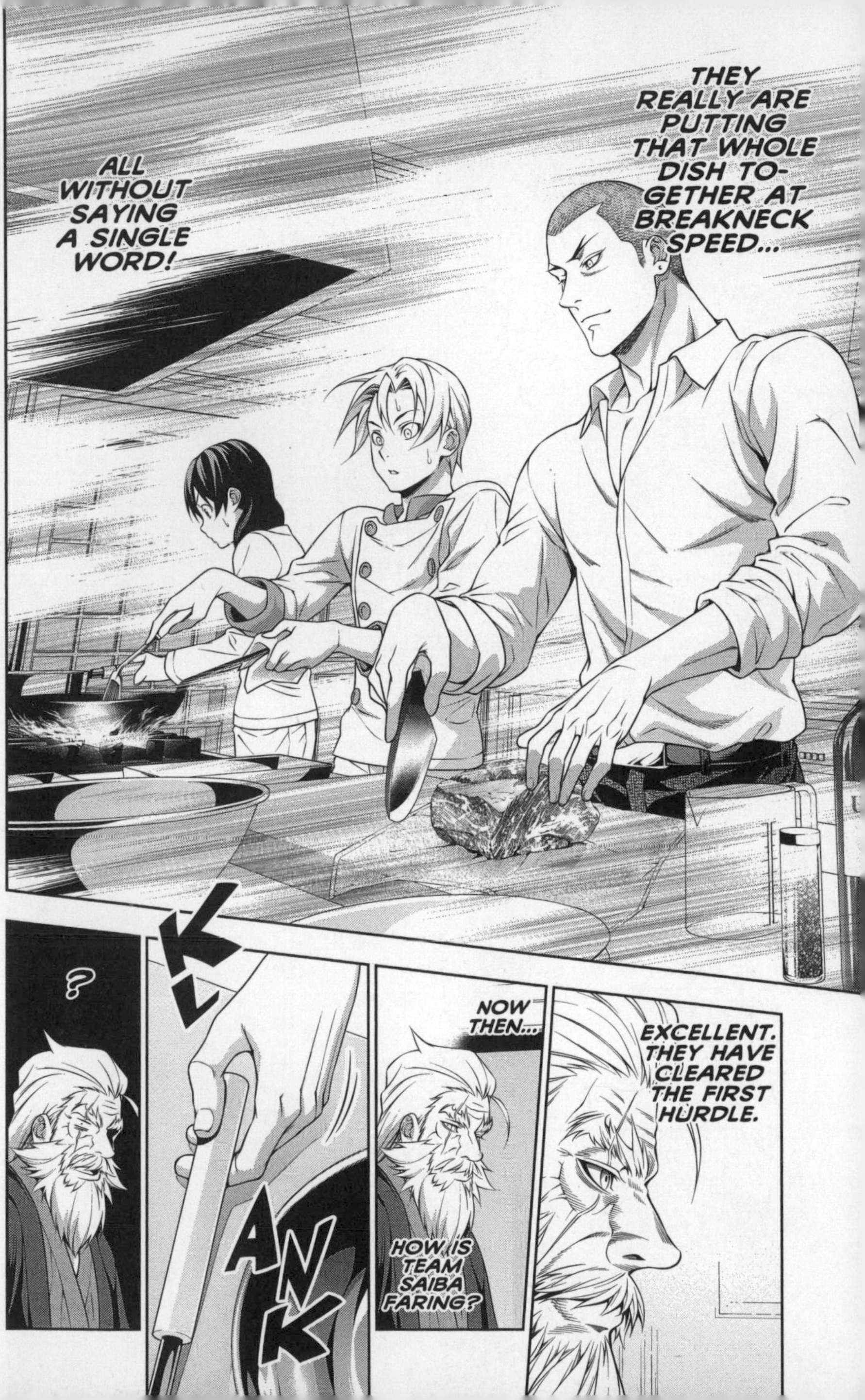
THEY REALLY ARE PUTTING THAT WHOLE DISH TO-GETHER AT BREAKNECK SPEED...
ALL WITHOUT SAYING A SINGLE WORD!
EXCELLENT. THEY HAVE CLEARED THE FIRST HURDLE.
NOW THEN...
HOW IS TEAM SAIBA FARING?
KLANK
?

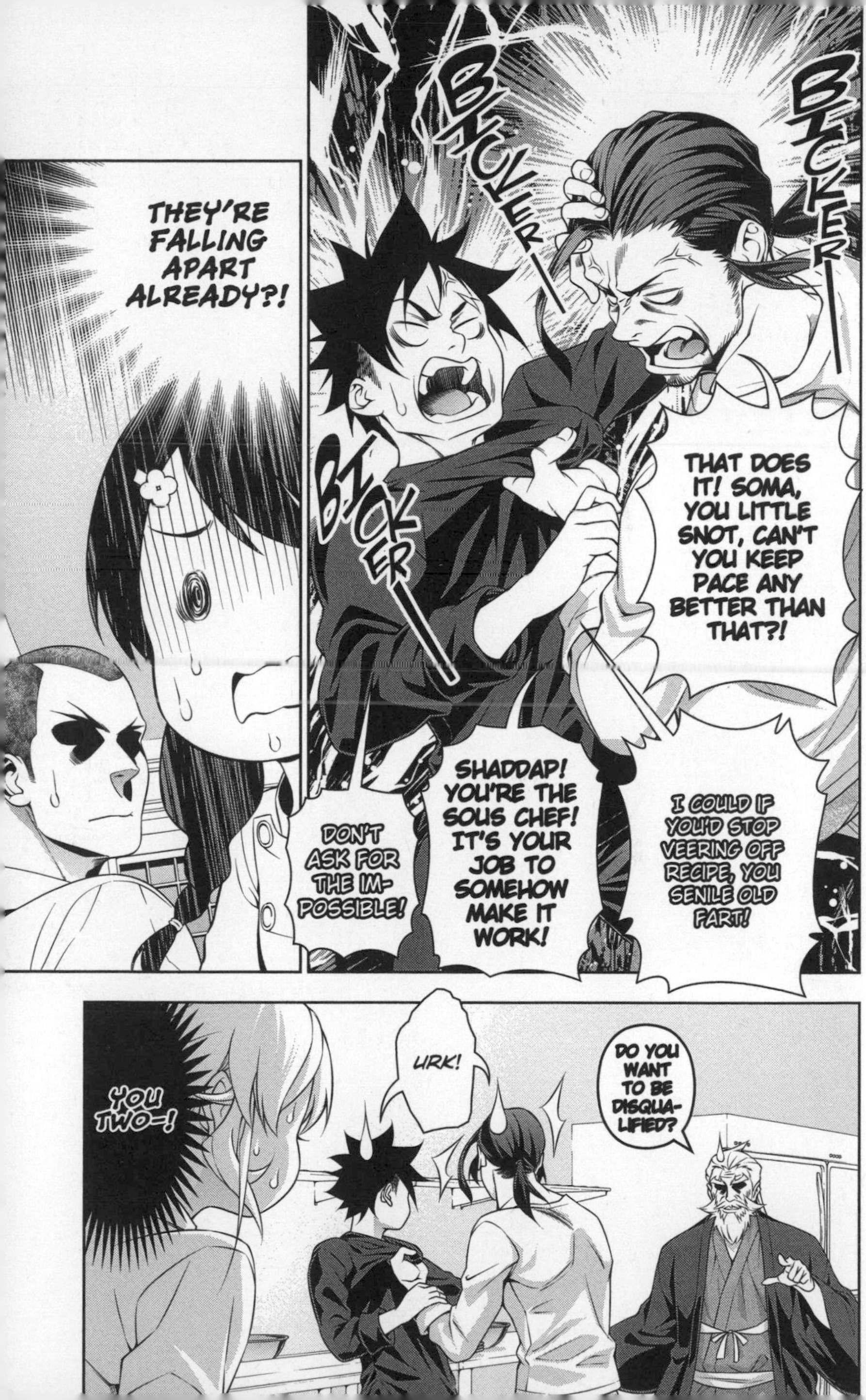
BICKER
BICKER
THAT DOES IT! SOMA, YOU LITTLE SNOT, CAN'T YOU KEEP PACE ANY BETTER THAN THAT?!
I COULD IF YOU'D STOP VEERING OFF RECIPE, YOU SENILE OLD FART!
SHADDAP! YOU'RE THE SOUS CHEF! IT'S YOUR JOB TO SOMEHOW MAKE IT WORK!
DON'T ASK FOR THE IM-POSSIBLE!
BICKER
THEY'RE FALLING APART ALREADY?!
DO YOU WANT TO BE DISQUA-LIFIED?
URK!
YOU TWO--!

THE SCRIMMAGE STRAWS
(ACTUALLY DISPOSABLE CHOPSTICKS)

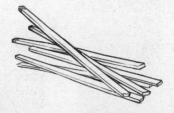

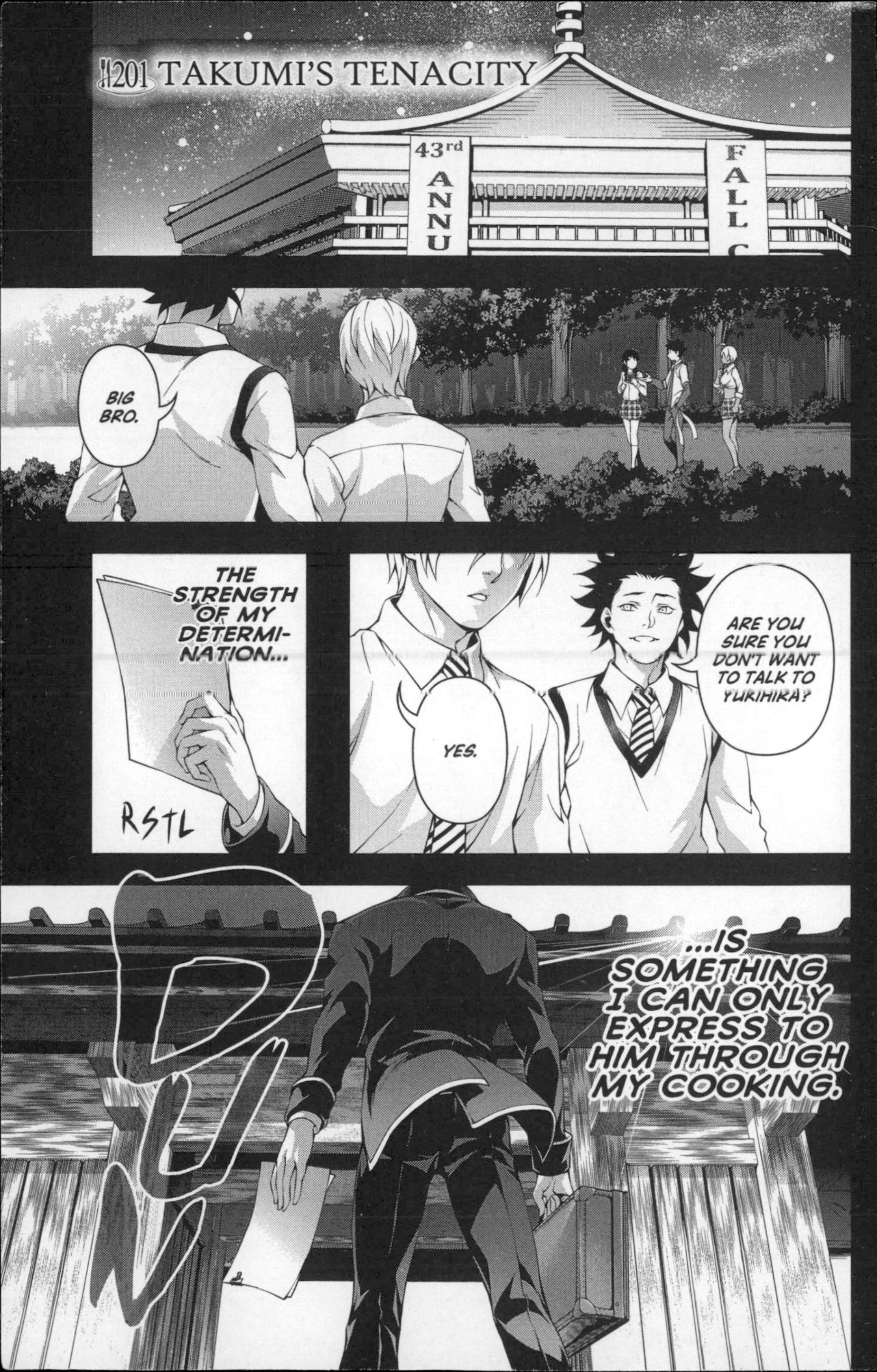
201 TAKUMI'S TENACITY
43rd ANNU
FALL
BIG BRO.
ARE YOU SURE YOU DON'T WANT TO TALK TO YUKIHIRA?
YES.
THE STRENGTH OF MY DETERMINATION...
RSTL
...IS SOMETHING I CAN ONLY EXPRESS TO HIM THROUGH MY COOKING.

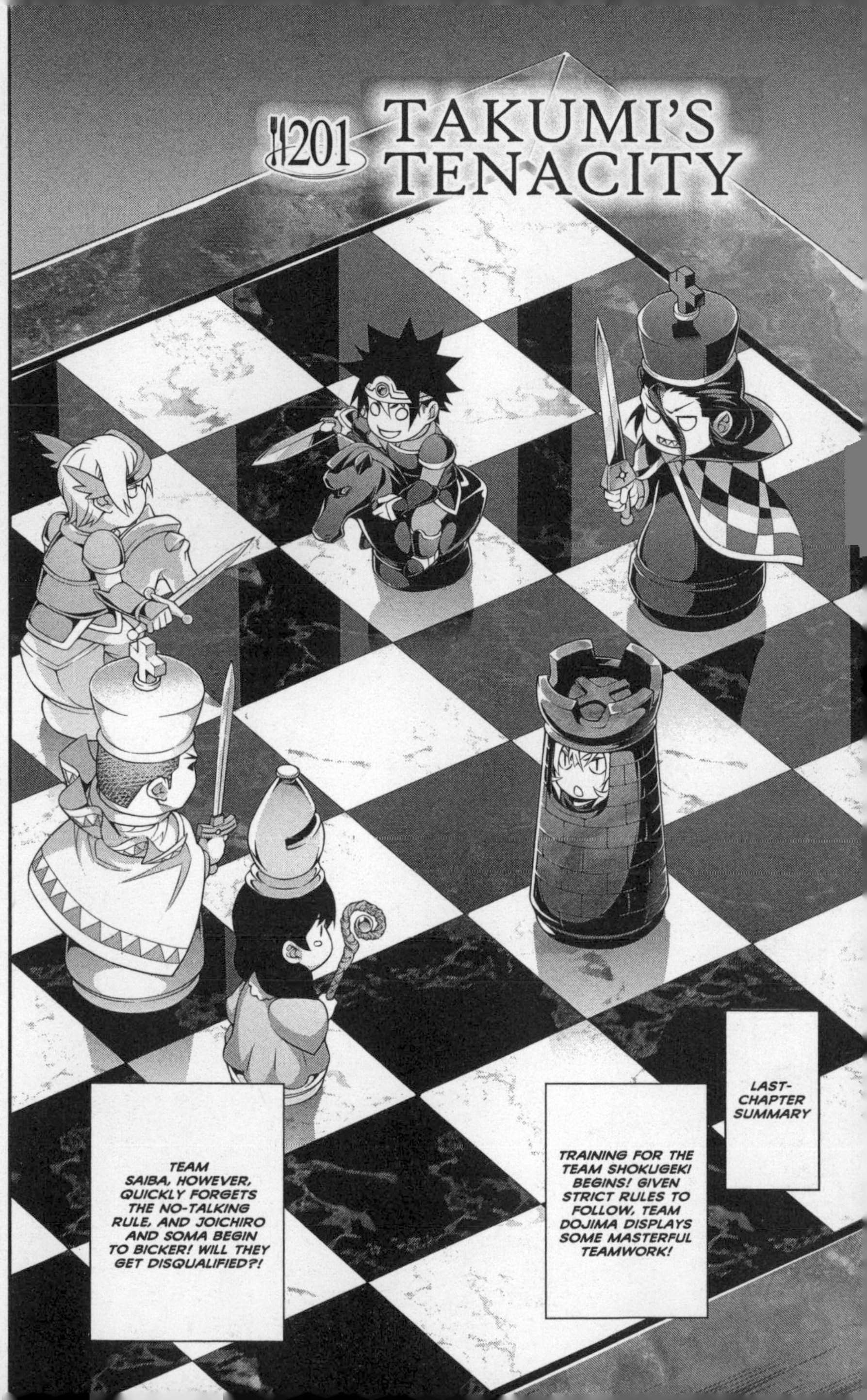

201 TAKUMI'S TENACITY
LAST-CHAPTER SUMMARY
TRAINING FOR THE TEAM SHOKUGEKI BEGINS! GIVEN STRICT RULES TO FOLLOW, TEAM DOJIMA DISPLAYS SOME MASTERFUL TEAMWORK!
TEAM SAIBA, HOWEVER, QUICKLY FORGETS THE NO-TALKING RULE, AND JOICHIRO AND SOMA BEGIN TO BICKER! WILL THEY GET DISQUALIFIED?!

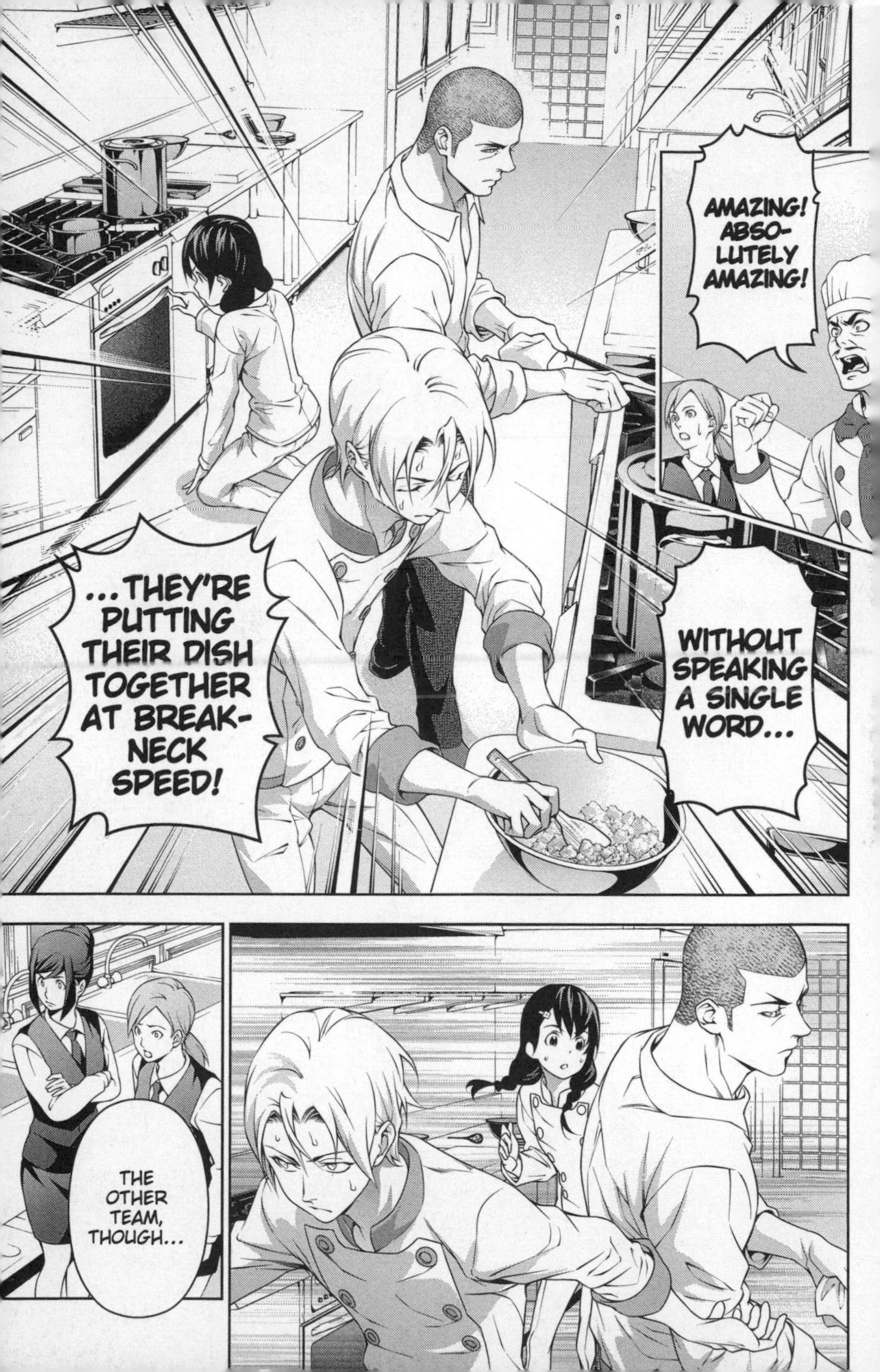
AMAZING! ABSO-LUTELY AMAZING!
WITHOUT SPEAKING A SINGLE WORD...
...THEY'RE PUTTING THEIR DISH TOGETHER AT BREAK-NECK SPEED!
THE OTHER TEAM, THOUGH...

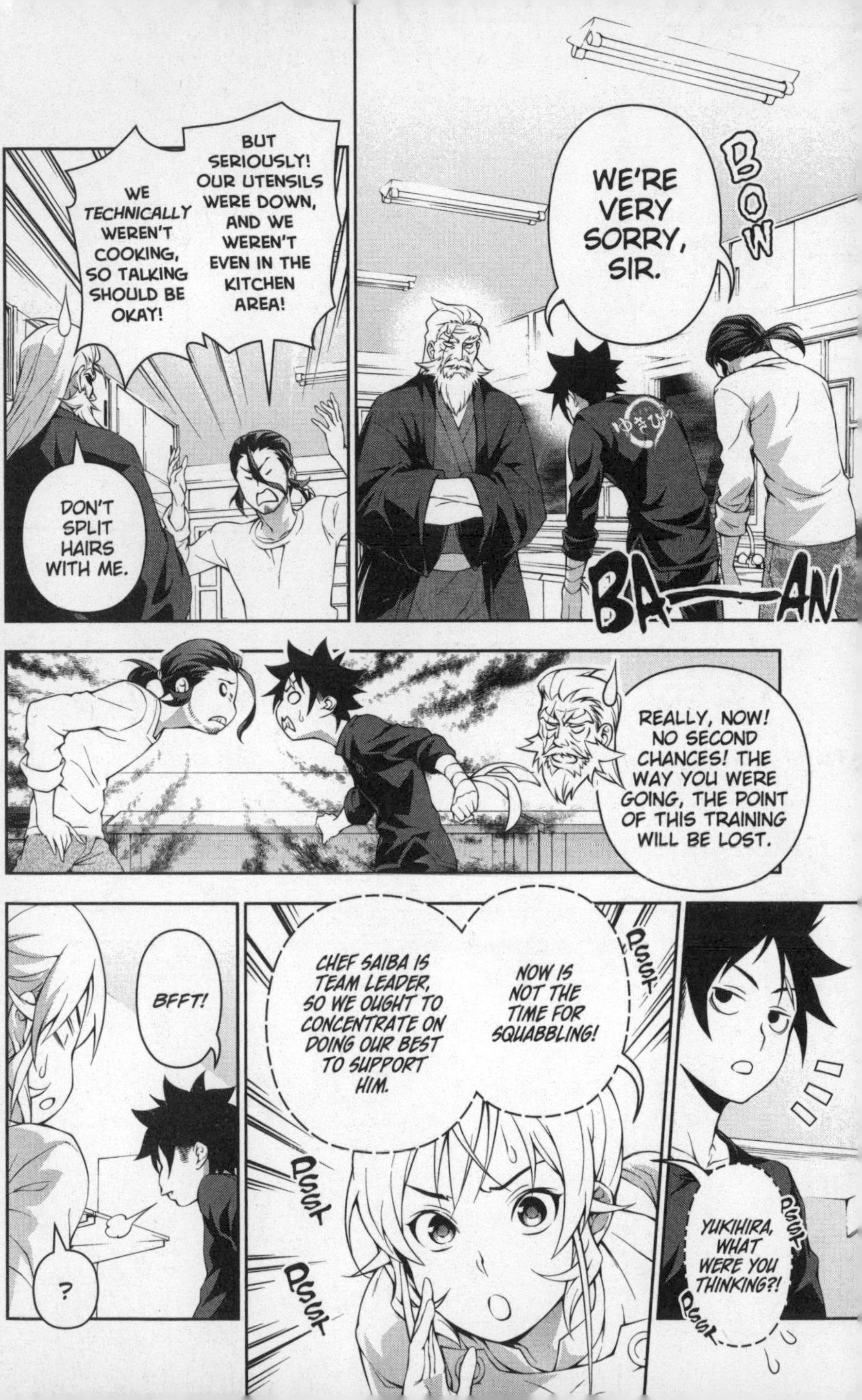
BOW
WE'RE VERY SORRY, SIR.
BA—AN
BUT SERIOUSLY! OUR UTENSILS WERE DOWN, AND WE WEREN'T EVEN IN THE KITCHEN AREA!
WE TECHNICALLY WEREN'T COOKING, SO TALKING SHOULD BE OKAY!
DON'T SPLIT HAIRS WITH ME.
REALLY, NOW! NO SECOND CHANCES! THE WAY YOU WERE GOING, THE POINT OF THIS TRAINING WILL BE LOST.
PSSST
YUKIHIRA, WHAT WERE YOU THINKING?!
PSSST
PSSST
NOW IS NOT THE TIME FOR SQUABBLING!
CHEF SAIBA IS TEAM LEADER, SO WE OUGHT TO CONCENTRATE ON DOING OUR BEST TO SUPPORT HIM.
PSSST
PSSST
BFFT!
?

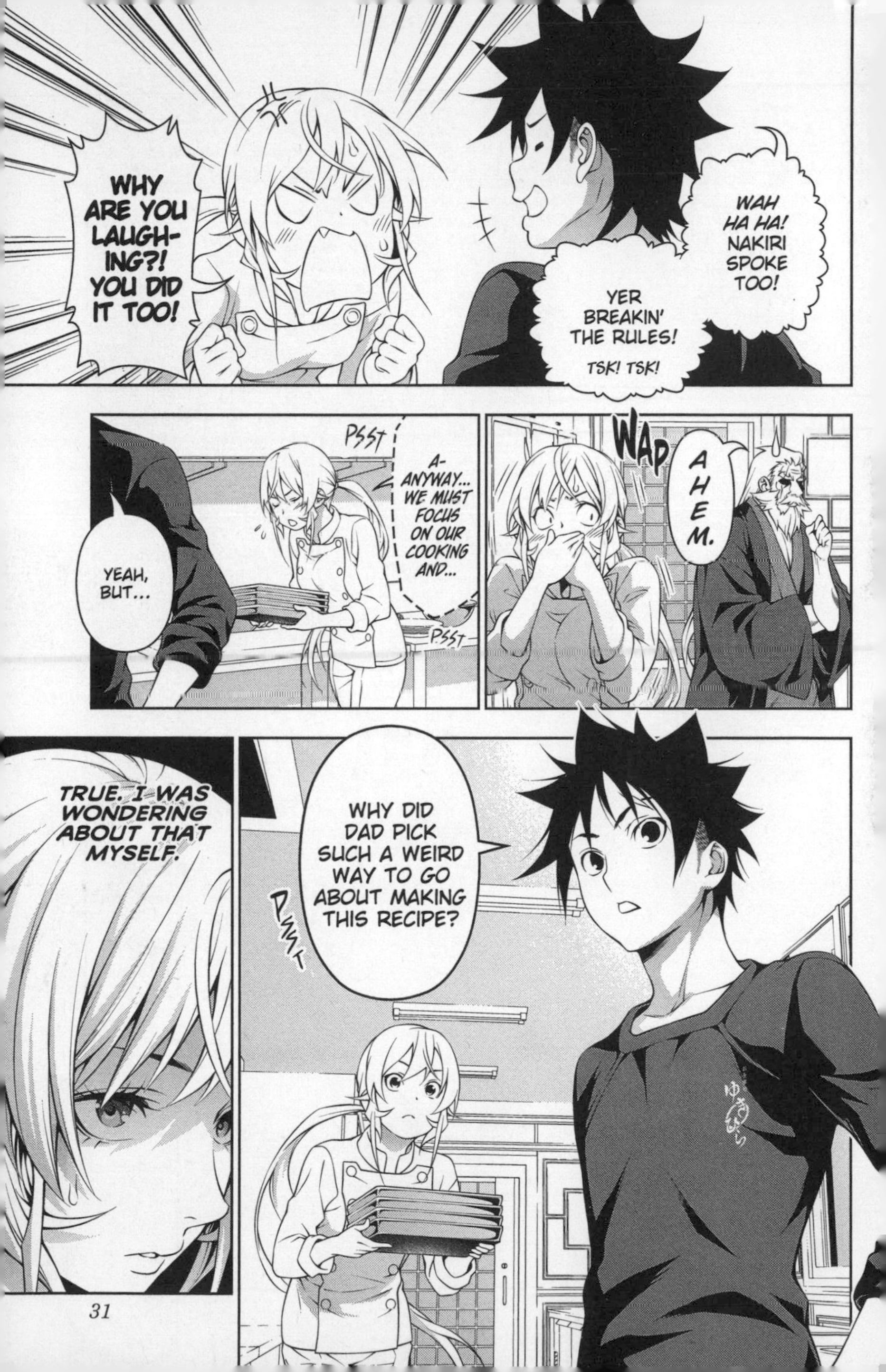
WAH HA HA! NAKIRI SPOKE TOO!
YER BREAKIN' THE RULES!
TSK! TSK!
WHY ARE YOU LAUGHING?! YOU DID IT TOO!
WAP
AHEM.
PSST
A-ANYWAY... WE MUST FOCUS ON OUR COOKING AND...
YEAH, BUT...
PSST
WHY DID DAD PICK SUCH A WEIRD WAY TO GO ABOUT MAKING THIS RECIPE?
PSST
TRUE. I WAS WONDERING ABOUT THAT MYSELF.

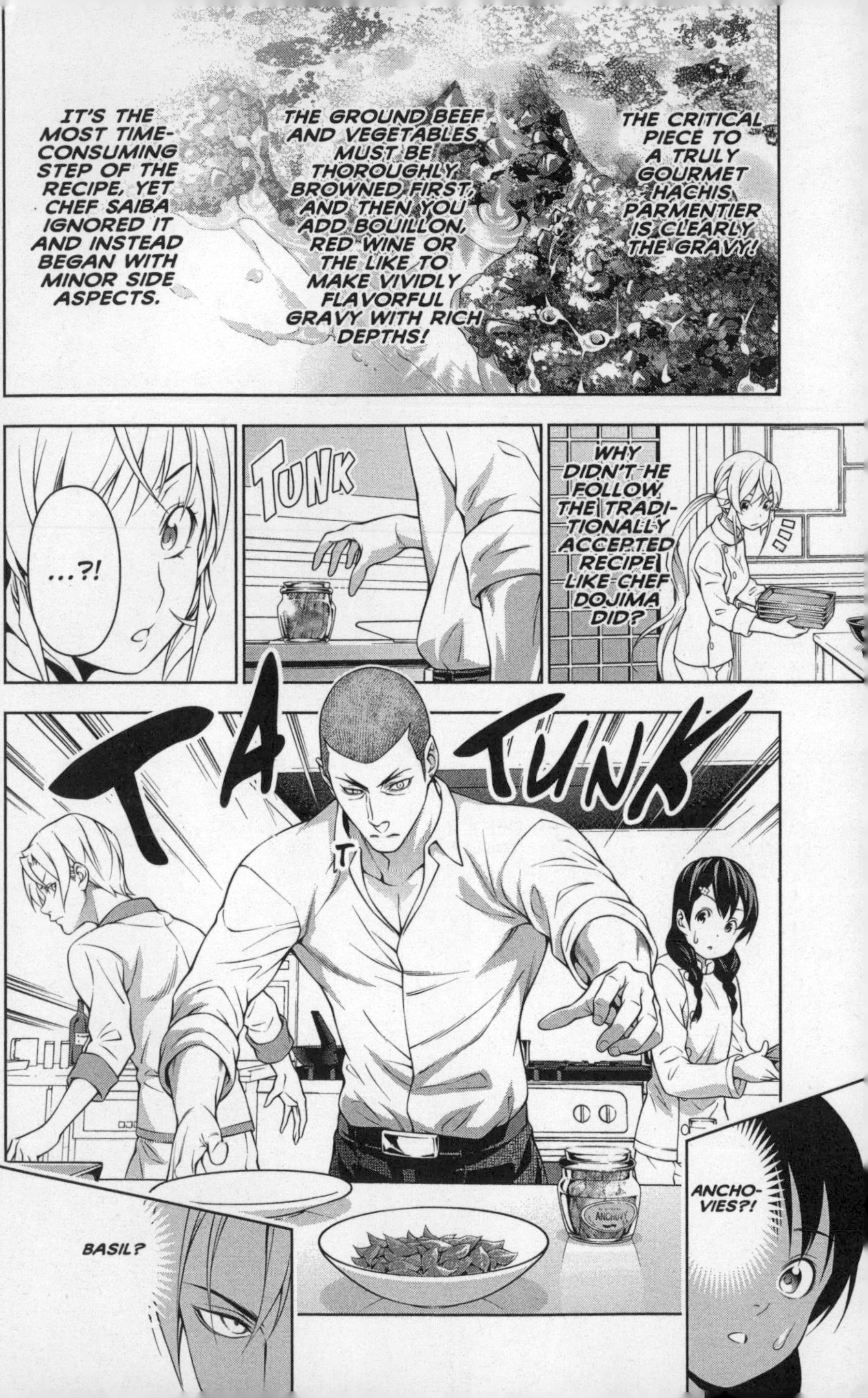
THE CRITICAL PIECE TO A TRULY GOURMET HACHIS PARMENTIER IS CLEARLY THE GRAVY!
THE GROUND BEEF AND VEGETABLES MUST BE THOROUGHLY BROWNED FIRST, AND THEN YOU ADD BOUILLON, RED WINE OR THE LIKE TO MAKE VIVIDLY FLAVORFUL GRAVY WITH RICH DEPTHS!
IT'S THE MOST TIME-CONSUMING STEP OF THE RECIPE, YET CHEF SAIBA IGNORED IT AND INSTEAD BEGAN WITH MINOR SIDE ASPECTS.
WHY DIDN'T HE FOLLOW THE TRADITIONALLY ACCEPTED RECIPE LIKE CHEF DOJIMA DID?
TUNK
...?!
TA TUNK
T
ANCHOVIES?!
BASIL?

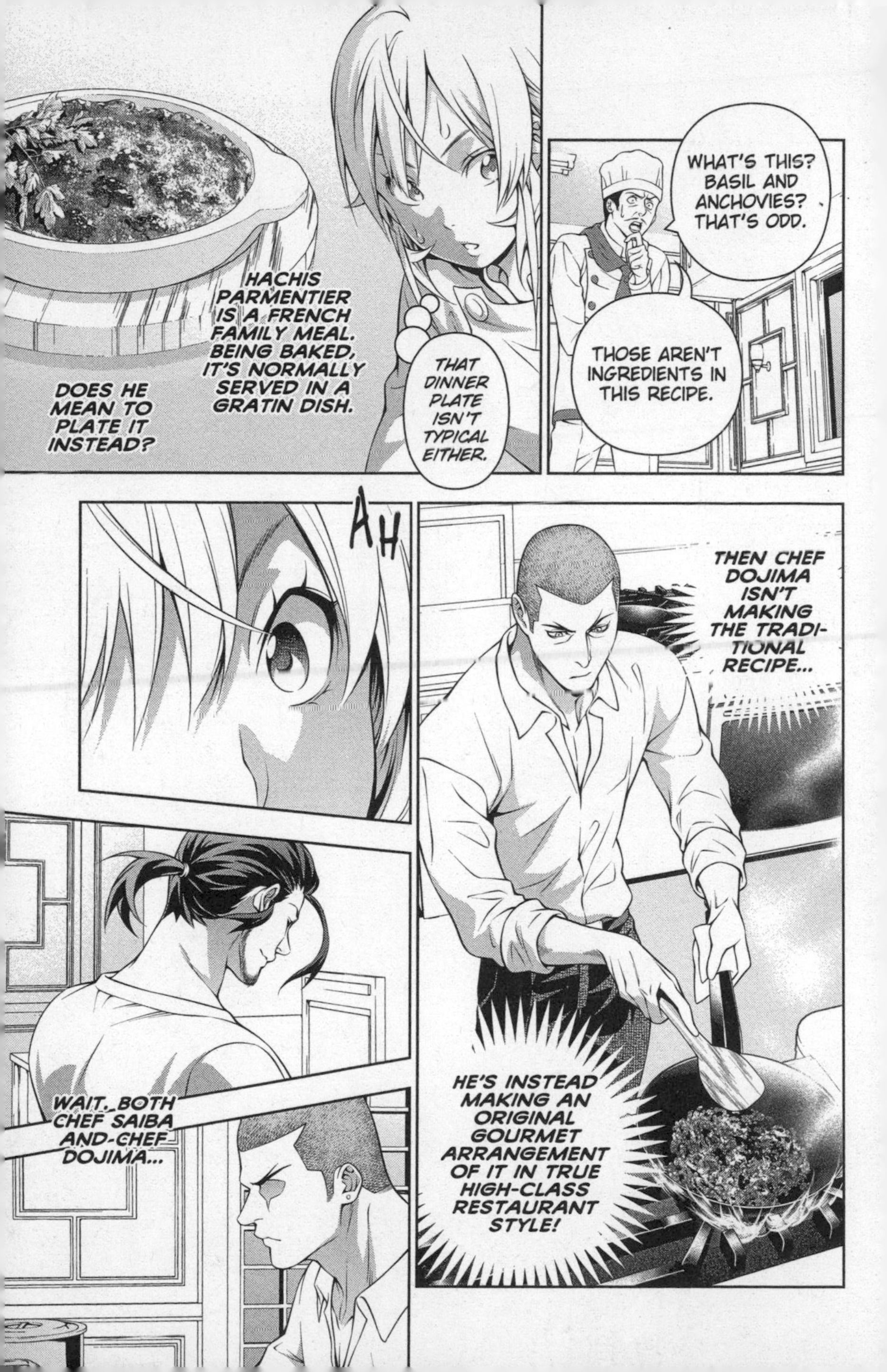
WHAT'S THIS? BASIL AND ANCHOVIES? THAT'S ODD.
THOSE AREN'T INGREDIENTS IN THIS RECIPE.
THAT DINNER PLATE ISN'T TYPICAL EITHER.
HACHIS PARMENTIER IS A FRENCH FAMILY MEAL. BEING BAKED, IT'S NORMALLY SERVED IN A GRATIN DISH.
DOES HE MEAN TO PLATE IT INSTEAD?
THEN CHEF DOJIMA ISN'T MAKING THE TRADI-TIONAL RECIPE...
HE'S INSTEAD MAKING AN ORIGINAL GOURMET ARRANGEMENT OF IT IN TRUE HIGH-CLASS RESTAURANT STYLE!
AH
WAIT, BOTH CHEF SAIBA AND CHEF DOJIMA...

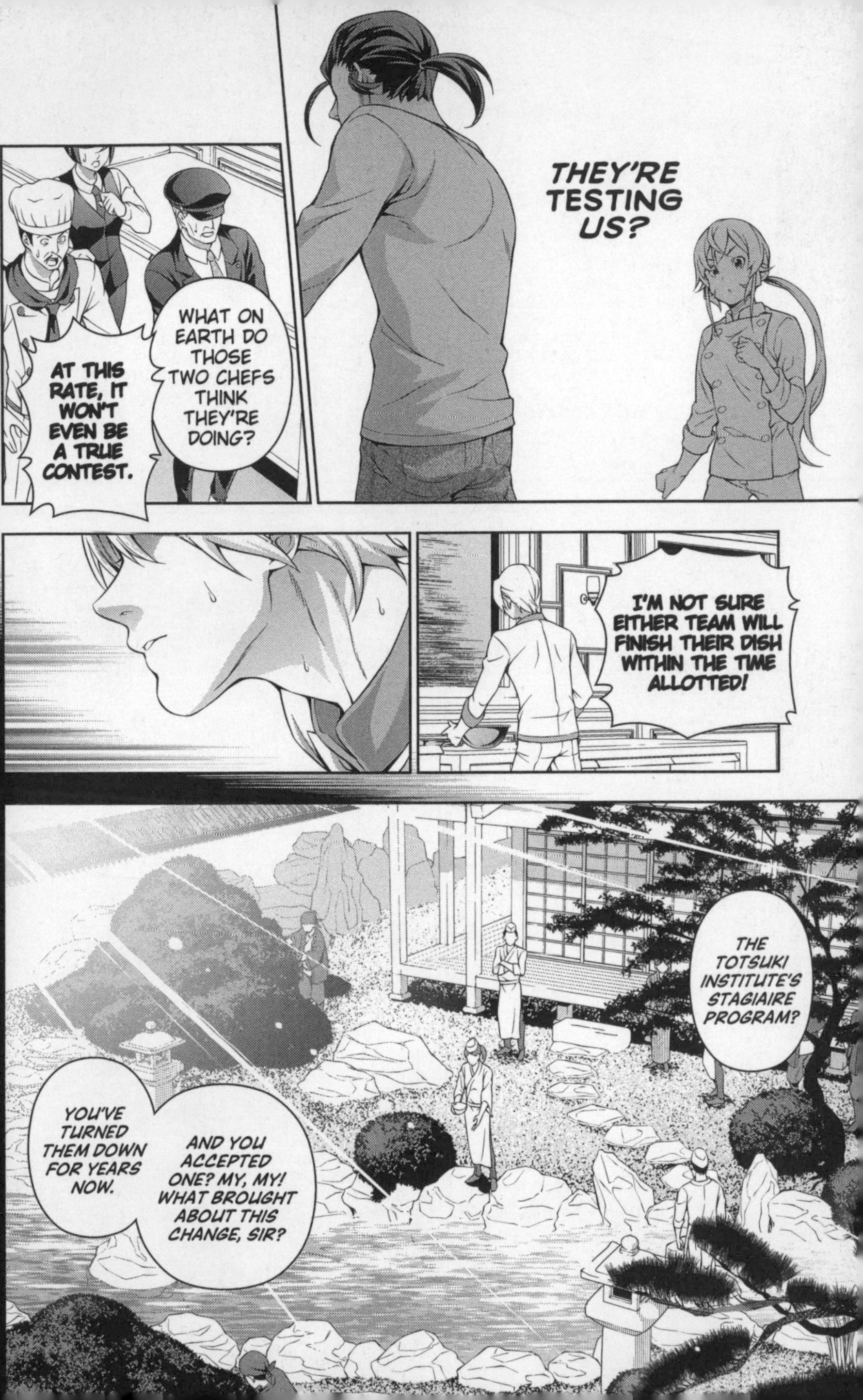
THEY'RE TESTING US?
WHAT ON EARTH DO THOSE TWO CHEFS THINK THEY'RE DOING?
AT THIS RATE, IT WON'T EVEN BE A TRUE CONTEST.
I'M NOT SURE EITHER TEAM WILL FINISH THEIR DISH WITHIN THE TIME ALLOTTED!
THE TOTSUKI INSTITUTE'S STAGIAIRE PROGRAM?
YOU'VE TURNED THEM DOWN FOR YEARS NOW.
AND YOU ACCEPTED ONE? MY, MY! WHAT BROUGHT ABOUT THIS CHANGE, SIR?

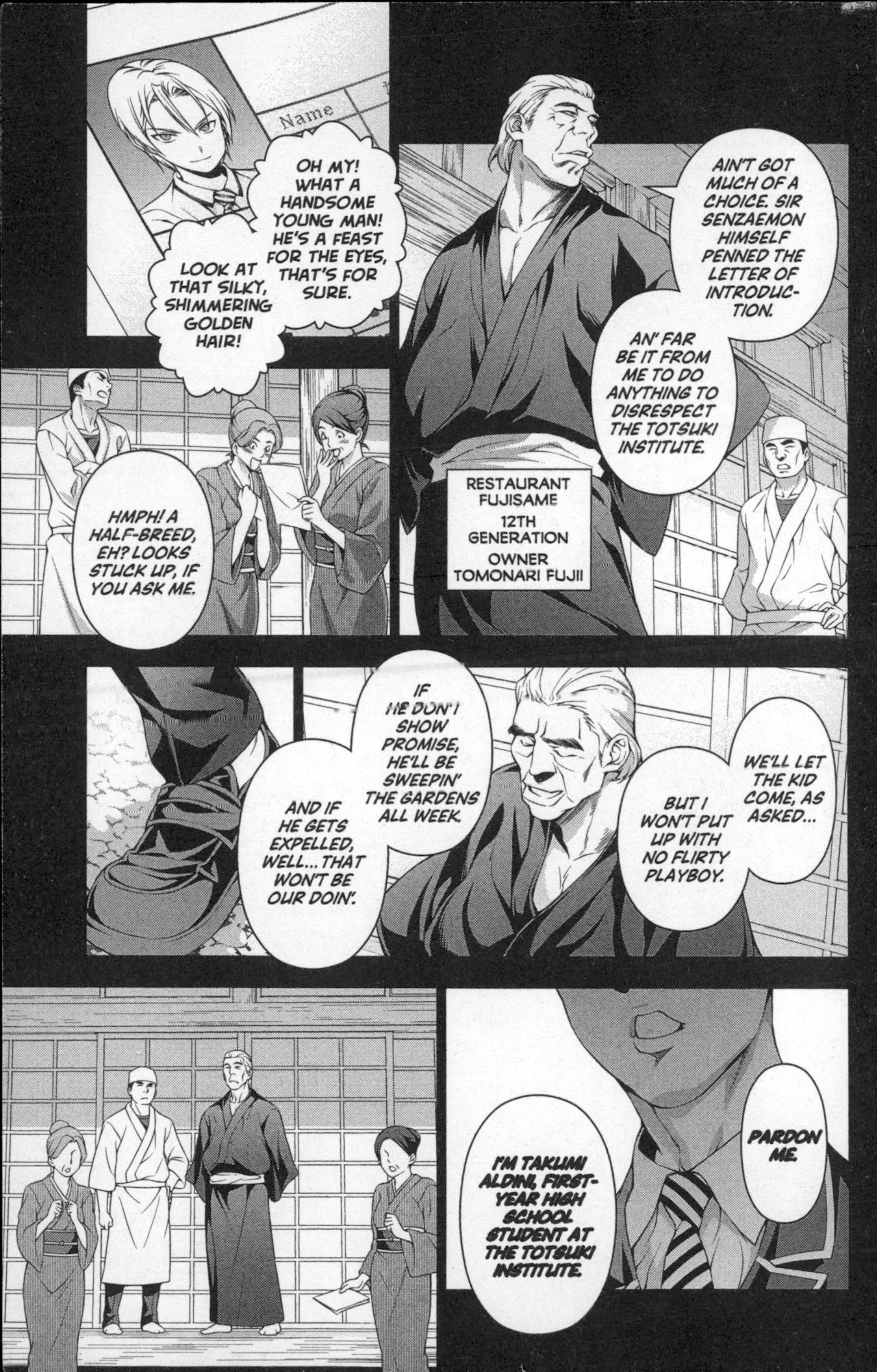
AIN'T GOT MUCH OF A CHOICE. SIR SENZAEMON HIMSELF PENNED THE LETTER OF INTRODUCTION.
AN' FAR BE IT FROM ME TO DO ANYTHING TO DISRESPECT THE TOTSUKI INSTITUTE.
RESTAURANT FUJISAME 12TH GENERATION OWNER TOMONARI FUJII
Name
OH MY! WHAT A HANDSOME YOUNG MAN! HE'S A FEAST FOR THE EYES, THAT'S FOR SURE.
LOOK AT THAT SILKY, SHIMMERING GOLDEN HAIR!
HMPH! A HALF-BREED, EH? LOOKS STUCK UP, IF YOU ASK ME.
WE'LL LET THE KID COME, AS ASKED...
BUT I WON'T PUT UP WITH NO FLIRTY PLAYBOY.
IF HE DON'T SHOW PROMISE, HE'LL BE SWEEPIN' THE GARDENS ALL WEEK.
AND IF HE GETS EXPELLED, WELL... THAT WON'T BE OUR DOIN'.
PARDON ME.
I'M TAKUMI ALDINI, FIRST-YEAR HIGH SCHOOL STUDENT AT THE TOTSUKI INSTITUTE.

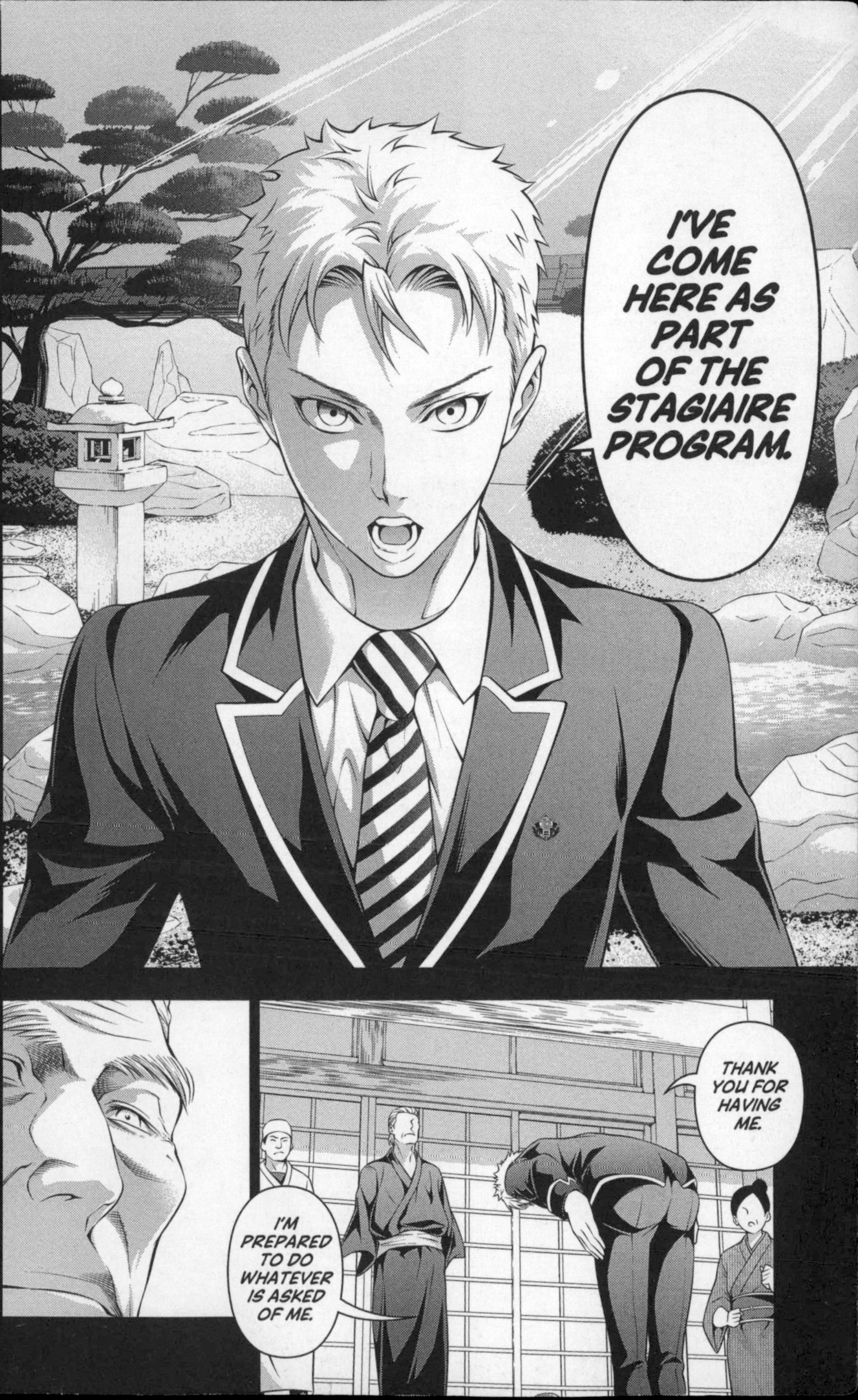
I'VE COME HERE AS PART OF THE STAGIAIRE PROGRAM.
THANK YOU FOR HAVING ME.
I'M PREPARED TO DO WHATEVER IS ASKED OF ME.

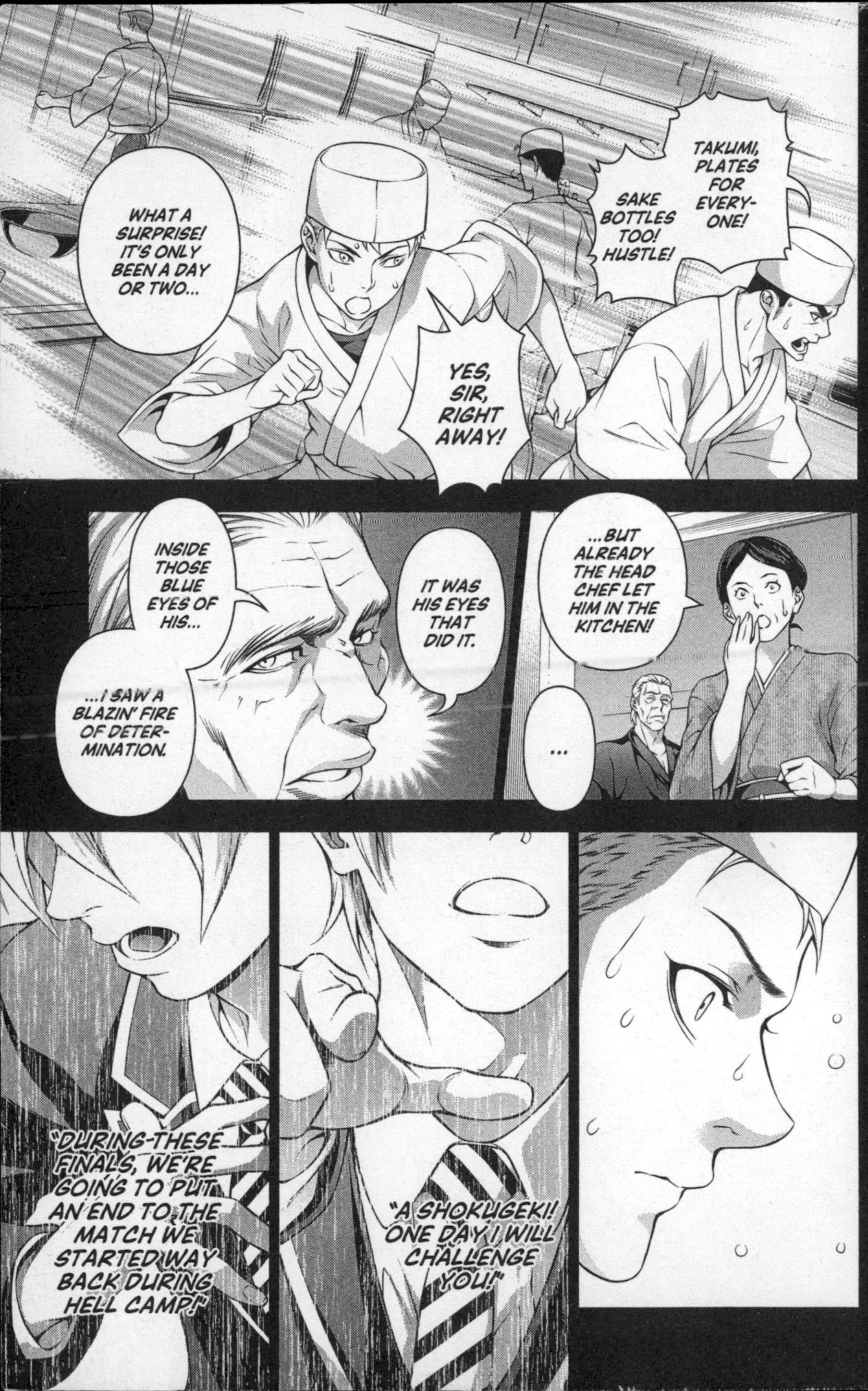
TAKUMI, PLATES FOR EVERY-ONE!
SAKE BOTTLES TOO! HUSTLE!
WHAT A SURPRISE! IT'S ONLY BEEN A DAY OR TWO...
YES, SIR, RIGHT AWAY!
...BUT ALREADY THE HEAD CHEF LET HIM IN THE KITCHEN!
...
IT WAS HIS EYES THAT DID IT.
INSIDE THOSE BLUE EYES OF HIS...
...I SAW A BLAZIN' FIRE OF DETER-MINATION.
"A SHOKUGEKI! ONE DAY I WILL CHALLENGE YOU!"
"DURING THESE FINALS, WE'RE GOING TO PUT AN END TO THE MATCH WE STARTED WAY BACK DURING HELL CAMP!"

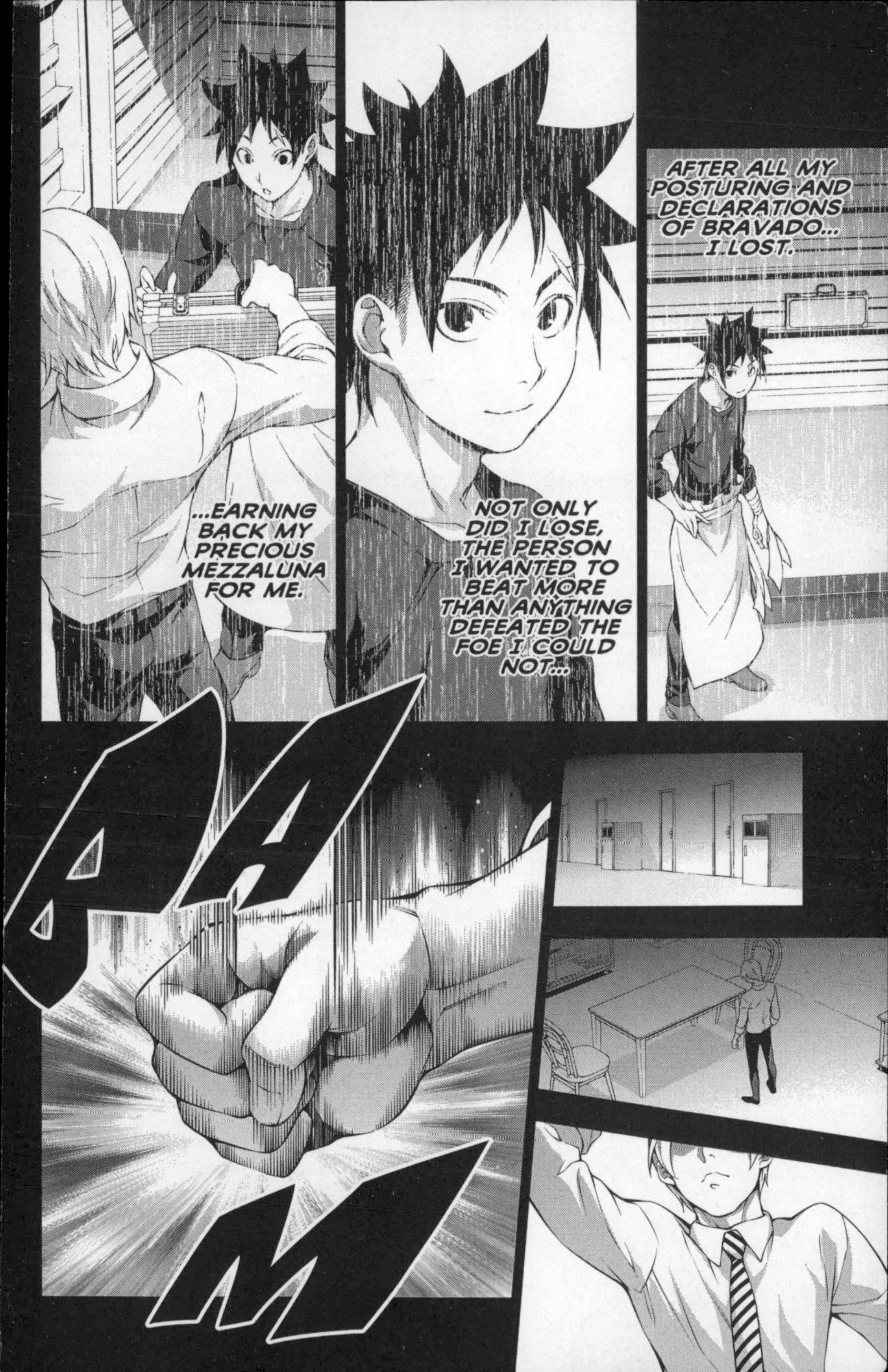
AFTER ALL MY POSTURING AND DECLARATIONS OF BRAVADO... I LOST.
NOT ONLY DID I LOSE, THE PERSON I WANTED TO BEAT MORE THAN ANYTHING DEFEATED THE FOE I COULD NOT...
...EARNING BACK MY PRECIOUS MEZZALUNA FOR ME.
BAM

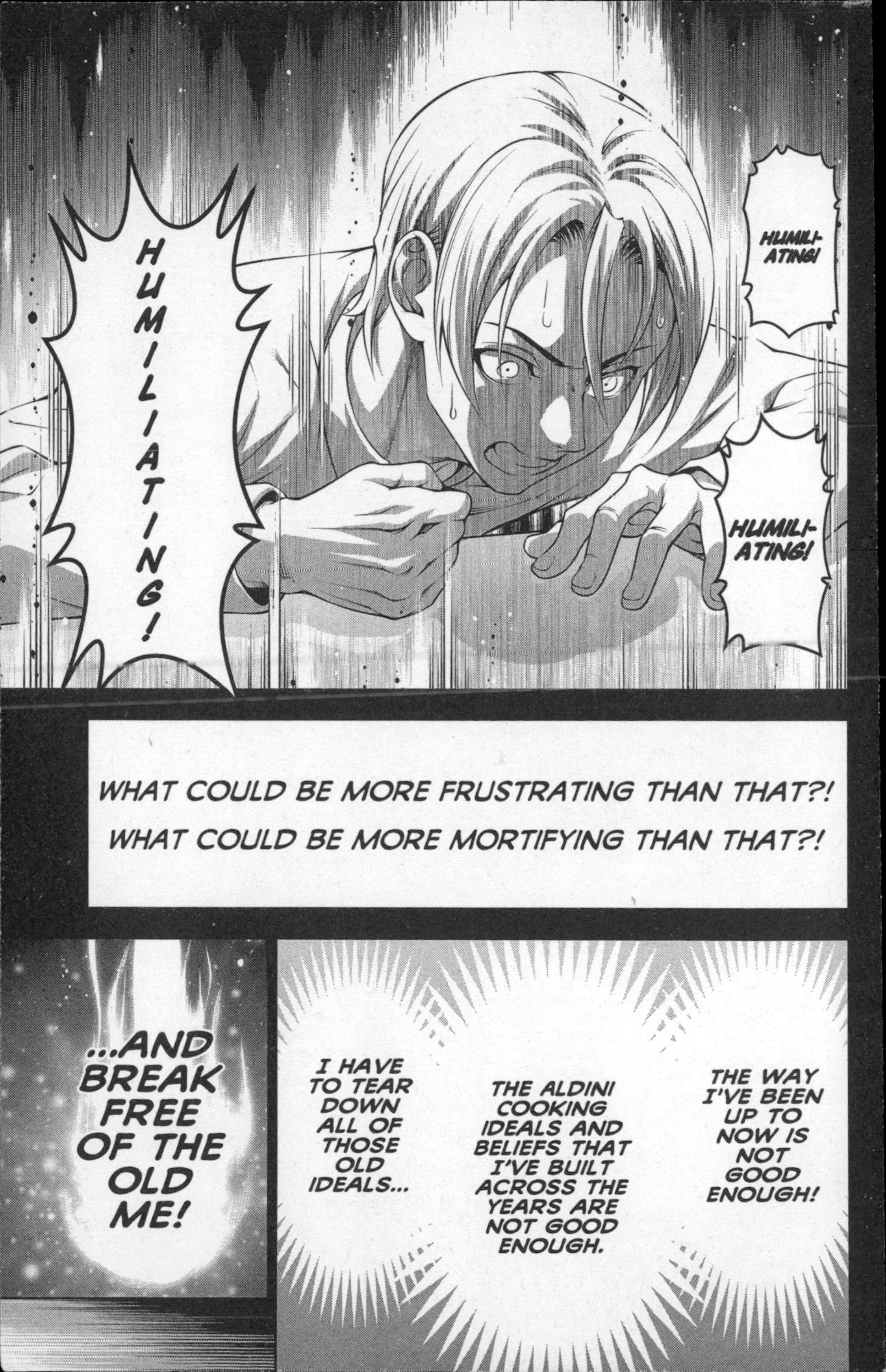
HUMILI-ATING!
HUMILI-ATING!
HUMILIATING!
WHAT COULD BE MORE FRUSTRATING THAN THAT?!
WHAT COULD BE MORE MORTIFYING THAN THAT?!
THE WAY I'VE BEEN UP TO NOW IS NOT GOOD ENOUGH!
THE ALDINI COOKING IDEALS AND BELIEFS THAT I'VE BUILT ACROSS THE YEARS ARE NOT GOOD ENOUGH.
I HAVE TO TEAR DOWN ALL OF THOSE OLD IDEALS...
...AND BREAK FREE OF THE OLD ME!

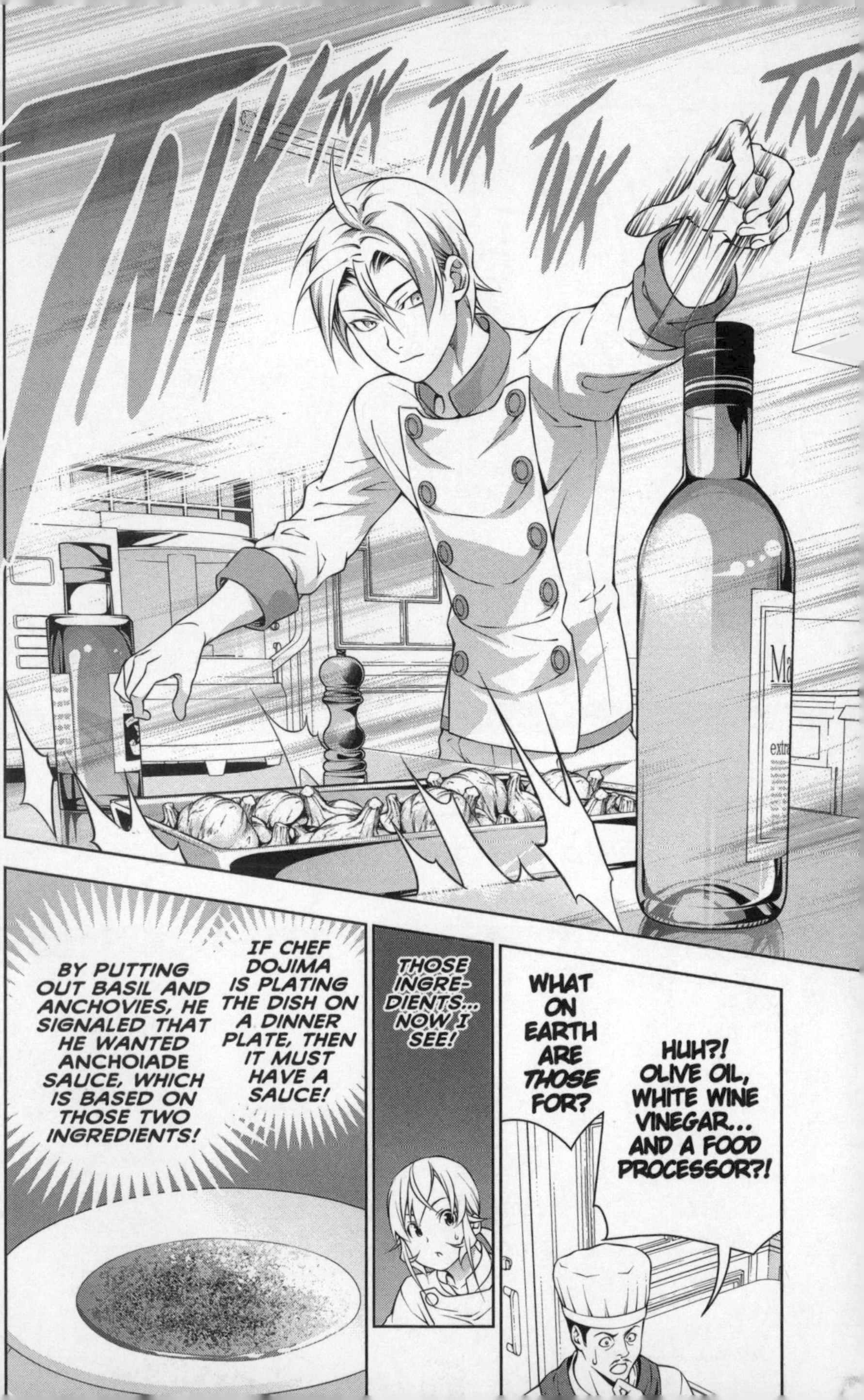
TAK TAK TAK TAK TAK
HUH?! OLIVE OIL, WHITE WINE VINEGAR... AND A FOOD PROCESSOR?!
WHAT ON EARTH ARE THOSE FOR?
THOSE INGREDIENTS... NOW I SEE!
IF CHEF DOJIMA IS PLATING THE DISH ON A DINNER PLATE, THEN IT MUST HAVE A SAUCE!
BY PUTTING OUT BASIL AND ANCHOVIES, HE SIGNALED THAT HE WANTED ANCHOIADE SAUCE, WHICH IS BASED ON THOSE TWO INGREDIENTS!

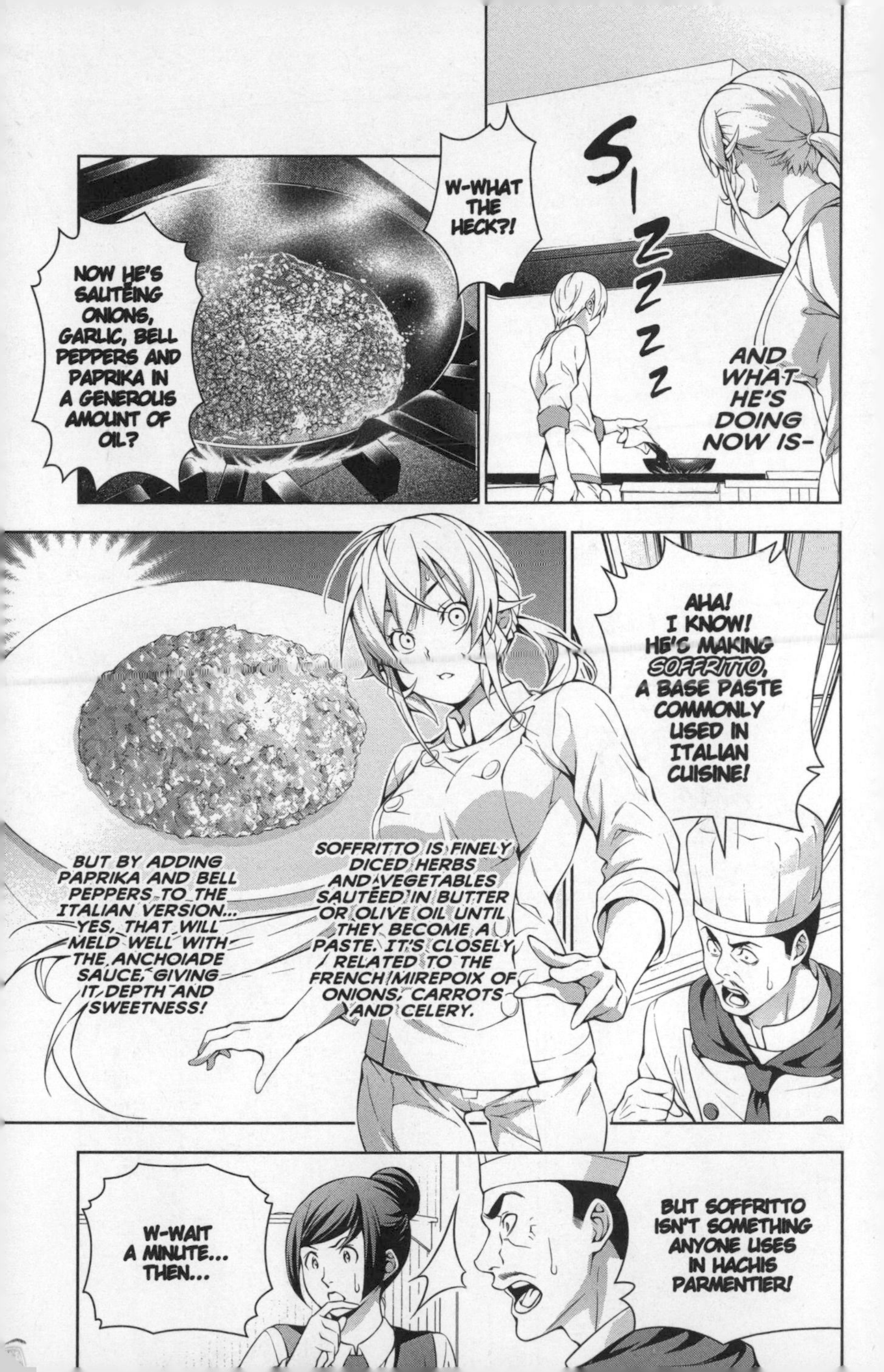
W-WHAT THE HECK?!
SIZZZZ
AND WHAT HE'S DOING NOW IS-
NOW HE'S SAUTÉING ONIONS, GARLIC, BELL PEPPERS AND PAPRIKA IN A GENEROUS AMOUNT OF OIL?
AHA! I KNOW! HE'S MAKING SOFFRITTO, A BASE PASTE COMMONLY USED IN ITALIAN CUISINE!
SOFFRITTO IS FINELY DICED HERBS AND VEGETABLES SAUTÉED IN BUTTER OR OLIVE OIL UNTIL THEY BECOME A PASTE. IT'S CLOSELY RELATED TO THE FRENCH MIREPOIX OF ONIONS, CARROTS AND CELERY.
BUT BY ADDING PAPRIKA AND BELL PEPPERS TO THE ITALIAN VERSION... YES, THAT WILL MELD WELL WITH THE ANCHOIADE SAUCE, GIVING IT DEPTH AND SWEETNESS!
BUT SOFFRITTO ISN'T SOMETHING ANYONE USES IN HACHIS PARMENTIER!
W-WAIT A MINUTE... THEN...

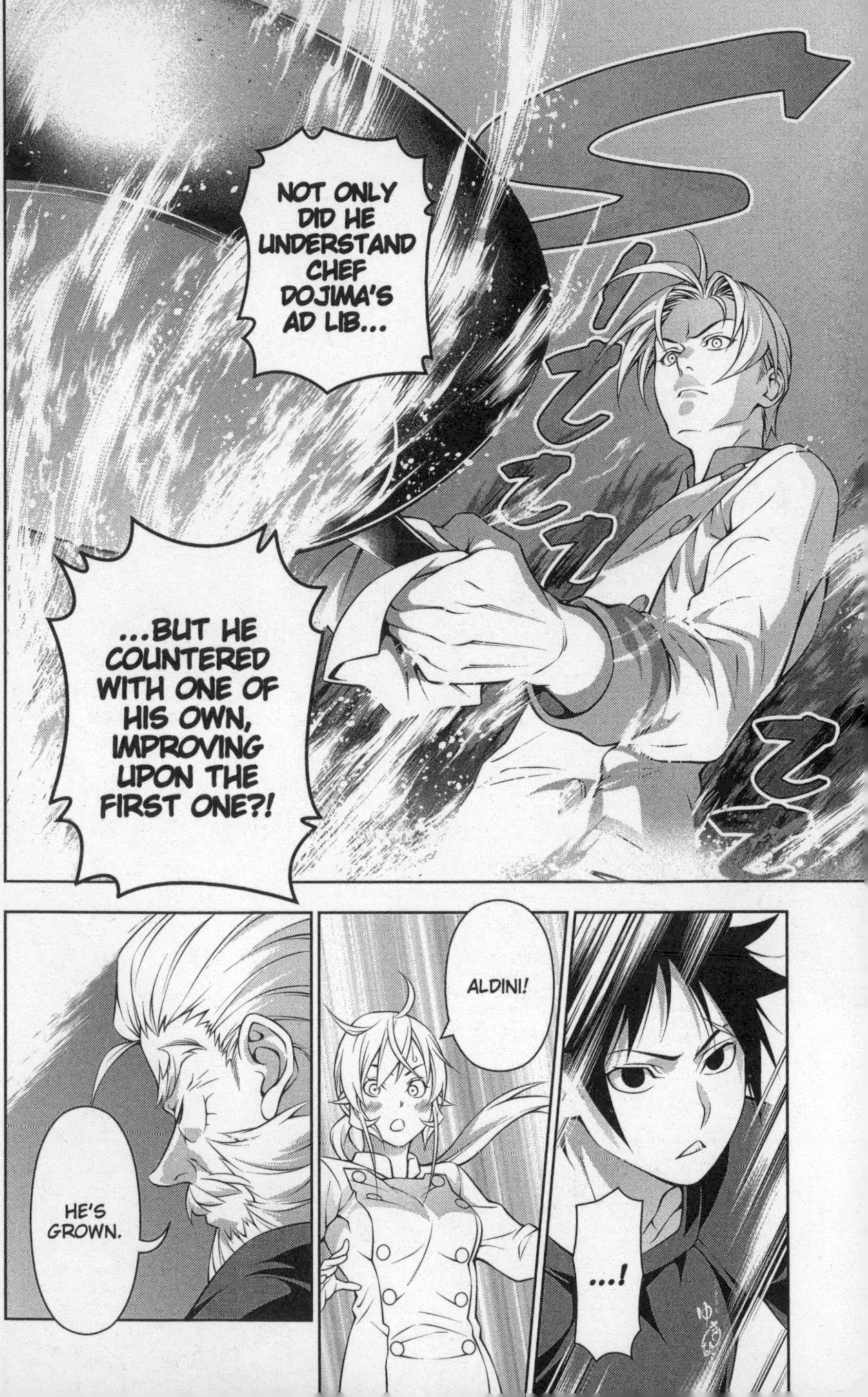
NOT ONLY DID HE UNDERSTAND CHEF DOJIMA'S AD LIB...
...BUT HE COUNTERED WITH ONE OF HIS OWN, IMPROVING UPON THE FIRST ONE?!
...!
ALDINI!
HE'S GROWN.

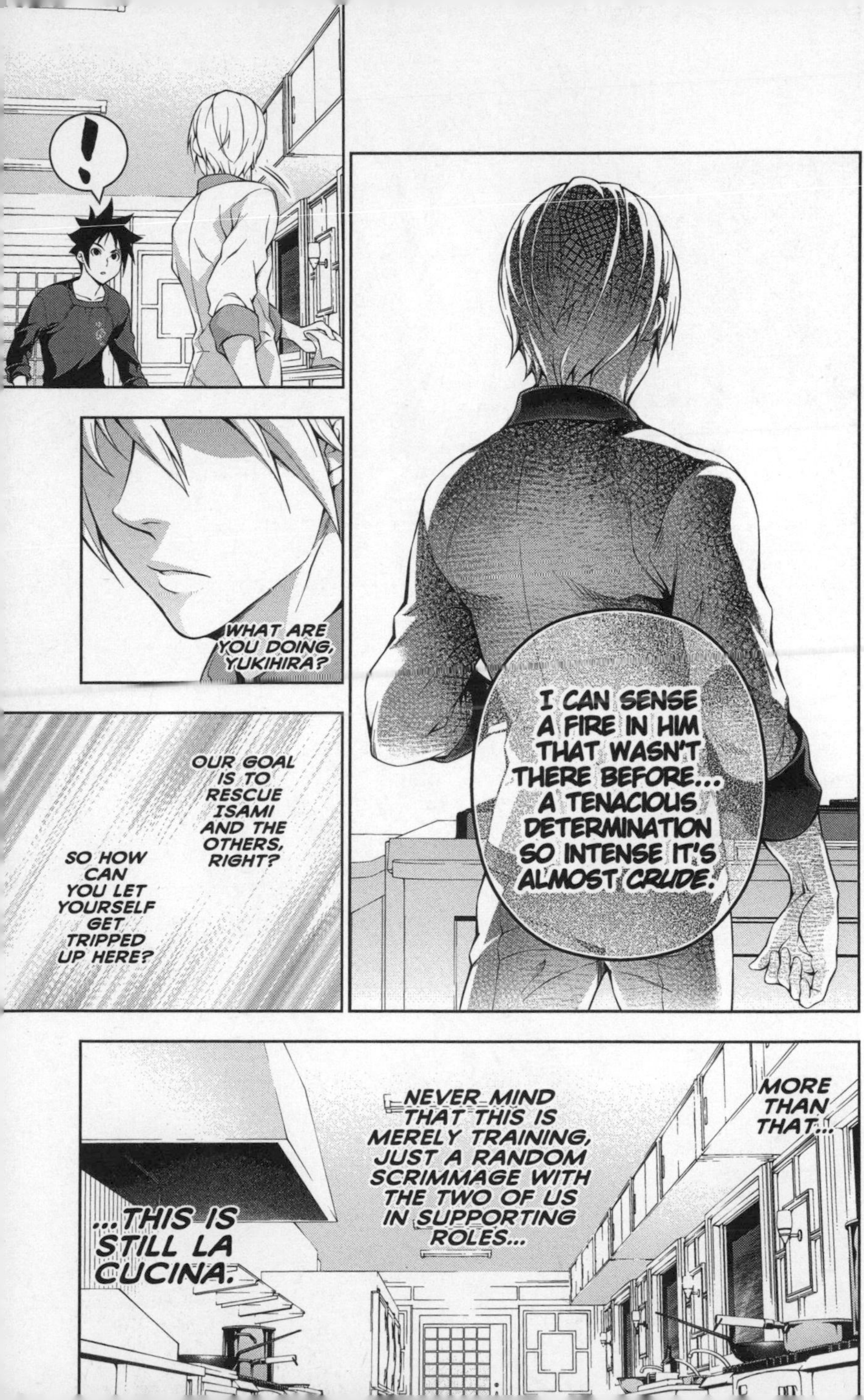
I CAN SENSE A FIRE IN HIM THAT WASN'T THERE BEFORE... A TENACIOUS DETERMINATION SO INTENSE IT'S ALMOST CRUDE.
!
WHAT ARE YOU DOING, YUKIHIRA?
OUR GOAL IS TO RESCUE ISAMI AND THE OTHERS, RIGHT?
SO HOW CAN YOU LET YOURSELF GET TRIPPED UP HERE?
MORE THAN THAT...
NEVER MIND THAT THIS IS MERELY TRAINING, JUST A RANDOM SCRIMMAGE WITH THE TWO OF US IN SUPPORTING ROLES...
...THIS IS STILL LA CUCINA.

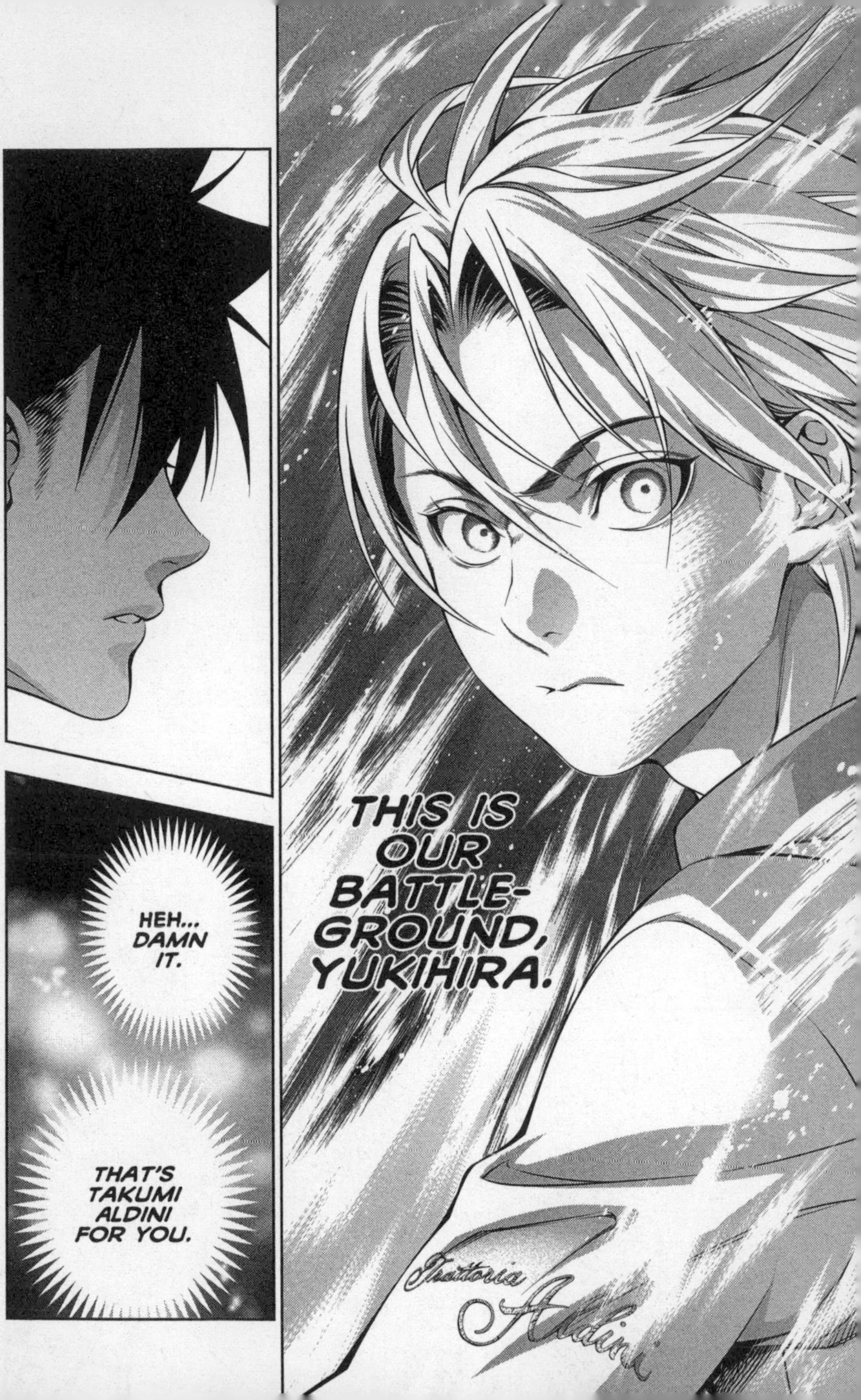
THIS IS OUR BATTLE-GROUND, YUKIHIRA.
Trattoria Aldini
HEH... DAMN IT.
THAT'S TAKUMI ALDINI FOR YOU.

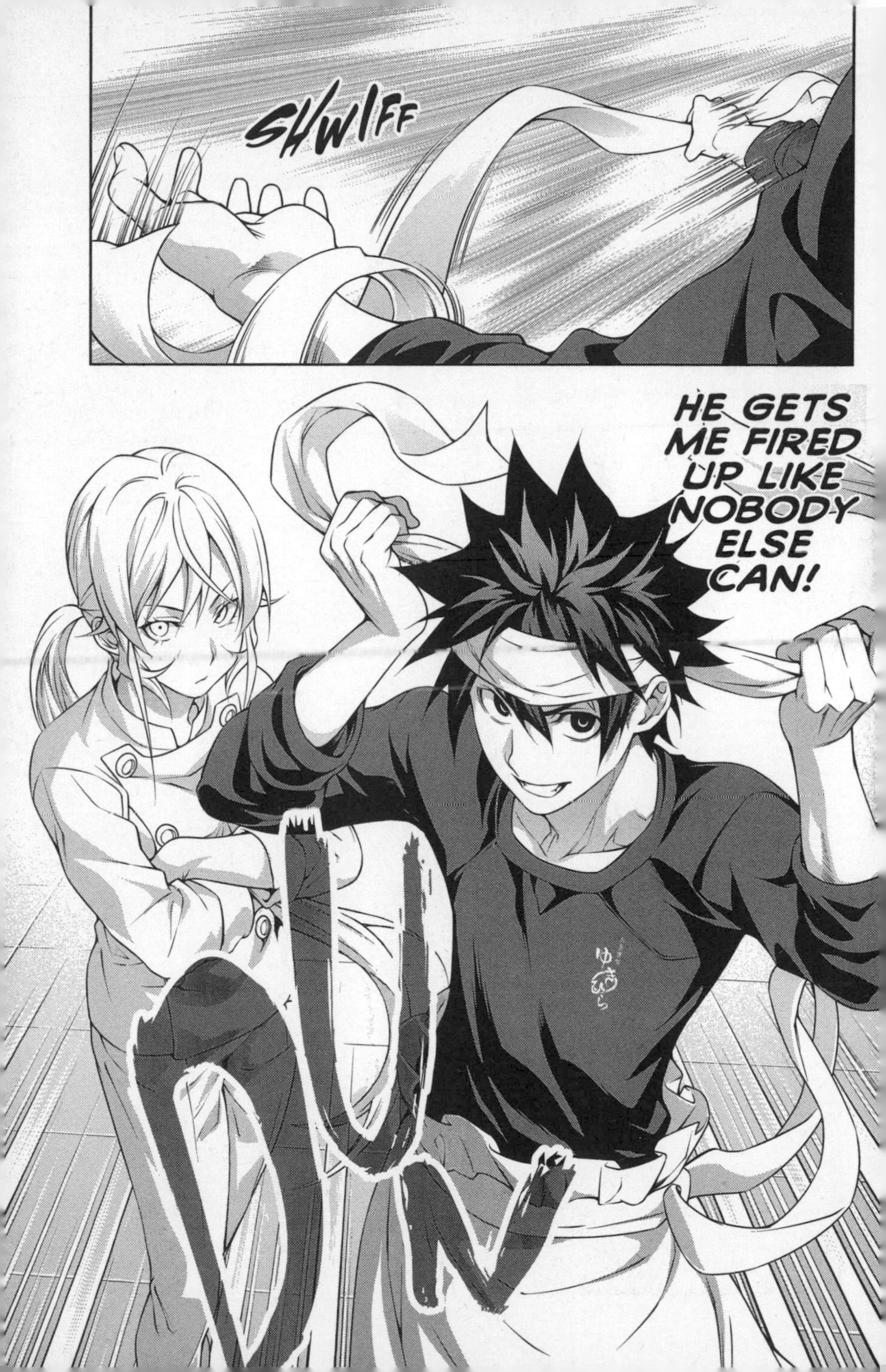
SHWIFF
HE GETS ME FIRED UP LIKE NOBODY ELSE CAN!
ゆきひら

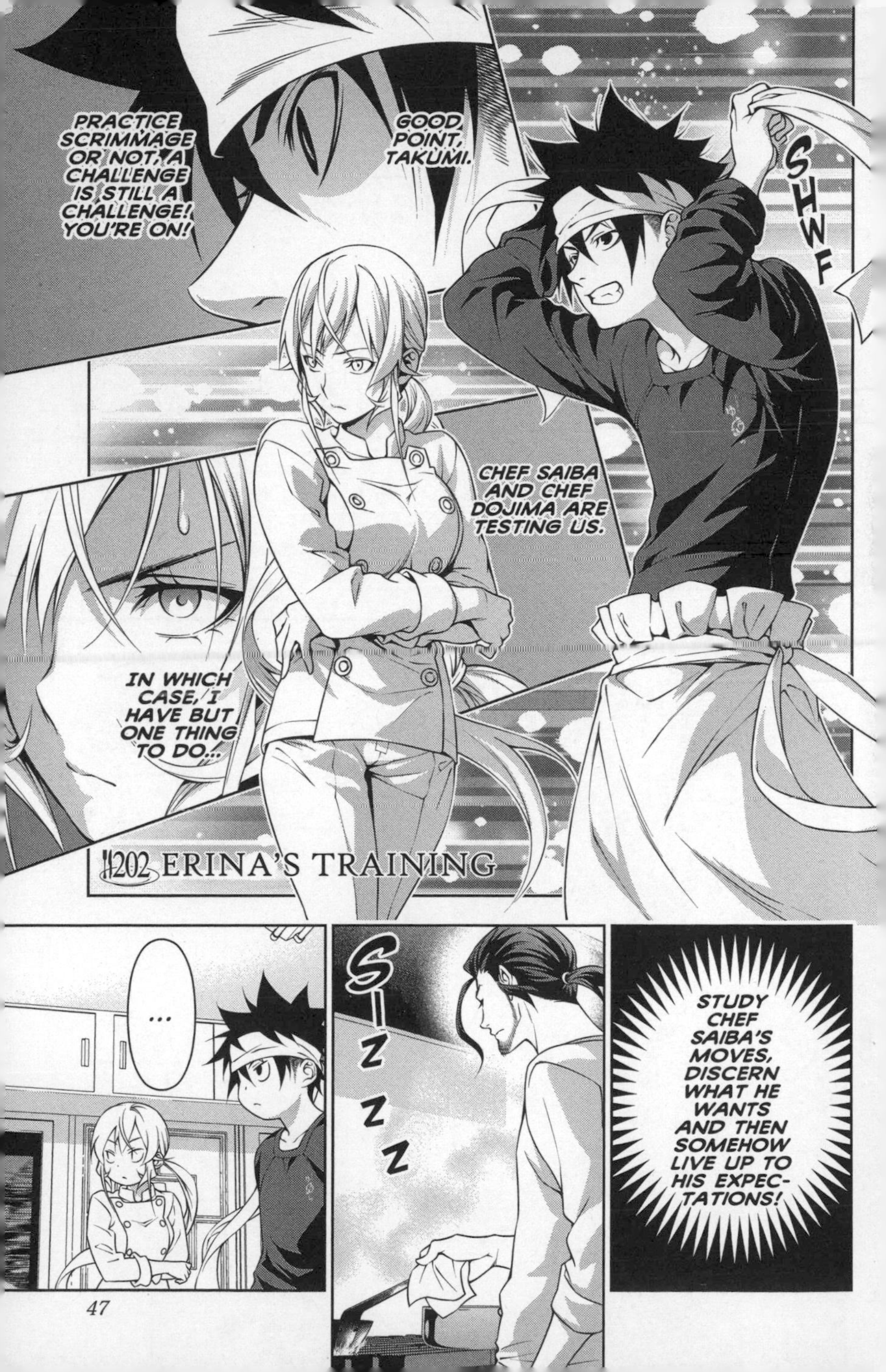
SHWF
GOOD POINT, TAKUMI.
PRACTICE SCRIMMAGE OR NOT, A CHALLENGE IS STILL A CHALLENGE! YOU'RE ON!
CHEF SAIBA AND CHEF DOJIMA ARE TESTING US.
IN WHICH CASE, I HAVE BUT ONE THING TO DO...
#202 ERINA'S TRAINING
STUDY CHEF SAIBA'S MOVES, DISCERN WHAT HE WANTS AND THEN SOMEHOW LIVE UP TO HIS EXPEC-TATIONS!
SIZZZ
...

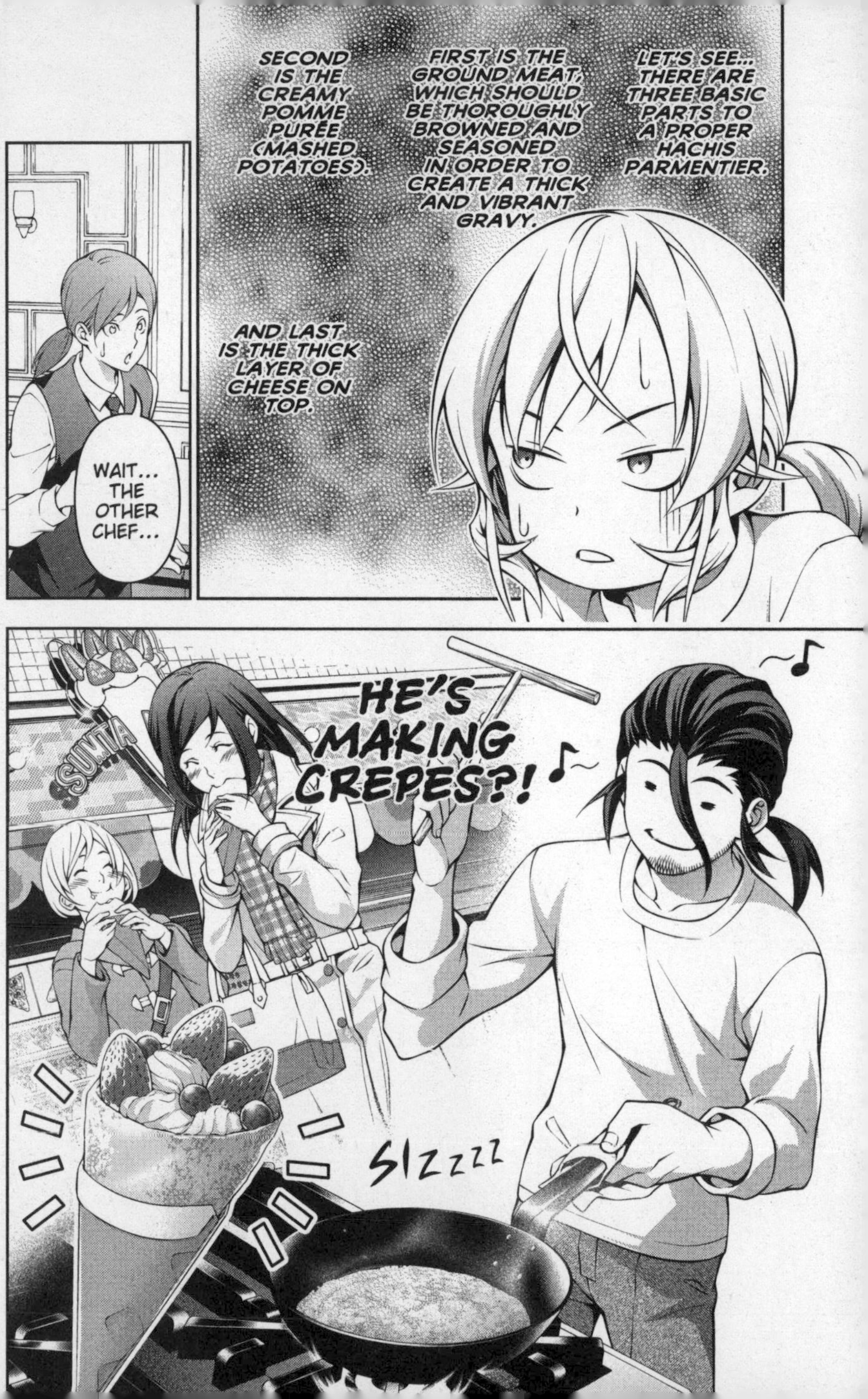
LET'S SEE... THERE ARE THREE BASIC PARTS TO A PROPER HACHIS PARMENTIER.
FIRST IS THE GROUND MEAT, WHICH SHOULD BE THOROUGHLY BROWNED AND SEASONED IN ORDER TO CREATE A THICK AND VIBRANT GRAVY.
SECOND IS THE CREAMY POMME PURÉE (MASHED POTATOES).
AND LAST IS THE THICK LAYER OF CHEESE ON TOP.
WAIT... THE OTHER CHEF...
HE'S MAKING CREPES?!
SIZZZZZ

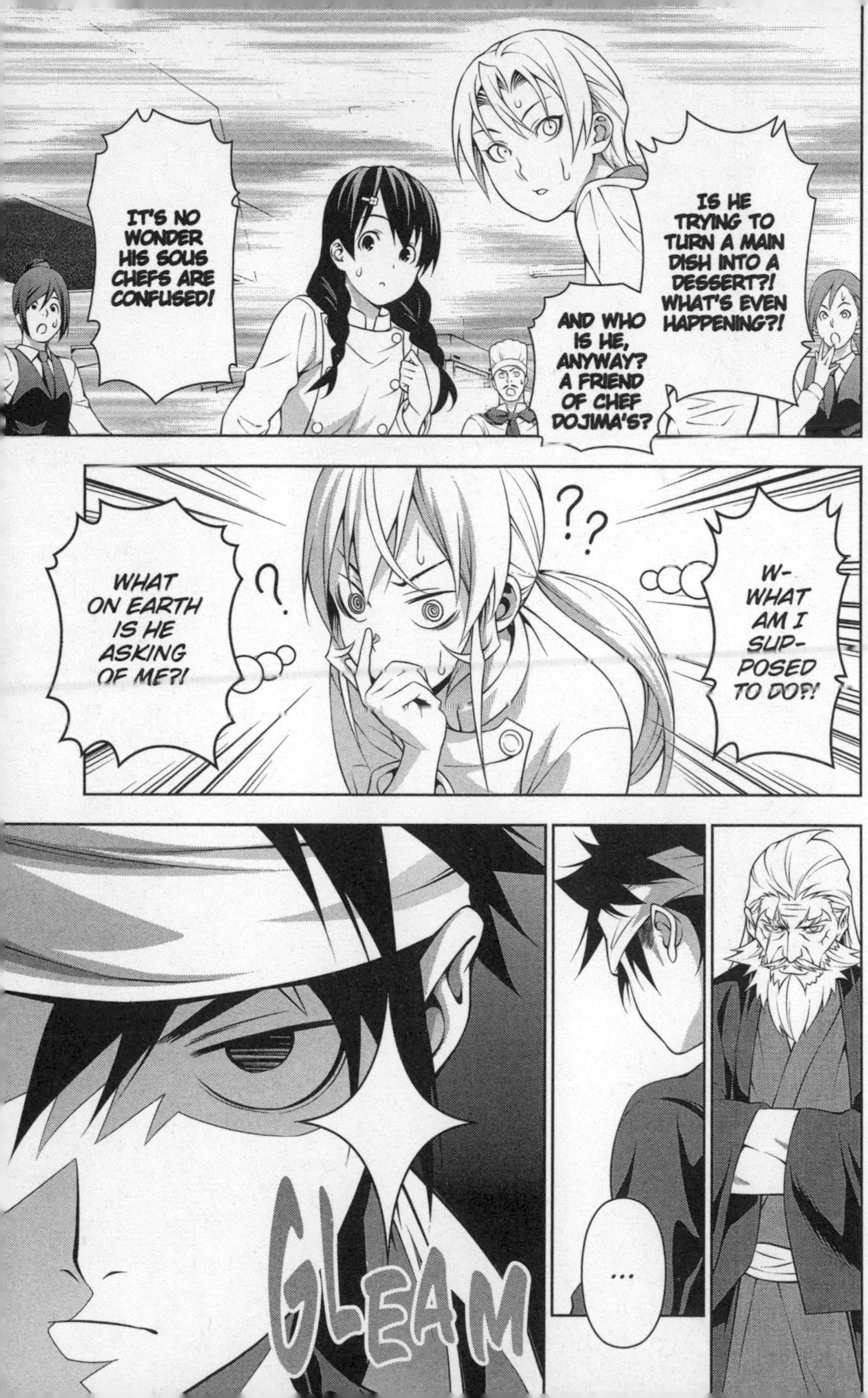
IS HE TRYING TO TURN A MAIN DISH INTO A DESSERT?! WHAT'S EVEN HAPPENING?!
AND WHO IS HE, ANYWAY? A FRIEND OF CHEF DOJIMA'S?
IT'S NO WONDER HIS SOUS CHEFS ARE CONFUSED!
W-WHAT AM I SUP-POSED TO DO?!
WHAT ON EARTH IS HE ASKING OF ME?!
...
GLEAM

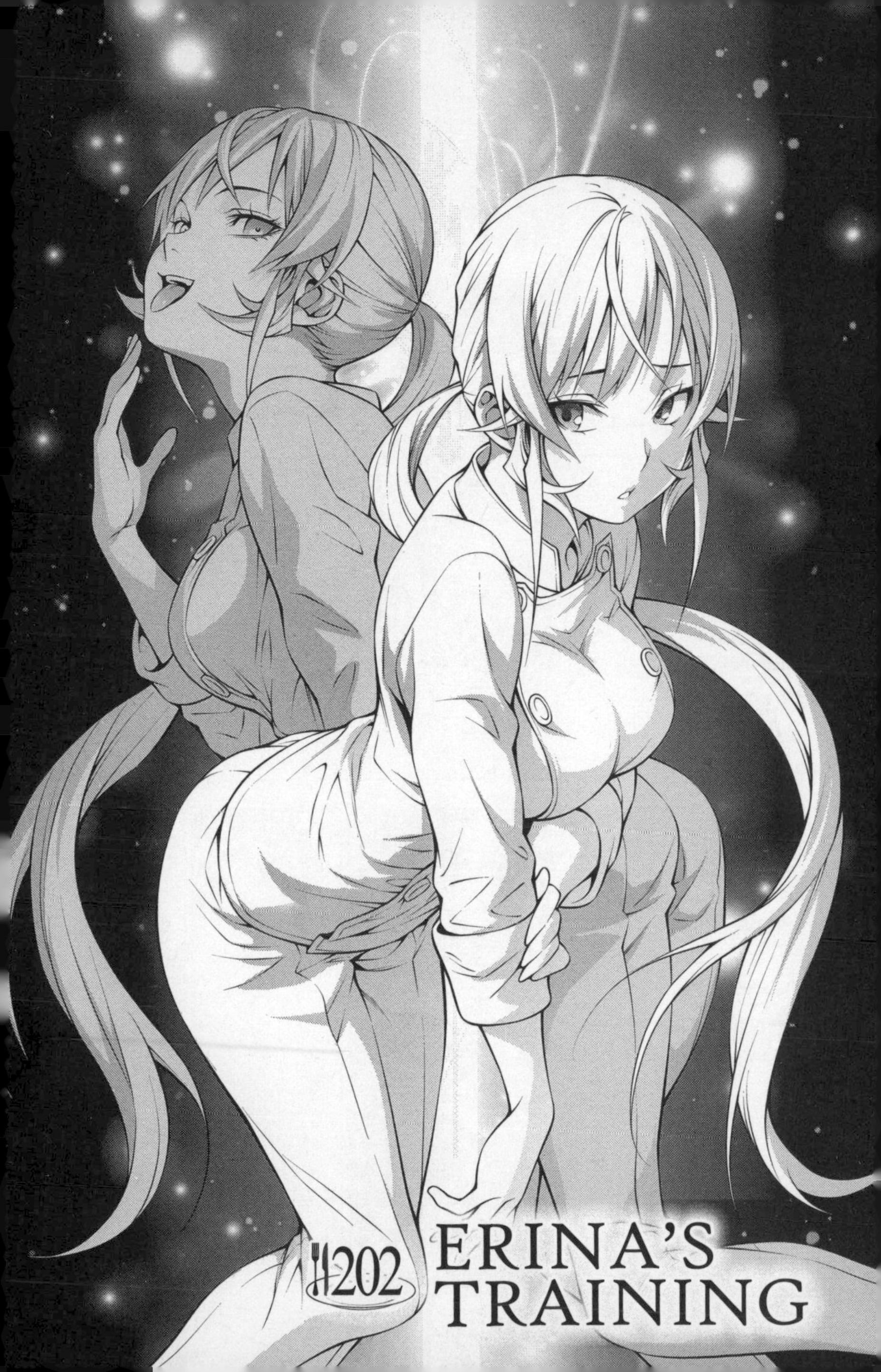
202
ERINA'S
TRAINING

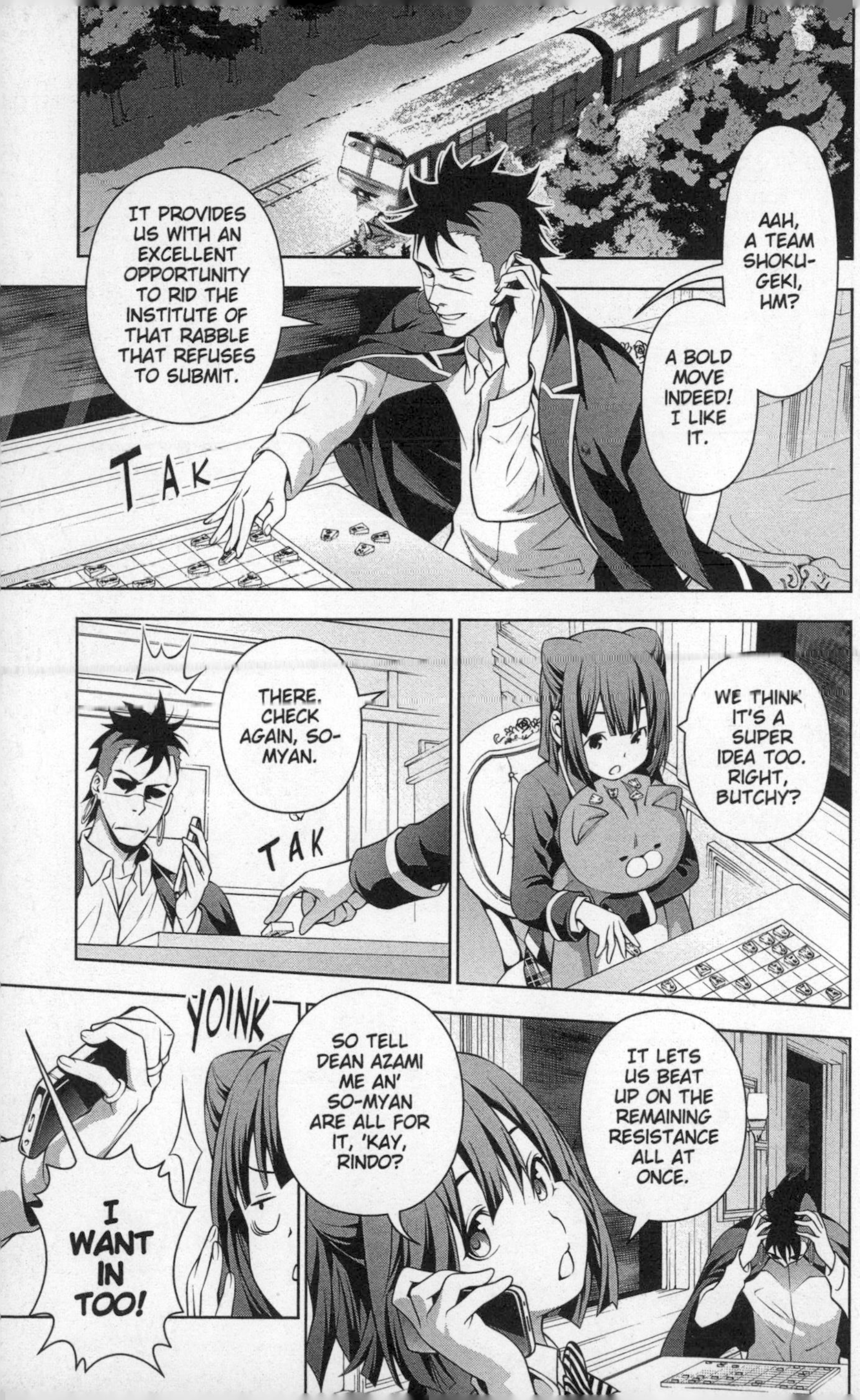
AAH, A TEAM SHOKU-GEKI, HM?
A BOLD MOVE INDEED! I LIKE IT.
IT PROVIDES US WITH AN EXCELLENT OPPORTUNITY TO RID THE INSTITUTE OF THAT RABBLE THAT REFUSES TO SUBMIT.
TAK
WE THINK IT'S A SUPER IDEA TOO. RIGHT, BUTCHY?
THERE. CHECK AGAIN, SO-MYAN.
TAK
IT LETS US BEAT UP ON THE REMAINING RESISTANCE ALL AT ONCE.
SO TELL DEAN AZAMI ME AN' SO-MYAN ARE ALL FOR IT, 'KAY, RINDO?
YOINK
I WANT IN TOO!

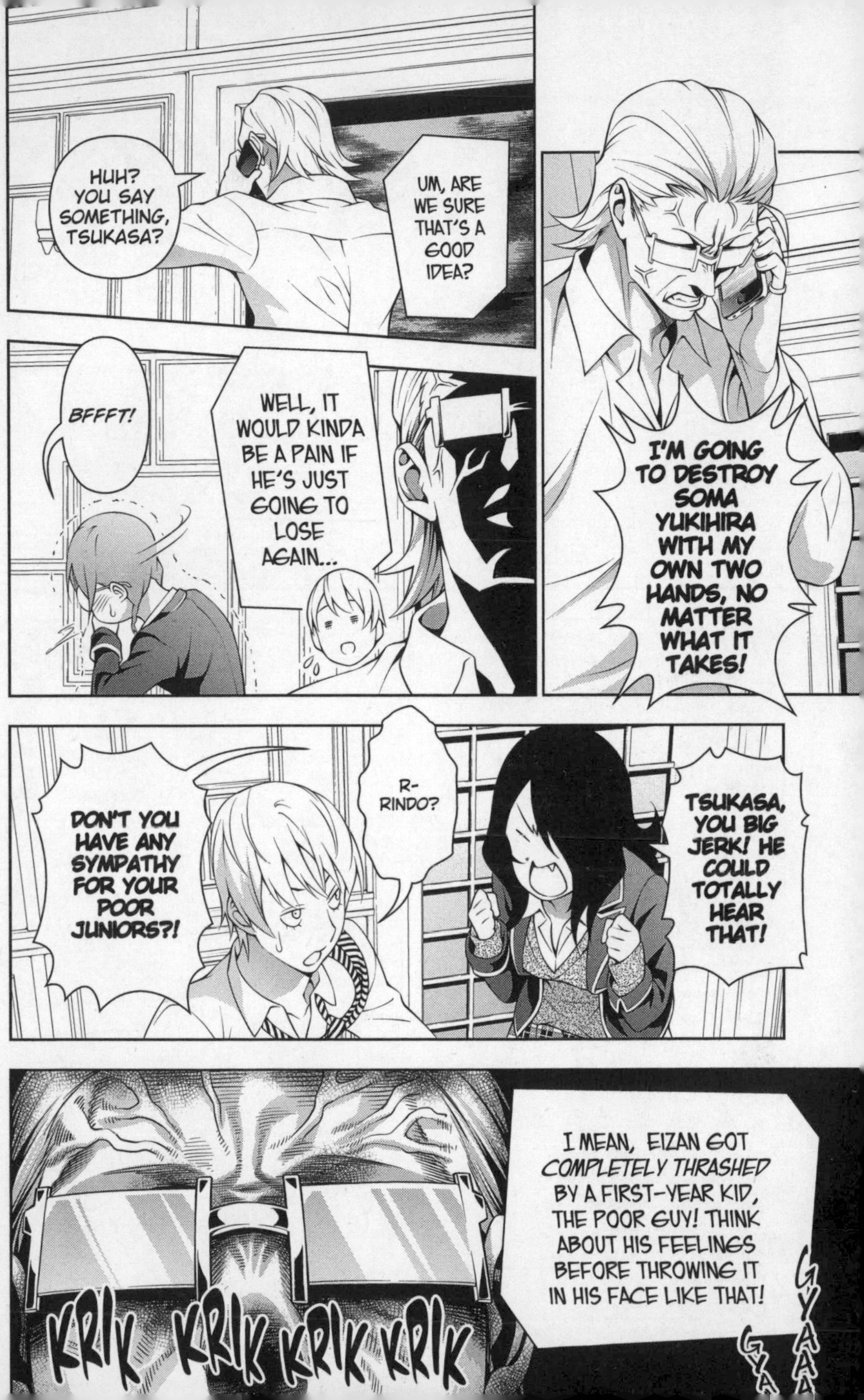
I'M GOING TO DESTROY SOMA YUKIHIRA WITH MY OWN TWO HANDS, NO MATTER WHAT IT TAKES!
UM, ARE WE SURE THAT'S A GOOD IDEA?
HUH? YOU SAY SOMETHING, TSUKASA?
WELL, IT WOULD KINDA BE A PAIN IF HE'S JUST GOING TO LOSE AGAIN...
BFFFT!
TSUKASA, YOU BIG JERK! HE COULD TOTALLY HEAR THAT!
R-RINDO?
DON'T YOU HAVE ANY SYMPATHY FOR YOUR POOR JUNIORS?!
I MEAN, EIZAN GOT *COMPLETELY THRASHED* BY A FIRST-YEAR KID, THE POOR GUY! THINK ABOUT HIS FEELINGS BEFORE THROWING IT IN HIS FACE LIKE THAT!
GYAAA
KRIK KRIK KRIK KRIK

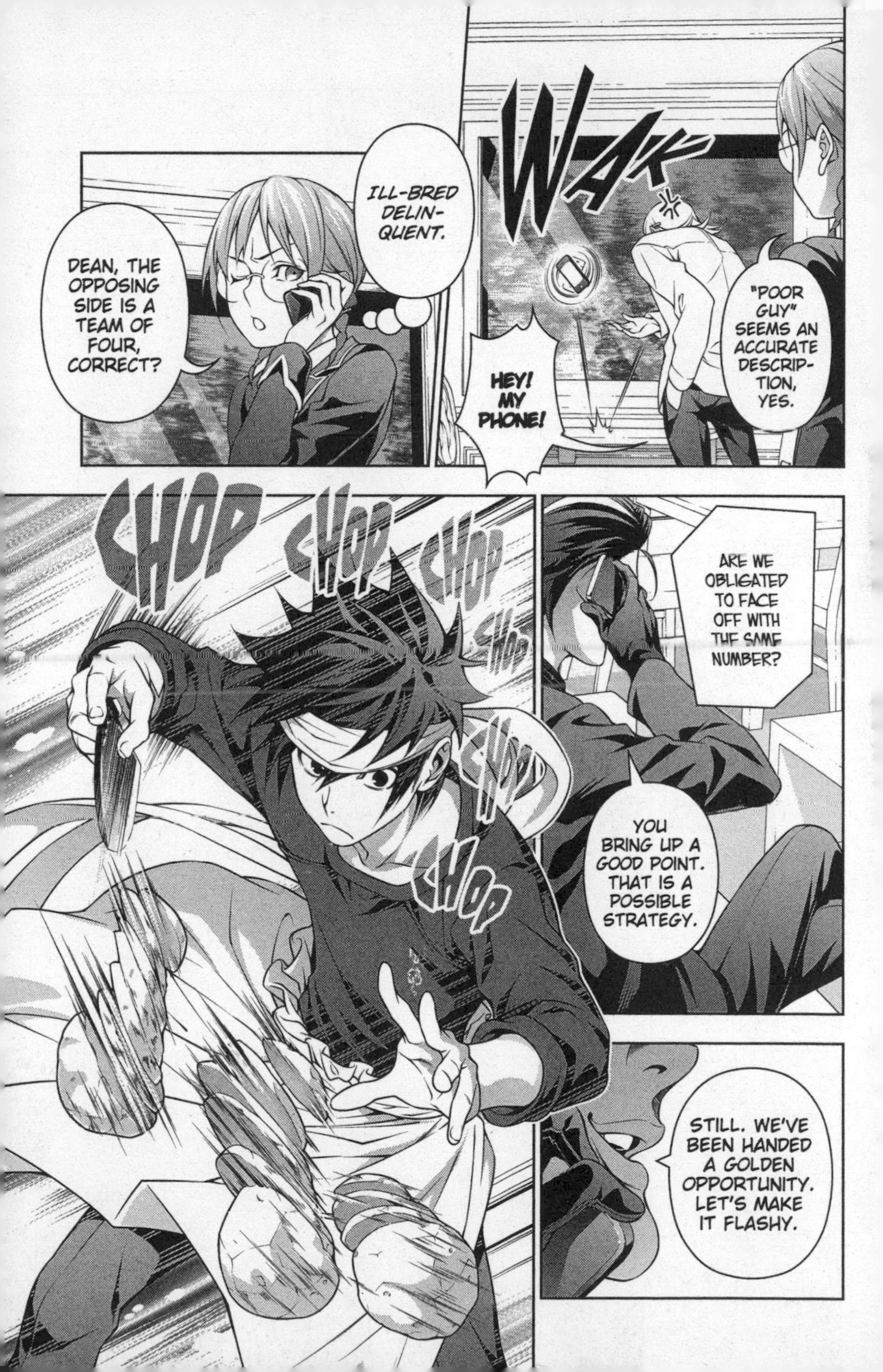
WAK
"POOR GUY" SEEMS AN ACCURATE DESCRIP-TION, YES.
HEY! MY PHONE!
ILL-BRED DELIN-QUENT.
DEAN, THE OPPOSING SIDE IS A TEAM OF FOUR, CORRECT?
ARE WE OBLIGATED TO FACE OFF WITH THE SAME NUMBER?
YOU BRING UP A GOOD POINT. THAT IS A POSSIBLE STRATEGY.
STILL. WE'VE BEEN HANDED A GOLDEN OPPORTUNITY. LET'S MAKE IT FLASHY.
CHOP CHOP CHOP CHOP CHOP CHOP

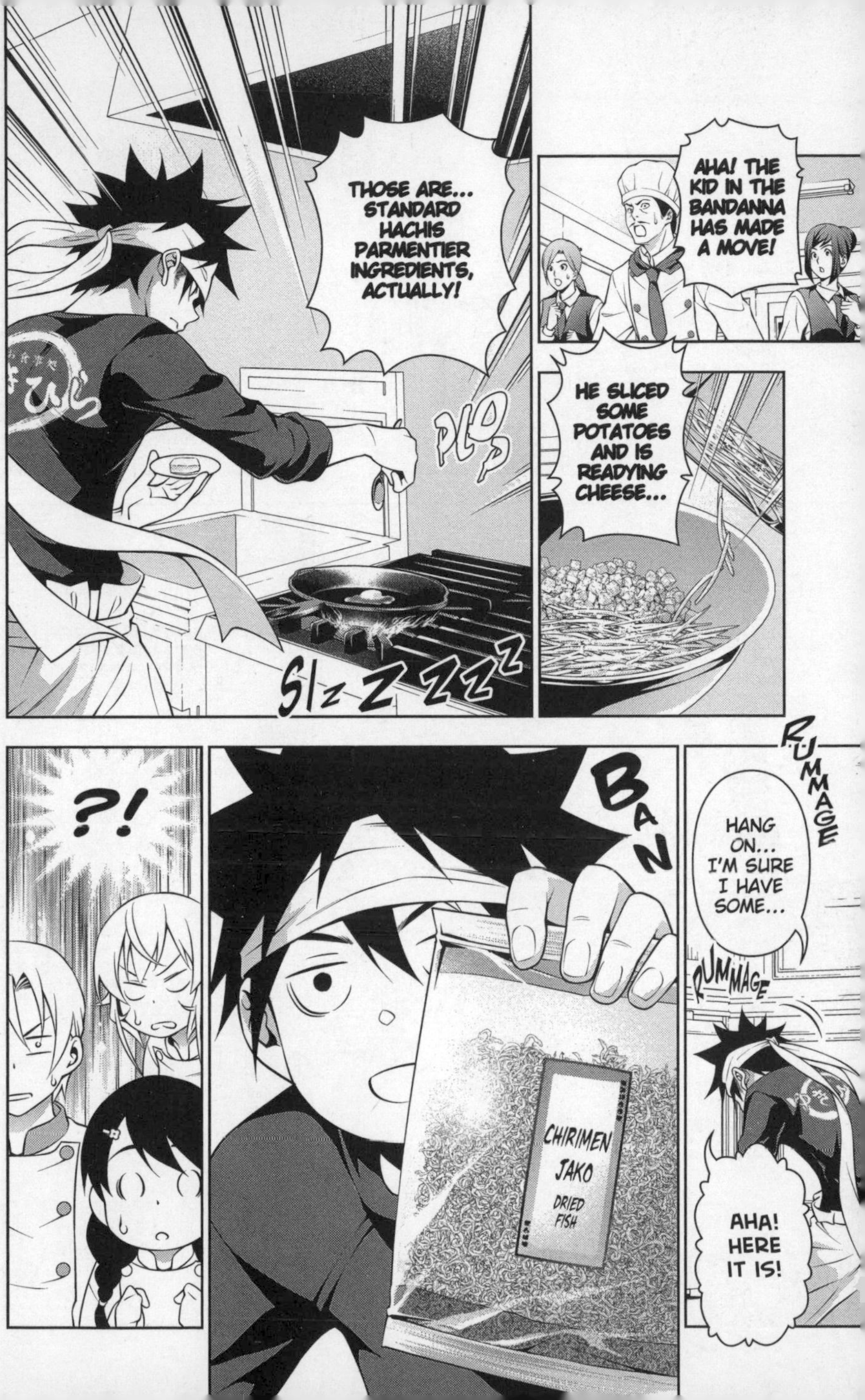
AHA! THE KID IN THE BANDANNA HAS MADE A MOVE!
HE SLICED SOME POTATOES AND IS READYING CHEESE...
THOSE ARE... STANDARD HACHIS PARMENTIER INGREDIENTS, ACTUALLY!
PLOP
SIZZZZZZ
RUMMAGE
HANG ON... I'M SURE I HAVE SOME...
RUMMAGE
AHA! HERE IT IS!
BAN
CHIRIMEN JAKO
DRIED FISH
?!

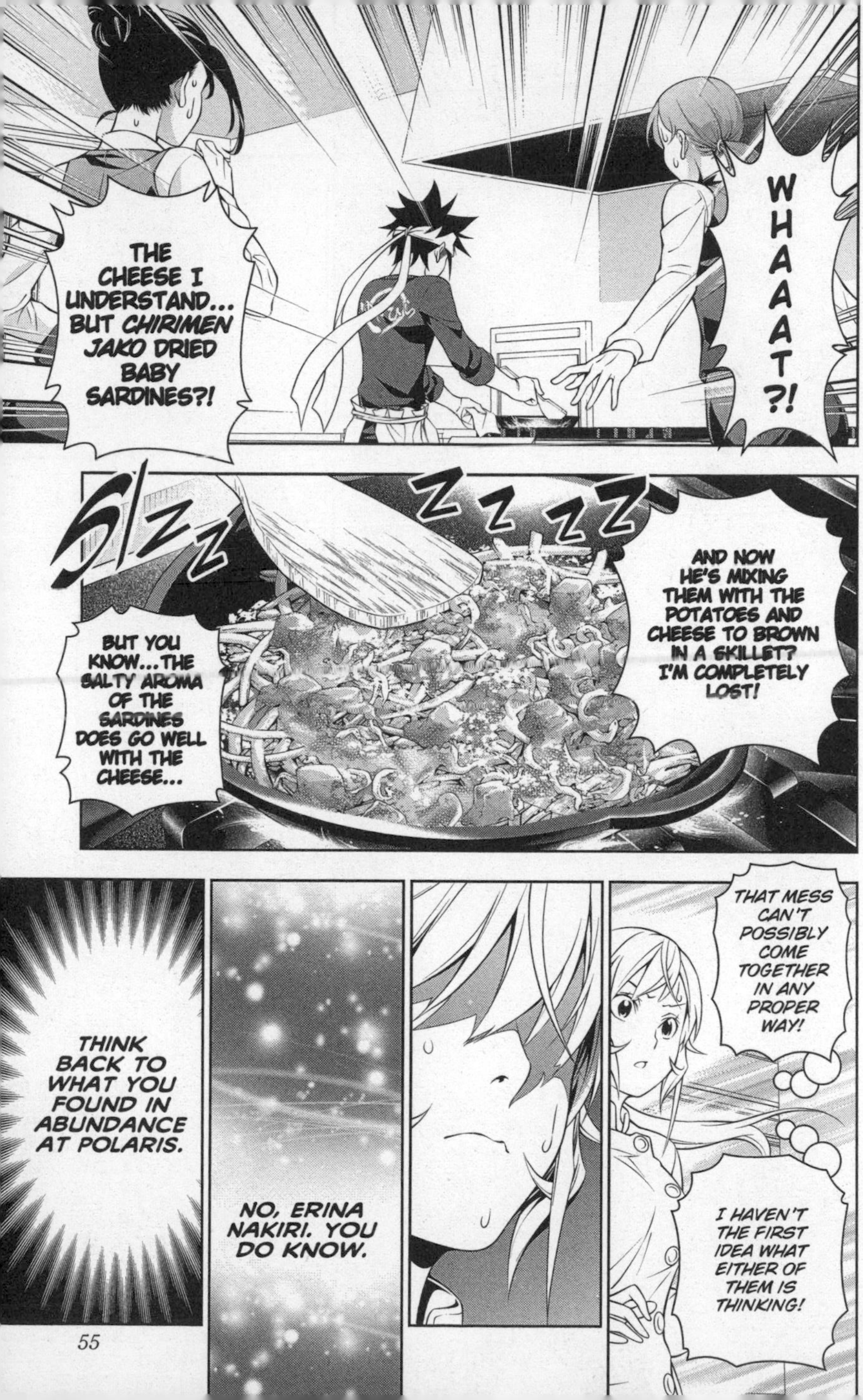
WHAAAT?!
THE CHEESE I UNDERSTAND... BUT CHIRIMEN JAKO DRIED BABY SARDINES?!
SIZZZZZZ
AND NOW HE'S MIXING THEM WITH THE POTATOES AND CHEESE TO BROWN IN A SKILLET? I'M COMPLETELY LOST!
BUT YOU KNOW...THE SALTY AROMA OF THE SARDINES DOES GO WELL WITH THE CHEESE...
THAT MESS CAN'T POSSIBLY COME TOGETHER IN ANY PROPER WAY!
I HAVEN'T THE FIRST IDEA WHAT EITHER OF THEM IS THINKING!
NO, ERINA NAKIRI. YOU DO KNOW.
THINK BACK TO WHAT YOU FOUND IN ABUNDANCE AT POLARIS.

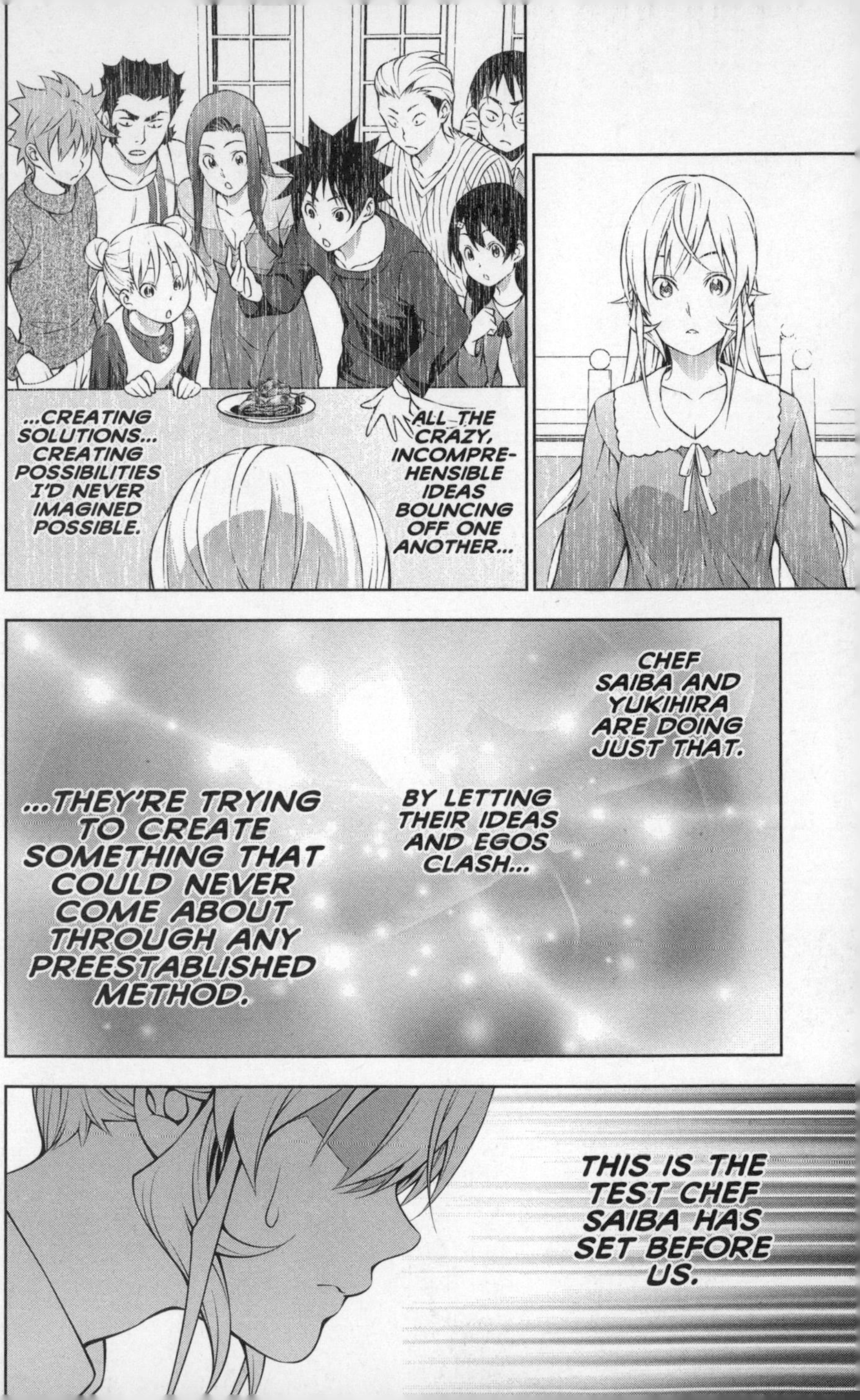
ALL THE CRAZY, INCOMPREHENSIBLE IDEAS BOUNCING OFF ONE ANOTHER...
...CREATING SOLUTIONS... CREATING POSSIBILITIES I'D NEVER IMAGINED POSSIBLE.
CHEF SAIBA AND YUKIHIRA ARE DOING JUST THAT.
BY LETTING THEIR IDEAS AND EGOS CLASH...
...THEY'RE TRYING TO CREATE SOMETHING THAT COULD NEVER COME ABOUT THROUGH ANY PREESTABLISHED METHOD.
THIS IS THE TEST CHEF SAIBA HAS SET BEFORE US.

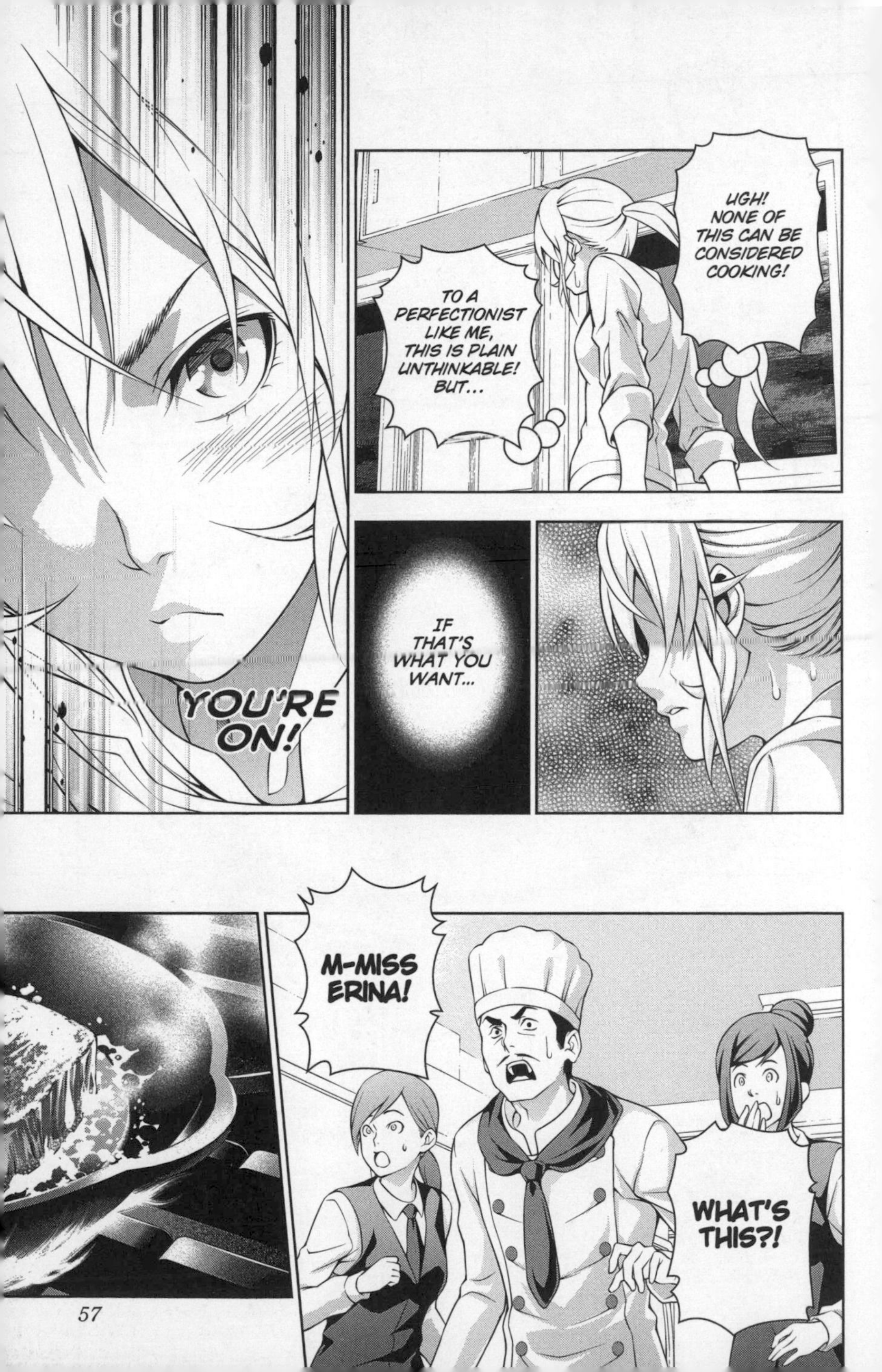
UGH! NONE OF THIS CAN BE CONSIDERED COOKING!
TO A PERFECTIONIST LIKE ME, THIS IS PLAIN UNTHINKABLE! BUT...
IF THAT'S WHAT YOU WANT...
YOU'RE ON!
M-MISS ERINA!
WHAT'S THIS?!

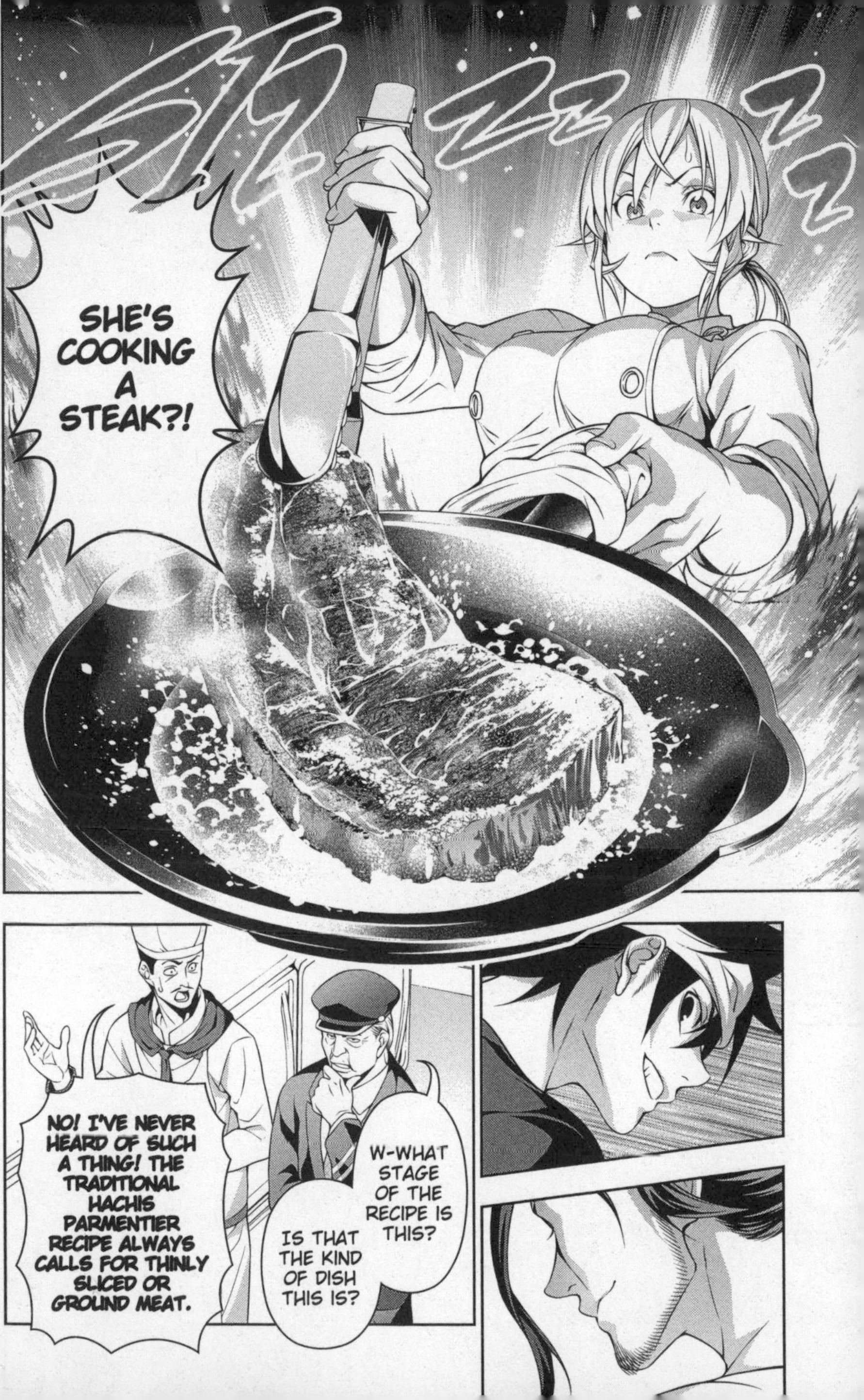
SHE'S COOKING A STEAK?!
W-WHAT STAGE OF THE RECIPE IS THIS?
IS THAT THE KIND OF DISH THIS IS?
NO! I'VE NEVER HEARD OF SUCH A THING! THE TRADITIONAL HACHIS PARMENTIER RECIPE ALWAYS CALLS FOR THINLY SLICED OR GROUND MEAT.

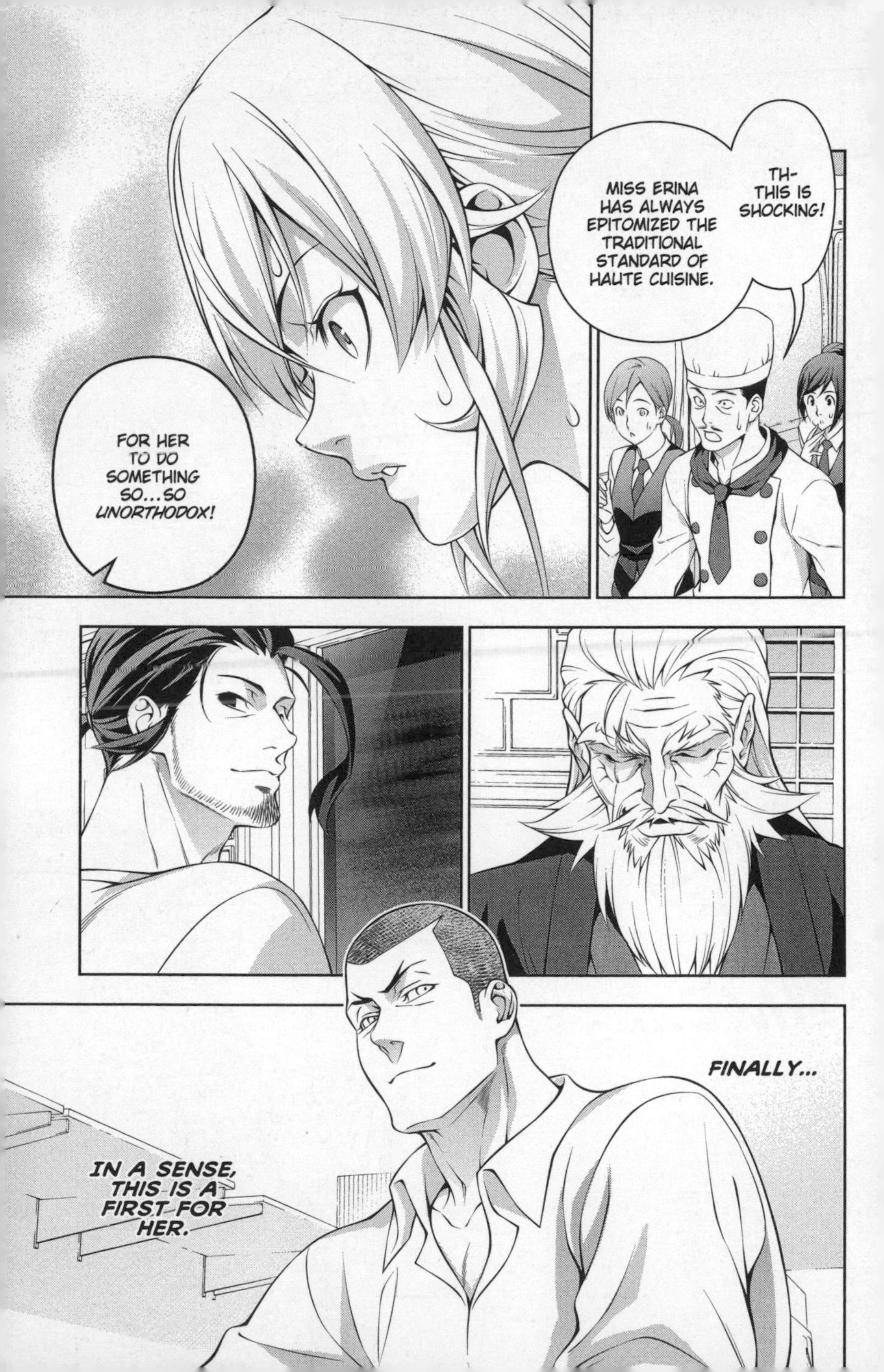
TH- THIS IS SHOCKING!
MISS ERINA HAS ALWAYS EPITOMIZED THE TRADITIONAL STANDARD OF HAUTE CUISINE.
FOR HER TO DO SOMETHING SO...SO *UNORTHODOX!*
FINALLY...
IN A SENSE, THIS IS A FIRST FOR HER.

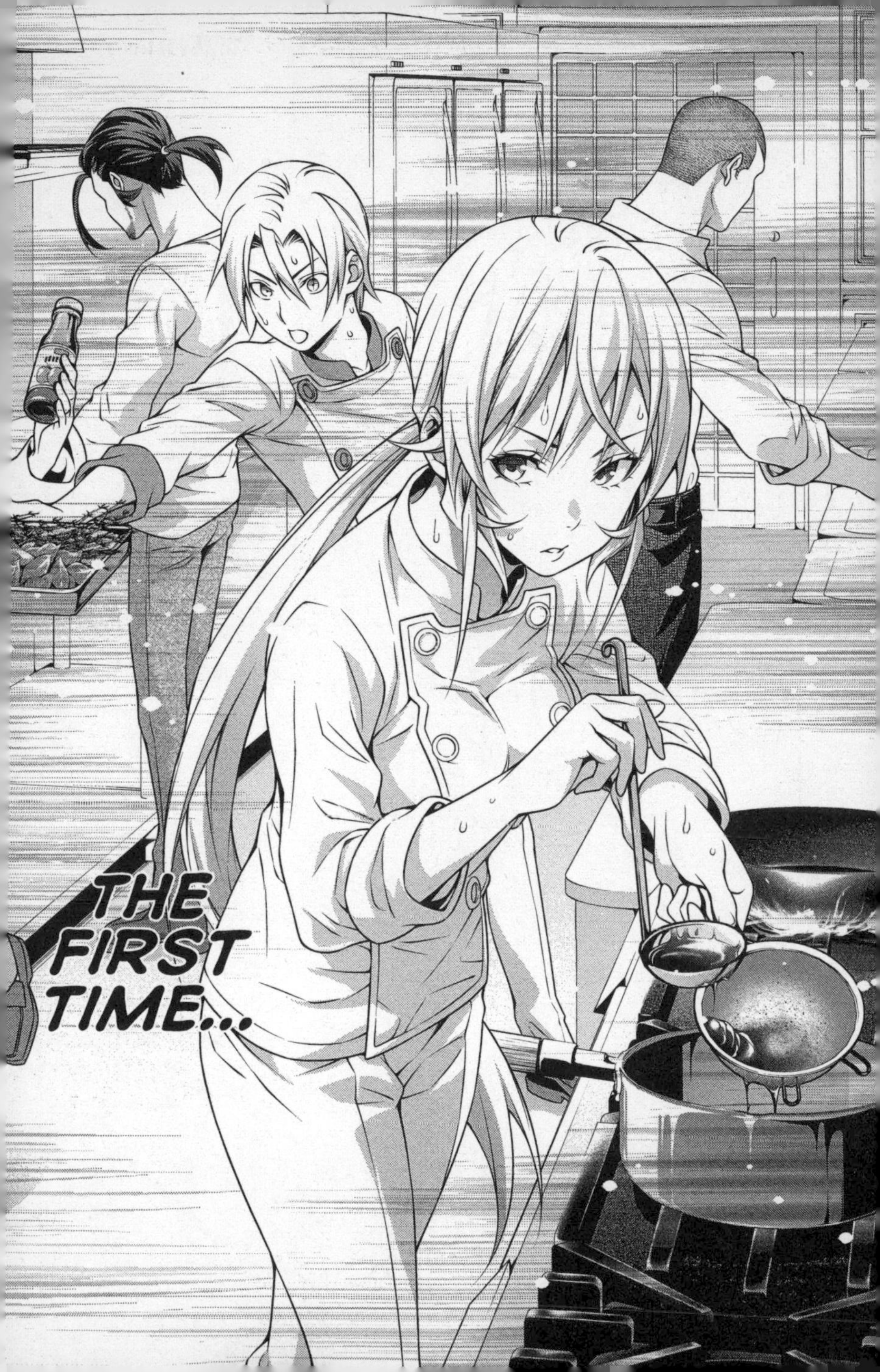
THE FIRST TIME...

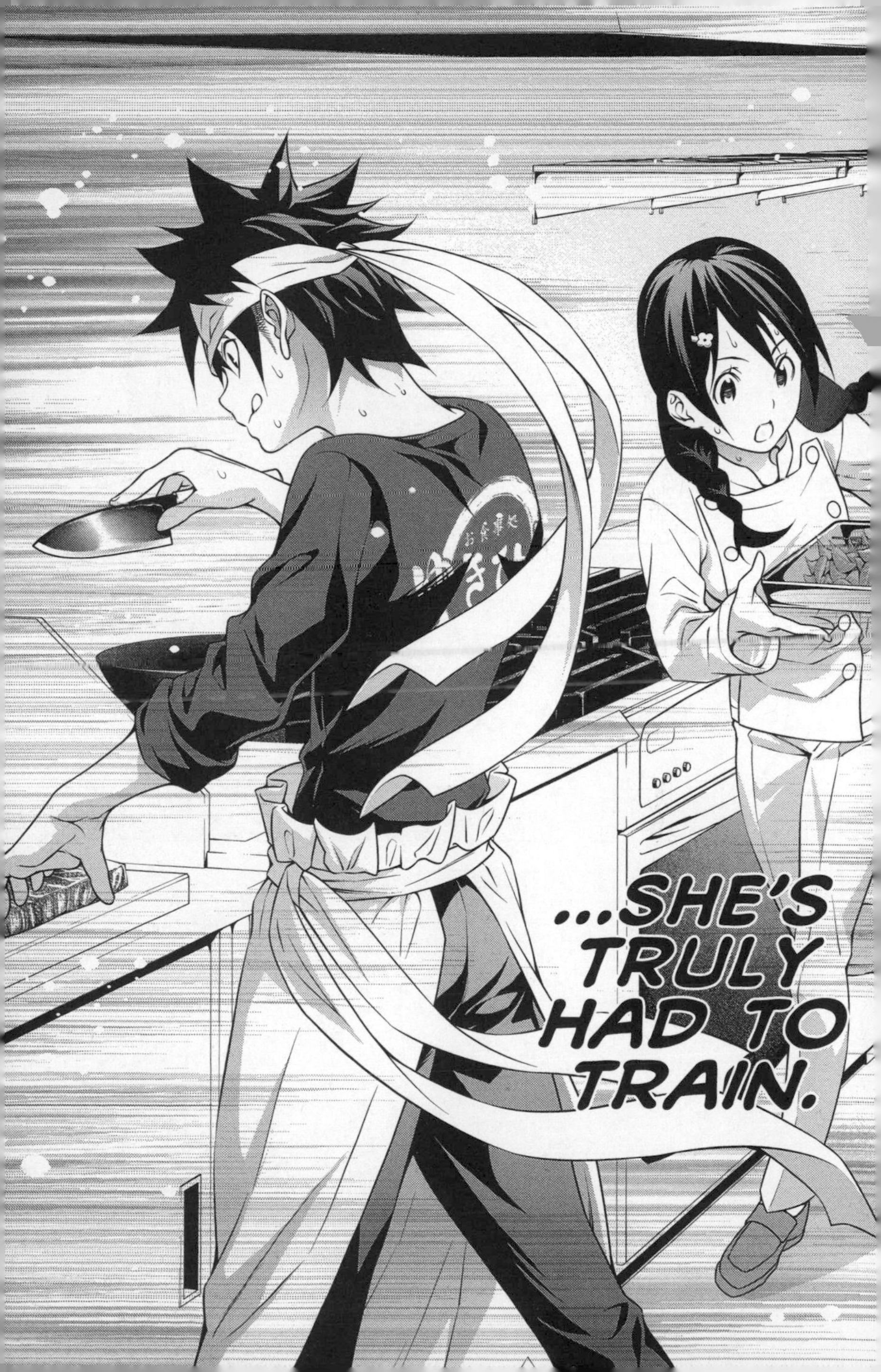
...SHE'S TRULY HAD TO TRAIN.

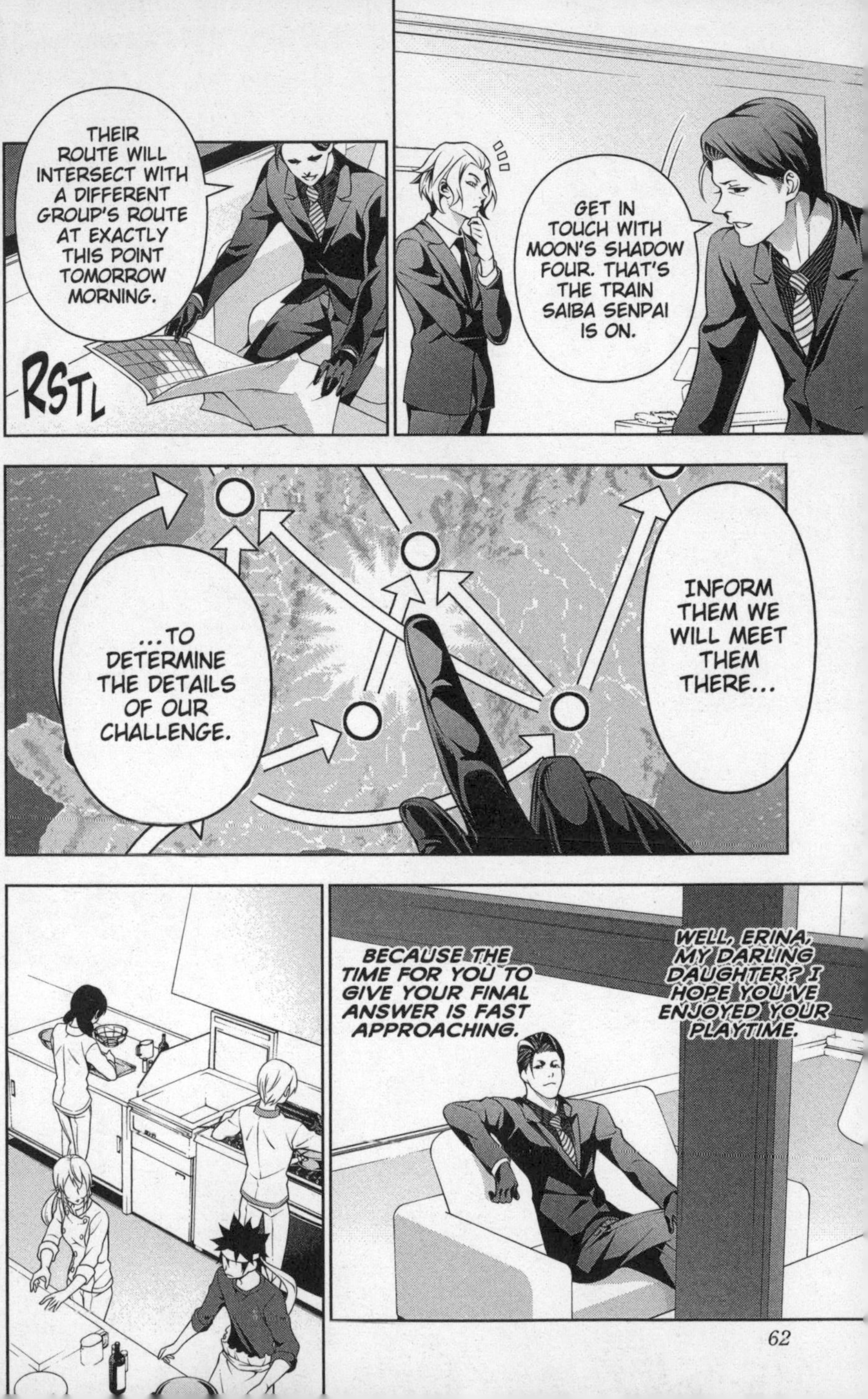
GET IN TOUCH WITH MOON'S SHADOW FOUR. THAT'S THE TRAIN SAIBA SENPAI IS ON.
THEIR ROUTE WILL INTERSECT WITH A DIFFERENT GROUP'S ROUTE AT EXACTLY THIS POINT TOMORROW MORNING.
RSTL
INFORM THEM WE WILL MEET THEM THERE...
...TO DETERMINE THE DETAILS OF OUR CHALLENGE.
WELL, ERINA, MY DARLING DAUGHTER? I HOPE YOU'VE ENJOYED YOUR PLAYTIME.
BECAUSE THE TIME FOR YOU TO GIVE YOUR FINAL ANSWER IS FAST APPROACHING.

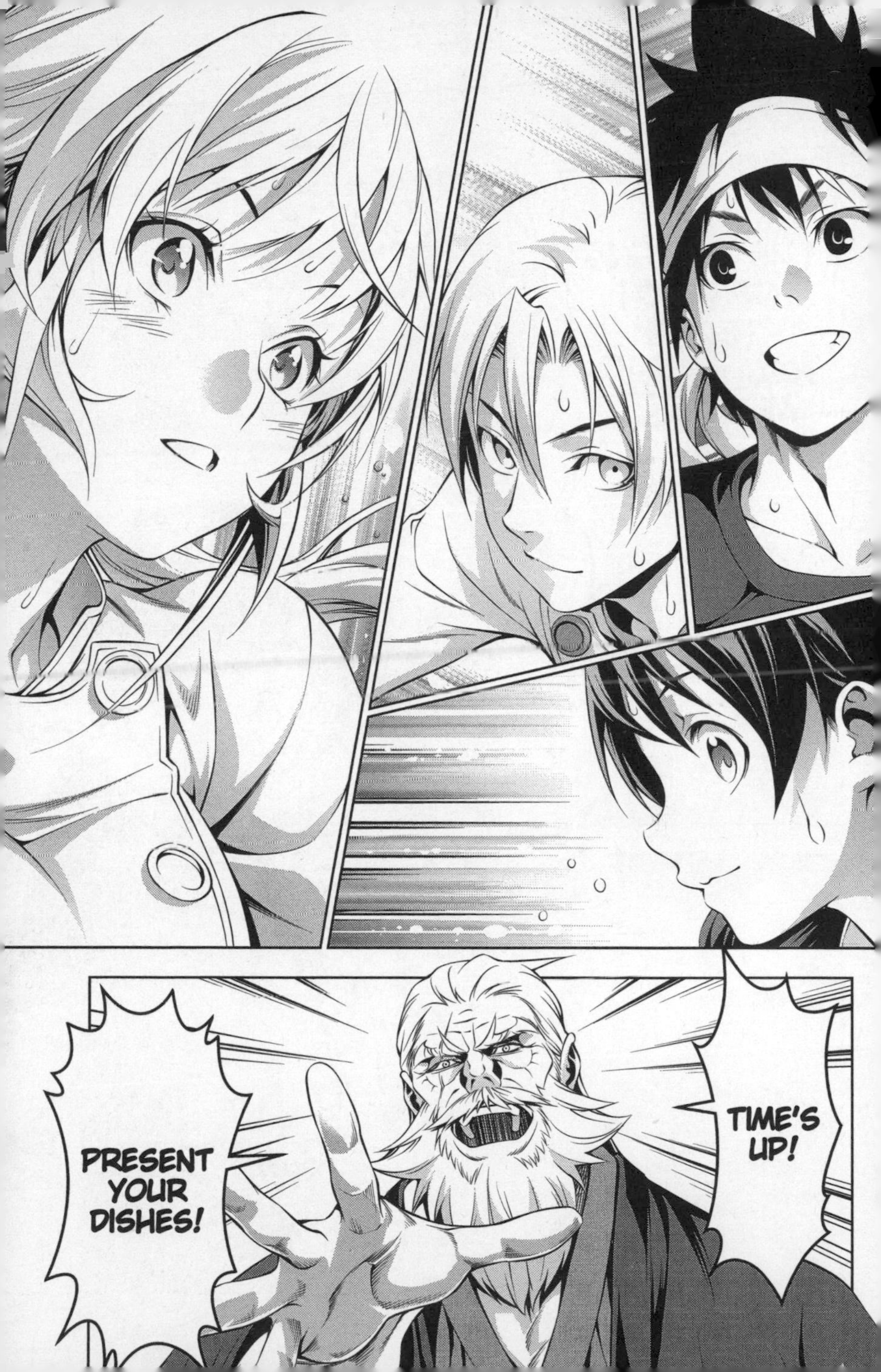
TIME'S UP!
PRESENT YOUR DISHES!

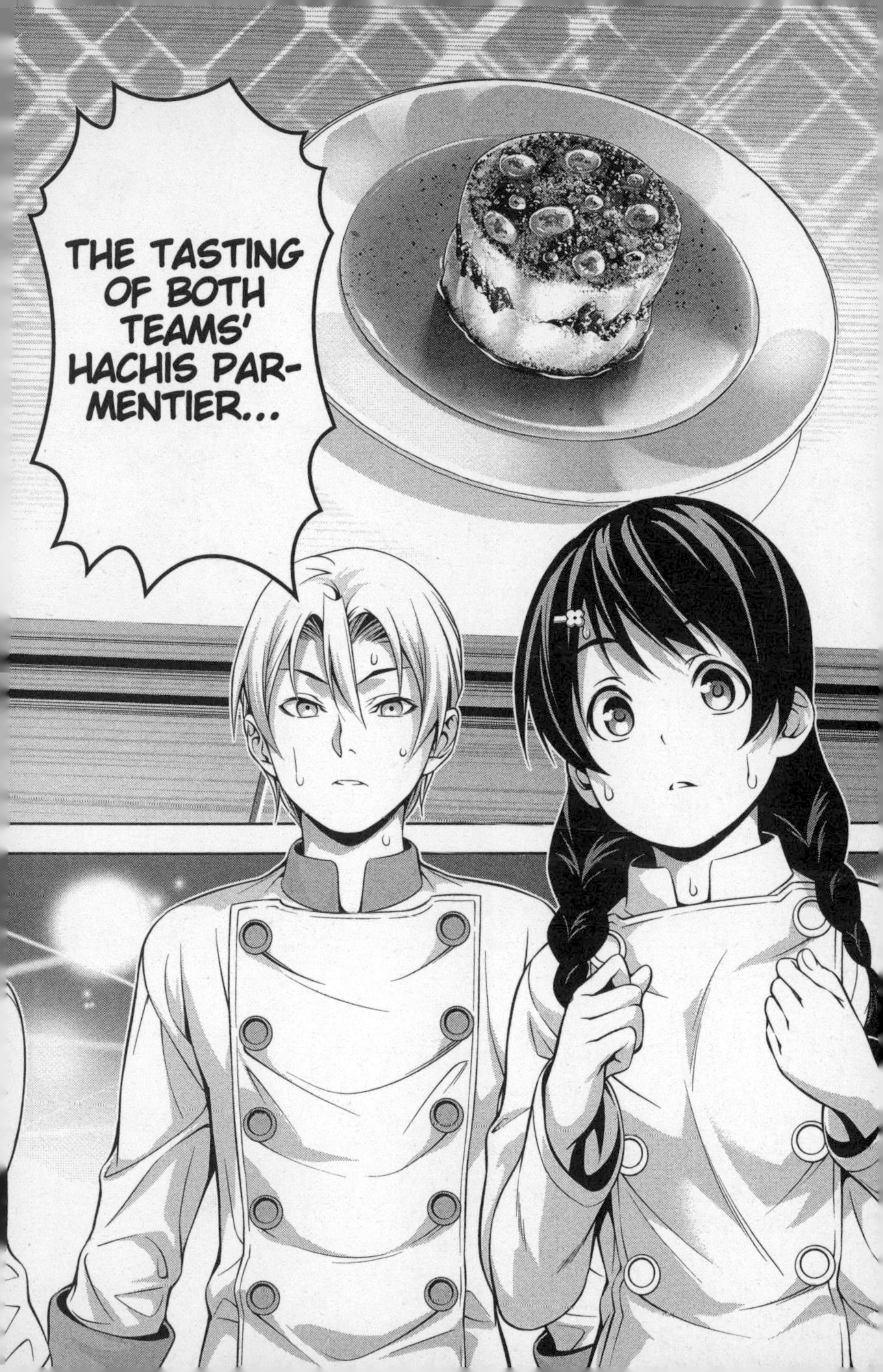
THE TASTING OF BOTH TEAMS' HACHIS PARMENTIER...

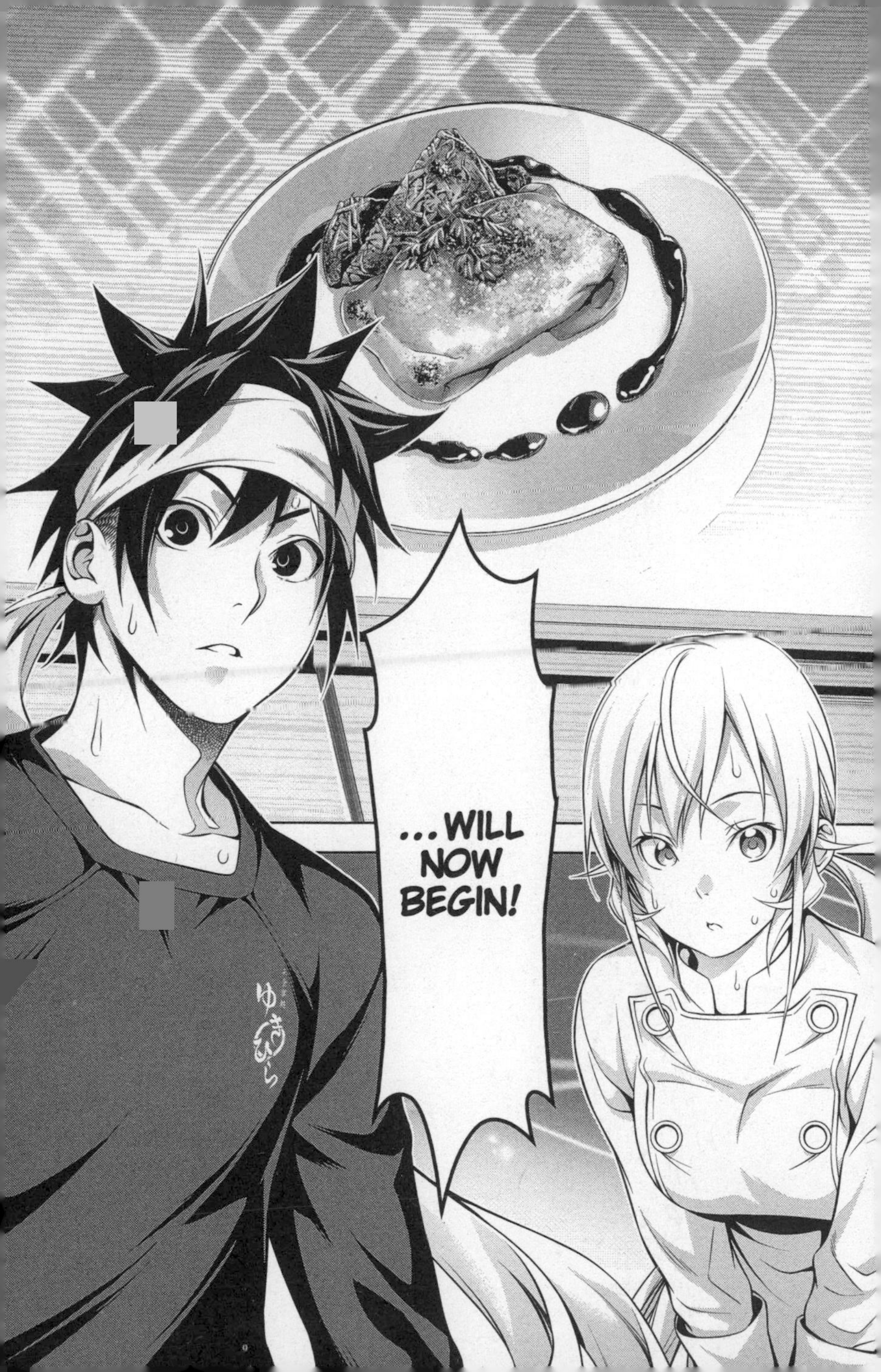
...WILL NOW BEGIN!
ゆきひら

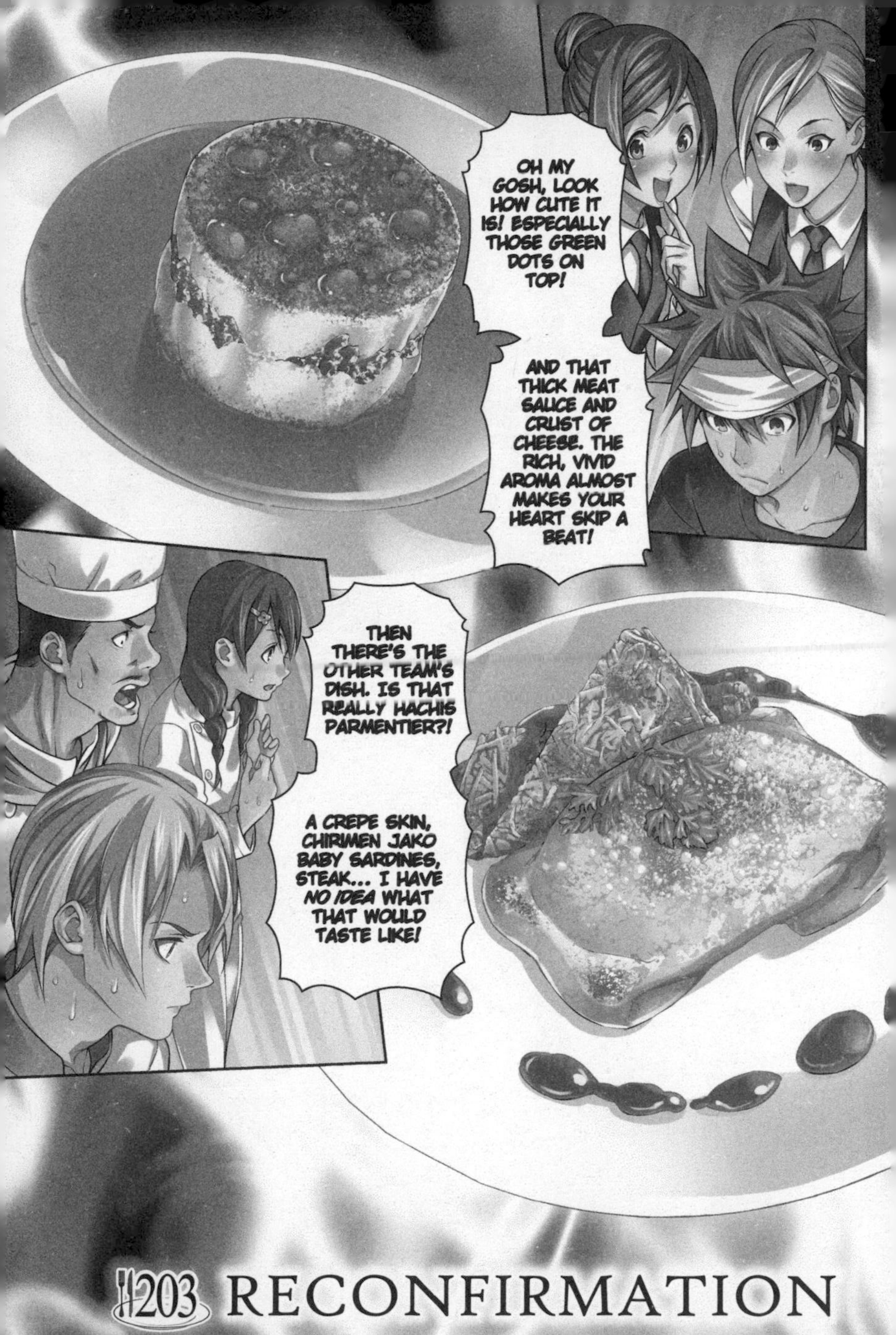
OH MY GOSH, LOOK HOW CUTE IT IS! ESPECIALLY THOSE GREEN DOTS ON TOP!
AND THAT THICK MEAT SAUCE AND CRUST OF CHEESE. THE RICH, VIVID AROMA ALMOST MAKES YOUR HEART SKIP A BEAT!
THEN THERE'S THE OTHER TEAM'S DISH. IS THAT REALLY HACHIS PARMENTIER?!
A CREPE SKIN, CHIRIMEN JAKO BABY SARDINES, STEAK... I HAVE *NO IDEA* WHAT THAT WOULD TASTE LIKE!

203 RECONFIRMATION

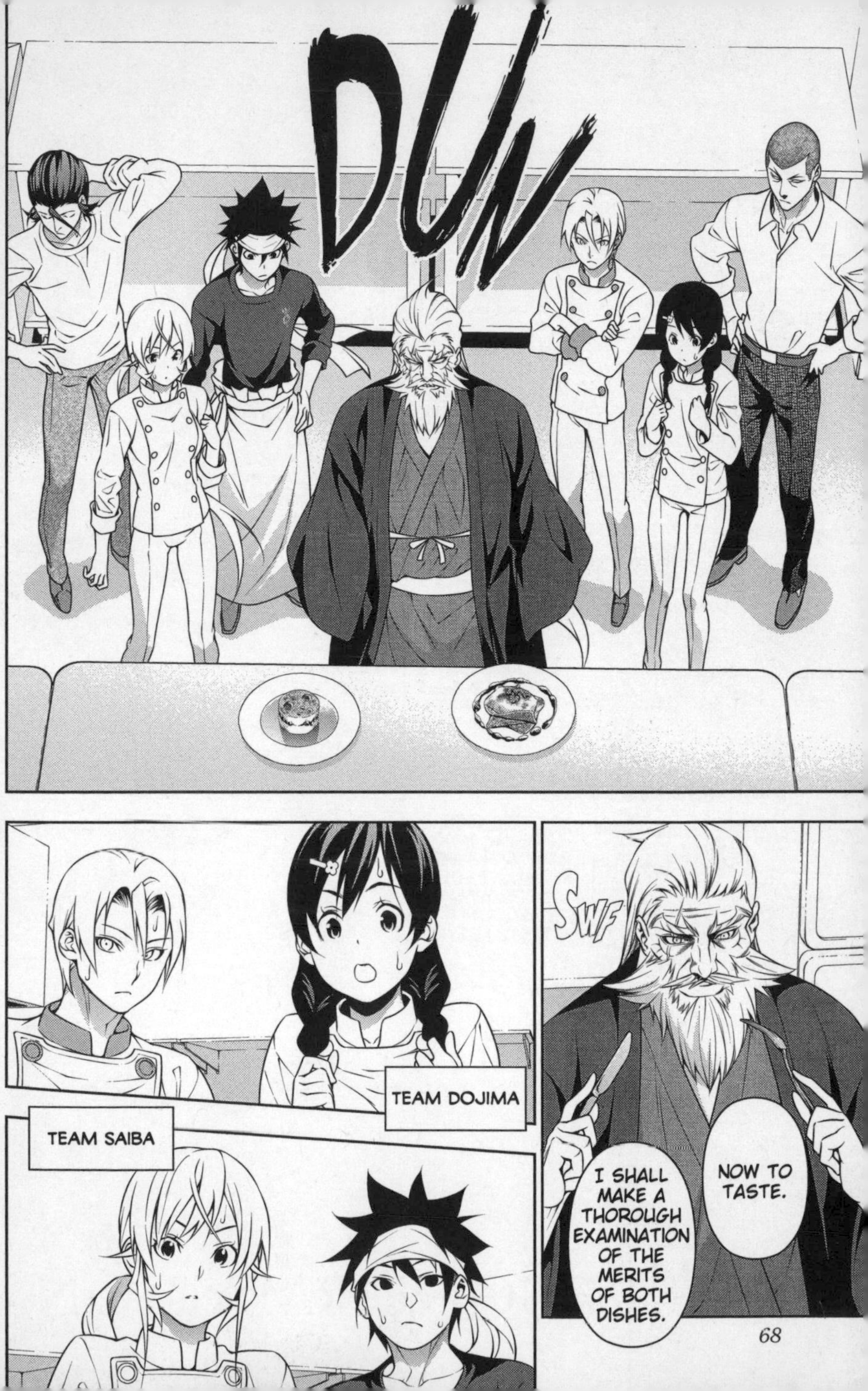
DW
SWF
NOW TO TASTE.
I SHALL MAKE A THOROUGH EXAMINATION OF THE MERITS OF BOTH DISHES.
TEAM DOJIMA
TEAM SAIBA

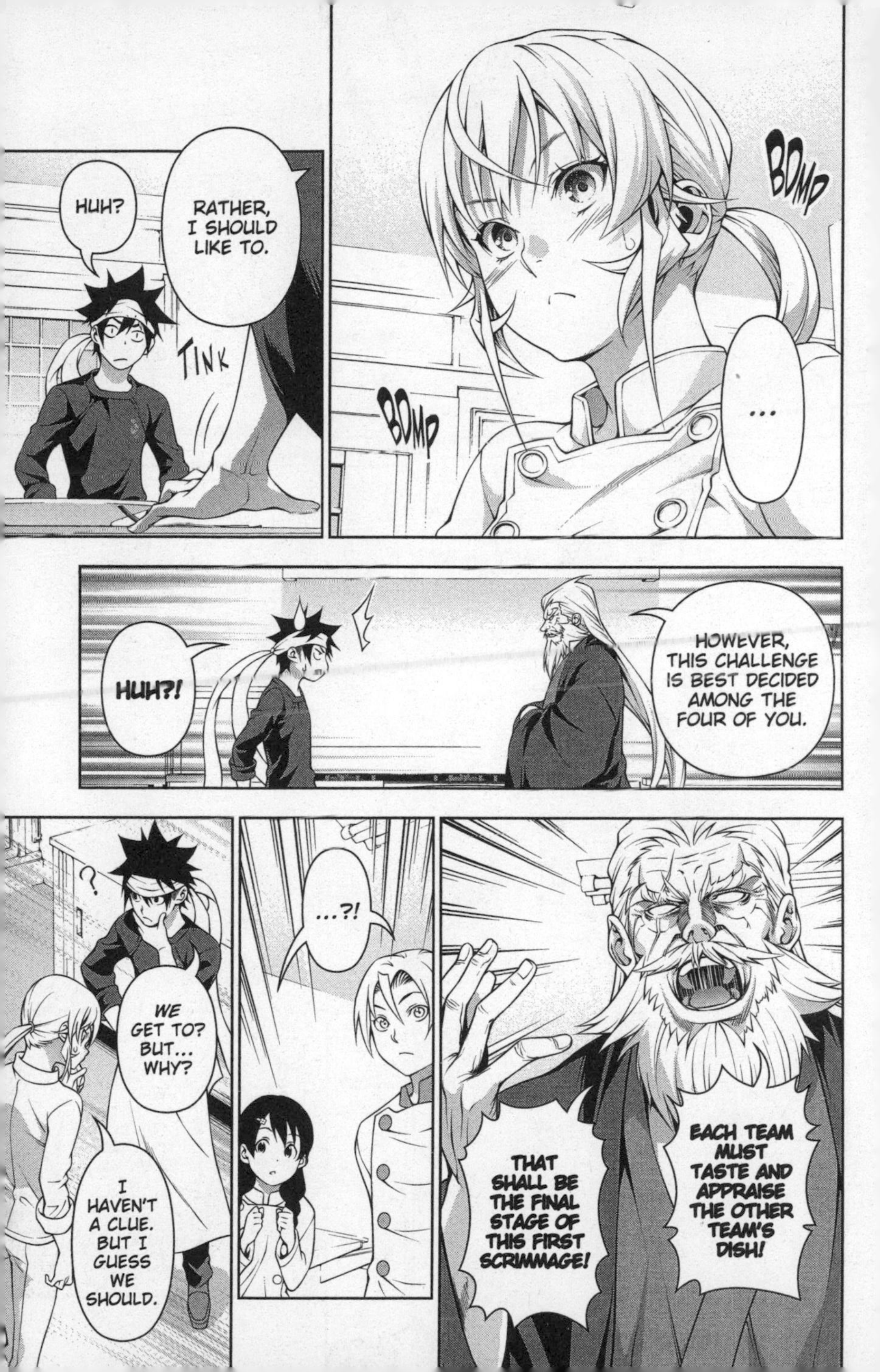
BOMP
...
BOMP
RATHER, I SHOULD LIKE TO.
HUH?
TINK
HOWEVER, THIS CHALLENGE IS BEST DECIDED AMONG THE FOUR OF YOU.
HUH?!
EACH TEAM MUST TASTE AND APPRAISE THE OTHER TEAM'S DISH!
THAT SHALL BE THE FINAL STAGE OF THIS FIRST SCRIMMAGE!
...?!
WE GET TO? BUT... WHY?
I HAVEN'T A CLUE. BUT I GUESS WE SHOULD.

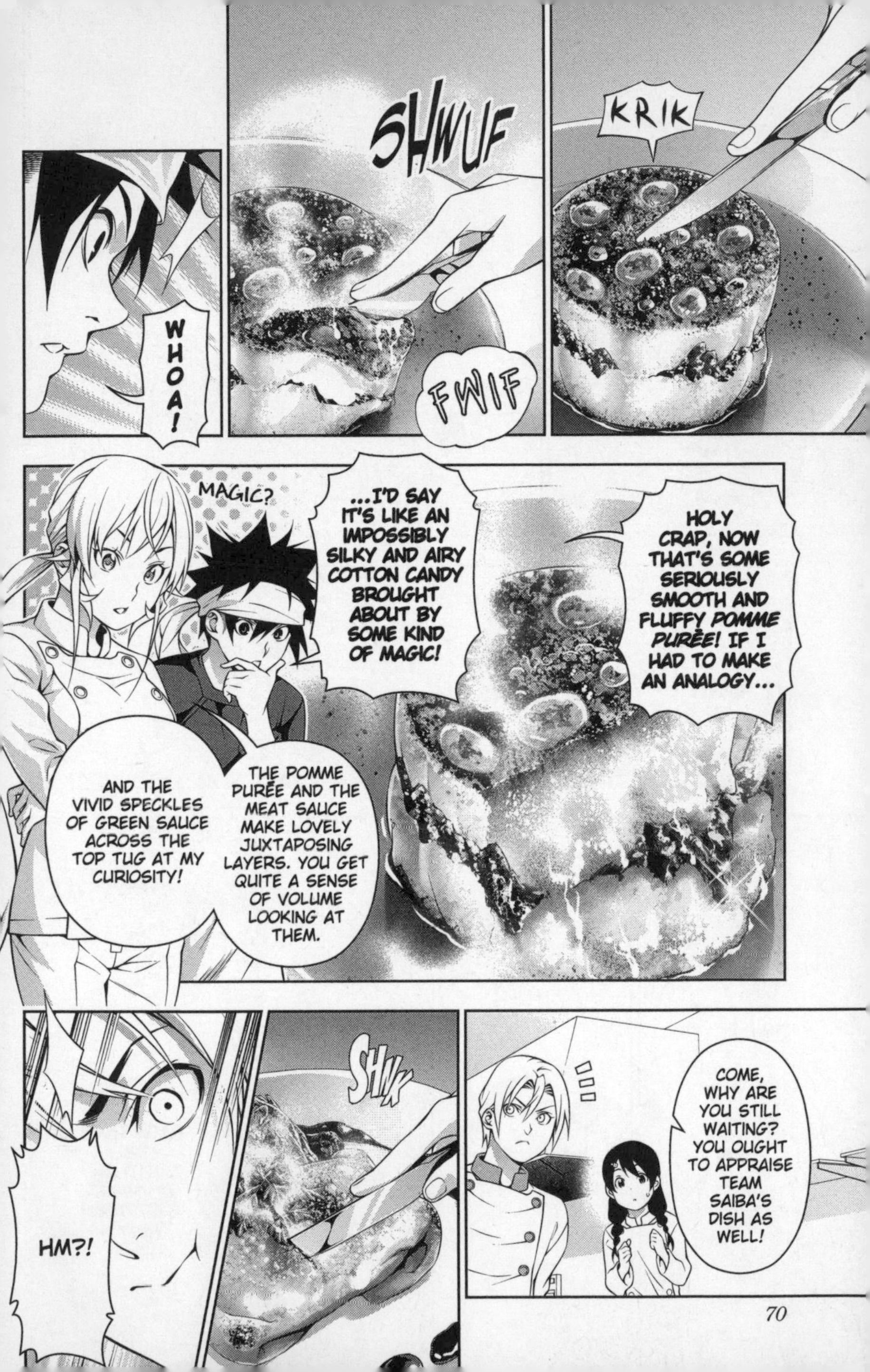
KRIK
SHWUF
FWIF
WHOA!
HOLY CRAP, NOW THAT'S SOME SERIOUSLY SMOOTH AND FLUFFY *POMME PURÉE*! IF I HAD TO MAKE AN ANALOGY...
...I'D SAY IT'S LIKE AN IMPOSSIBLY SILKY AND AIRY COTTON CANDY BROUGHT ABOUT BY SOME KIND OF MAGIC!
MAGIC?
THE POMME PURÉE AND THE MEAT SAUCE MAKE LOVELY JUXTAPOSING LAYERS. YOU GET QUITE A SENSE OF VOLUME LOOKING AT THEM.
AND THE VIVID SPECKLES OF GREEN SAUCE ACROSS THE TOP TUG AT MY CURIOSITY!
COME, WHY ARE YOU STILL WAITING? YOU OUGHT TO APPRAISE TEAM SAIBA'S DISH AS WELL!
SHNK
HM?!

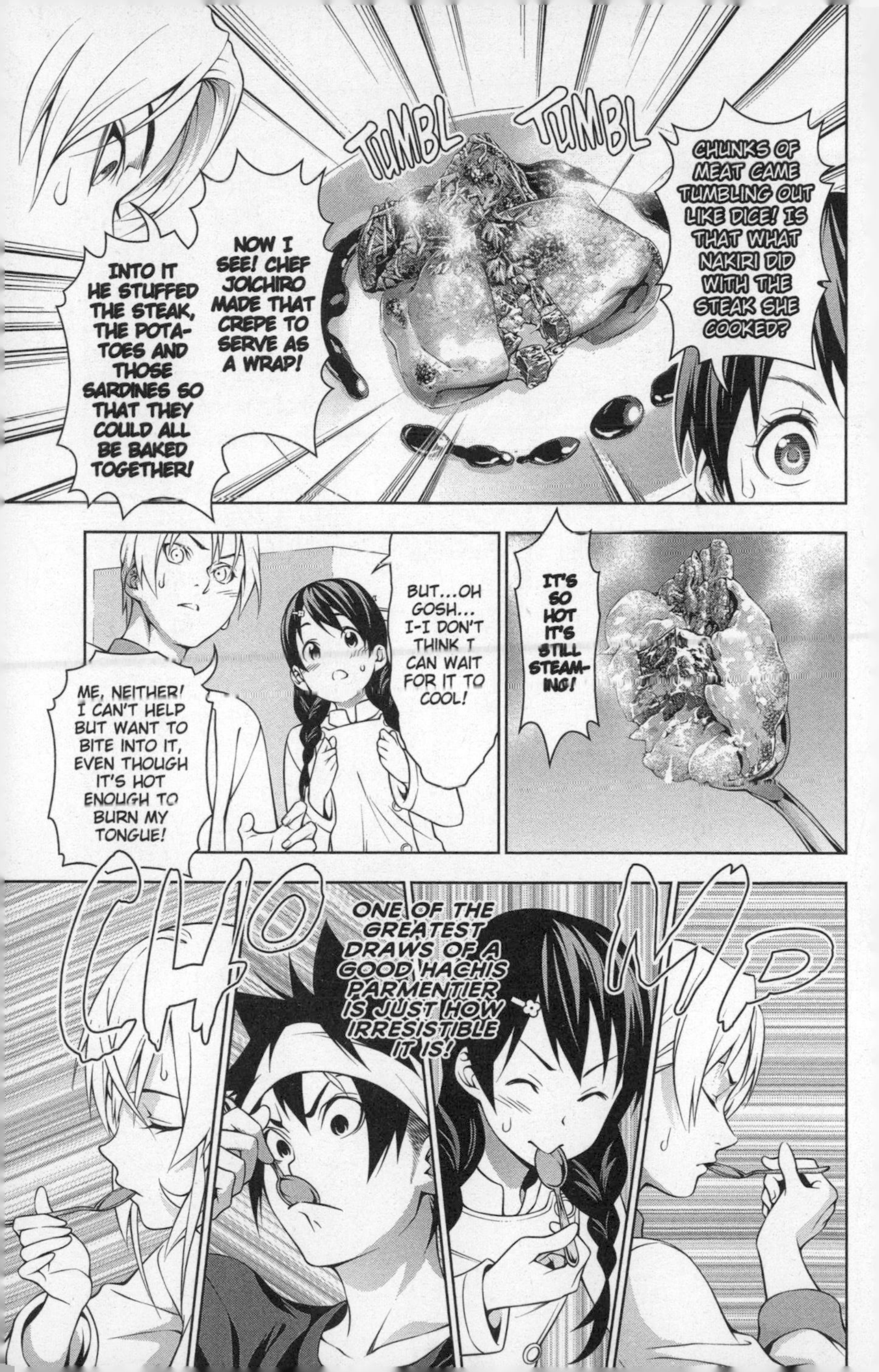
CHUNKS OF MEAT CAME TUMBLING OUT LIKE DICE! IS THAT WHAT NAKIRI DID WITH THE STEAK SHE COOKED?
TUMBL
TUMBL
NOW I SEE! CHEF JOICHIRO MADE THAT CREPE TO SERVE AS A WRAP!
INTO IT HE STUFFED THE STEAK, THE POTA-TOES AND THOSE SARDINES SO THAT THEY COULD ALL BE BAKED TOGETHER!
IT'S SO HOT IT'S STILL STEAM-ING!
BUT...OH GOSH... I-I DON'T THINK T CAN WAIT FOR IT TO COOL!
ME, NEITHER! I CAN'T HELP BUT WANT TO BITE INTO IT, EVEN THOUGH IT'S HOT ENOUGH TO BURN MY TONGUE!
CHOMP
ONE OF THE GREATEST DRAWS OF A GOOD HACHIS PARMENTIER IS JUST HOW IRRESISTIBLE IT IS!

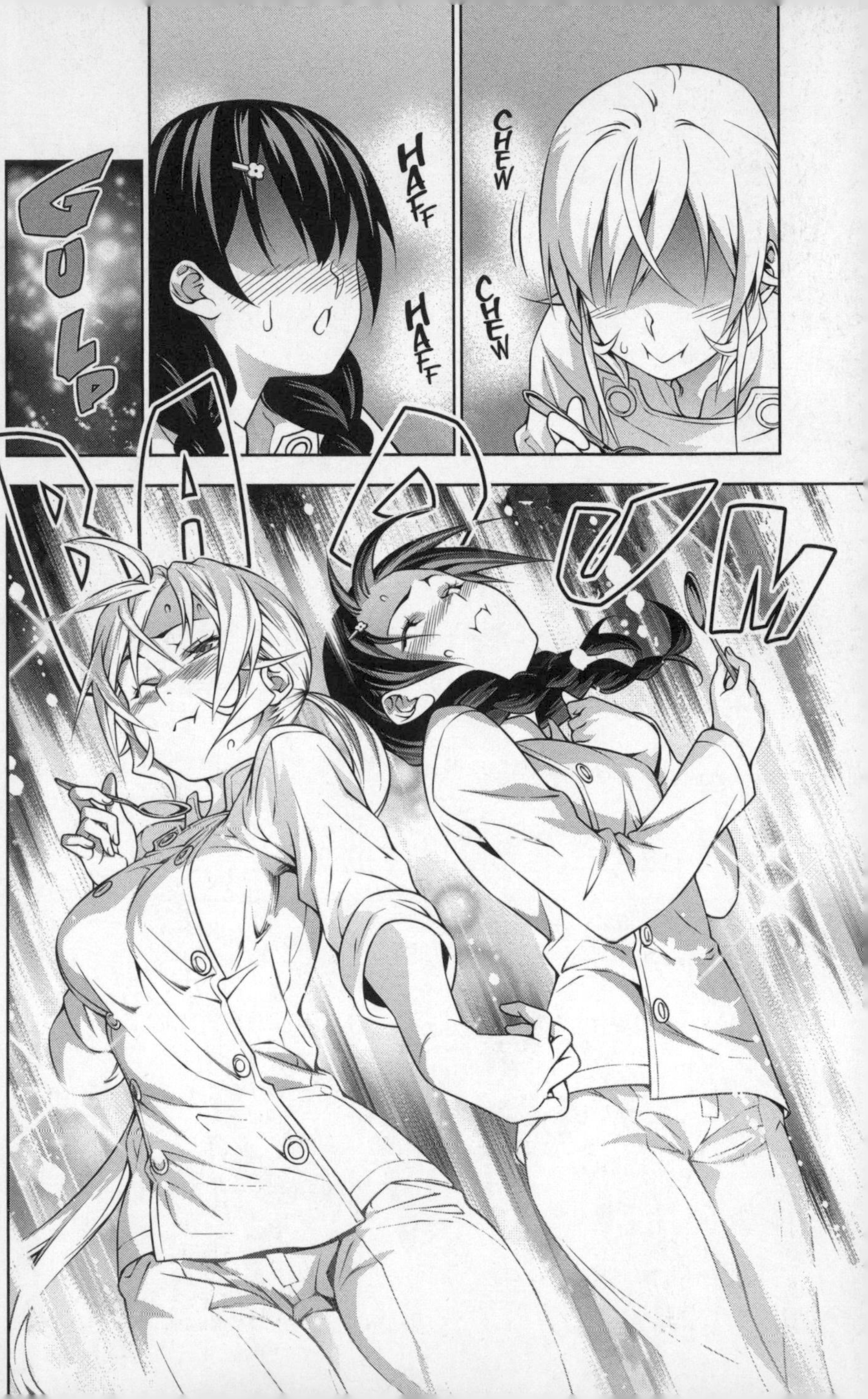
CHEW
CHEW
HAFF
HAFF
GULP
BADUM

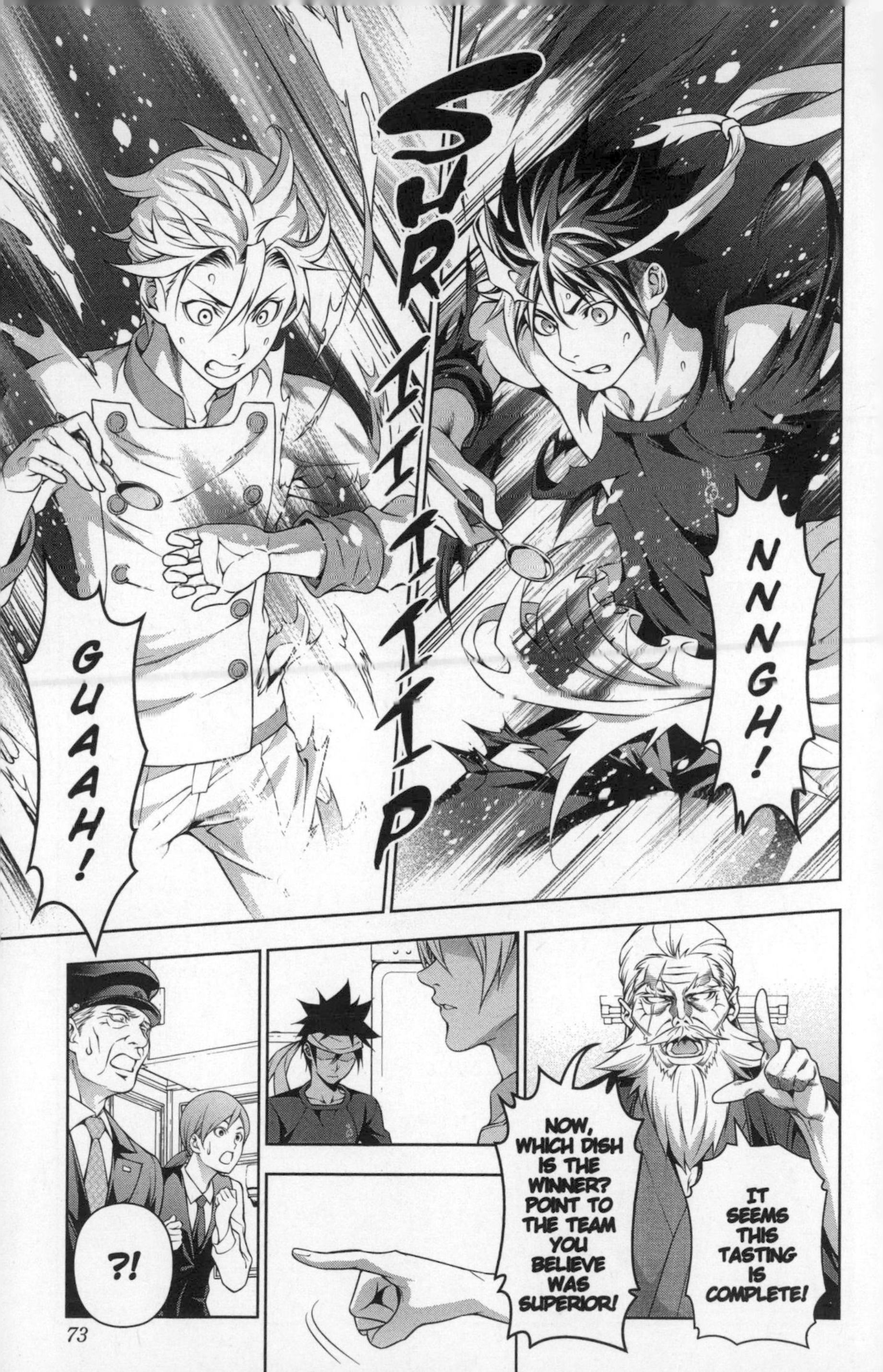
NNNGH!
SHRIIIIIP
GUAAH!
IT SEEMS THIS TASTING IS COMPLETE!
NOW, WHICH DISH IS THE WINNER? POINT TO THE TEAM YOU BELIEVE WAS SUPERIOR!
?!

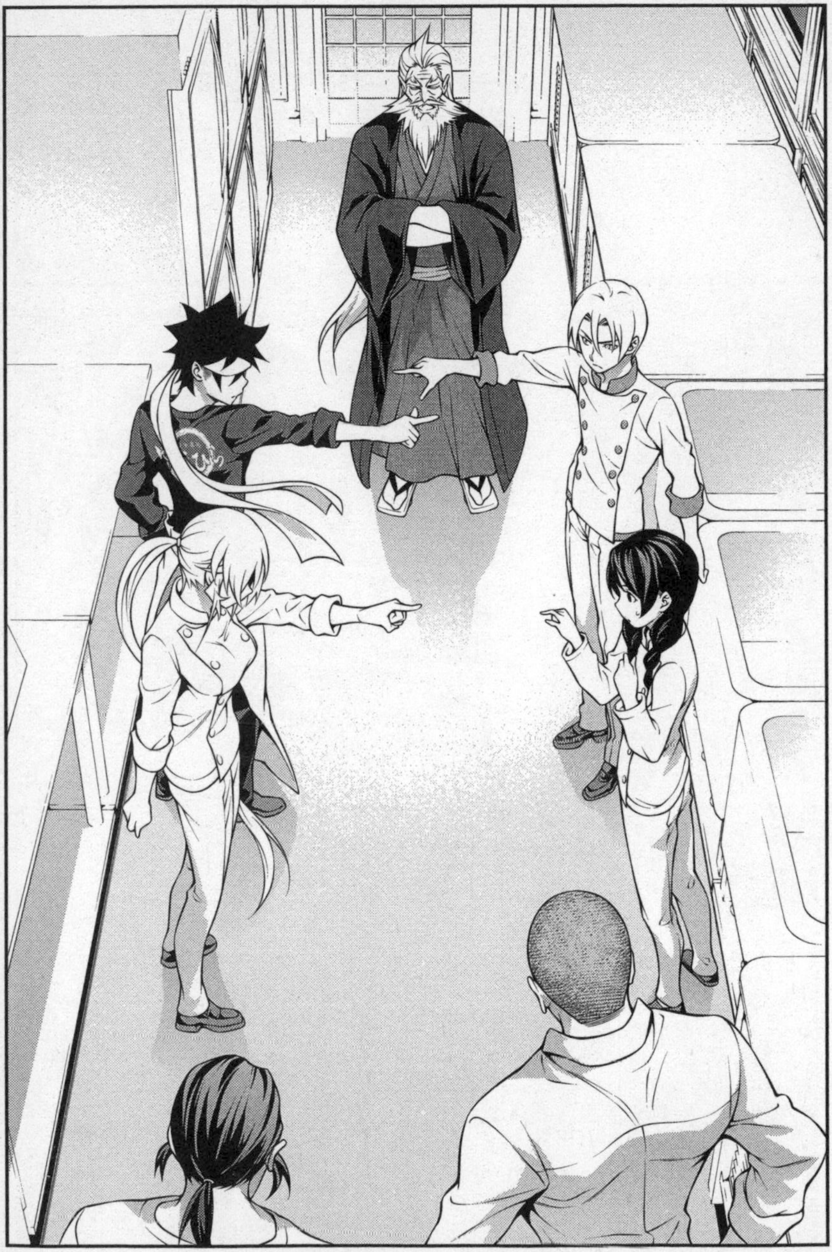

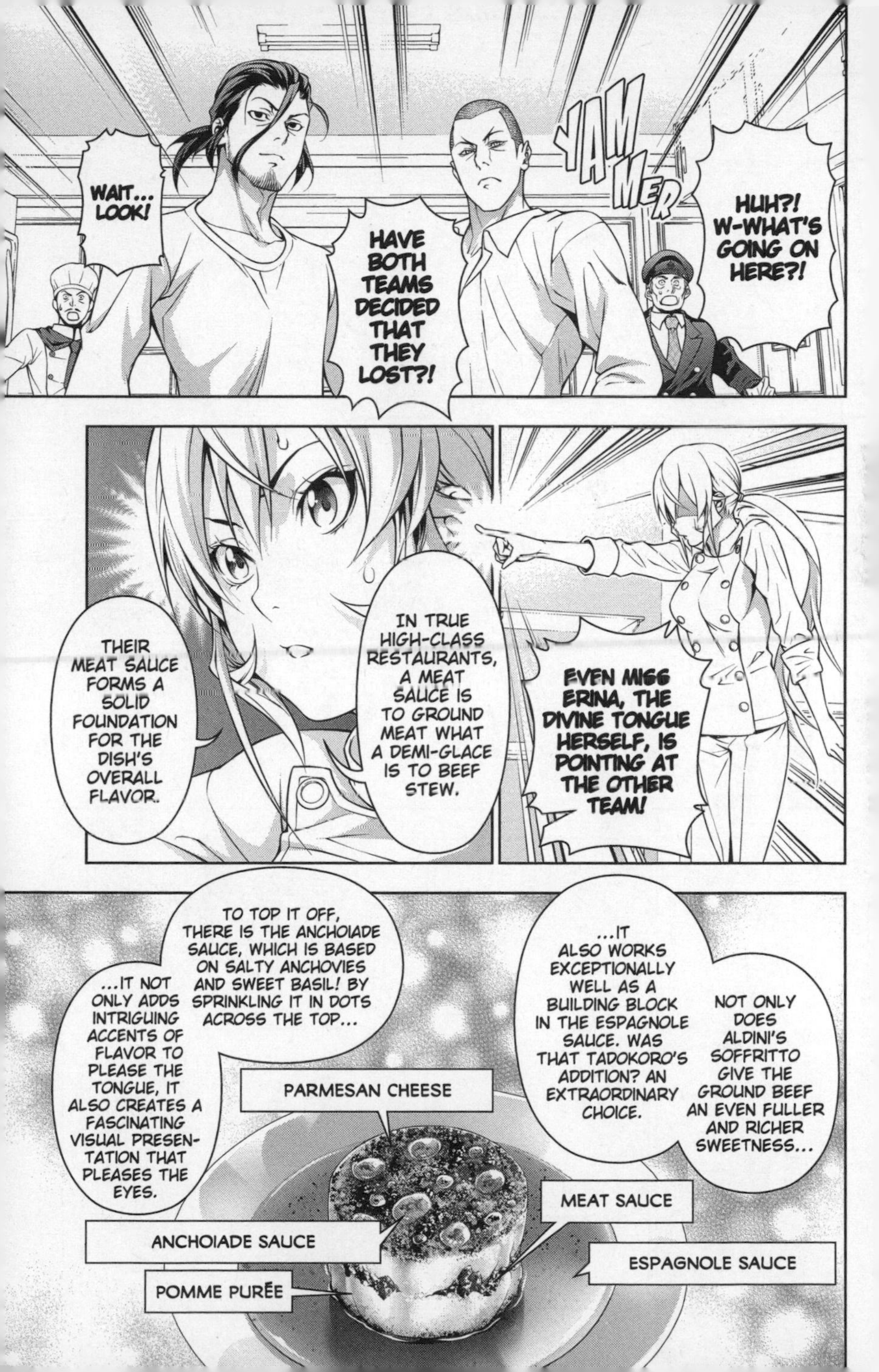
HUH?! W-WHAT'S GOING ON HERE?!
YAMMER
HAVE BOTH TEAMS DECIDED THAT THEY LOST?!
WAIT... LOOK!
EVEN MISS ERINA, THE DIVINE TONGUE HERSELF, IS POINTING AT THE OTHER TEAM!
IN TRUE HIGH-CLASS RESTAURANTS, A MEAT SAUCE IS TO GROUND MEAT WHAT A DEMI-GLACE IS TO BEEF STEW.
THEIR MEAT SAUCE FORMS A SOLID FOUNDATION FOR THE DISH'S OVERALL FLAVOR.
NOT ONLY DOES ALDINI'S SOFFRITTO GIVE THE GROUND BEEF AN EVEN FULLER AND RICHER SWEETNESS...
...IT ALSO WORKS EXCEPTIONALLY WELL AS A BUILDING BLOCK IN THE ESPAGNOLE SAUCE. WAS THAT TADOKORO'S ADDITION? AN EXTRAORDINARY CHOICE.
TO TOP IT OFF, THERE IS THE ANCHOIADE SAUCE, WHICH IS BASED ON SALTY ANCHOVIES AND SWEET BASIL! BY SPRINKLING IT IN DOTS ACROSS THE TOP...
...IT NOT ONLY ADDS INTRIGUING ACCENTS OF FLAVOR TO PLEASE THE TONGUE, IT ALSO CREATES A FASCINATING VISUAL PRESENTATION THAT PLEASES THE EYES.
PARMESAN CHEESE
MEAT SAUCE
ESPAGNOLE SAUCE
ANCHOIADE SAUCE
POMME PURÉE

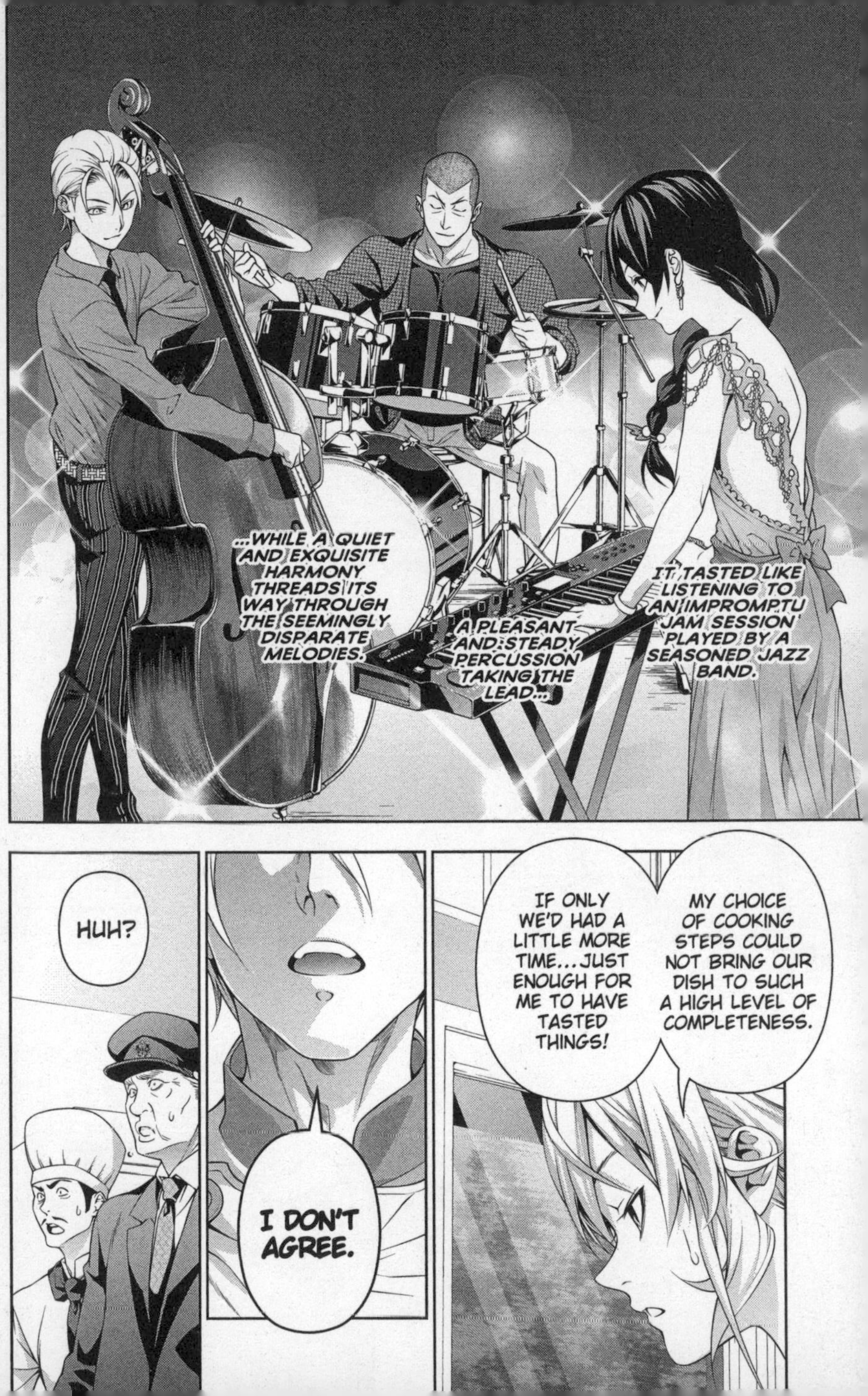
IT TASTED LIKE LISTENING TO AN IMPROMPTU JAM SESSION PLAYED BY A SEASONED JAZZ BAND.
A PLEASANT AND STEADY PERCUSSION TAKING THE LEAD...
...WHILE A QUIET AND EXQUISITE HARMONY THREADS ITS WAY THROUGH THE SEEMINGLY DISPARATE MELODIES.
MY CHOICE OF COOKING STEPS COULD NOT BRING OUR DISH TO SUCH A HIGH LEVEL OF COMPLETENESS.
IF ONLY WE'D HAD A LITTLE MORE TIME... JUST ENOUGH FOR ME TO HAVE TASTED THINGS!
I DON'T AGREE.
HUH?

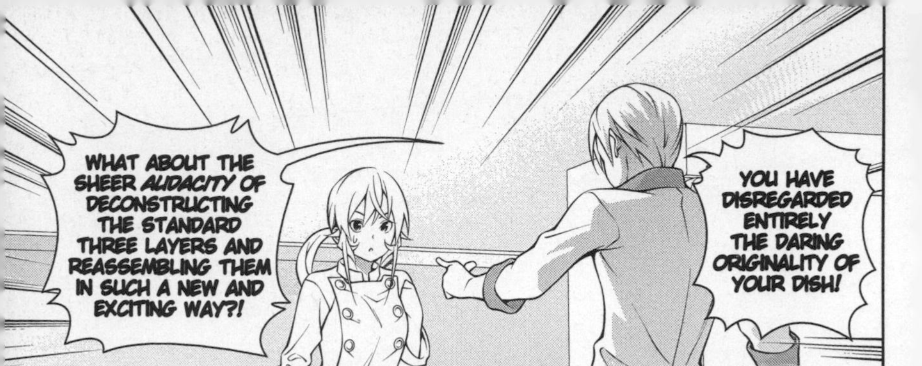
YOU HAVE DISREGARDED ENTIRELY THE DARING ORIGINALITY OF YOUR DISH!
WHAT ABOUT THE SHEER *AUDACITY* OF DECONSTRUCTING THE STANDARD THREE LAYERS AND REASSEMBLING THEM IN SUCH A NEW AND EXCITING WAY?!
GRATED POTATO WAS ADDED TO THE CREPE BATTER, CREATING A THICK AND CHEWY CREPE ALSACIENNE! YUKIHIRA REALIZED THIS WAS MEANT AS A WRAP FOR THE INGREDIENTS...
...AND THAT SPURRED HIS IDEA TO MIX CHEESE, SLICED POTATO AND SARDINES TOGETHER TO MAKE A CRISPY GALETTE DE POMME AS A GARNISH TO THE DISH!
LOOK WHAT THAT DOES TO THE DISH! IT GIVES IT CONTRASTING TEXTURES OF CRISPY AND CHEWY, ALONG WITH THE INVIGORATING SALTINESS OF SEAFOOD, NONE OF WHICH ARE PRESENT IN THE TRADITIONAL RECIPE!

*GALETTE DE POMME IS A LIGHTLY FRIED CAKE OF JULIENNED POTATOES.

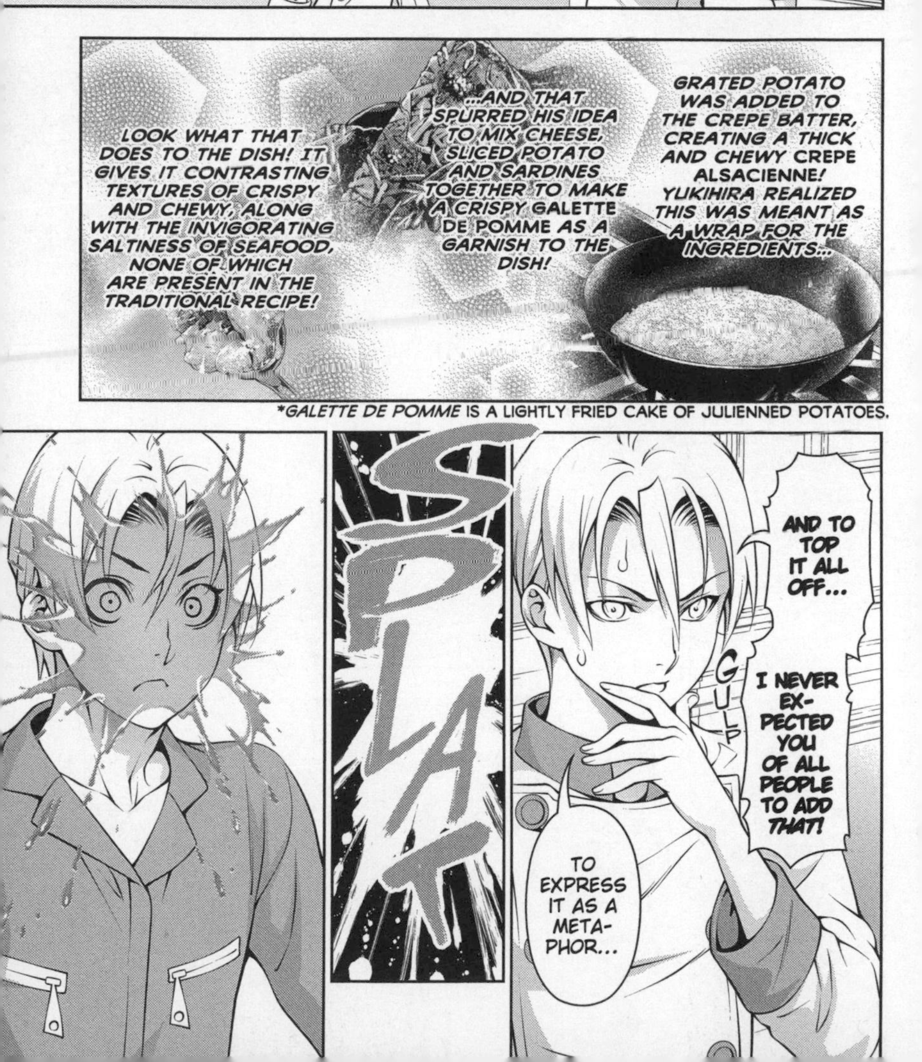
AND TO TOP IT ALL OFF...
GULP
I NEVER EX-PECTED YOU OF ALL PEOPLE TO ADD *THAT*!
TO EXPRESS IT AS A META-PHOR...
SPLAT

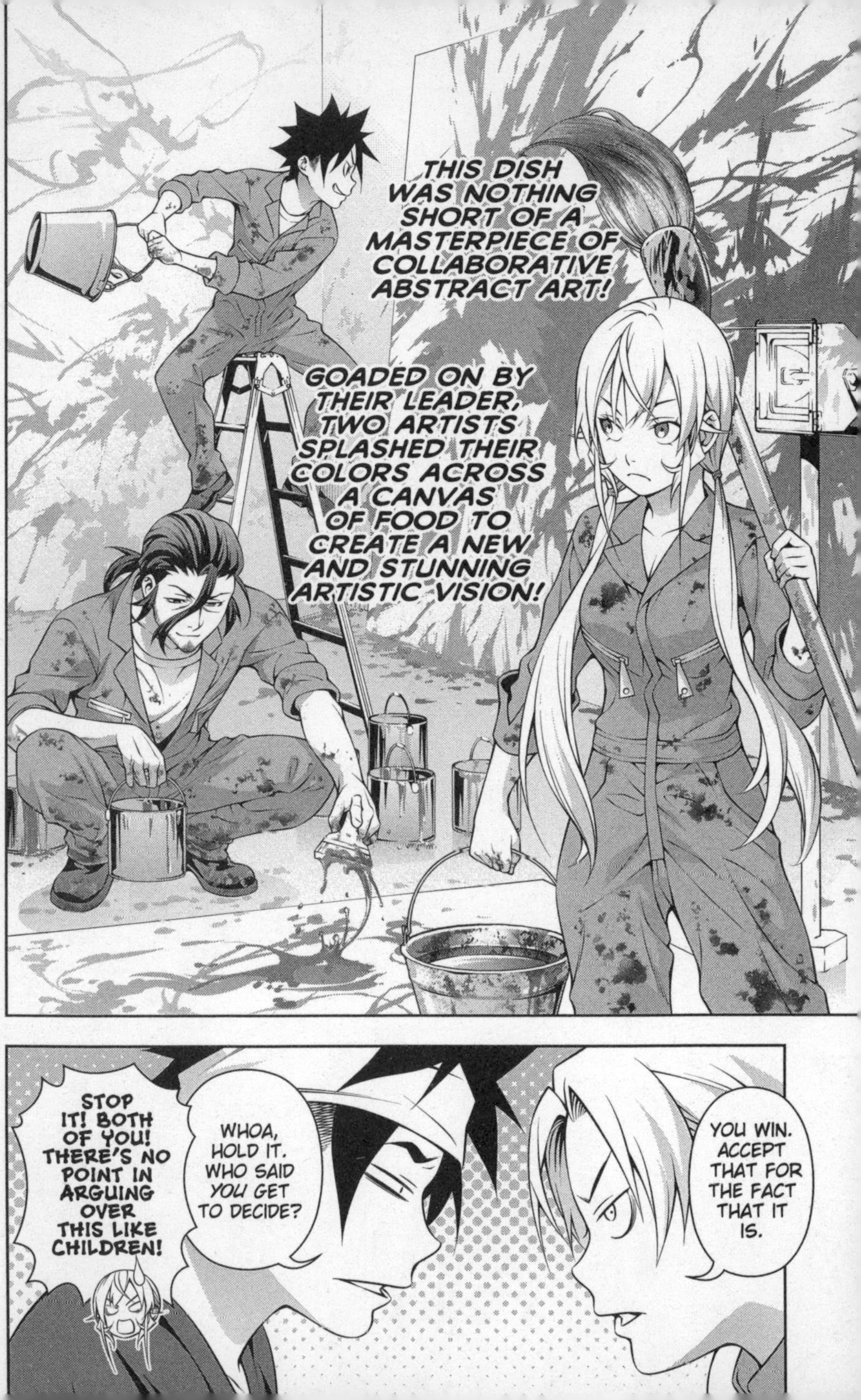
THIS DISH WAS NOTHING SHORT OF A MASTERPIECE OF COLLABORATIVE ABSTRACT ART!
GOADED ON BY THEIR LEADER, TWO ARTISTS SPLASHED THEIR COLORS ACROSS A CANVAS OF FOOD TO CREATE A NEW AND STUNNING ARTISTIC VISION!
YOU WIN. ACCEPT THAT FOR THE FACT THAT IT IS.
WHOA, HOLD IT. WHO SAID *YOU* GET TO DECIDE?
STOP IT! BOTH OF YOU! THERE'S NO POINT IN ARGUING OVER THIS LIKE CHILDREN!

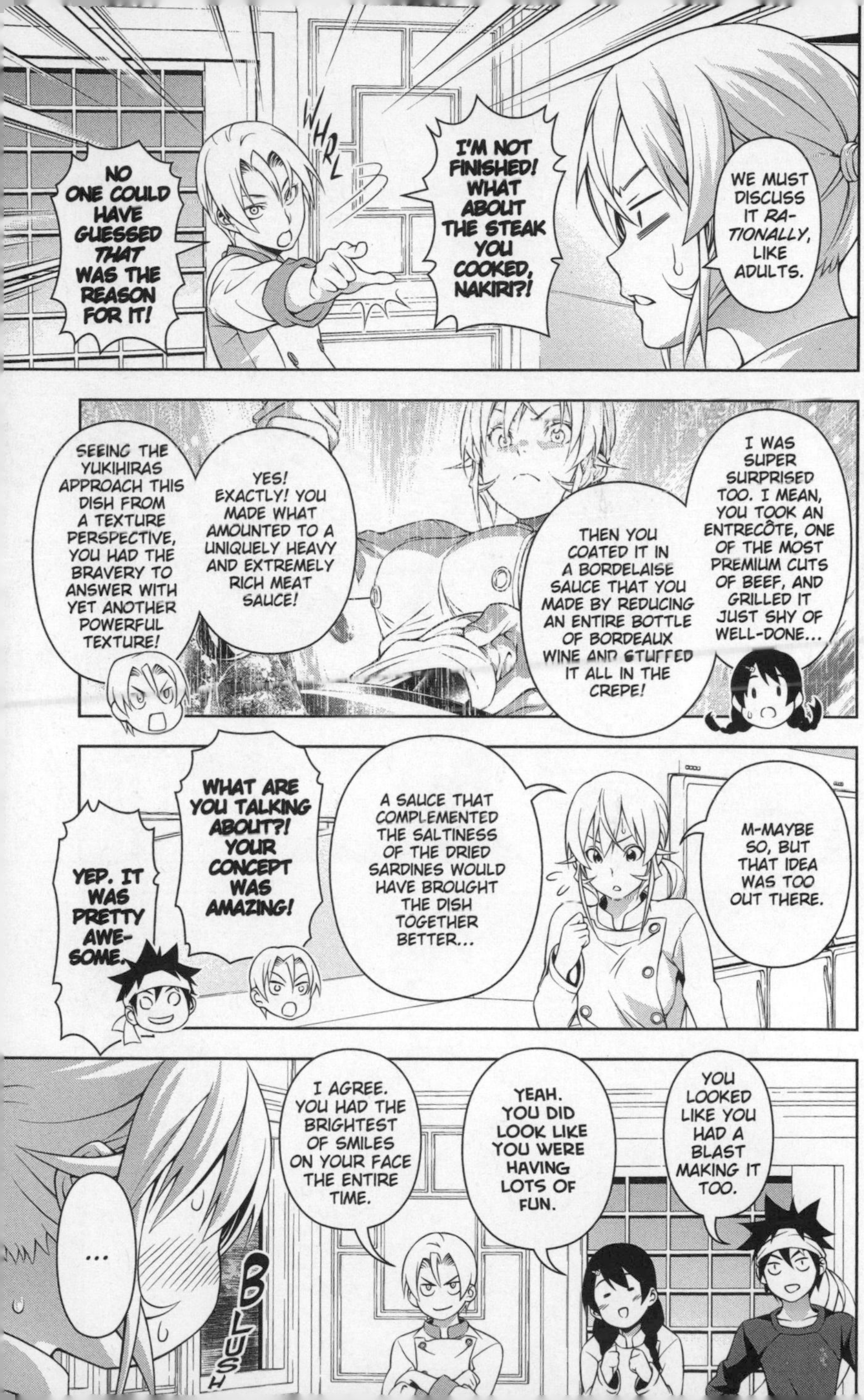
WE MUST DISCUSS IT RATIONALLY, LIKE ADULTS.
I'M NOT FINISHED! WHAT ABOUT THE STEAK YOU COOKED, NAKIRI?!
WHRL
NO ONE COULD HAVE GUESSED THAT WAS THE REASON FOR IT!
I WAS SUPER SURPRISED TOO. I MEAN, YOU TOOK AN ENTRECÔTE, ONE OF THE MOST PREMIUM CUTS OF BEEF, AND GRILLED IT JUST SHY OF WELL-DONE...
THEN YOU COATED IT IN A BORDELAISE SAUCE THAT YOU MADE BY REDUCING AN ENTIRE BOTTLE OF BORDEAUX WINE AND STUFFED IT ALL IN THE CREPE!
YES! EXACTLY! YOU MADE WHAT AMOUNTED TO A UNIQUELY HEAVY AND EXTREMELY RICH MEAT SAUCE!
SEEING THE YUKIHIRAS APPROACH THIS DISH FROM A TEXTURE PERSPECTIVE, YOU HAD THE BRAVERY TO ANSWER WITH YET ANOTHER POWERFUL TEXTURE!
M-MAYBE SO, BUT THAT IDEA WAS TOO OUT THERE.
A SAUCE THAT COMPLEMENTED THE SALTINESS OF THE DRIED SARDINES WOULD HAVE BROUGHT THE DISH TOGETHER BETTER...
WHAT ARE YOU TALKING ABOUT?! YOUR CONCEPT WAS AMAZING!
YEP. IT WAS PRETTY AWESOME.
YOU LOOKED LIKE YOU HAD A BLAST MAKING IT TOO.
YEAH. YOU DID LOOK LIKE YOU WERE HAVING LOTS OF FUN.
I AGREE. YOU HAD THE BRIGHTEST OF SMILES ON YOUR FACE THE ENTIRE TIME.
BLUSH
...

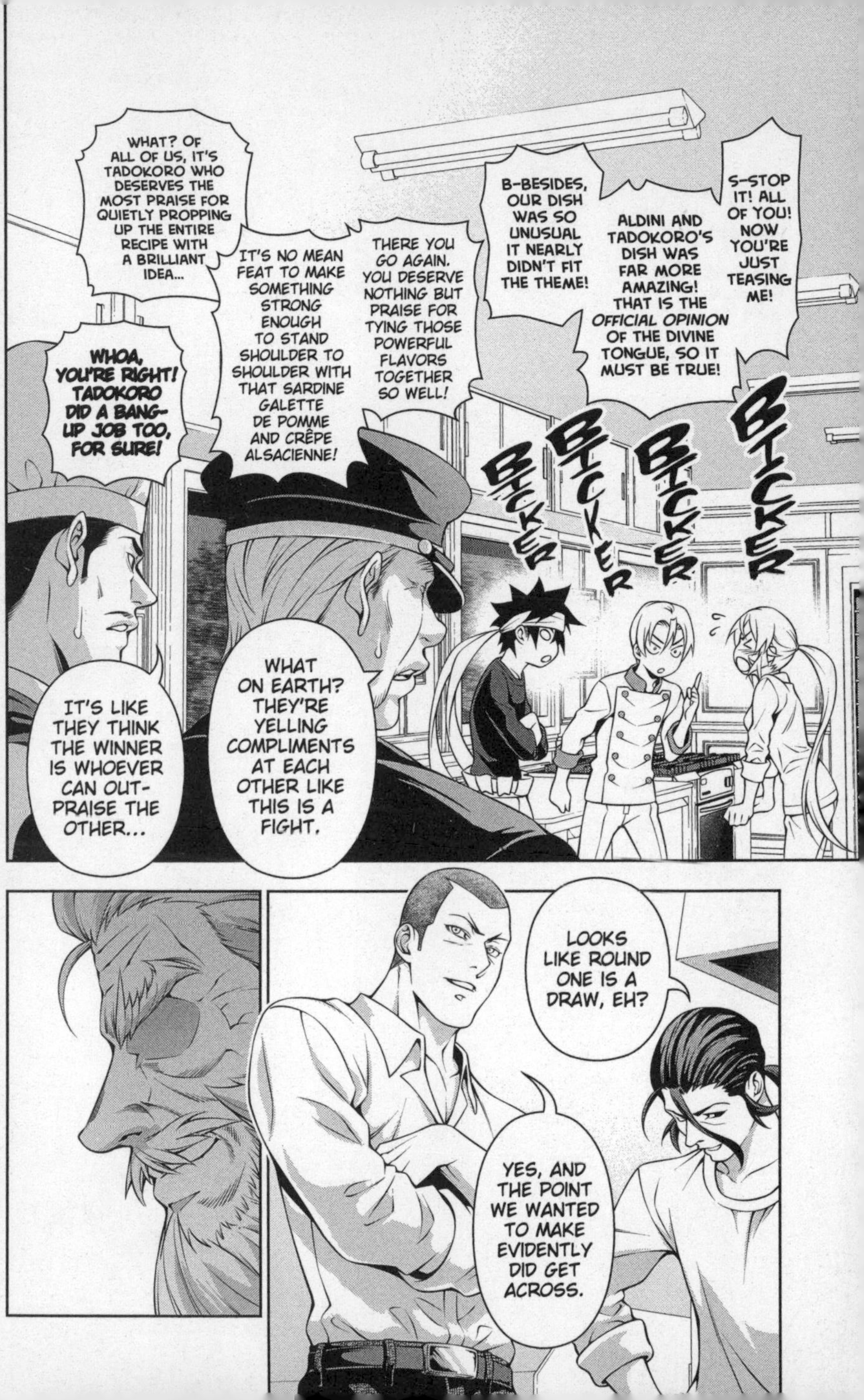
S-STOP IT! ALL OF YOU! NOW YOU'RE JUST TEASING ME!
ALDINI AND TADOKORO'S DISH WAS FAR MORE AMAZING! THAT IS THE *OFFICIAL OPINION* OF THE DIVINE TONGUE, SO IT MUST BE TRUE!
B-BESIDES, OUR DISH WAS SO UNUSUAL IT NEARLY DIDN'T FIT THE THEME!
THERE YOU GO AGAIN. YOU DESERVE NOTHING BUT PRAISE FOR TYING THOSE POWERFUL FLAVORS TOGETHER SO WELL!
IT'S NO MEAN FEAT TO MAKE SOMETHING STRONG ENOUGH TO STAND SHOULDER TO SHOULDER WITH THAT SARDINE GALETTE DE POMME AND CRÊPE ALSACIENNE!
WHAT? OF ALL OF US, IT'S TADOKORO WHO DESERVES THE MOST PRAISE FOR QUIETLY PROPPING UP THE ENTIRE RECIPE WITH A BRILLIANT IDEA...
WHOA, YOU'RE RIGHT! TADOKORO DID A BANG-UP JOB TOO, FOR SURE!
BICKER
BICKER
BICKER
BICKER
WHAT ON EARTH? THEY'RE YELLING COMPLIMENTS AT EACH OTHER LIKE THIS IS A FIGHT.
IT'S LIKE THEY THINK THE WINNER IS WHOEVER CAN OUT-PRAISE THE OTHER...
LOOKS LIKE ROUND ONE IS A DRAW, EH?
YES, AND THE POINT WE WANTED TO MAKE EVIDENTLY DID GET ACROSS.

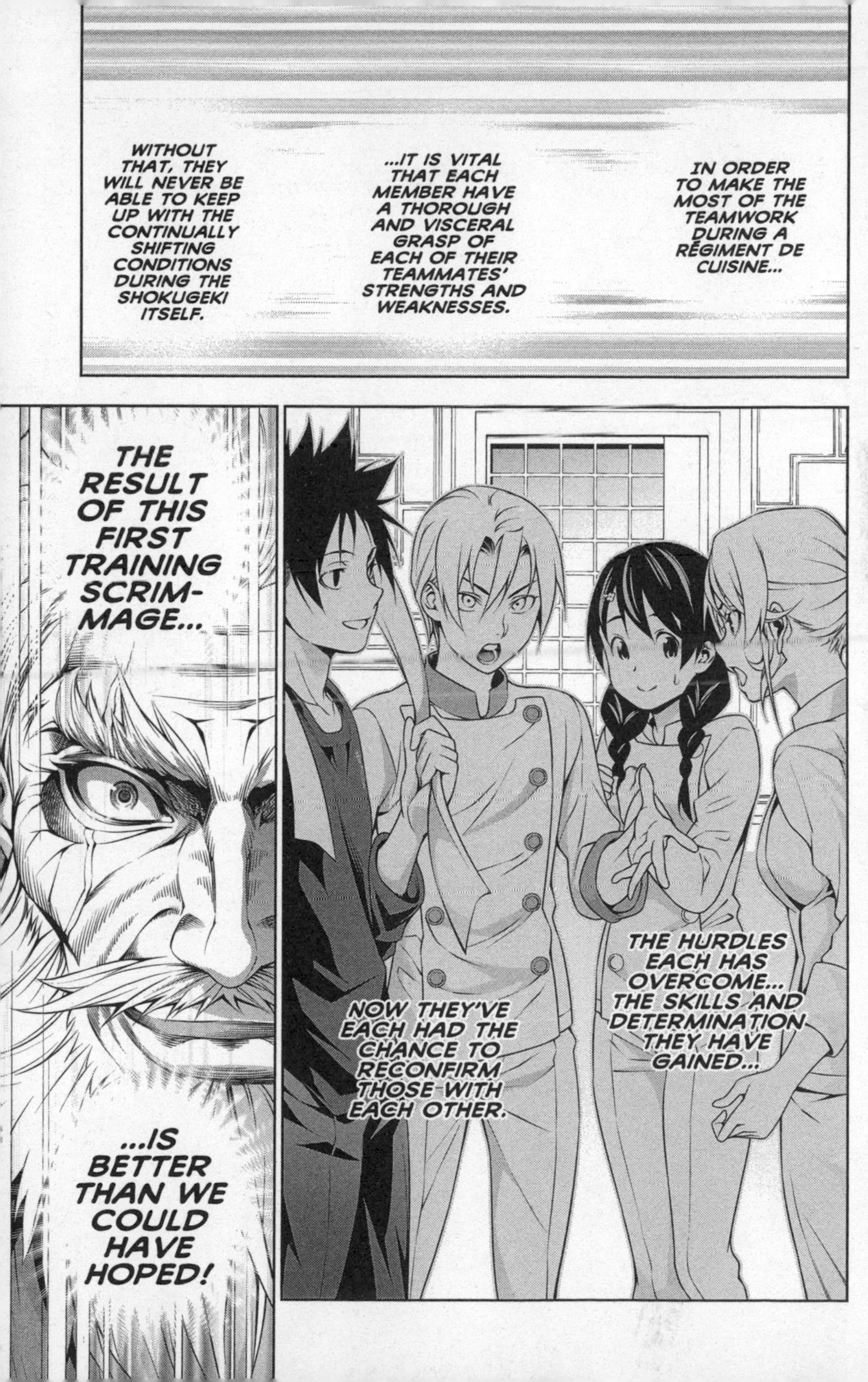
IN ORDER TO MAKE THE MOST OF THE TEAMWORK DURING A RÉGIMENT DE CUISINE...
...IT IS VITAL THAT EACH MEMBER HAVE A THOROUGH AND VISCERAL GRASP OF EACH OF THEIR TEAMMATES' STRENGTHS AND WEAKNESSES.
WITHOUT THAT, THEY WILL NEVER BE ABLE TO KEEP UP WITH THE CONTINUALLY SHIFTING CONDITIONS DURING THE SHOKUGEKI ITSELF.
THE HURDLES EACH HAS OVERCOME... THE SKILLS AND DETERMINATION THEY HAVE GAINED...
NOW THEY'VE EACH HAD THE CHANCE TO RECONFIRM THOSE WITH EACH OTHER.
THE RESULT OF THIS FIRST TRAINING SCRIM-MAGE...
...IS BETTER THAN WE COULD HAVE HOPED!

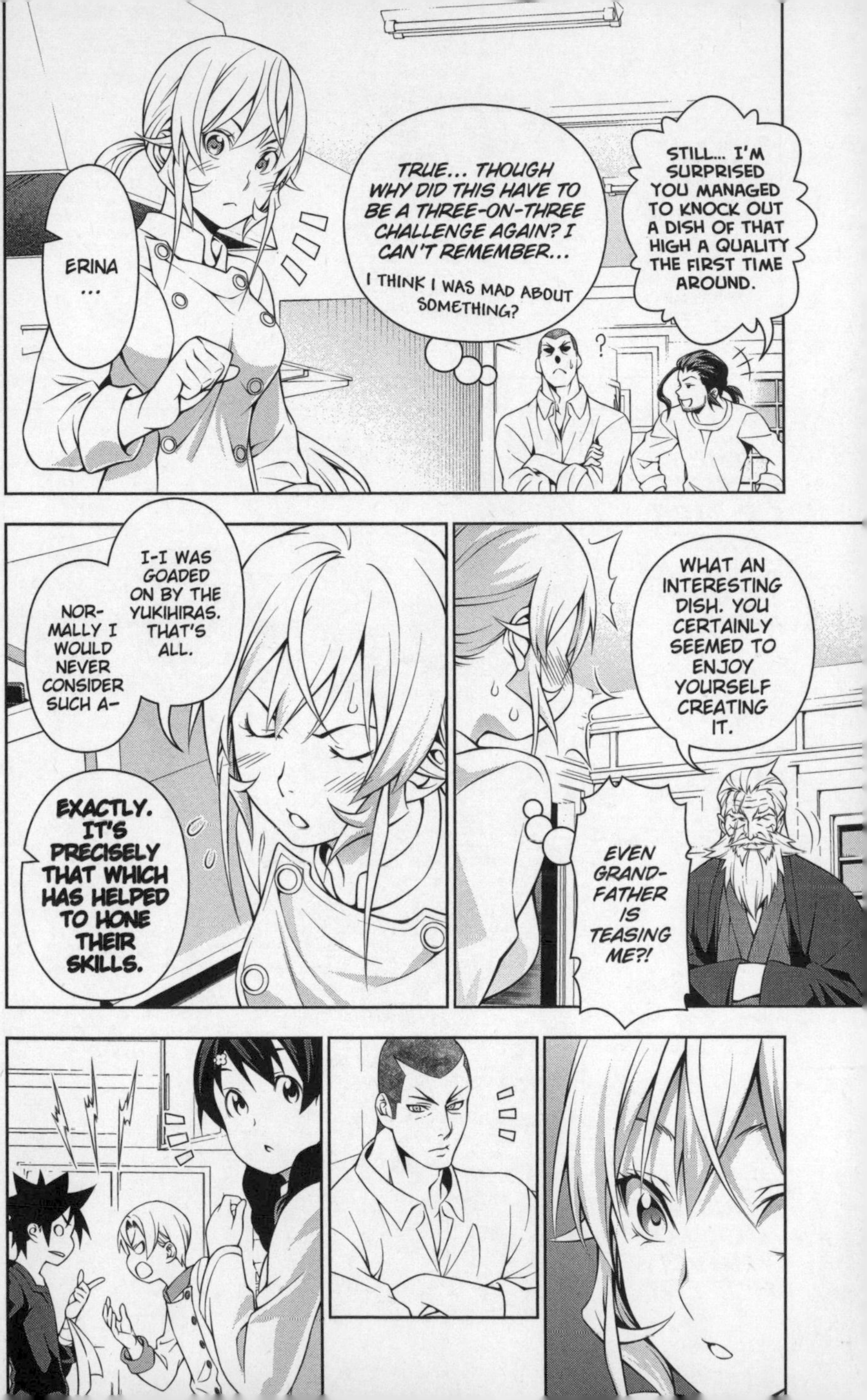
STILL... I'M SURPRISED YOU MANAGED TO KNOCK OUT A DISH OF THAT HIGH A QUALITY THE FIRST TIME AROUND.
TRUE... THOUGH WHY DID THIS HAVE TO BE A THREE-ON-THREE CHALLENGE AGAIN? I CAN'T REMEMBER...
I THINK I WAS MAD ABOUT SOMETHING?
ERINA...
WHAT AN INTERESTING DISH. YOU CERTAINLY SEEMED TO ENJOY YOURSELF CREATING IT.
EVEN GRAND-FATHER IS TEASING ME?!
I-I WAS GOADED ON BY THE YUKIHIRAS. THAT'S ALL.
NOR-MALLY I WOULD NEVER CONSIDER SUCH A-
EXACTLY. IT'S PRECISELY THAT WHICH HAS HELPED TO HONE THEIR SKILLS.

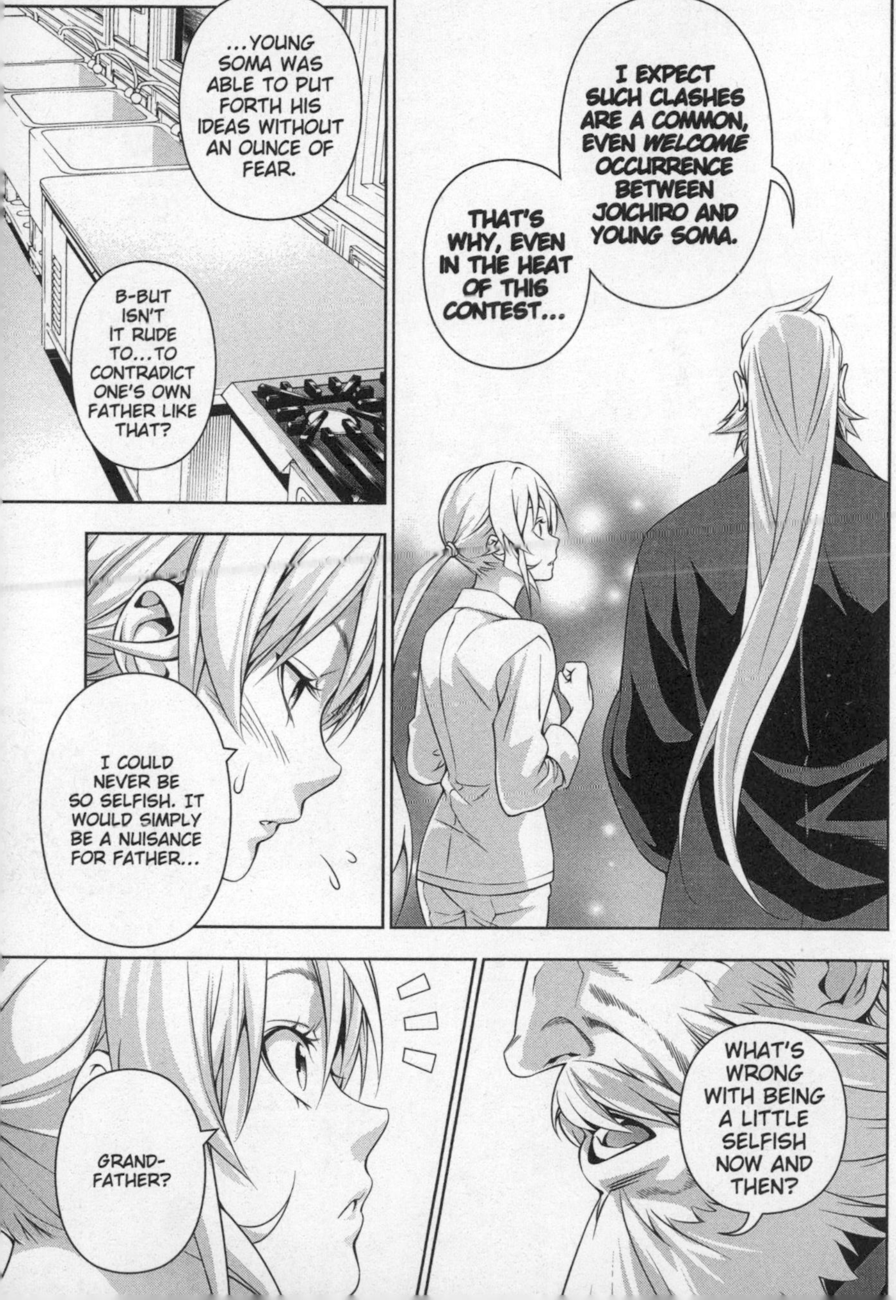
I EXPECT SUCH CLASHES ARE A COMMON, EVEN *WELCOME* OCCURRENCE BETWEEN JOICHIRO AND YOUNG SOMA.
THAT'S WHY, EVEN IN THE HEAT OF THIS CONTEST...
...YOUNG SOMA WAS ABLE TO PUT FORTH HIS IDEAS WITHOUT AN OUNCE OF FEAR.
B-BUT ISN'T IT RUDE TO...TO CONTRADICT ONE'S OWN FATHER LIKE THAT?
I COULD NEVER BE SO SELFISH. IT WOULD SIMPLY BE A NUISANCE FOR FATHER...
WHAT'S WRONG WITH BEING A LITTLE SELFISH NOW AND THEN?
GRAND-FATHER?

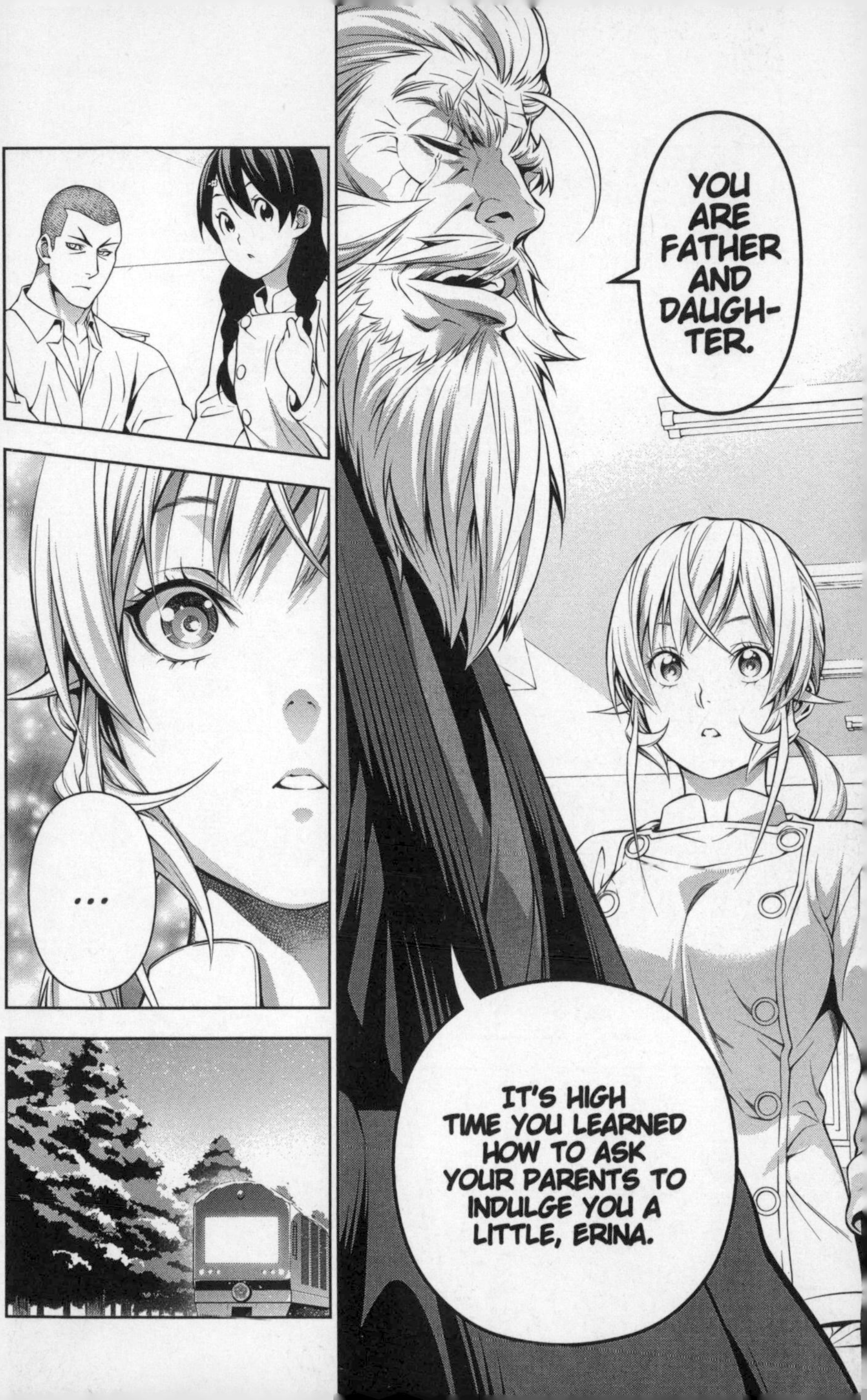
YOU ARE FATHER AND DAUGHTER.
IT'S HIGH TIME YOU LEARNED HOW TO ASK YOUR PARENTS TO INDULGE YOU A LITTLE, ERINA.
...

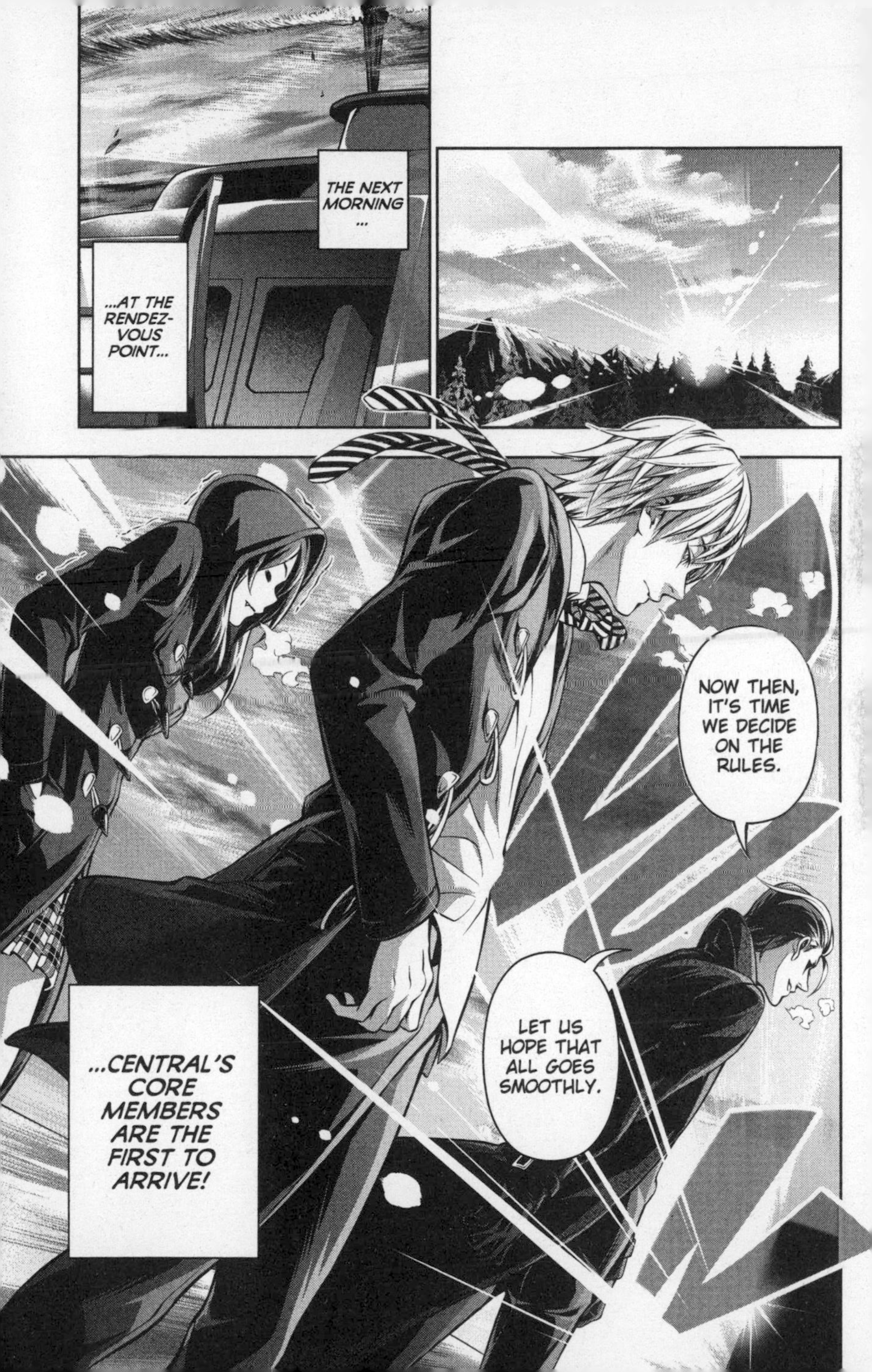
THE NEXT MORNING ...
...AT THE RENDEZ-VOUS POINT...
NOW THEN, IT'S TIME WE DECIDE ON THE RULES.
LET US HOPE THAT ALL GOES SMOOTHLY.
...CENTRAL'S CORE MEMBERS ARE THE FIRST TO ARRIVE!

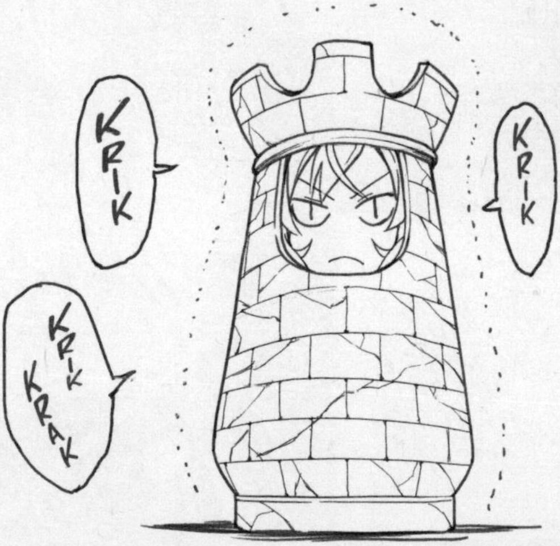
KRIK
KRIK
KRIK KRAK

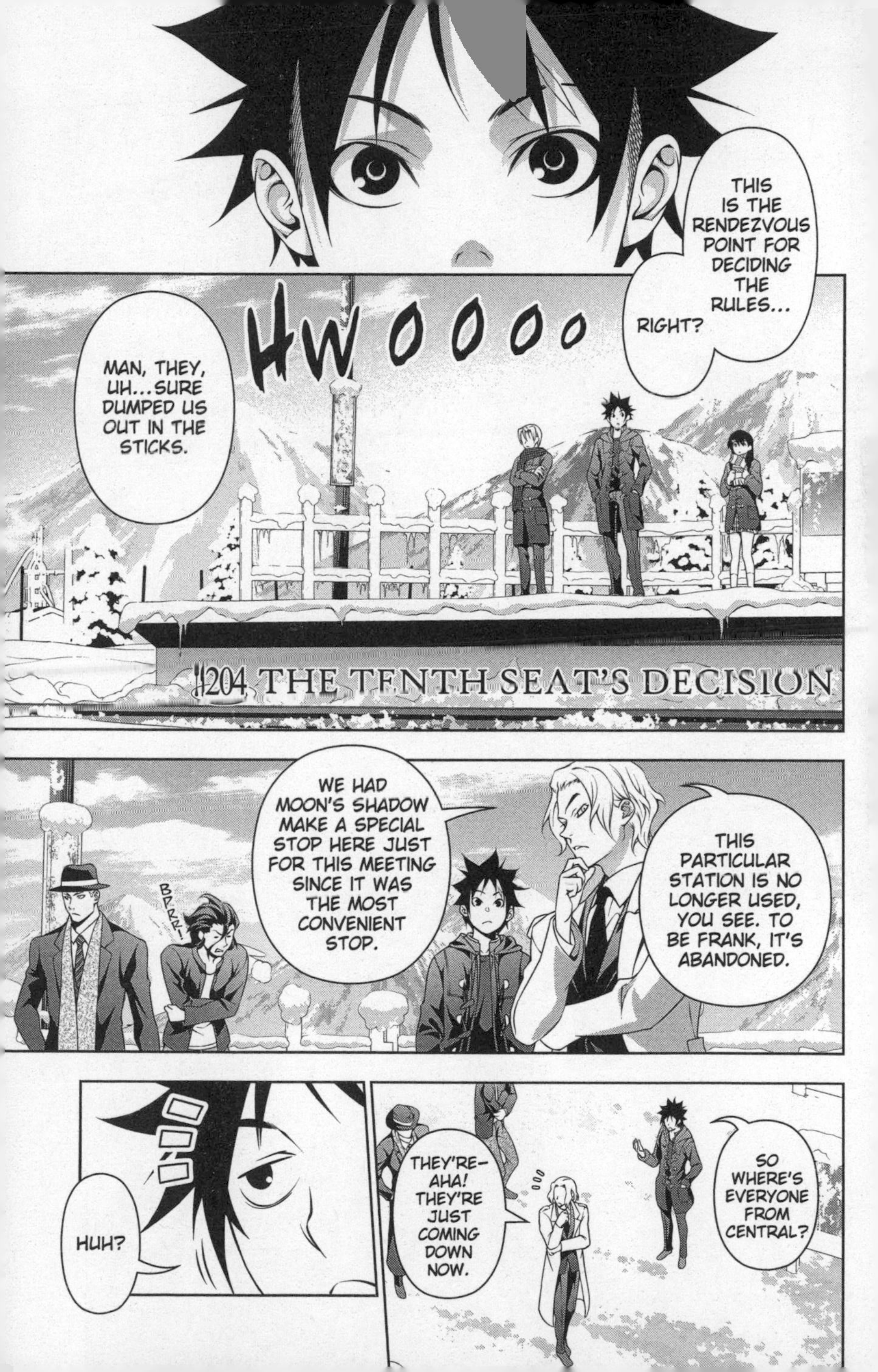
THIS IS THE RENDEZVOUS POINT FOR DECIDING THE RULES... RIGHT?
HWOOOO
MAN, THEY, UH...SURE DUMPED US OUT IN THE STICKS.
204 THE TENTH SEAT'S DECISION
THIS PARTICULAR STATION IS NO LONGER USED, YOU SEE. TO BE FRANK, IT'S ABANDONED.
WE HAD MOON'S SHADOW MAKE A SPECIAL STOP HERE JUST FOR THIS MEETING SINCE IT WAS THE MOST CONVENIENT STOP.
BRRR!
SO WHERE'S EVERYONE FROM CENTRAL?
THEY'RE— AHA! THEY'RE JUST COMING DOWN NOW.
HUH?

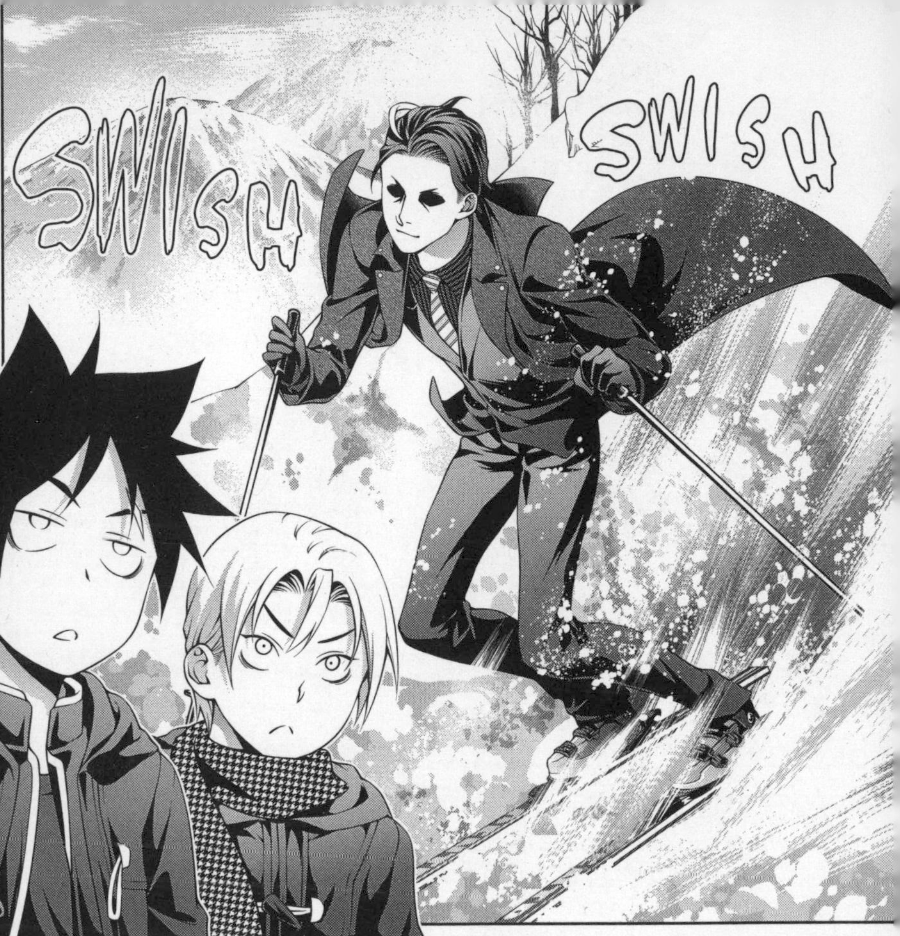
SWISH
SWISH
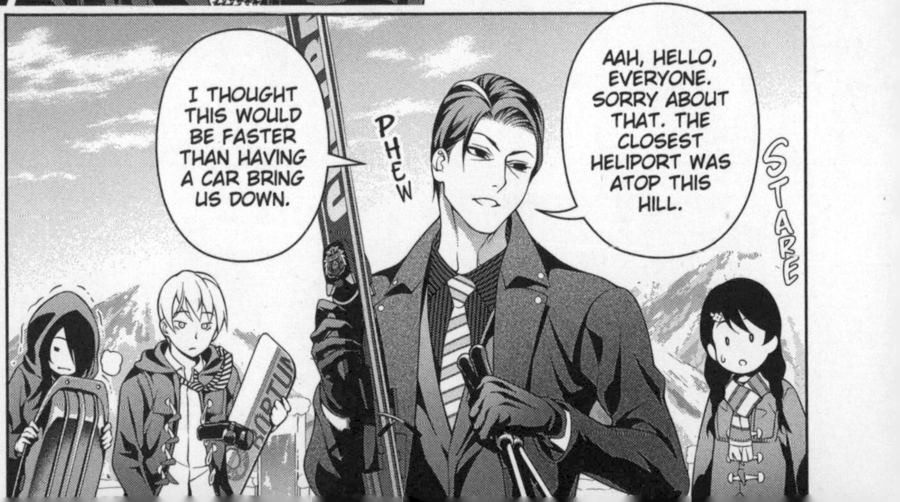
STARE
AAH, HELLO, EVERYONE. SORRY ABOUT THAT. THE CLOSEST HELIPORT WAS ATOP THIS HILL.
PHEW
I THOUGHT THIS WOULD BE FASTER THAN HAVING A CAR BRING US DOWN.

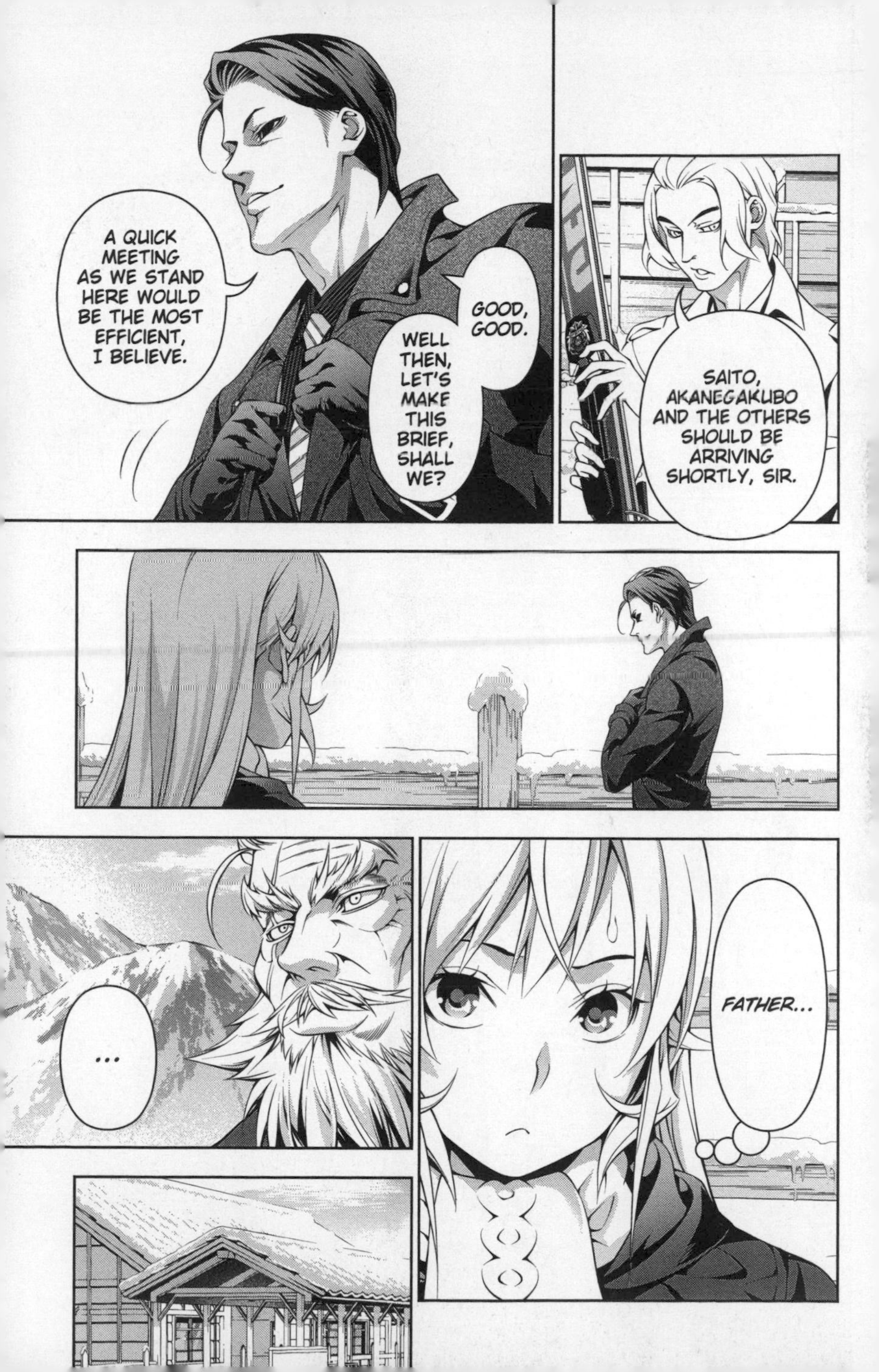
SAITO, AKANEGAKUBO AND THE OTHERS SHOULD BE ARRIVING SHORTLY, SIR.
GOOD, GOOD.
WELL THEN, LET'S MAKE THIS BRIEF, SHALL WE?
A QUICK MEETING AS WE STAND HERE WOULD BE THE MOST EFFICIENT, I BELIEVE.
FATHER...
...

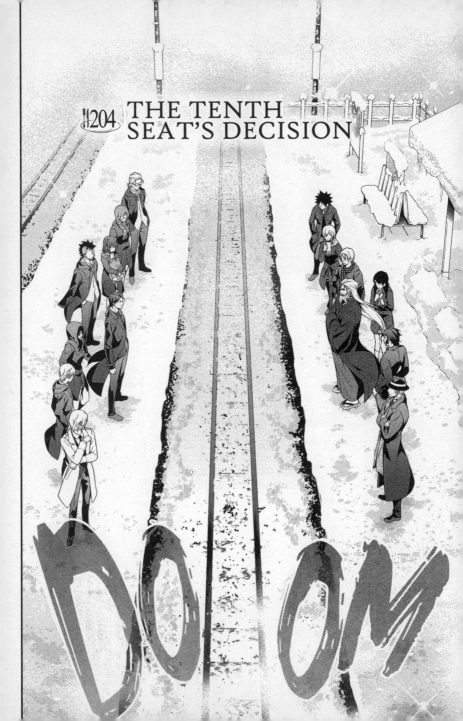

204 THE TENTH
SEAT'S DECISION

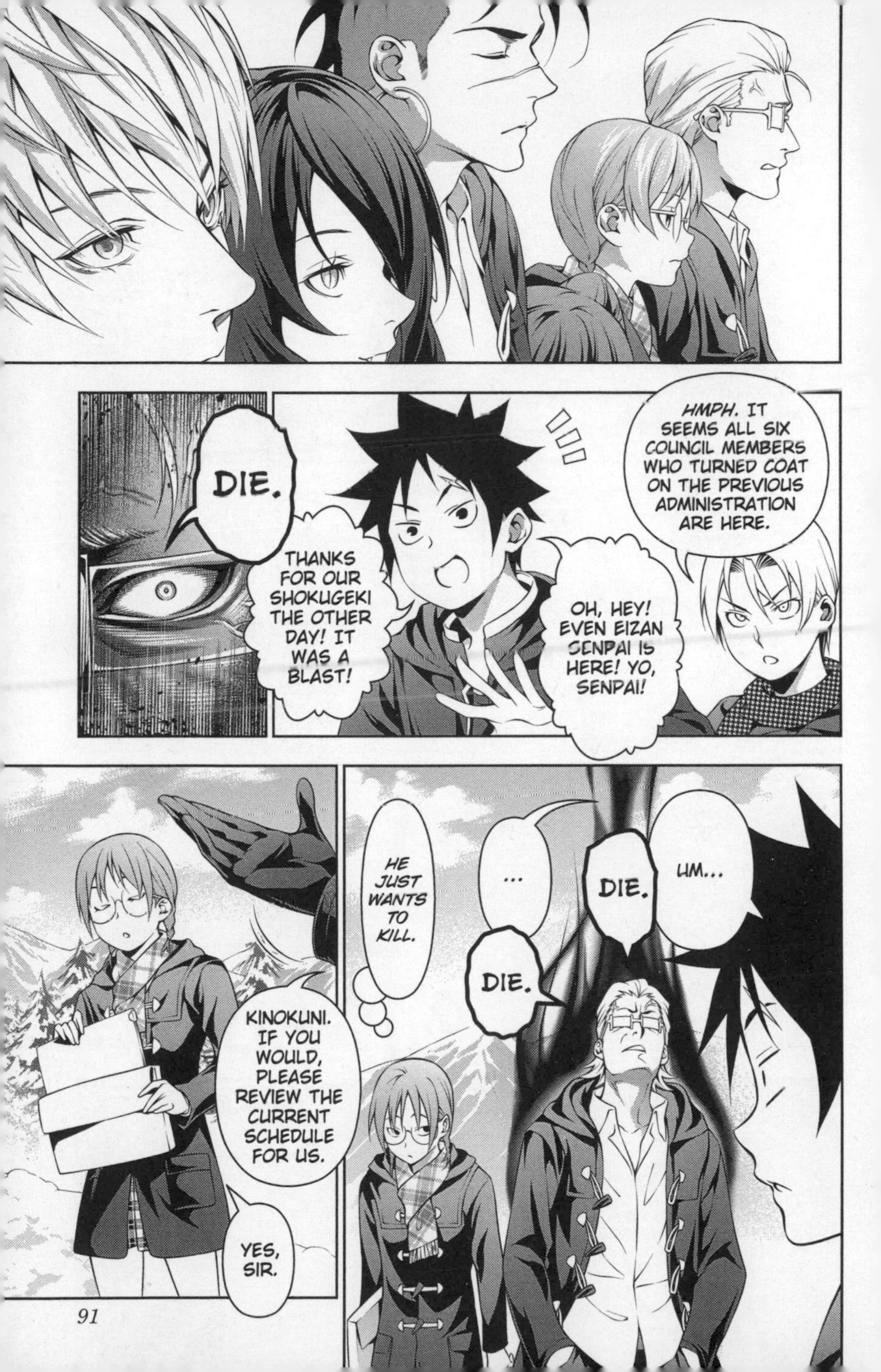
HMPH. IT SEEMS ALL SIX COUNCIL MEMBERS WHO TURNED COAT ON THE PREVIOUS ADMINISTRATION ARE HERE.
OH, HEY! EVEN EIZAN SENPAI IS HERE! YO, SENPAI!
THANKS FOR OUR SHOKUGEKI THE OTHER DAY! IT WAS A BLAST!
DIE.
UM...
DIE.
DIE.
...
HE JUST WANTS TO KILL.
KINOKUNI. IF YOU WOULD, PLEASE REVIEW THE CURRENT SCHEDULE FOR US.
YES, SIR.

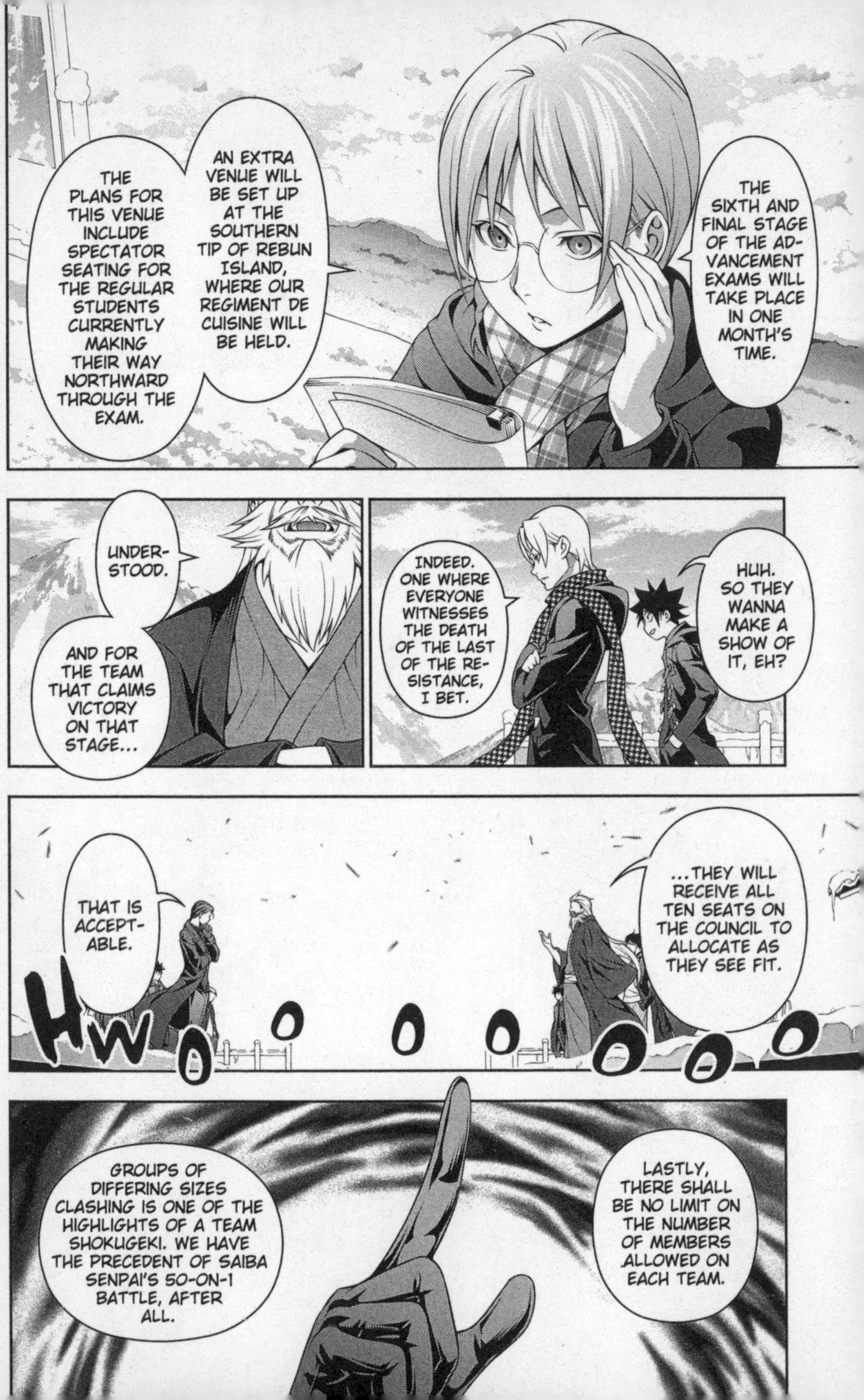
THE SIXTH AND FINAL STAGE OF THE ADVANCEMENT EXAMS WILL TAKE PLACE IN ONE MONTH'S TIME.
AN EXTRA VENUE WILL BE SET UP AT THE SOUTHERN TIP OF REBUN ISLAND, WHERE OUR REGIMENT DE CUISINE WILL BE HELD.
THE PLANS FOR THIS VENUE INCLUDE SPECTATOR SEATING FOR THE REGULAR STUDENTS CURRENTLY MAKING THEIR WAY NORTHWARD THROUGH THE EXAM.
HUH. SO THEY WANNA MAKE A SHOW OF IT, EH?
INDEED. ONE WHERE EVERYONE WITNESSES THE DEATH OF THE LAST OF THE RESISTANCE, I BET.
UNDERSTOOD.
AND FOR THE TEAM THAT CLAIMS VICTORY ON THAT STAGE...
...THEY WILL RECEIVE ALL TEN SEATS ON THE COUNCIL TO ALLOCATE AS THEY SEE FIT.
THAT IS ACCEPTABLE.
HWOOOOOOOOO
LASTLY, THERE SHALL BE NO LIMIT ON THE NUMBER OF MEMBERS ALLOWED ON EACH TEAM.
GROUPS OF DIFFERING SIZES CLASHING IS ONE OF THE HIGHLIGHTS OF A TEAM SHOKUGEKI. WE HAVE THE PRECEDENT OF SAIBA SENPAI'S 50-ON-1 BATTLE, AFTER ALL.

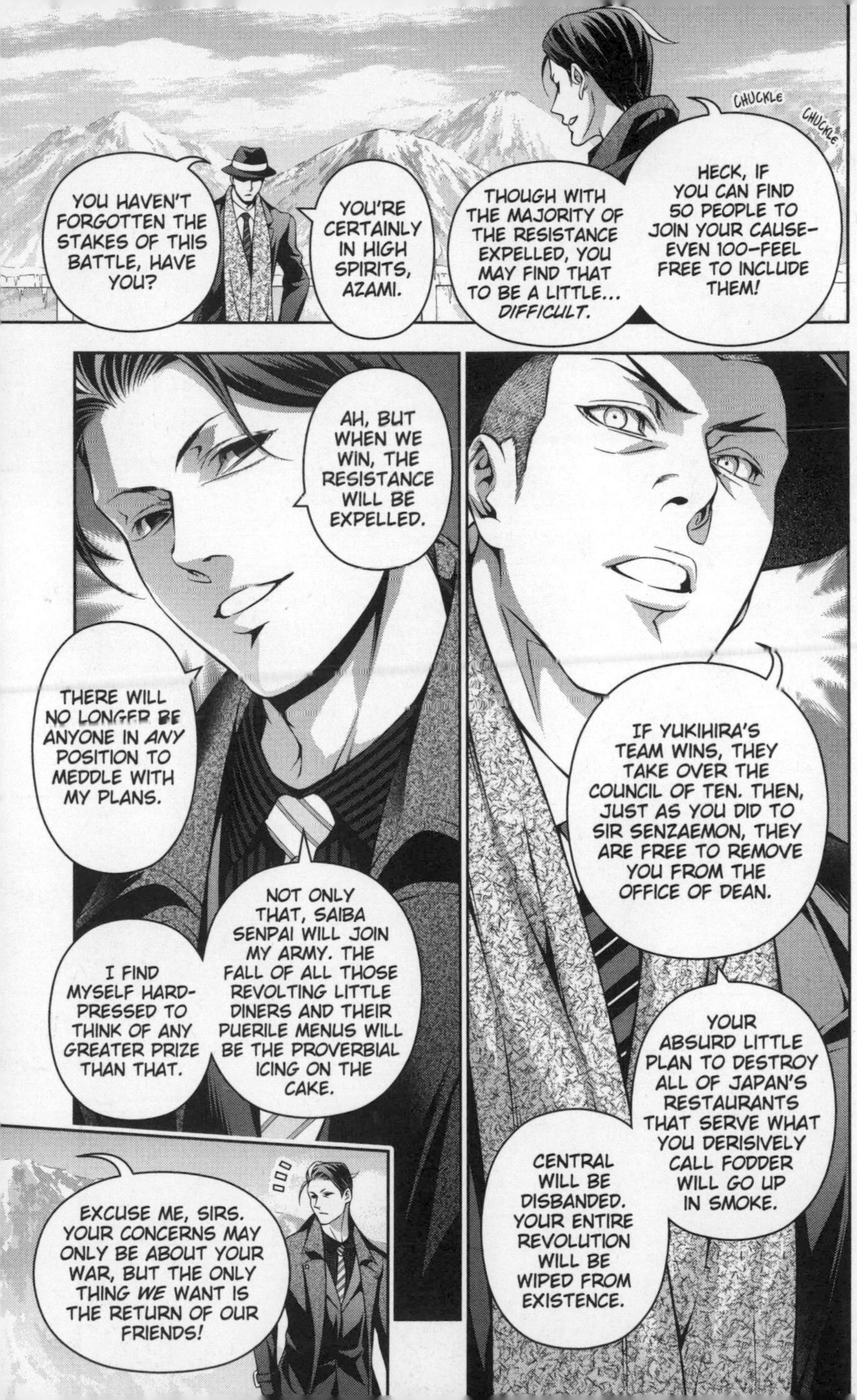
CHUCKLE
CHUCKLE
HECK, IF YOU CAN FIND 50 PEOPLE TO JOIN YOUR CAUSE–EVEN 100–FEEL FREE TO INCLUDE THEM!
THOUGH WITH THE MAJORITY OF THE RESISTANCE EXPELLED, YOU MAY FIND THAT TO BE A LITTLE... *DIFFICULT.*
YOU'RE CERTAINLY IN HIGH SPIRITS, AZAMI.
YOU HAVEN'T FORGOTTEN THE STAKES OF THIS BATTLE, HAVE YOU?
IF YUKIHIRA'S TEAM WINS, THEY TAKE OVER THE COUNCIL OF TEN. THEN, JUST AS YOU DID TO SIR SENZAEMON, THEY ARE FREE TO REMOVE YOU FROM THE OFFICE OF DEAN.
YOUR ABSURD LITTLE PLAN TO DESTROY ALL OF JAPAN'S RESTAURANTS THAT SERVE WHAT YOU DERISIVELY CALL FODDER WILL GO UP IN SMOKE.
CENTRAL WILL BE DISBANDED. YOUR ENTIRE REVOLUTION WILL BE WIPED FROM EXISTENCE.
AH, BUT WHEN WE WIN, THE RESISTANCE WILL BE EXPELLED.
THERE WILL NO LONGER BE ANYONE IN *ANY* POSITION TO MEDDLE WITH MY PLANS.
NOT ONLY THAT, SAIBA SENPAI WILL JOIN MY ARMY. THE FALL OF ALL THOSE REVOLTING LITTLE DINERS AND THEIR PUERILE MENUS WILL BE THE PROVERBIAL ICING ON THE CAKE.
I FIND MYSELF HARD-PRESSED TO THINK OF ANY GREATER PRIZE THAN THAT.
EXCUSE ME, SIRS. YOUR CONCERNS MAY ONLY BE ABOUT YOUR WAR, BUT THE ONLY THING *WE* WANT IS THE RETURN OF OUR FRIENDS!

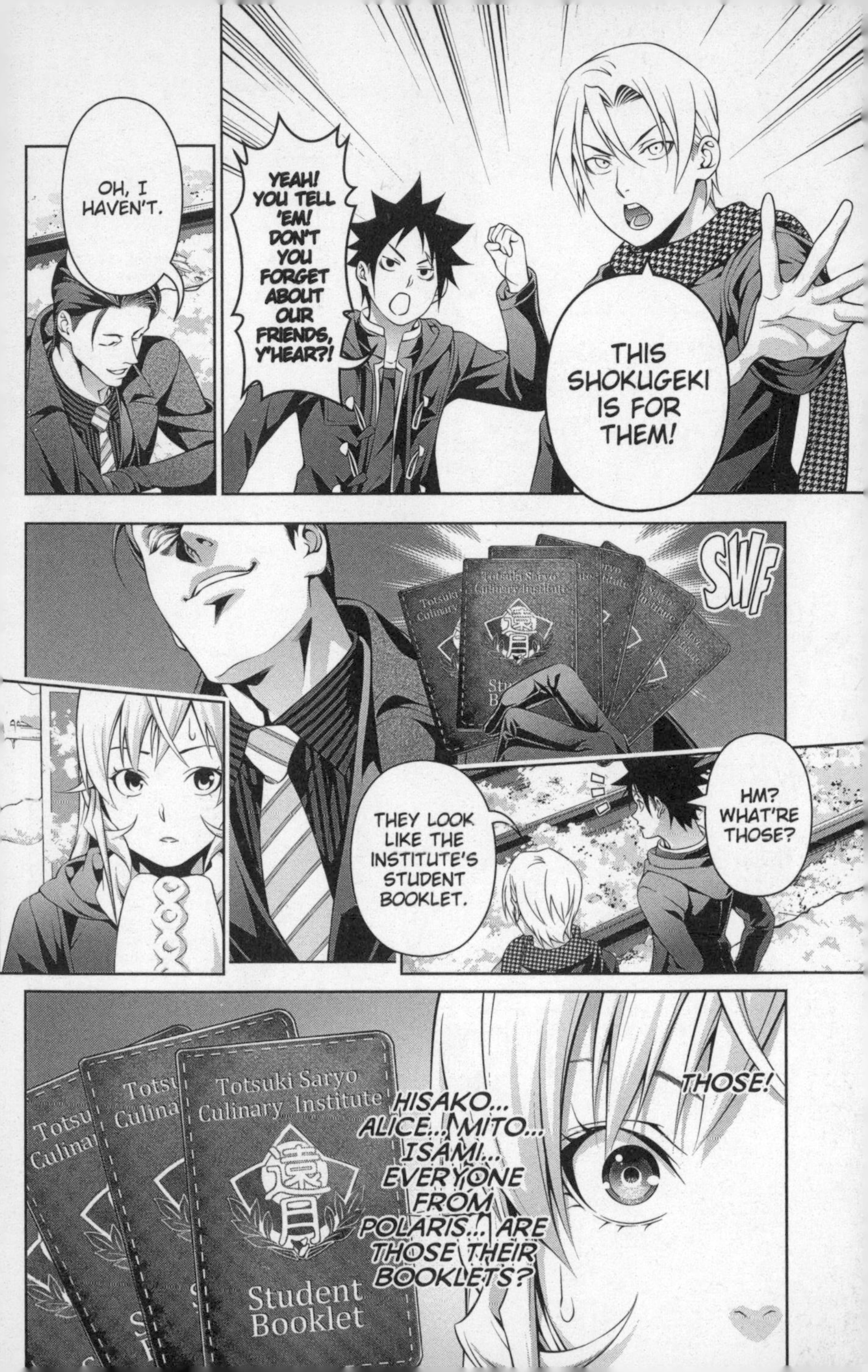
THIS SHOKUGEKI IS FOR THEM!
YEAH! YOU TELL 'EM! DON'T YOU FORGET ABOUT OUR FRIENDS, Y'HEAR?!
OH, I HAVEN'T.
SWF
HM? WHAT'RE THOSE?
THEY LOOK LIKE THE INSTITUTE'S STUDENT BOOKLET.
THOSE!
HISAKO... ALICE... MITO... ISAMI... EVERYONE FROM POLARIS... ARE THOSE THEIR BOOKLETS?
Totsuki Saryo Culinary Institute
Student Booklet

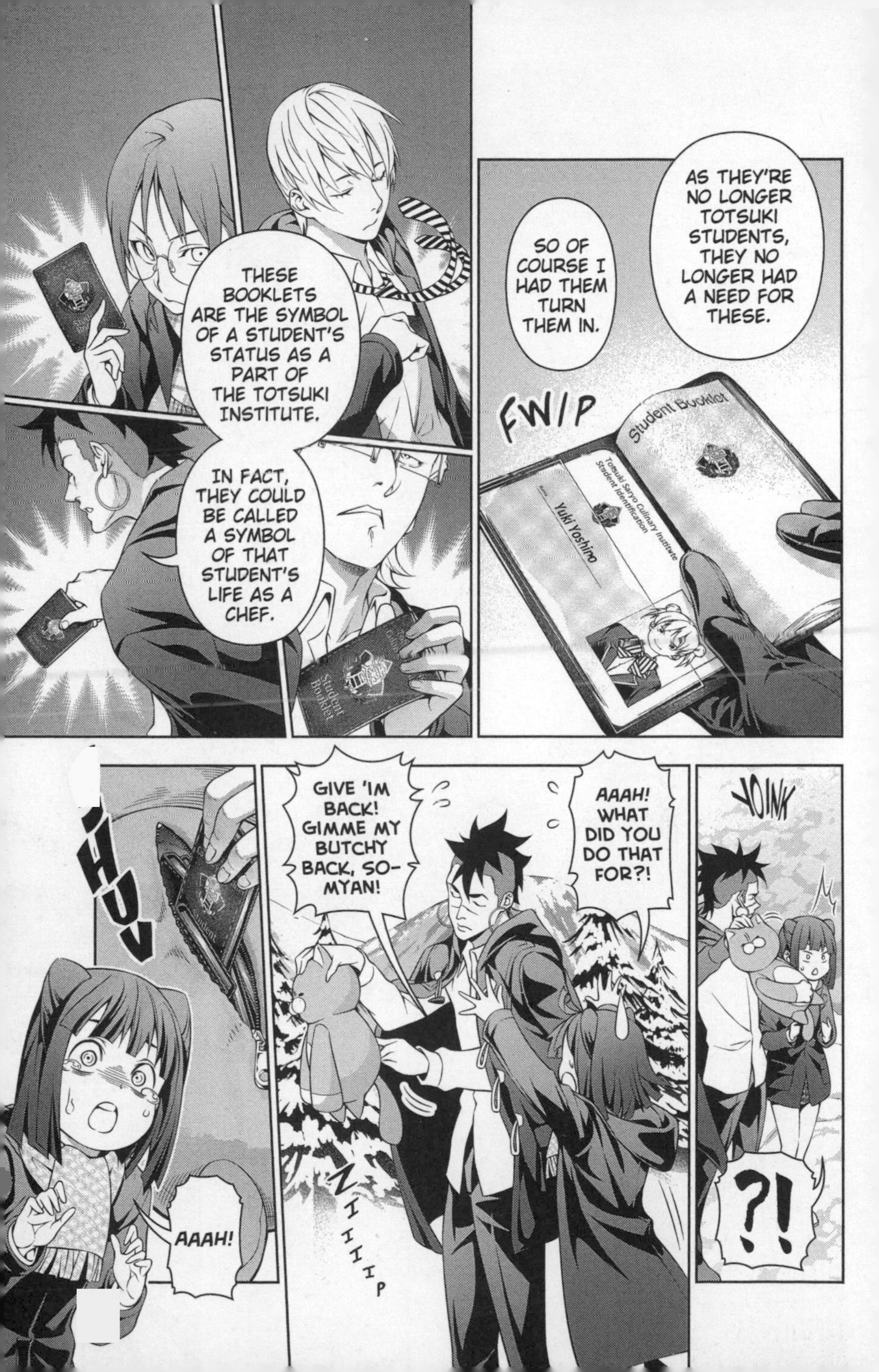
AS THEY'RE NO LONGER TOTSUKI STUDENTS, THEY NO LONGER HAD A NEED FOR THESE.
SO OF COURSE I HAD THEM TURN THEM IN.
FWIP
Student Booklet
Totsuki Saryo Culinary Institute Student Identification
Yuki Yoshino
THESE BOOKLETS ARE THE SYMBOL OF A STUDENT'S STATUS AS A PART OF THE TOTSUKI INSTITUTE.
IN FACT, THEY COULD BE CALLED A SYMBOL OF THAT STUDENT'S LIFE AS A CHEF.
Student Booklet
YOINK
?!
AAAH! WHAT DID YOU DO THAT FOR?!
GIVE 'IM BACK! GIMME MY BUTCHY BACK, SO-MYAN!
ZIIIIP
AAAH!

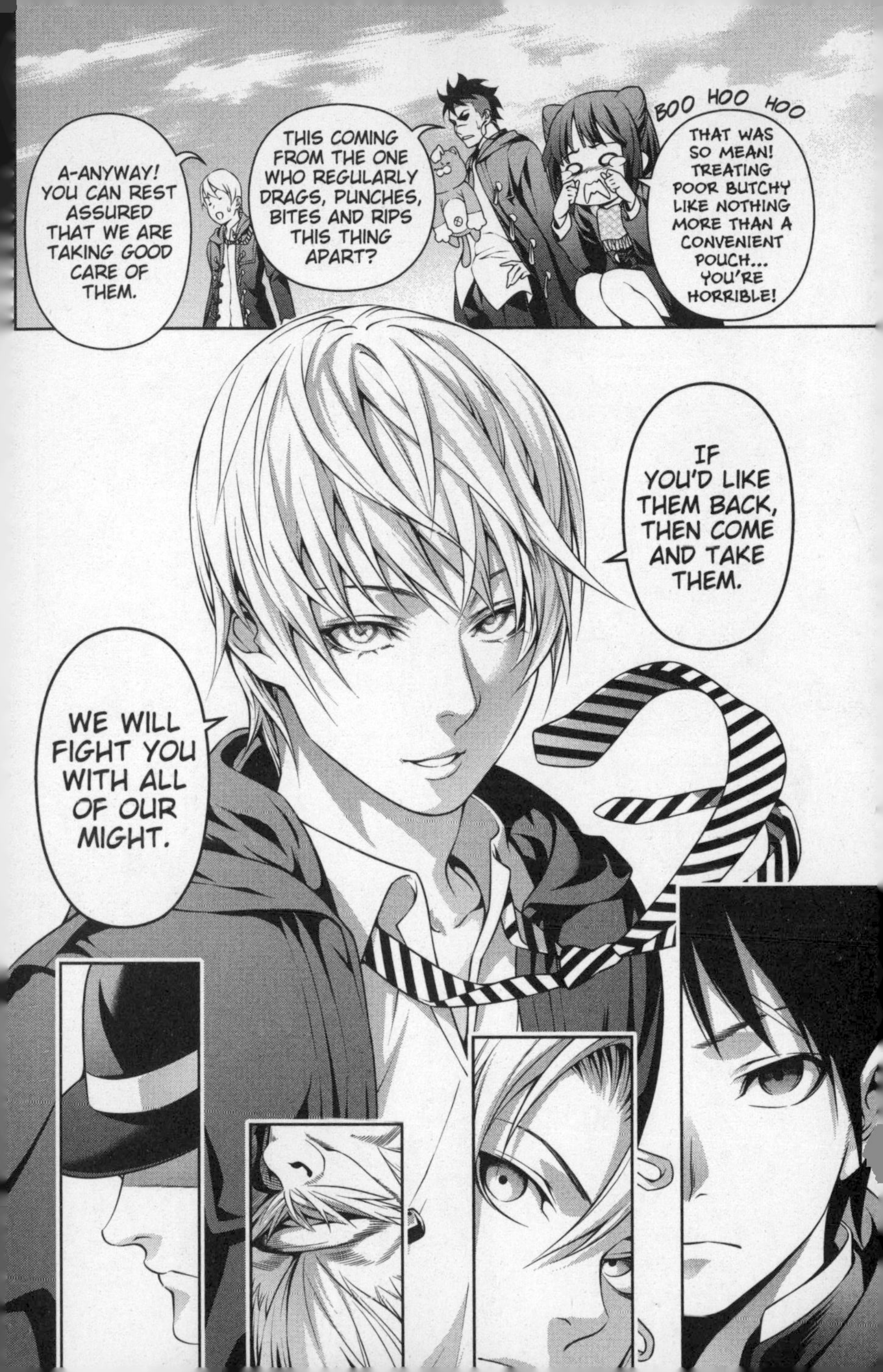
BOO HOO HOO
THAT WAS SO MEAN! TREATING POOR BUTCHY LIKE NOTHING MORE THAN A CONVENIENT POUCH... YOU'RE HORRIBLE!
THIS COMING FROM THE ONE WHO REGULARLY DRAGS, PUNCHES, BITES AND RIPS THIS THING APART?
A-ANYWAY! YOU CAN REST ASSURED THAT WE ARE TAKING GOOD CARE OF THEM.
IF YOU'D LIKE THEM BACK, THEN COME AND TAKE THEM.
WE WILL FIGHT YOU WITH ALL OF OUR MIGHT.

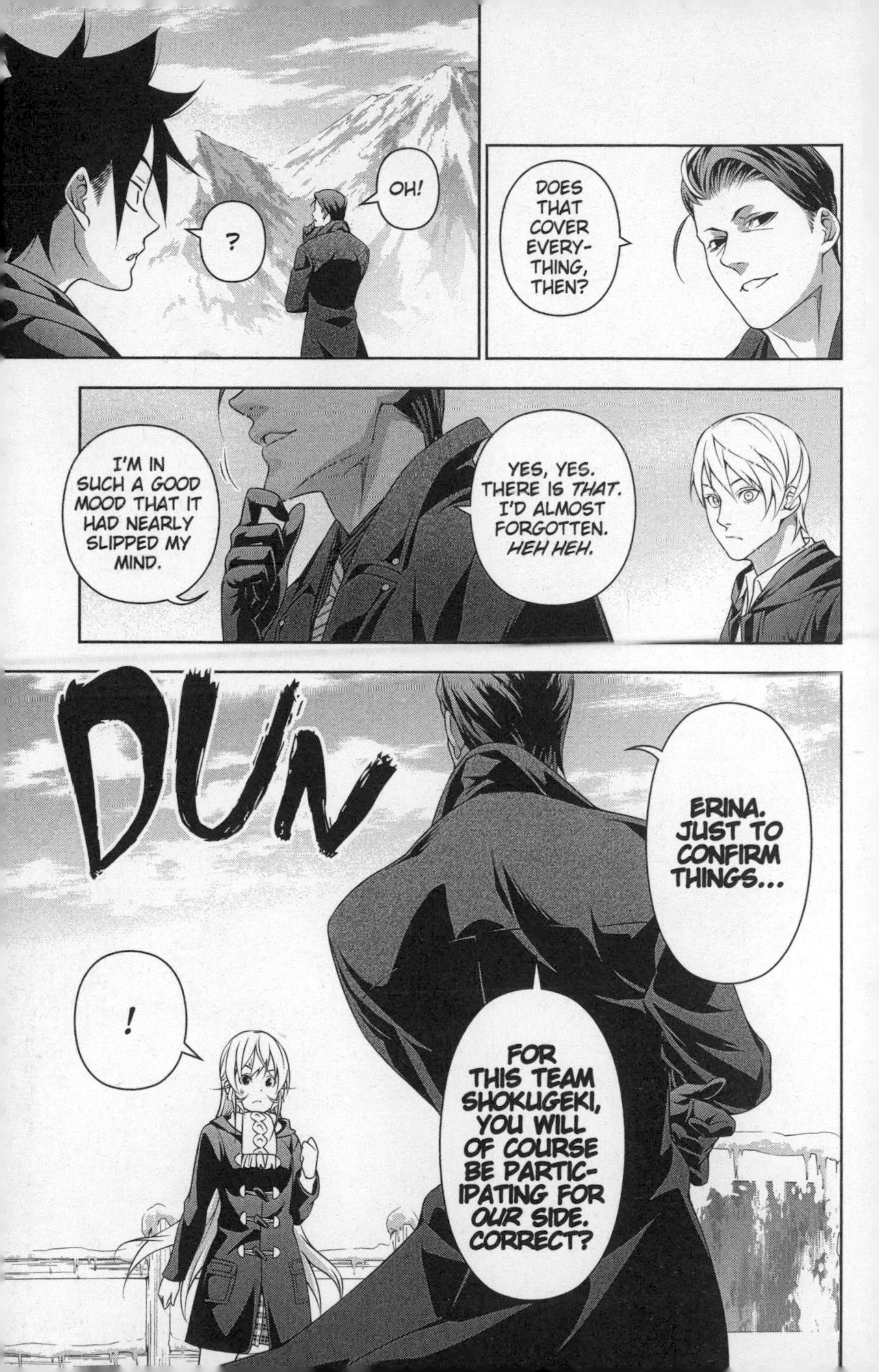
DOES THAT COVER EVERY-THING, THEN?
OH!
?
YES, YES. THERE IS *THAT*. I'D ALMOST FORGOTTEN. *HEH HEH.*
I'M IN SUCH A GOOD MOOD THAT IT HAD NEARLY SLIPPED MY MIND.
ERINA. JUST TO CONFIRM THINGS...
DUN
FOR THIS TEAM SHOKUGEKI, YOU WILL OF COURSE BE PARTIC-IPATING FOR *OUR* SIDE. CORRECT?
!

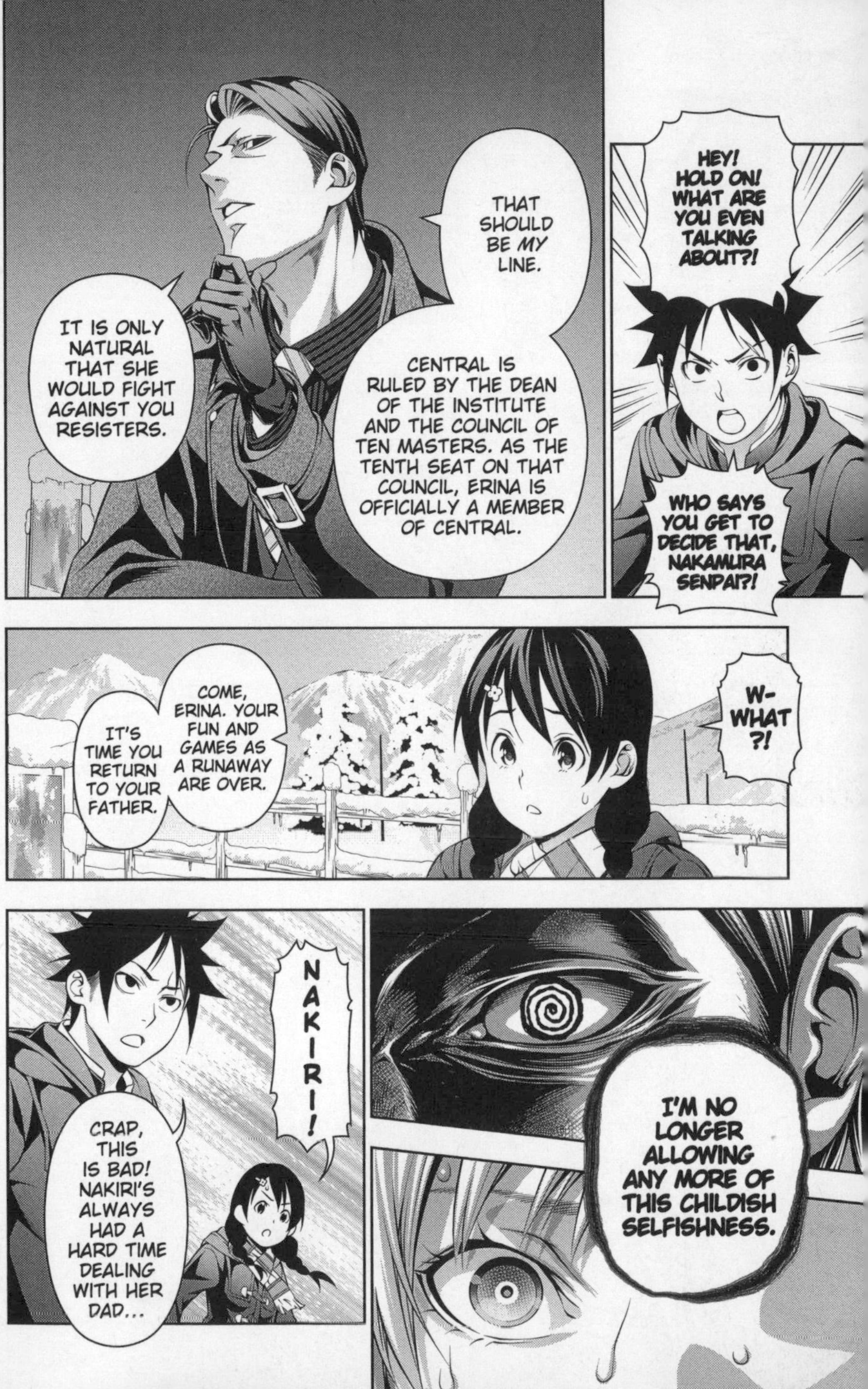
HEY! HOLD ON! WHAT ARE YOU EVEN TALKING ABOUT?!
WHO SAYS YOU GET TO DECIDE THAT, NAKAMURA SENPAI?!
THAT SHOULD BE *MY* LINE.
CENTRAL IS RULED BY THE DEAN OF THE INSTITUTE AND THE COUNCIL OF TEN MASTERS. AS THE TENTH SEAT ON THAT COUNCIL, ERINA IS OFFICIALLY A MEMBER OF CENTRAL.
IT IS ONLY NATURAL THAT SHE WOULD FIGHT AGAINST YOU RESISTERS.
W-WHAT?!
COME, ERINA. YOUR FUN AND GAMES AS A RUNAWAY ARE OVER.
IT'S TIME YOU RETURN TO YOUR FATHER.
I'M NO LONGER ALLOWING ANY MORE OF THIS CHILDISH SELFISHNESS.
NAKIRI!
CRAP, THIS IS BAD! NAKIRI'S ALWAYS HAD A HARD TIME DEALING WITH HER DAD...

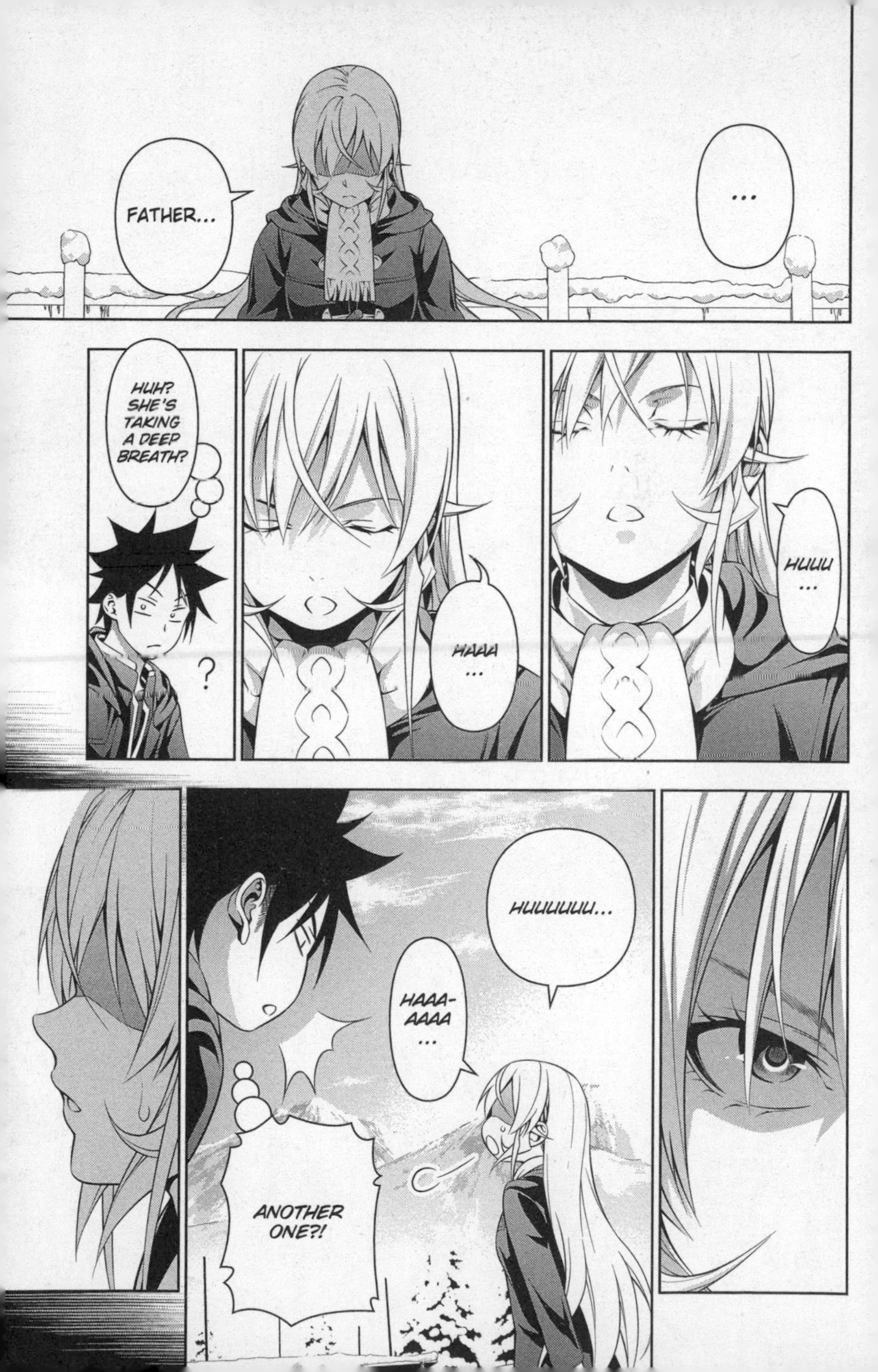
...
FATHER...
HUUU...
HAAA...
HUH? SHE'S TAKING A DEEP BREATH?
?
HUUUUUU...
HAAA-AAAA...
ANOTHER ONE?!

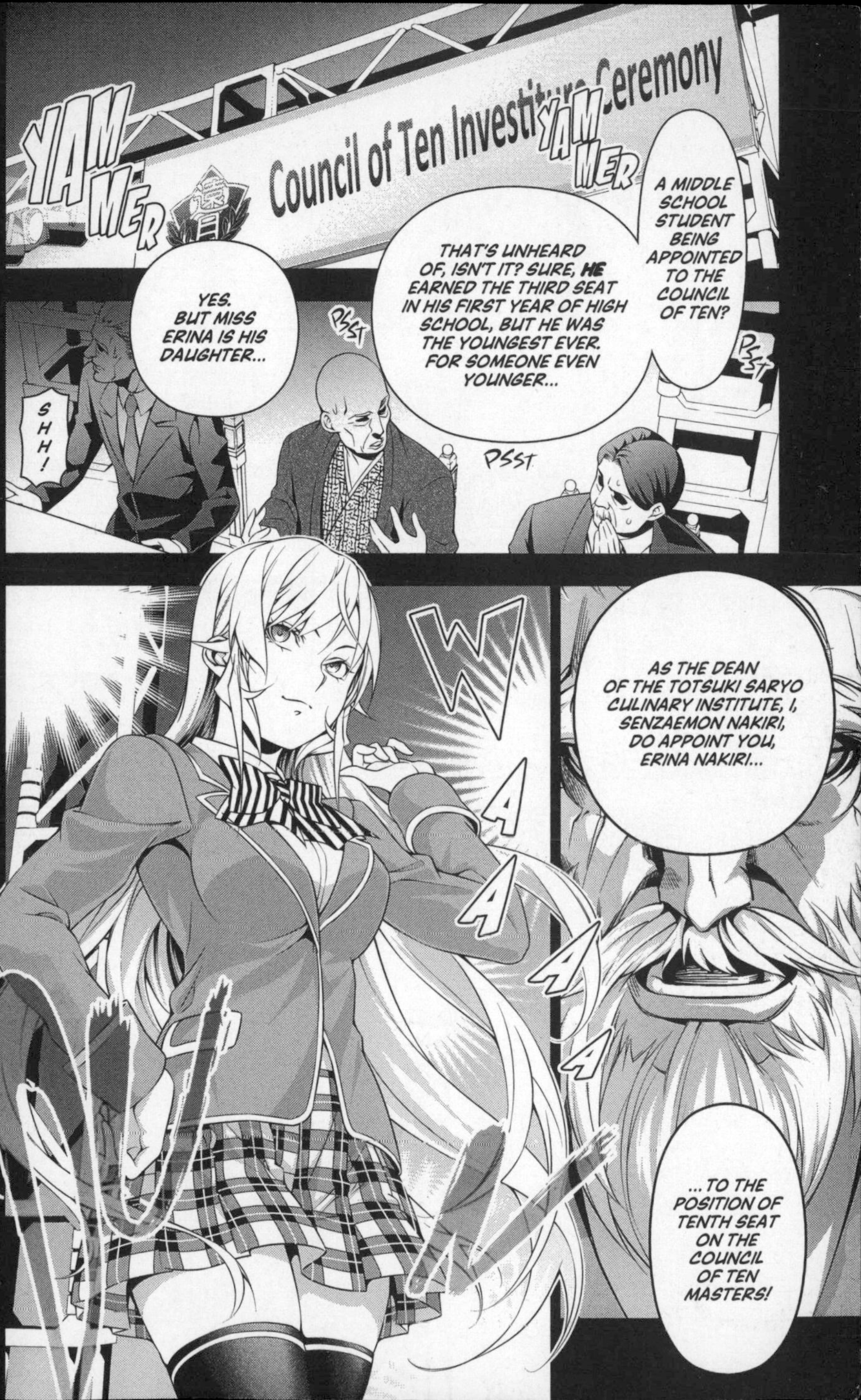
Council of Ten Investit
Ceremony
YAMMER
YAMMER
A MIDDLE SCHOOL STUDENT BEING APPOINTED TO THE COUNCIL OF TEN?
PSST
THAT'S UNHEARD OF, ISN'T IT? SURE, **HE** EARNED THE THIRD SEAT IN HIS FIRST YEAR OF HIGH SCHOOL, BUT HE WAS THE YOUNGEST EVER. FOR SOMEONE EVEN YOUNGER...
PSST
PSST.
YES. BUT MISS ERINA IS HIS DAUGHTER...
SHH!
AS THE DEAN OF THE TOTSUKI SARYO CULINARY INSTITUTE, I, SENZAEMON NAKIRI, DO APPOINT YOU, ERINA NAKIRI...
...TO THE POSITION OF TENTH SEAT ON THE COUNCIL OF TEN MASTERS!
WAAAAAA

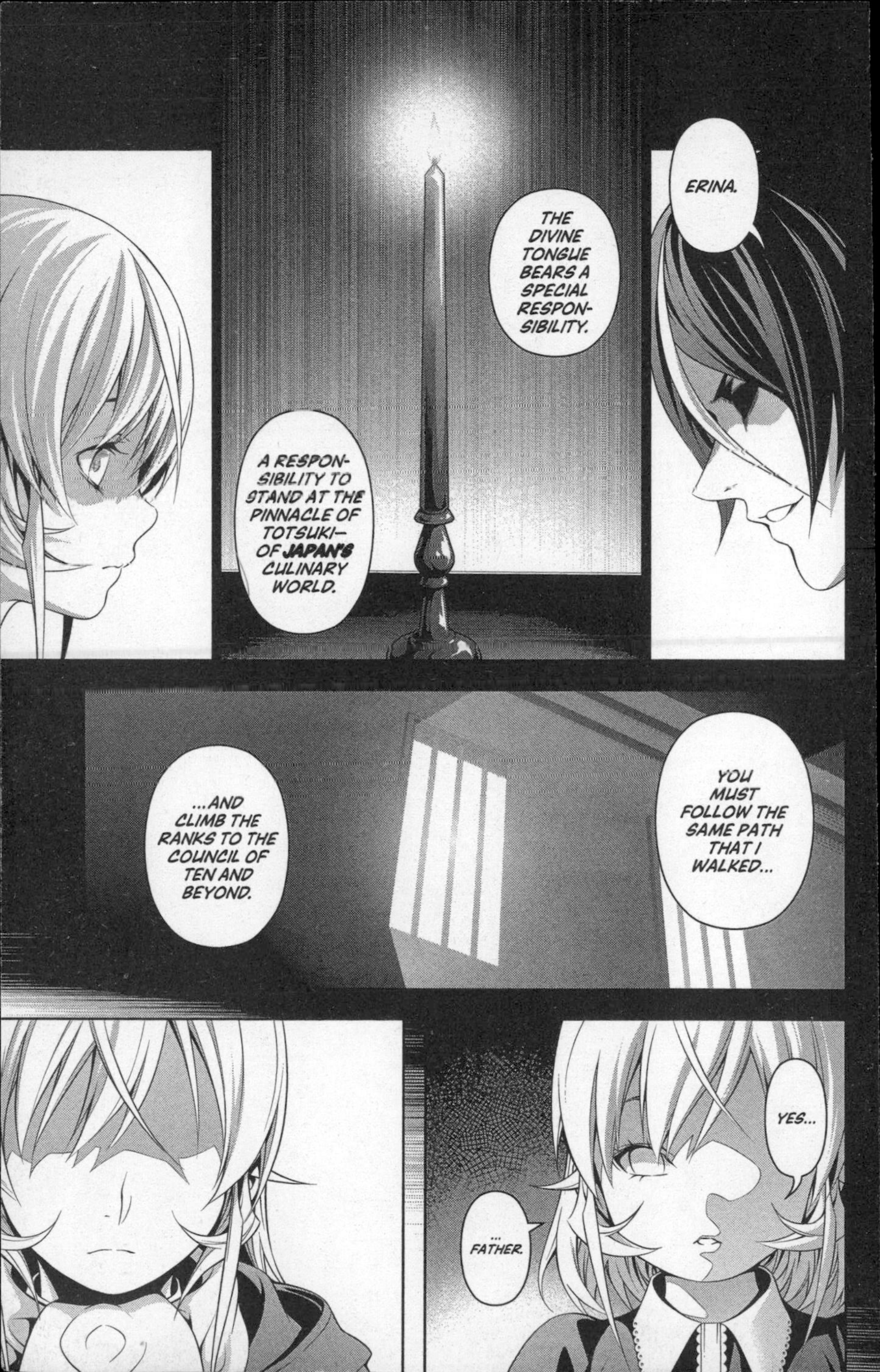
ERINA.
THE DIVINE TONGUE BEARS A SPECIAL RESPON-SIBILITY.
A RESPON-SIBILITY TO STAND AT THE PINNACLE OF TOTSUKI—OF **JAPAN'S** CULINARY WORLD.
YOU MUST FOLLOW THE SAME PATH THAT I WALKED...
...AND CLIMB THE RANKS TO THE COUNCIL OF TEN AND BEYOND.
YES...
... FATHER.

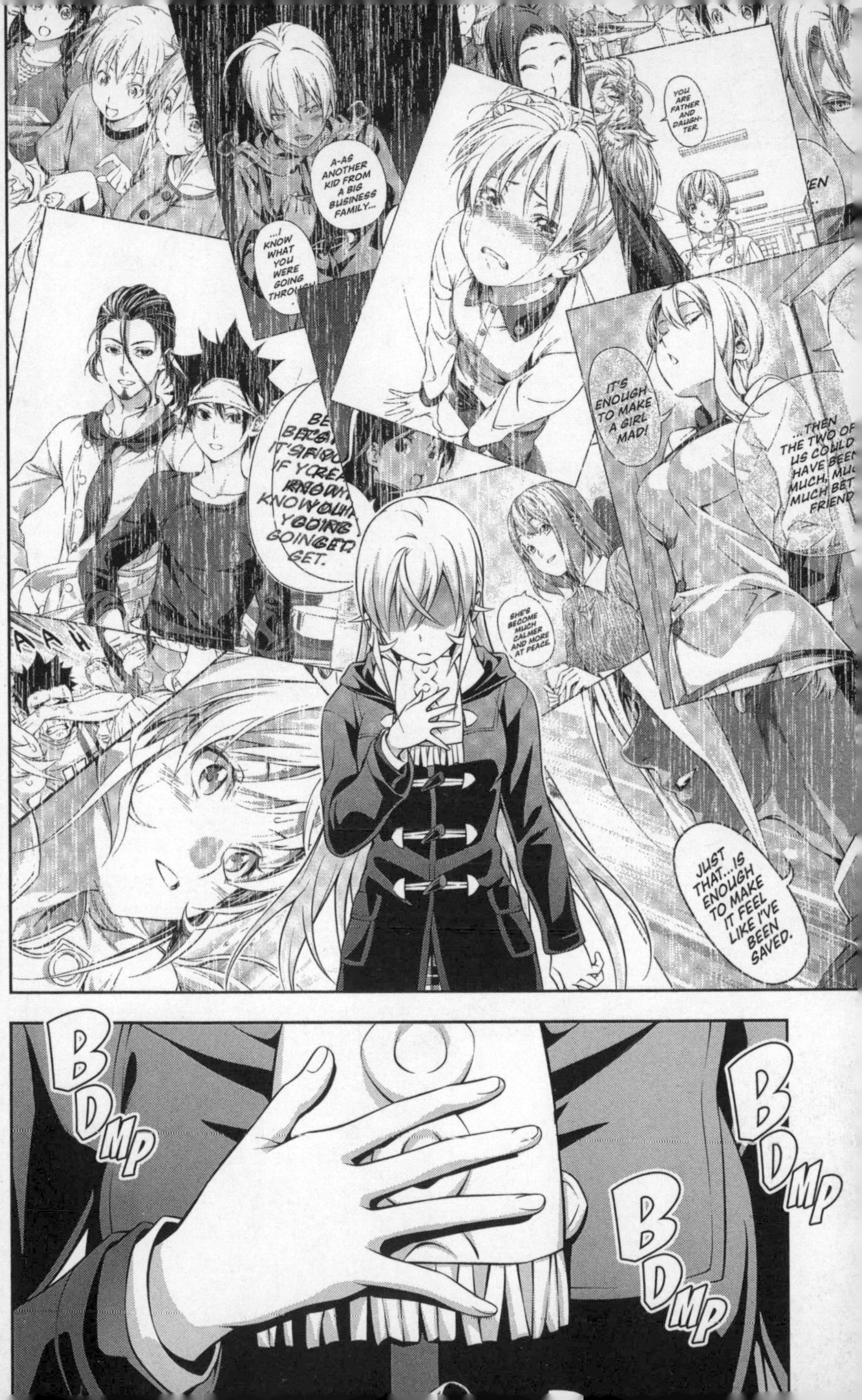

YOU ARE FATHER AND DAUGHTER.
...THEN THE TWO OF US COULD HAVE BEEN MUCH, MUC MUCH BET FRIEND
IT'S ENOUGH TO MAKE A GIRL MAD!
A-AS ANOTHER KID FROM A BIG BUSINESS FAMILY...
...I KNOW WHAT YOU WERE GOING THROUGH.
JUST THAT... IS ENOUGH TO MAKE IT FEEL LIKE I'VE BEEN SAVED.
SHE'S BECOME MUCH CALMER AND MORE AT PEACE.
AAAH
BDMP
BDMP
BDMP

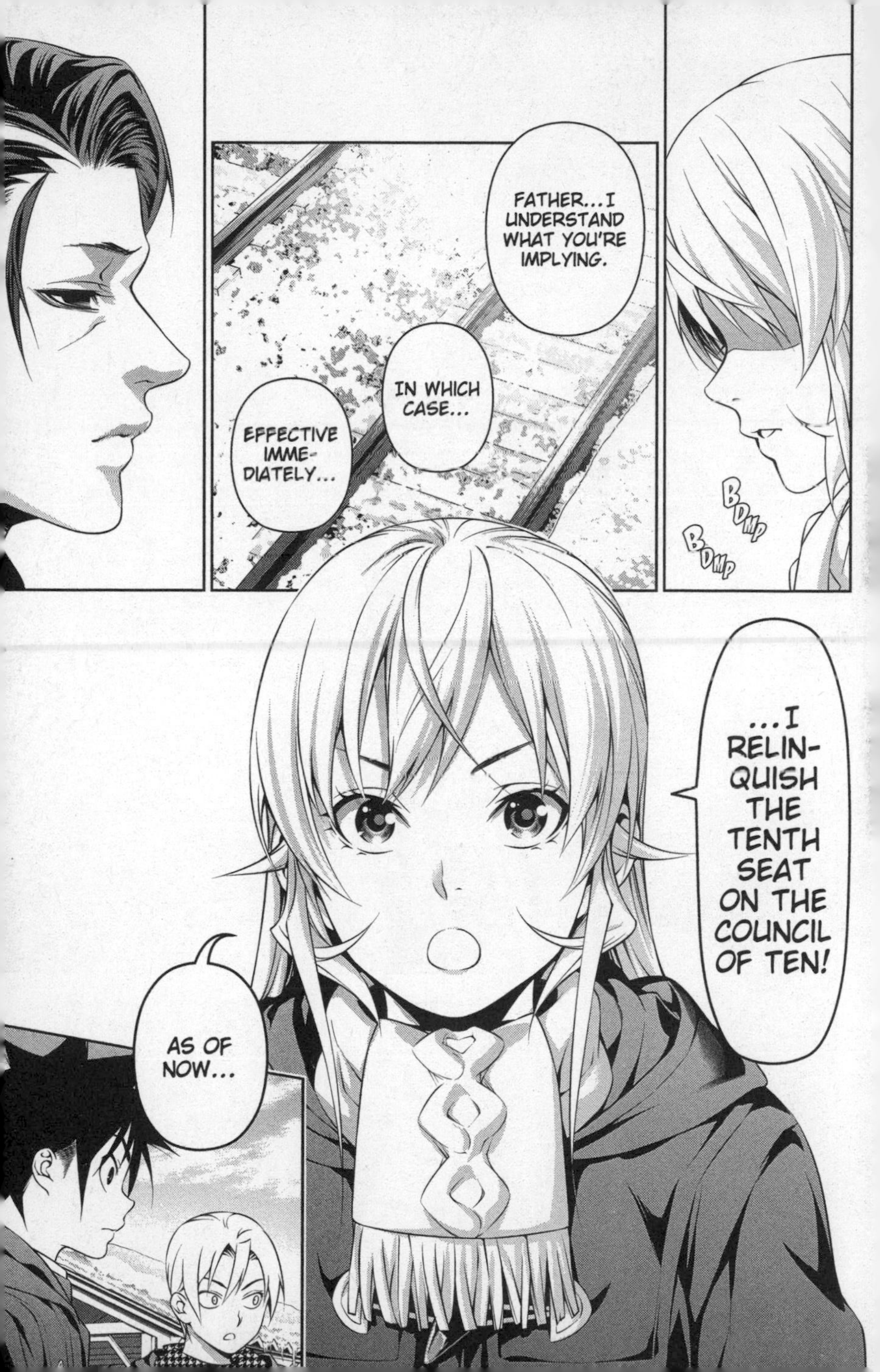
BDMP
BDMP
FATHER...I UNDERSTAND WHAT YOU'RE IMPLYING.
IN WHICH CASE...
EFFECTIVE IMME-DIATELY...
...I RELIN-QUISH THE TENTH SEAT ON THE COUNCIL OF TEN!
AS OF NOW...

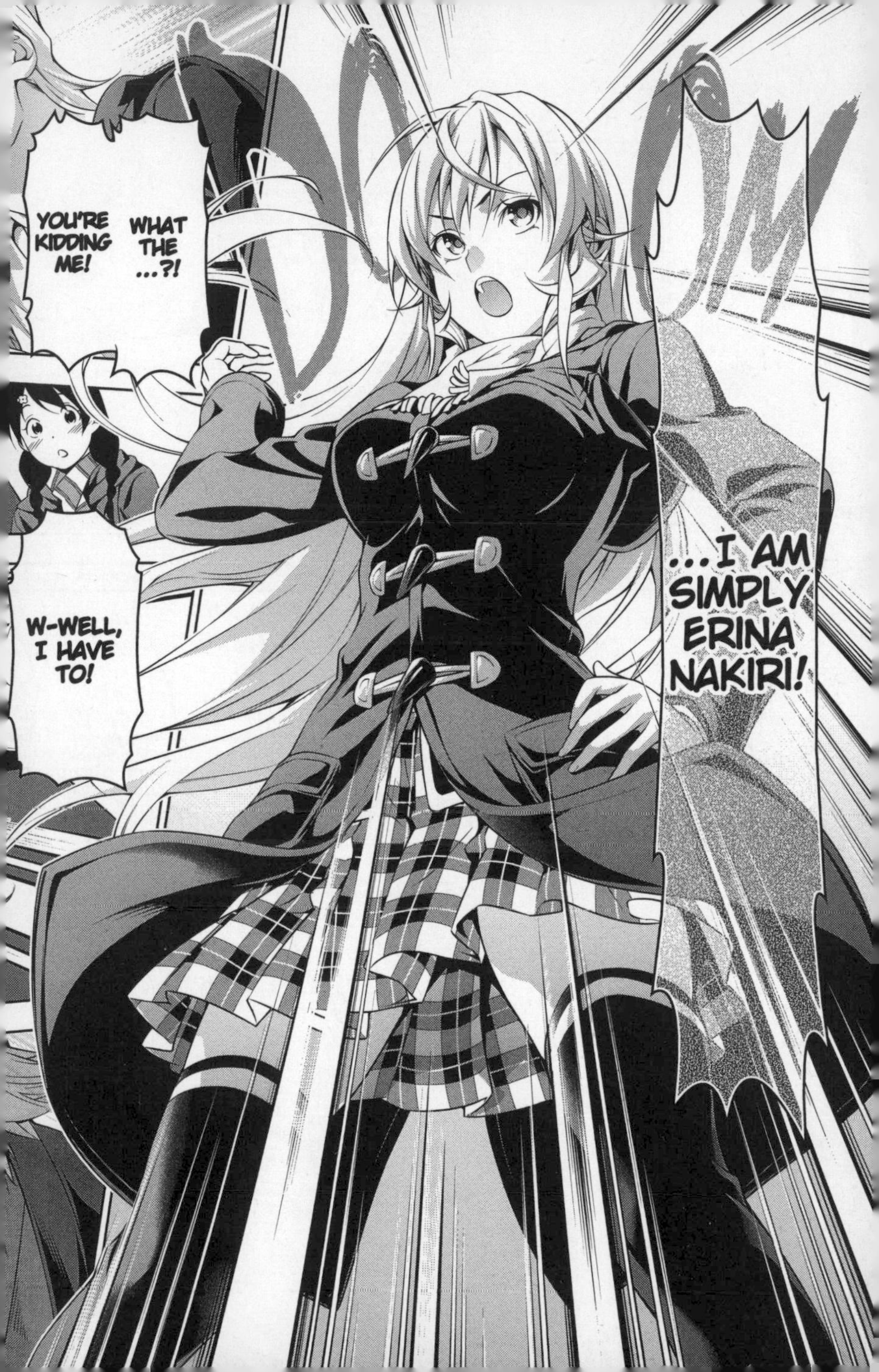
DOOM
...I AM SIMPLY ERINA NAKIRI!
WHAT THE ...?!
YOU'RE KIDDING ME!
W-WELL, I HAVE TO!

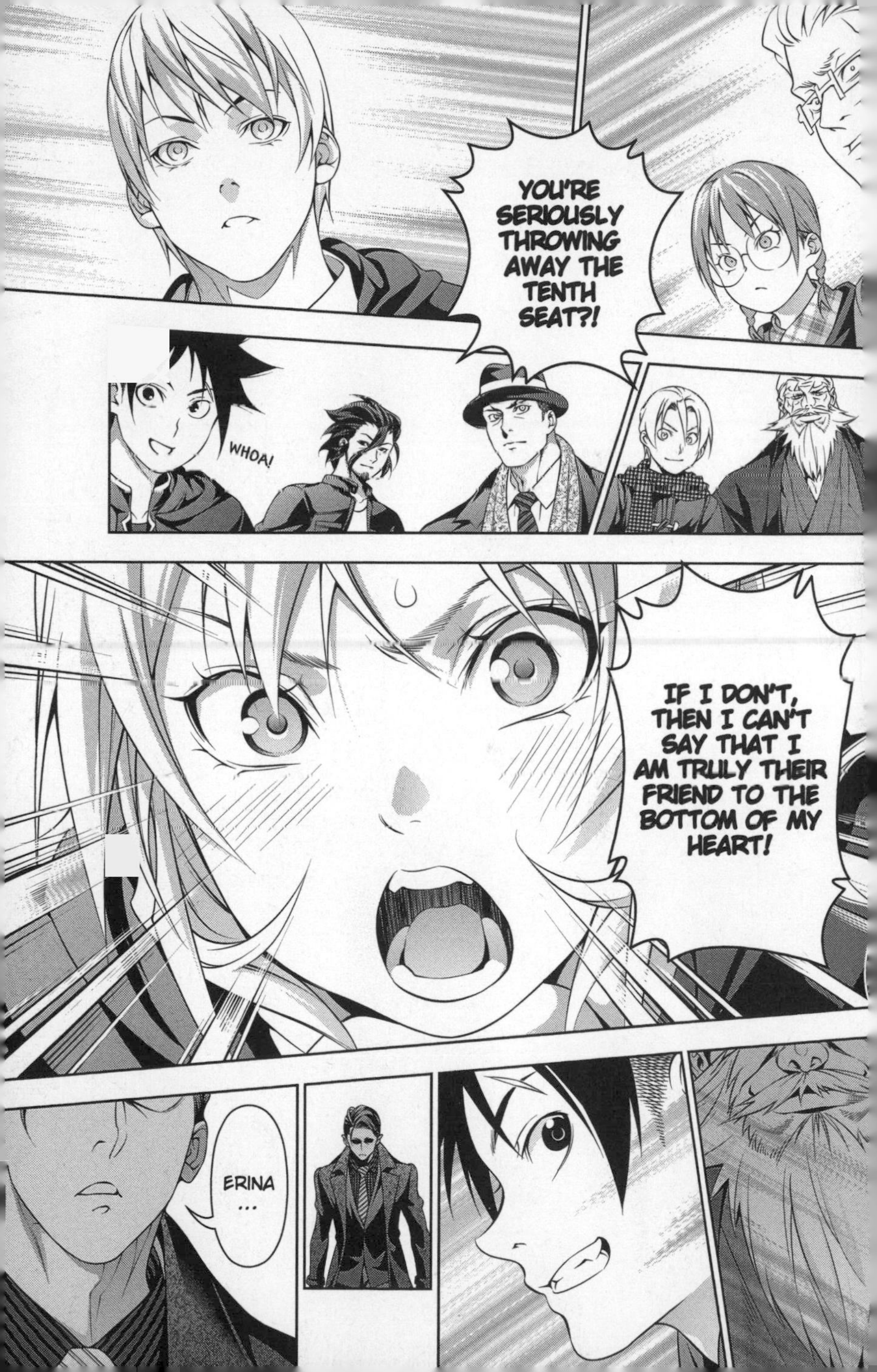
YOU'RE SERIOUSLY THROWING AWAY THE TENTH SEAT?!
WHOA!
IF I DON'T, THEN I CAN'T SAY THAT I AM TRULY THEIR FRIEND TO THE BOTTOM OF MY HEART!
ERINA ...

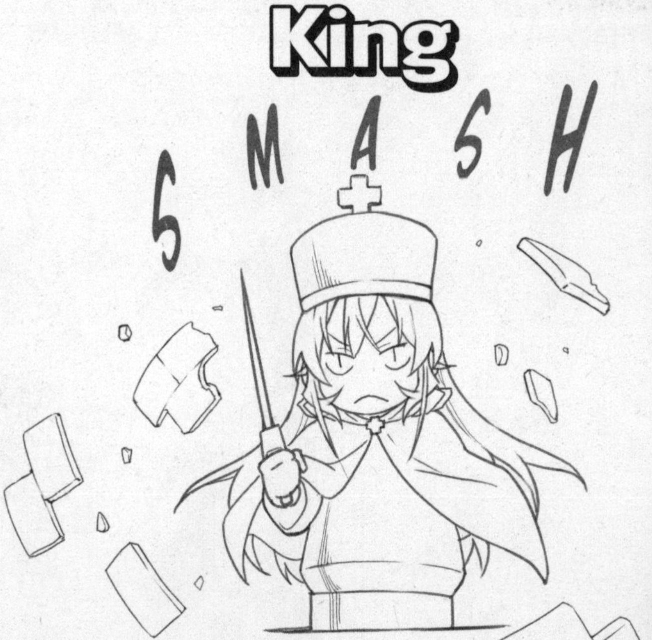
King
SMASH

205 CREATOR OF HAPPINESS

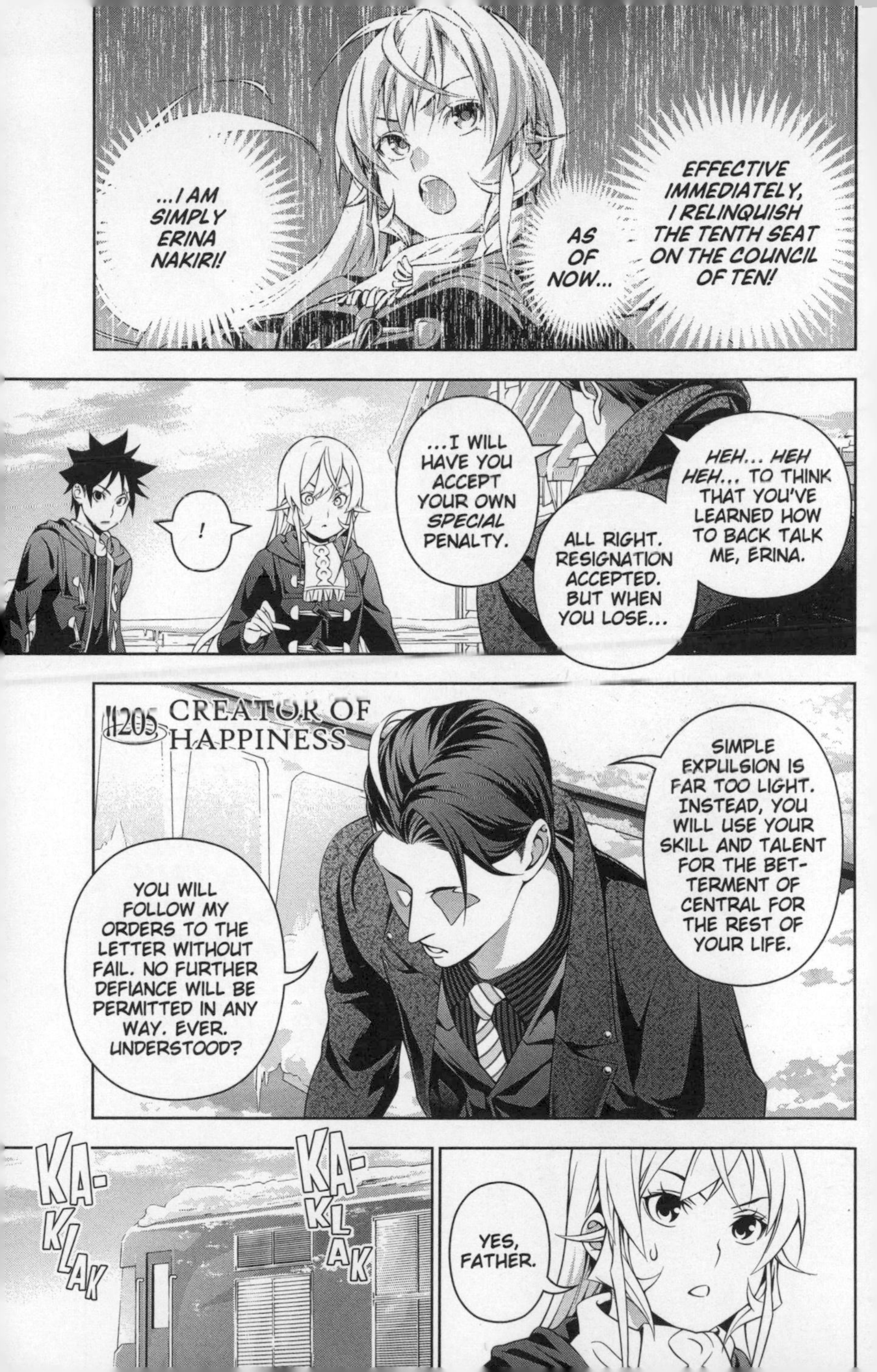
EFFECTIVE IMMEDIATELY, I RELINQUISH THE TENTH SEAT ON THE COUNCIL OF TEN!
AS OF NOW...
...I AM SIMPLY ERINA NAKIRI!
HEH... HEH HEH... TO THINK THAT YOU'VE LEARNED HOW TO BACK TALK ME, ERINA.
ALL RIGHT. RESIGNATION ACCEPTED. BUT WHEN YOU LOSE...
...I WILL HAVE YOU ACCEPT YOUR OWN SPECIAL PENALTY.
!
SIMPLE EXPULSION IS FAR TOO LIGHT. INSTEAD, YOU WILL USE YOUR SKILL AND TALENT FOR THE BETTERMENT OF CENTRAL FOR THE REST OF YOUR LIFE.
YOU WILL FOLLOW MY ORDERS TO THE LETTER WITHOUT FAIL. NO FURTHER DEFIANCE WILL BE PERMITTED IN ANY WAY. EVER. UNDERSTOOD?
YES, FATHER.
KA-KLAK
KA-KLAK

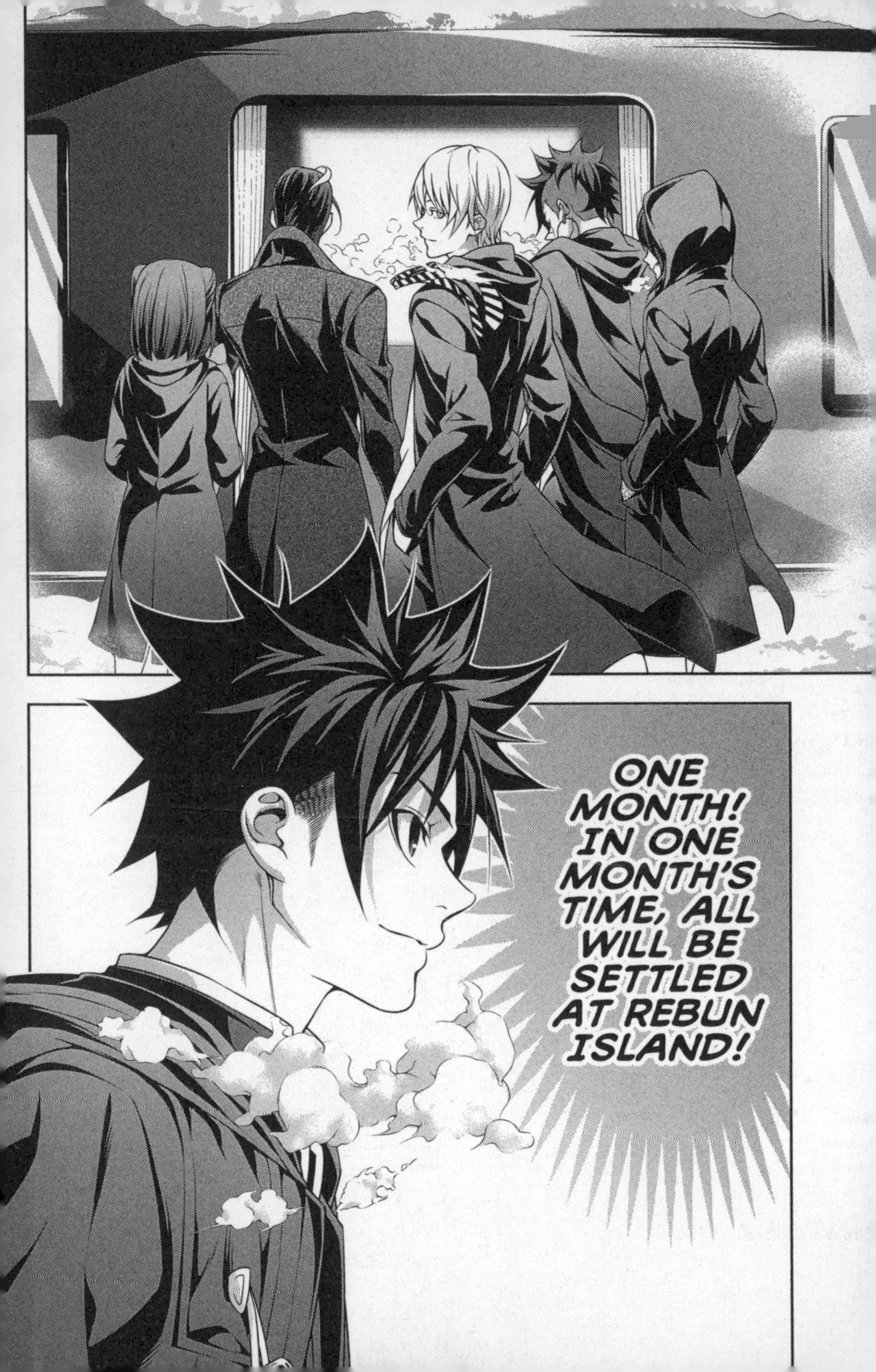
ONE MONTH! IN ONE MONTH'S TIME, ALL WILL BE SETTLED AT REBUN ISLAND!

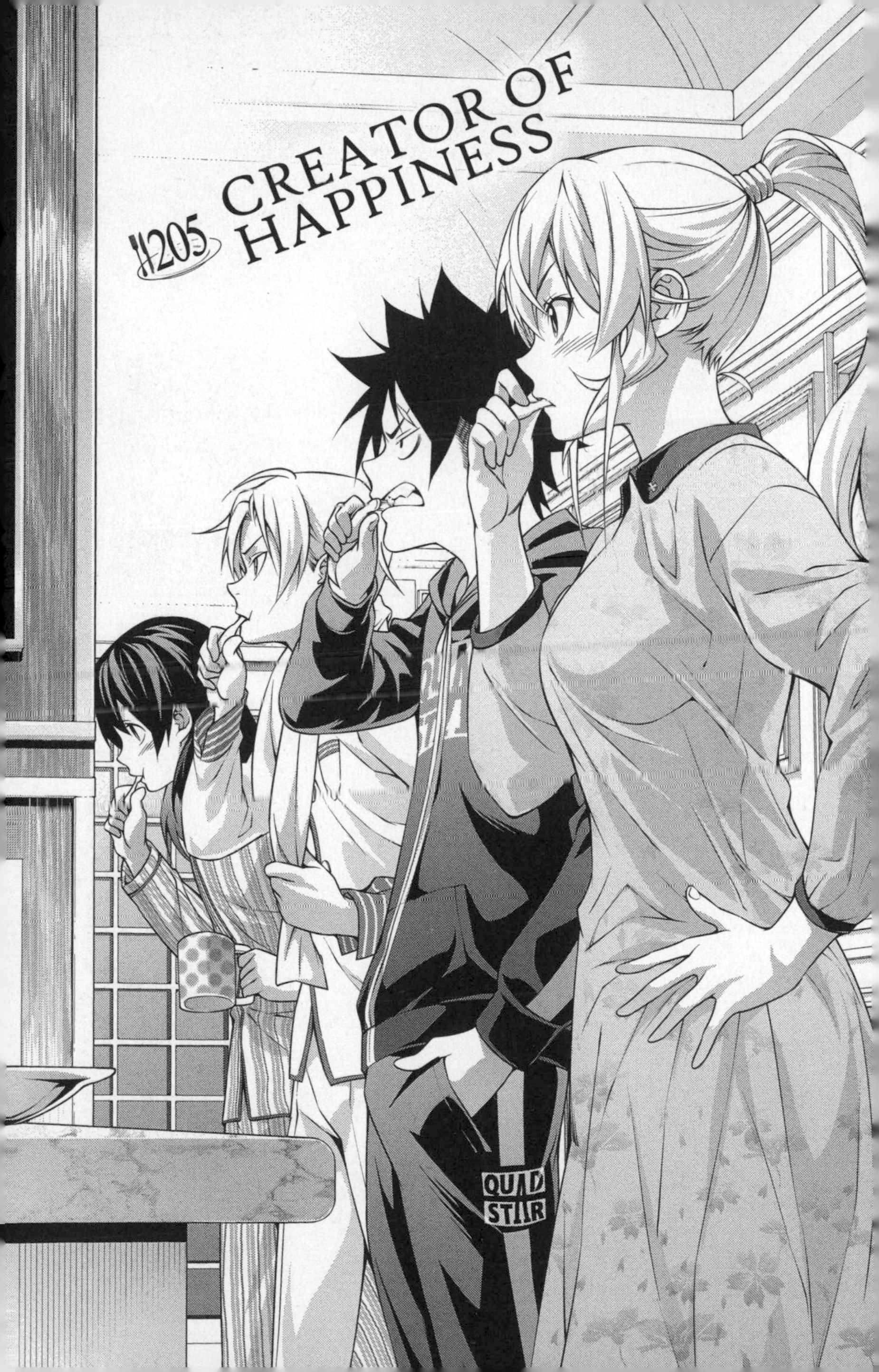

205
CREATOR OF HAPPINESS
QUAD STAR

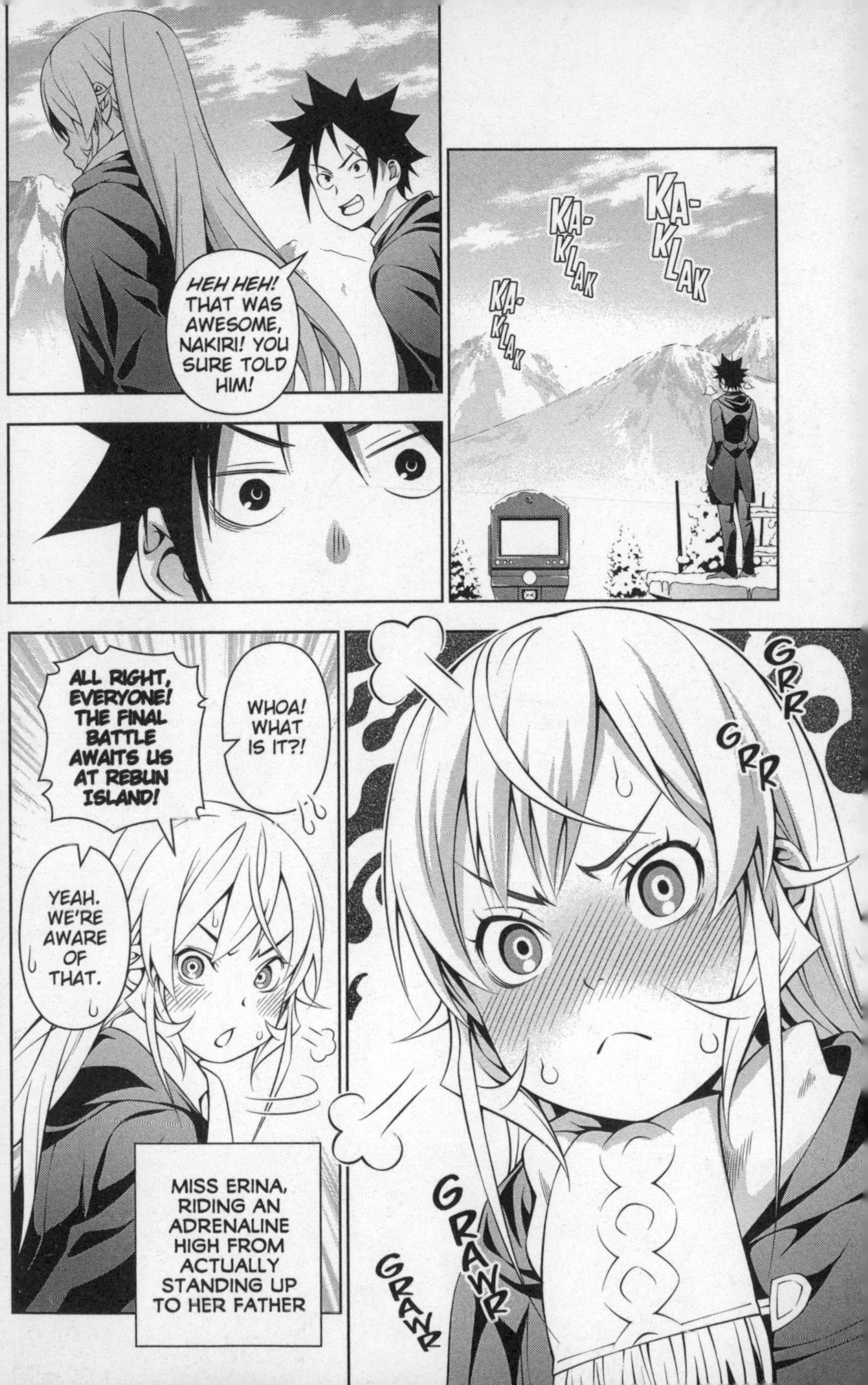
KA-KLAK
KA-KLAK
KA-KLAK
HEH HEH! THAT WAS AWESOME, NAKIRI! YOU SURE TOLD HIM!
GRR
GRR
GRAWR
GRAWR
WHOA! WHAT IS IT?!
ALL RIGHT, EVERYONE! THE FINAL BATTLE AWAITS US AT REBUN ISLAND!
YEAH. WE'RE AWARE OF THAT.
MISS ERINA, RIDING AN ADRENALINE HIGH FROM ACTUALLY STANDING UP TO HER FATHER

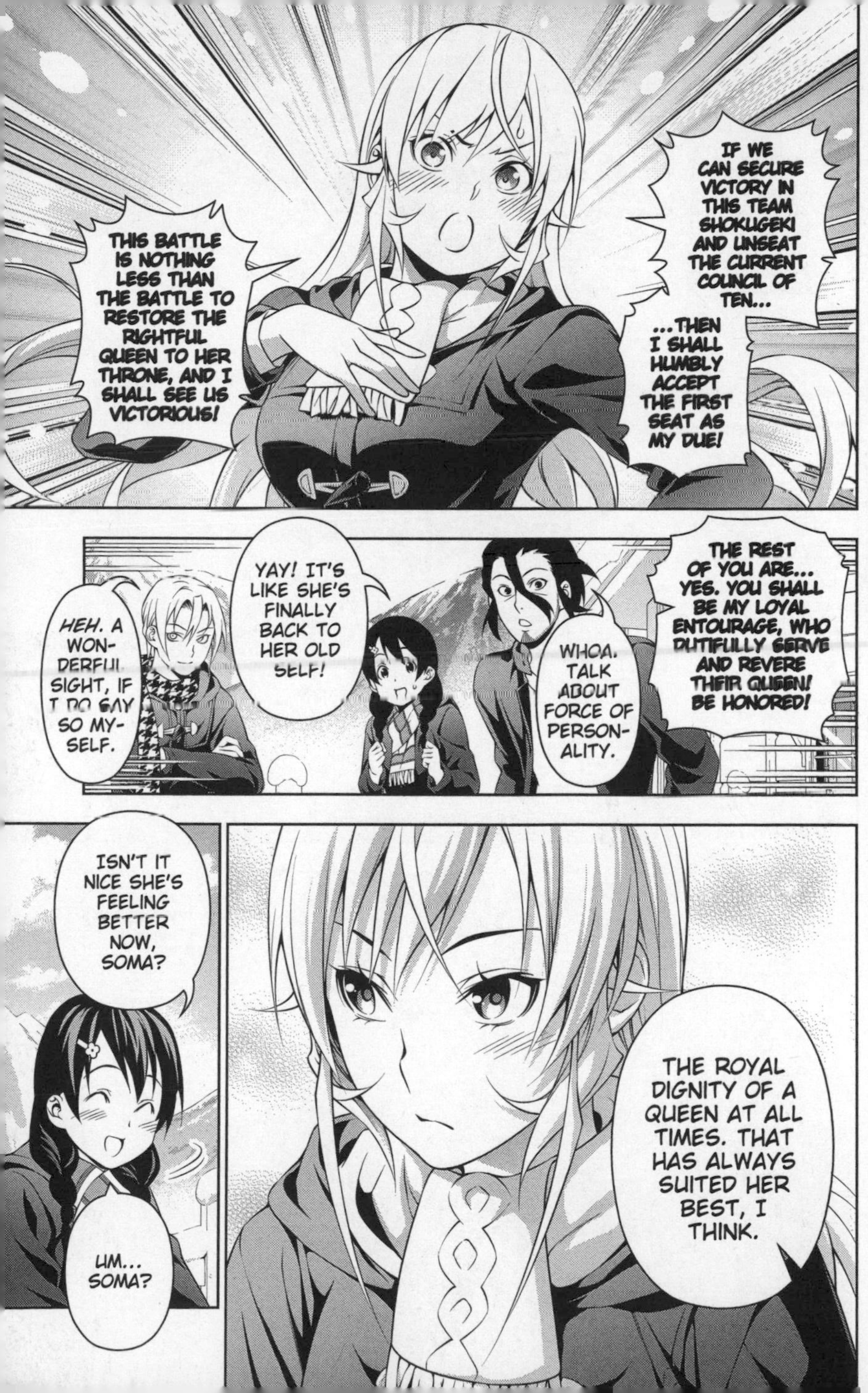
IF WE CAN SECURE VICTORY IN THIS TEAM SHOKUGEKI AND UNSEAT THE CURRENT COUNCIL OF TEN...
...THEN I SHALL HUMBLY ACCEPT THE FIRST SEAT AS MY DUE!
THIS BATTLE IS NOTHING LESS THAN THE BATTLE TO RESTORE THE RIGHTFUL QUEEN TO HER THRONE, AND I SHALL SEE US VICTORIOUS!
THE REST OF YOU ARE... YES. YOU SHALL BE MY LOYAL ENTOURAGE, WHO DUTIFULLY SERVE AND REVERE THEIR QUEEN! BE HONORED!
WHOA. TALK ABOUT FORCE OF PERSON-ALITY.
YAY! IT'S LIKE SHE'S FINALLY BACK TO HER OLD SELF!
HEH. A WON-DERFUL SIGHT, IF I DO SAY SO MY-SELF.
THE ROYAL DIGNITY OF A QUEEN AT ALL TIMES. THAT HAS ALWAYS SUITED HER BEST, I THINK.
ISN'T IT NICE SHE'S FEELING BETTER NOW, SOMA?
UM... SOMA?

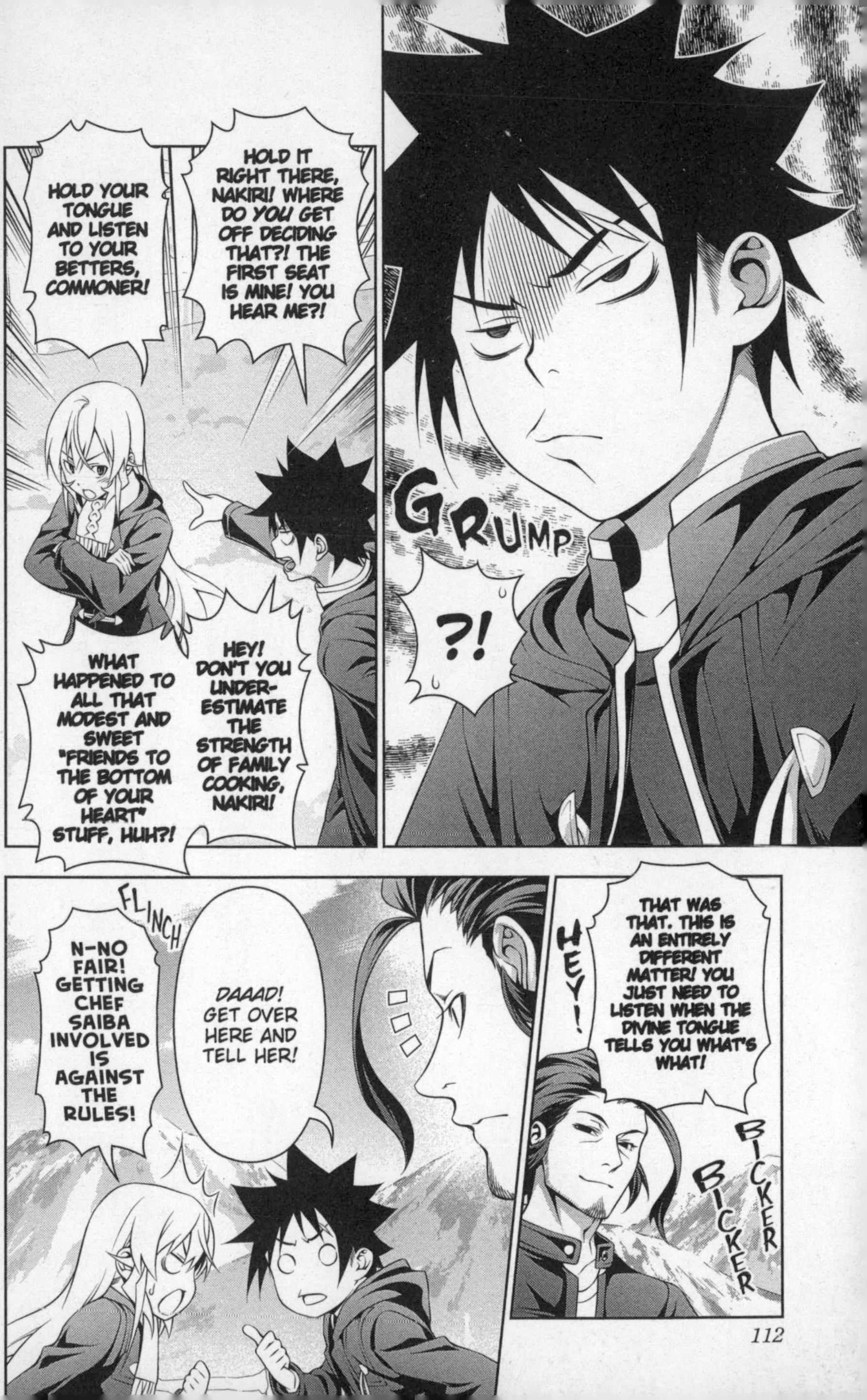
GRUMP
?!
HOLD IT RIGHT THERE, NAKIRI! WHERE DO *YOU* GET OFF DECIDING THAT?! THE FIRST SEAT IS MINE! YOU HEAR ME?!
HOLD YOUR TONGUE AND LISTEN TO YOUR BETTERS, COMMONER!
HEY! DON'T YOU UNDER-ESTIMATE THE STRENGTH OF FAMILY COOKING, NAKIRI!
WHAT HAPPENED TO ALL THAT MODEST AND SWEET "FRIENDS TO THE BOTTOM OF YOUR HEART" STUFF, HUH?!
HEY!
THAT WAS THAT. THIS IS AN ENTIRELY DIFFERENT MATTER! YOU JUST NEED TO LISTEN WHEN THE DIVINE TONGUE TELLS YOU WHAT'S WHAT!
BICKER
BICKER
DAAAD! GET OVER HERE AND TELL HER!
FLINCH
N-NO FAIR! GETTING CHEF SAIBA INVOLVED IS AGAINST THE RULES!

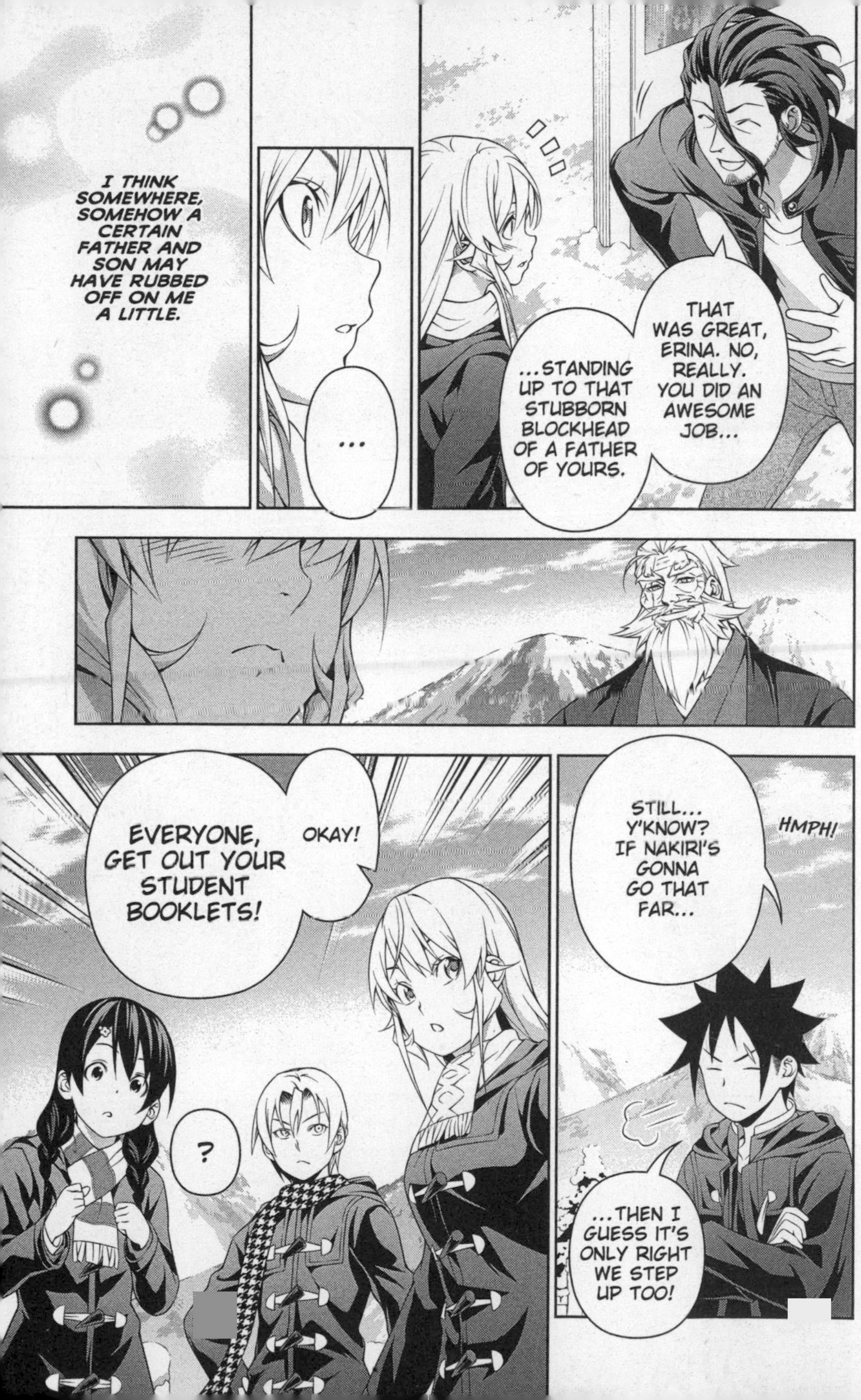
THAT WAS GREAT, ERINA. NO, REALLY. YOU DID AN AWESOME JOB...
...STANDING UP TO THAT STUBBORN BLOCKHEAD OF A FATHER OF YOURS.
...
I THINK SOMEWHERE, SOMEHOW A CERTAIN FATHER AND SON MAY HAVE RUBBED OFF ON ME A LITTLE.
HMPH!
STILL... Y'KNOW? IF NAKIRI'S GONNA GO THAT FAR...
...THEN I GUESS IT'S ONLY RIGHT WE STEP UP TOO!
OKAY!
EVERYONE, GET OUT YOUR STUDENT BOOKLETS!
?

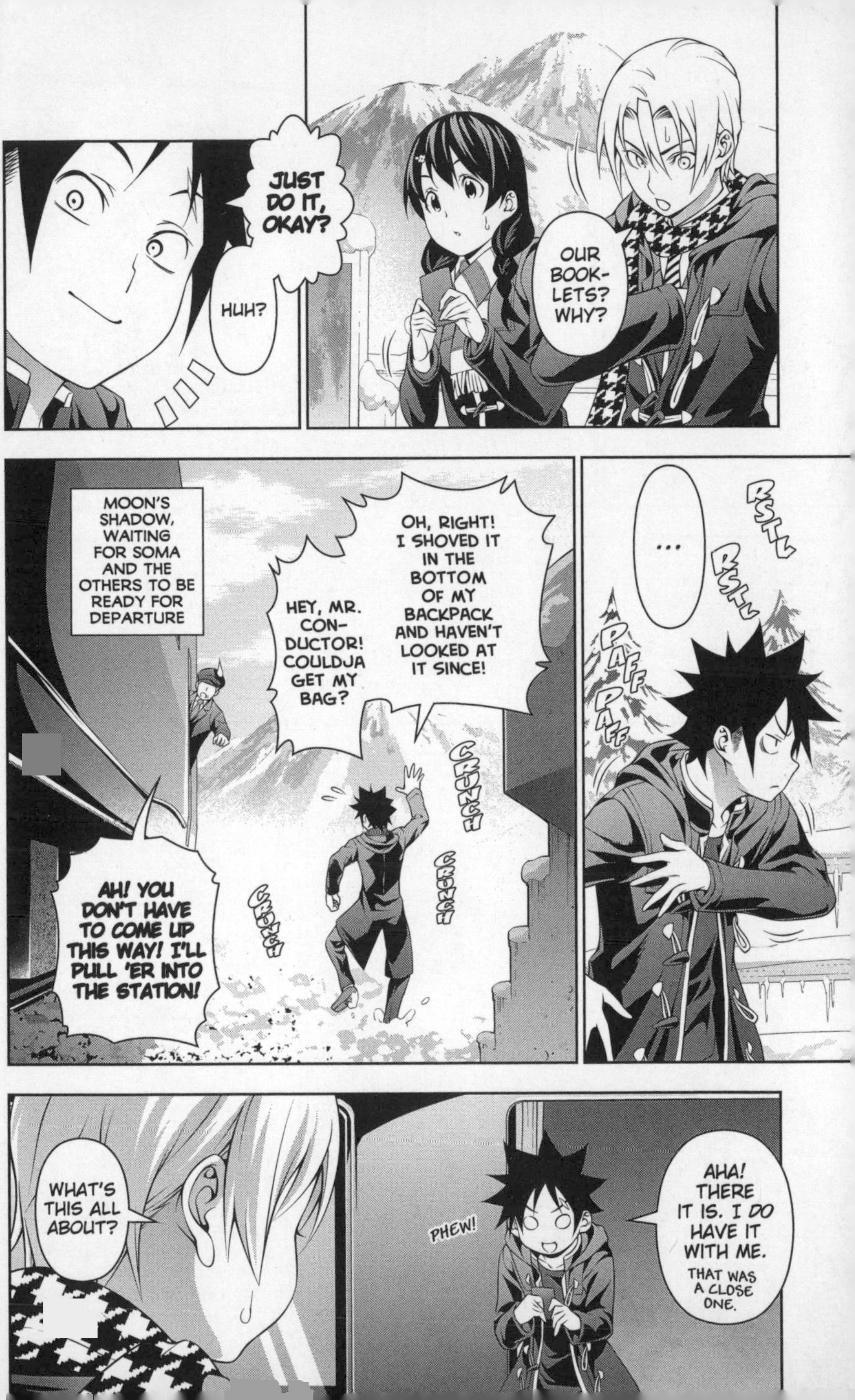
OUR BOOK-LETS? WHY?
JUST DO IT, OKAY?
HUH?
...
RSTL
RSTL
PAFF
PAFF
OH, RIGHT! I SHOVED IT IN THE BOTTOM OF MY BACKPACK AND HAVEN'T LOOKED AT IT SINCE!
HEY, MR. CONDUCTOR! COULDJA GET MY BAG?
MOON'S SHADOW, WAITING FOR SOMA AND THE OTHERS TO BE READY FOR DEPARTURE
CRUNCH
CRUNCH
CRUNCH
AH! YOU DON'T HAVE TO COME UP THIS WAY! I'LL PULL 'ER INTO THE STATION!
AHA! THERE IT IS. I DO HAVE IT WITH ME.
THAT WAS A CLOSE ONE.
PHEW!
WHAT'S THIS ALL ABOUT?

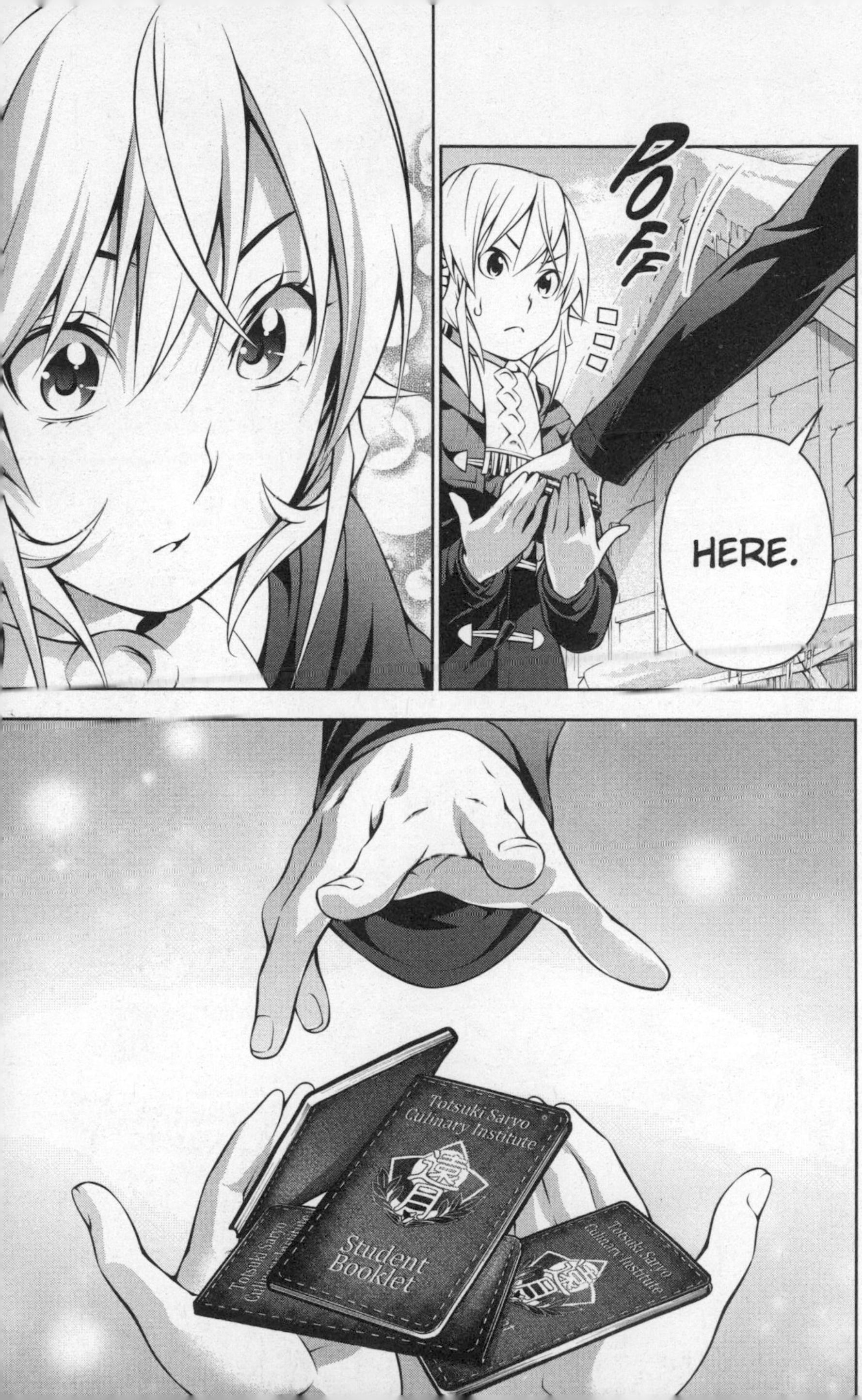
POFF
...
HERE.
Totsuki Saryo Culinary Institute
Student Booklet
Totsuki Saryo Culinary Institute

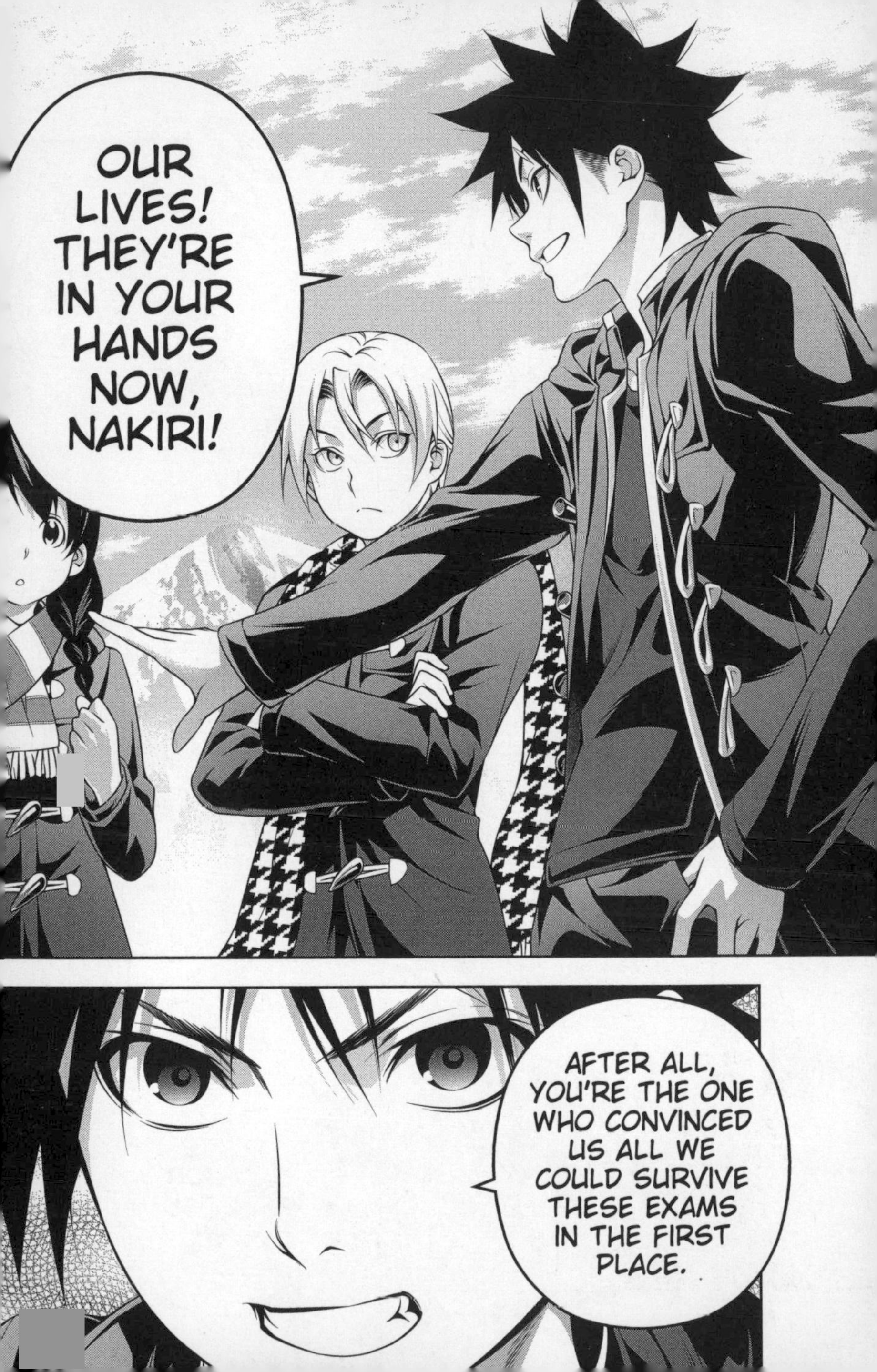
OUR LIVES! THEY'RE IN YOUR HANDS NOW, NAKIRI!
AFTER ALL, YOU'RE THE ONE WHO CONVINCED US ALL WE COULD SURVIVE THESE EXAMS IN THE FIRST PLACE.

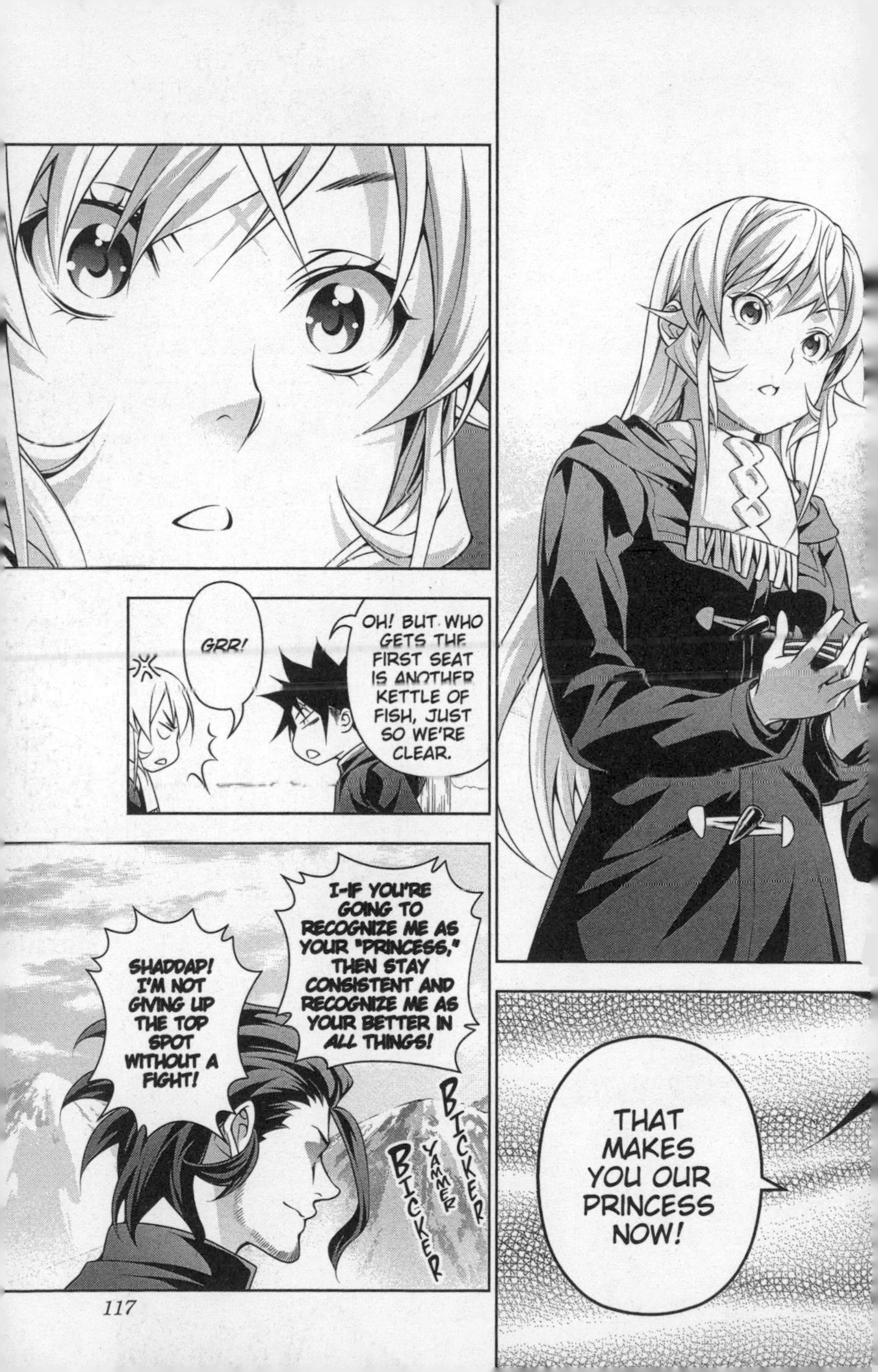
THAT MAKES YOU OUR PRINCESS NOW!
OH! BUT WHO GETS THE FIRST SEAT IS ANOTHER KETTLE OF FISH, JUST SO WE'RE CLEAR.
GRR!
I-IF YOU'RE GOING TO RECOGNIZE ME AS YOUR "PRINCESS," THEN STAY CONSISTENT AND RECOGNIZE ME AS YOUR BETTER IN ALL THINGS!
SHADDAP! I'M NOT GIVING UP THE TOP SPOT WITHOUT A FIGHT!
BICKER
YAMMER
BICKER

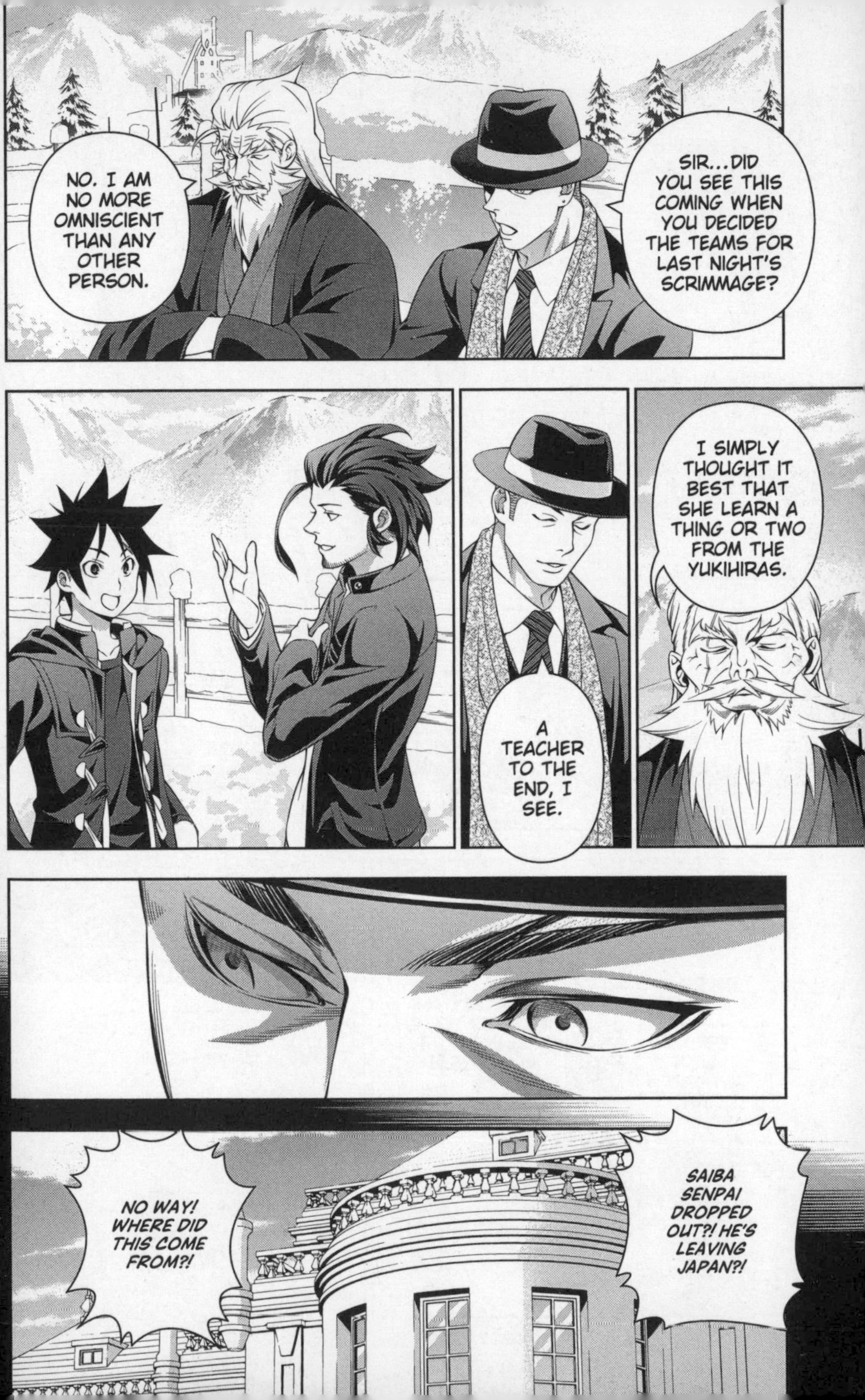
SIR...DID YOU SEE THIS COMING WHEN YOU DECIDED THE TEAMS FOR LAST NIGHT'S SCRIMMAGE?
NO. I AM NO MORE OMNISCIENT THAN ANY OTHER PERSON.
I SIMPLY THOUGHT IT BEST THAT SHE LEARN A THING OR TWO FROM THE YUKIHIRAS.
A TEACHER TO THE END, I SEE.
SAIBA SENPAI DROPPED OUT?! HE'S LEAVING JAPAN?!
NO WAY! WHERE DID THIS COME FROM?!

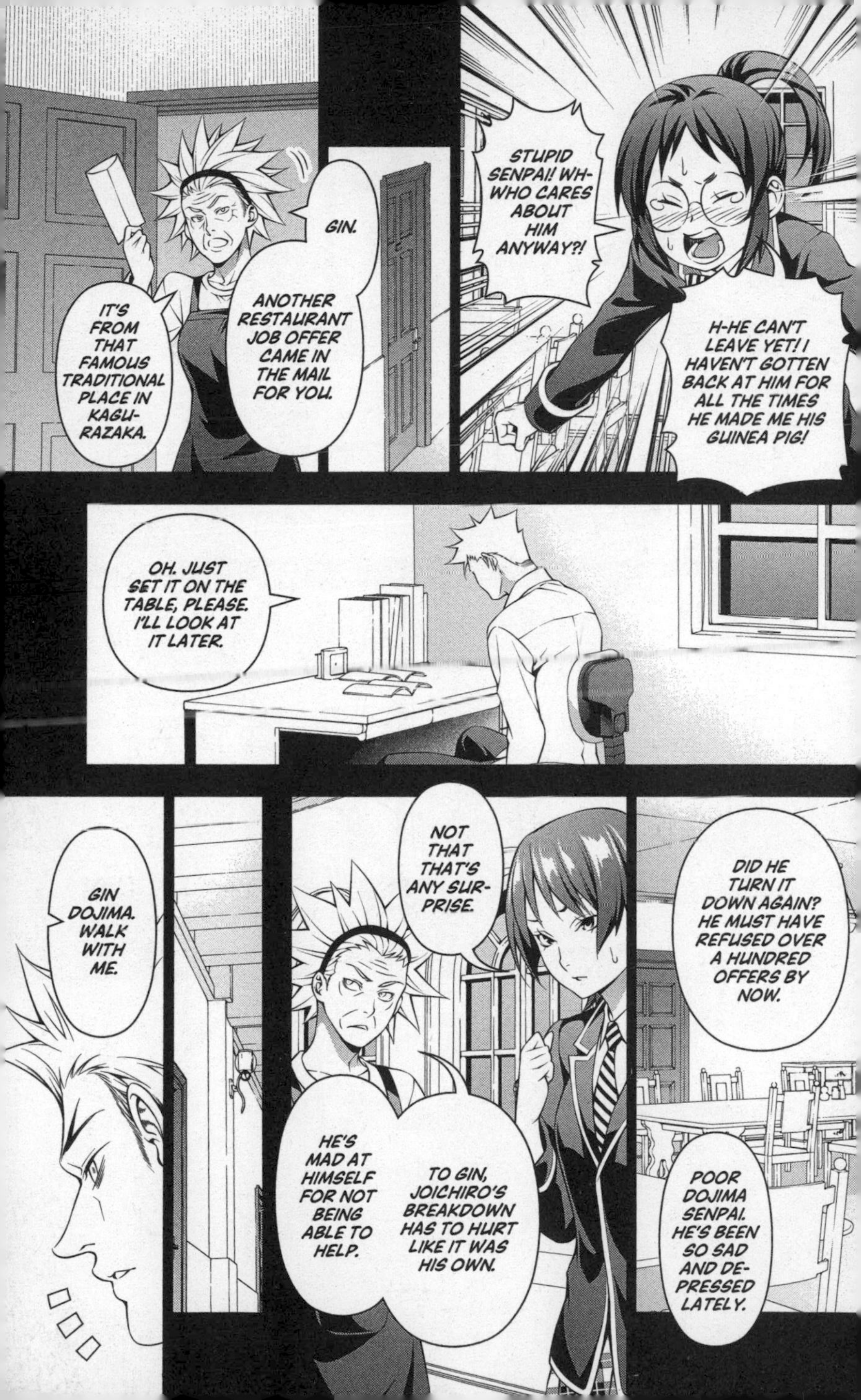
STUPID SENPAI! WH-WHO CARES ABOUT HIM ANYWAY?!
H-HE CAN'T LEAVE YET! I HAVEN'T GOTTEN BACK AT HIM FOR ALL THE TIMES HE MADE ME HIS GUINEA PIG!
GIN.
ANOTHER RESTAURANT JOB OFFER CAME IN THE MAIL FOR YOU.
IT'S FROM THAT FAMOUS TRADITIONAL PLACE IN KAGU-RAZAKA.
OH. JUST SET IT ON THE TABLE, PLEASE. I'LL LOOK AT IT LATER.
DID HE TURN IT DOWN AGAIN? HE MUST HAVE REFUSED OVER A HUNDRED OFFERS BY NOW.
POOR DOJIMA SENPAI. HE'S BEEN SO SAD AND DE-PRESSED LATELY.
NOT THAT THAT'S ANY SUR-PRISE.
TO GIN, JOICHIRO'S BREAKDOWN HAS TO HURT LIKE IT WAS HIS OWN.
HE'S MAD AT HIMSELF FOR NOT BEING ABLE TO HELP.
GIN DOJIMA. WALK WITH ME.

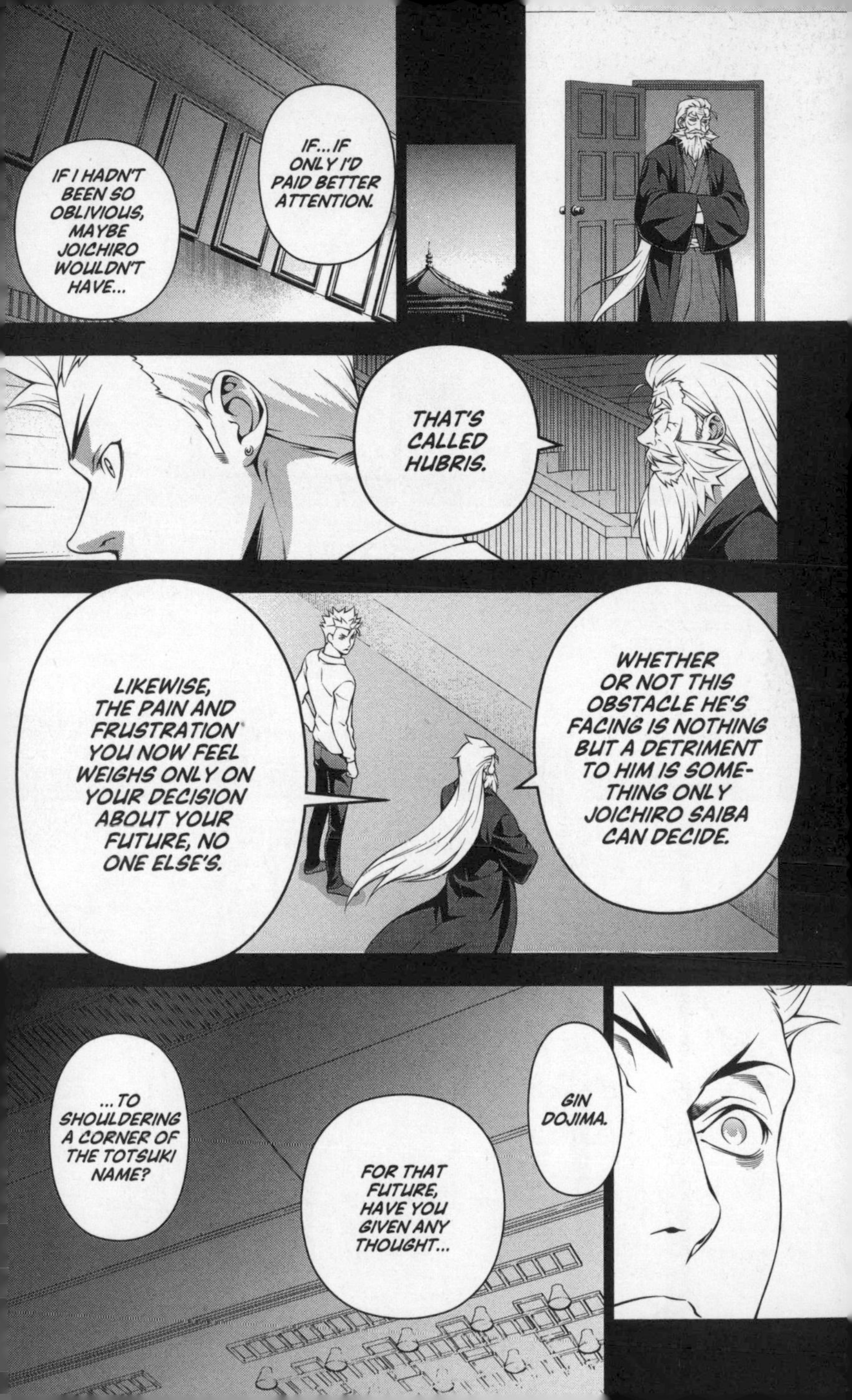
IF...IF ONLY I'D PAID BETTER ATTENTION.
IF I HADN'T BEEN SO OBLIVIOUS, MAYBE JOICHIRO WOULDN'T HAVE...
THAT'S CALLED HUBRIS.
WHETHER OR NOT THIS OBSTACLE HE'S FACING IS NOTHING BUT A DETRIMENT TO HIM IS SOME-THING ONLY JOICHIRO SAIBA CAN DECIDE.
LIKEWISE, THE PAIN AND FRUSTRATION YOU NOW FEEL WEIGHS ONLY ON YOUR DECISION ABOUT YOUR FUTURE, NO ONE ELSE'S.
GIN DOJIMA.
FOR THAT FUTURE, HAVE YOU GIVEN ANY THOUGHT...
...TO SHOULDERING A CORNER OF THE TOTSUKI NAME?

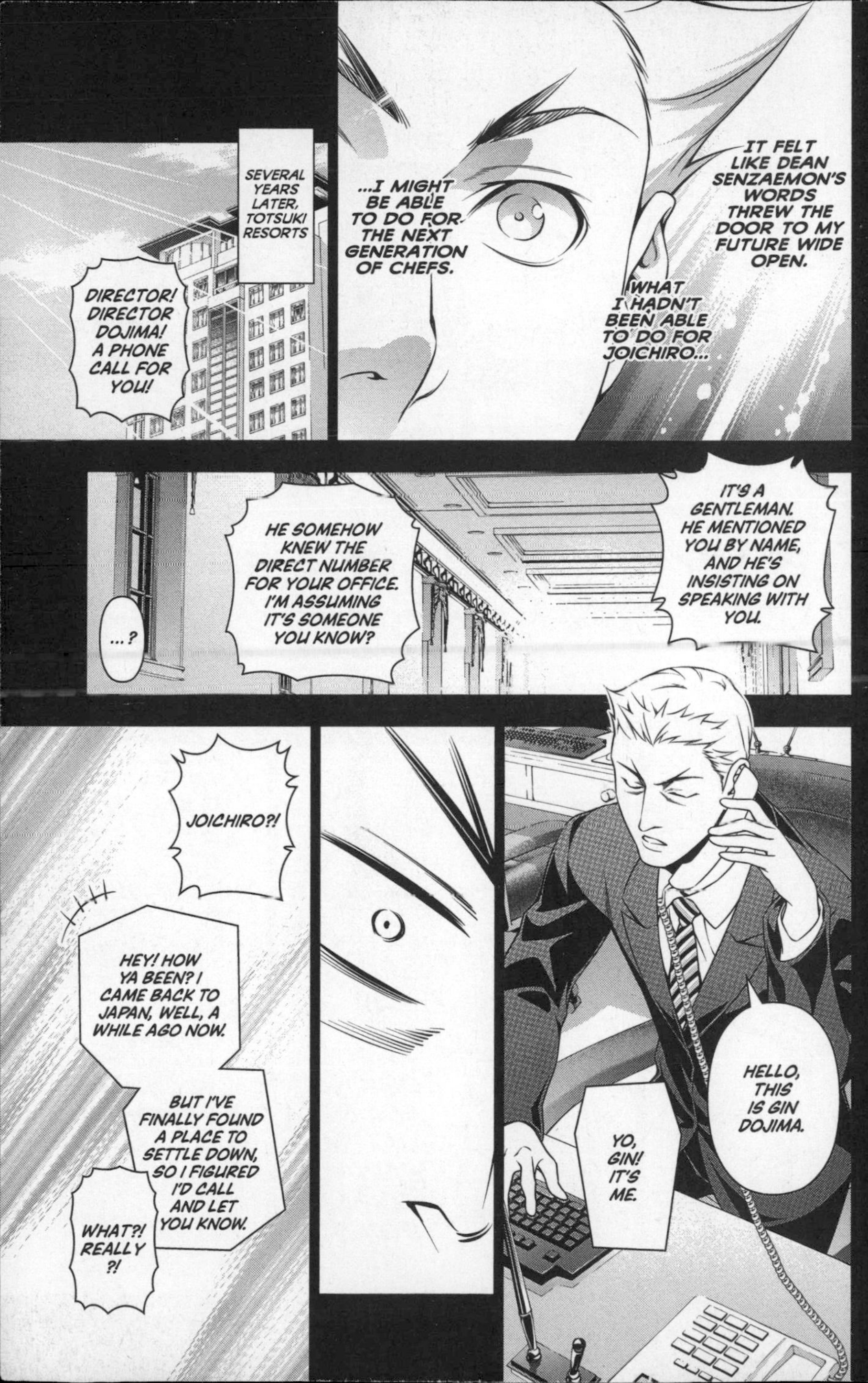
IT FELT LIKE DEAN SENZAEMON'S WORDS THREW THE DOOR TO MY FUTURE WIDE OPEN.
WHAT I HADN'T BEEN ABLE TO DO FOR JOICHIRO...
...I MIGHT BE ABLE TO DO FOR THE NEXT GENERATION OF CHEFS.
SEVERAL YEARS LATER, TOTSUKI RESORTS
DIRECTOR! DIRECTOR DOJIMA! A PHONE CALL FOR YOU!
IT'S A GENTLEMAN. HE MENTIONED YOU BY NAME, AND HE'S INSISTING ON SPEAKING WITH YOU.
HE SOMEHOW KNEW THE DIRECT NUMBER FOR YOUR OFFICE. I'M ASSUMING IT'S SOMEONE YOU KNOW?
...?
HELLO, THIS IS GIN DOJIMA.
YO, GIN! IT'S ME.
JOICHIRO?!
HEY! HOW YA BEEN? I CAME BACK TO JAPAN, WELL, A WHILE AGO NOW.
BUT I'VE FINALLY FOUND A PLACE TO SETTLE DOWN, SO I FIGURED I'D CALL AND LET YOU KNOW.
WHAT?! REALLY?!

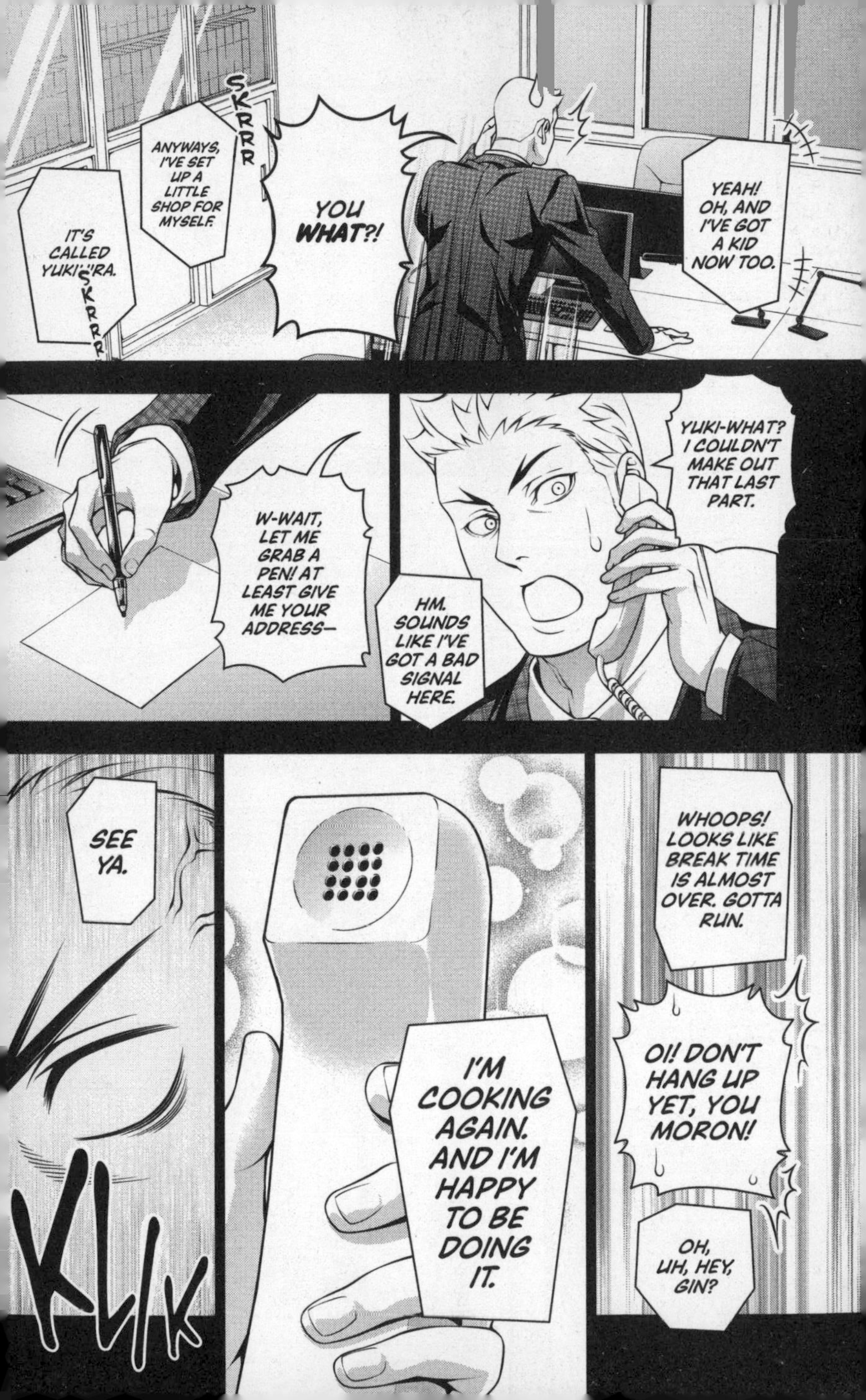
YEAH! OH, AND I'VE GOT A KID NOW TOO.
YOU WHAT?!
SKRRR
ANYWAYS, I'VE SET UP A LITTLE SHOP FOR MYSELF.
IT'S CALLED YUKI~~RA.
SKRRR
YUKI-WHAT? I COULDN'T MAKE OUT THAT LAST PART.
HM. SOUNDS LIKE I'VE GOT A BAD SIGNAL HERE.
W-WAIT, LET ME GRAB A PEN! AT LEAST GIVE ME YOUR ADDRESS—
WHOOPS! LOOKS LIKE BREAK TIME IS ALMOST OVER. GOTTA RUN.
OI! DON'T HANG UP YET, YOU MORON!
OH, UH, HEY, GIN?
I'M COOKING AGAIN. AND I'M HAPPY TO BE DOING IT.
SEE YA.
KLIK

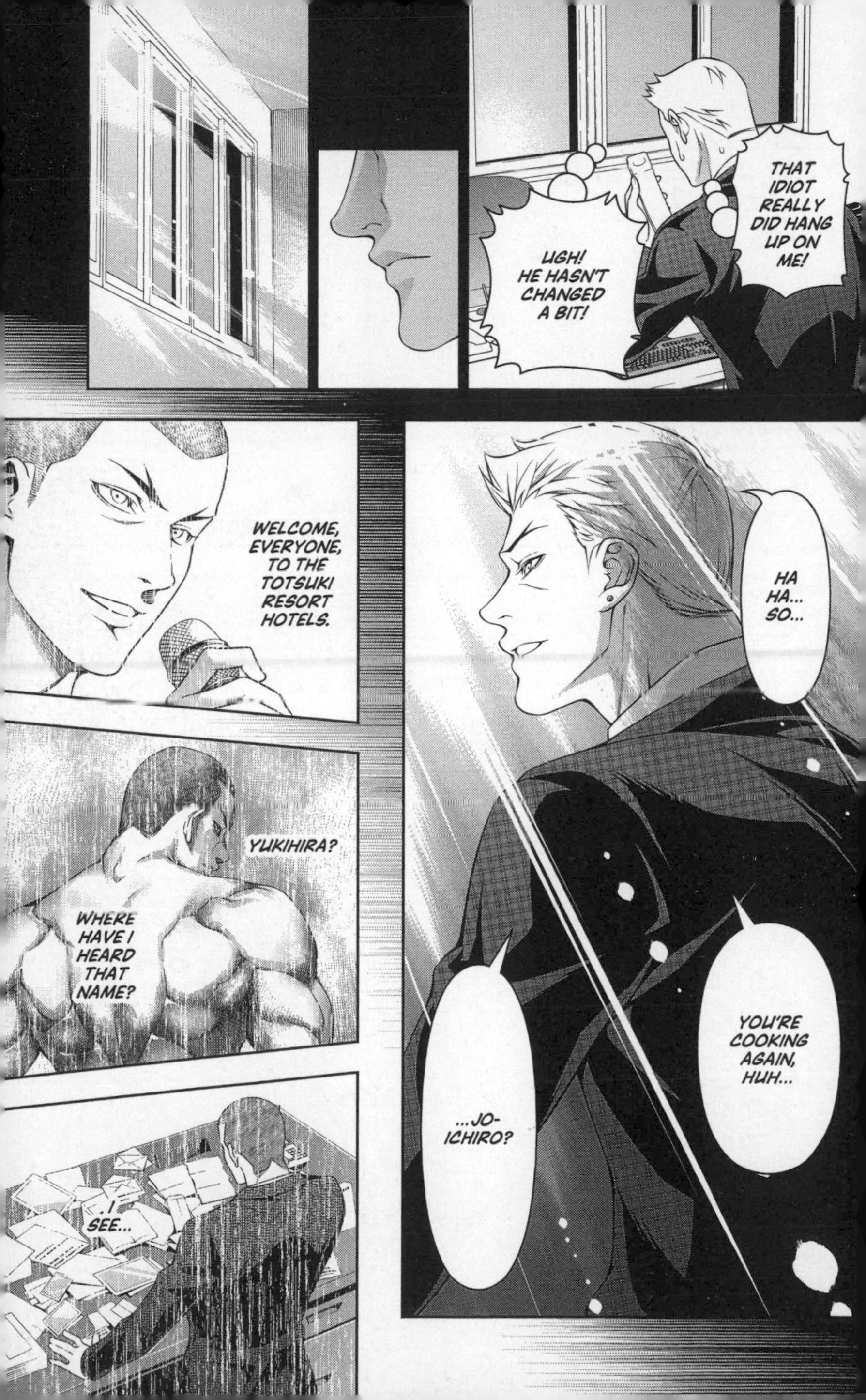
THAT IDIOT REALLY DID HANG UP ON ME!
UGH! HE HASN'T CHANGED A BIT!
HA HA... SO...
YOU'RE COOKING AGAIN, HUH...
...JO-ICHIRO?
WELCOME, EVERYONE, TO THE TOTSUKI RESORT HOTELS.
YUKIHIRA?
WHERE HAVE I HEARD THAT NAME?
I SEE...

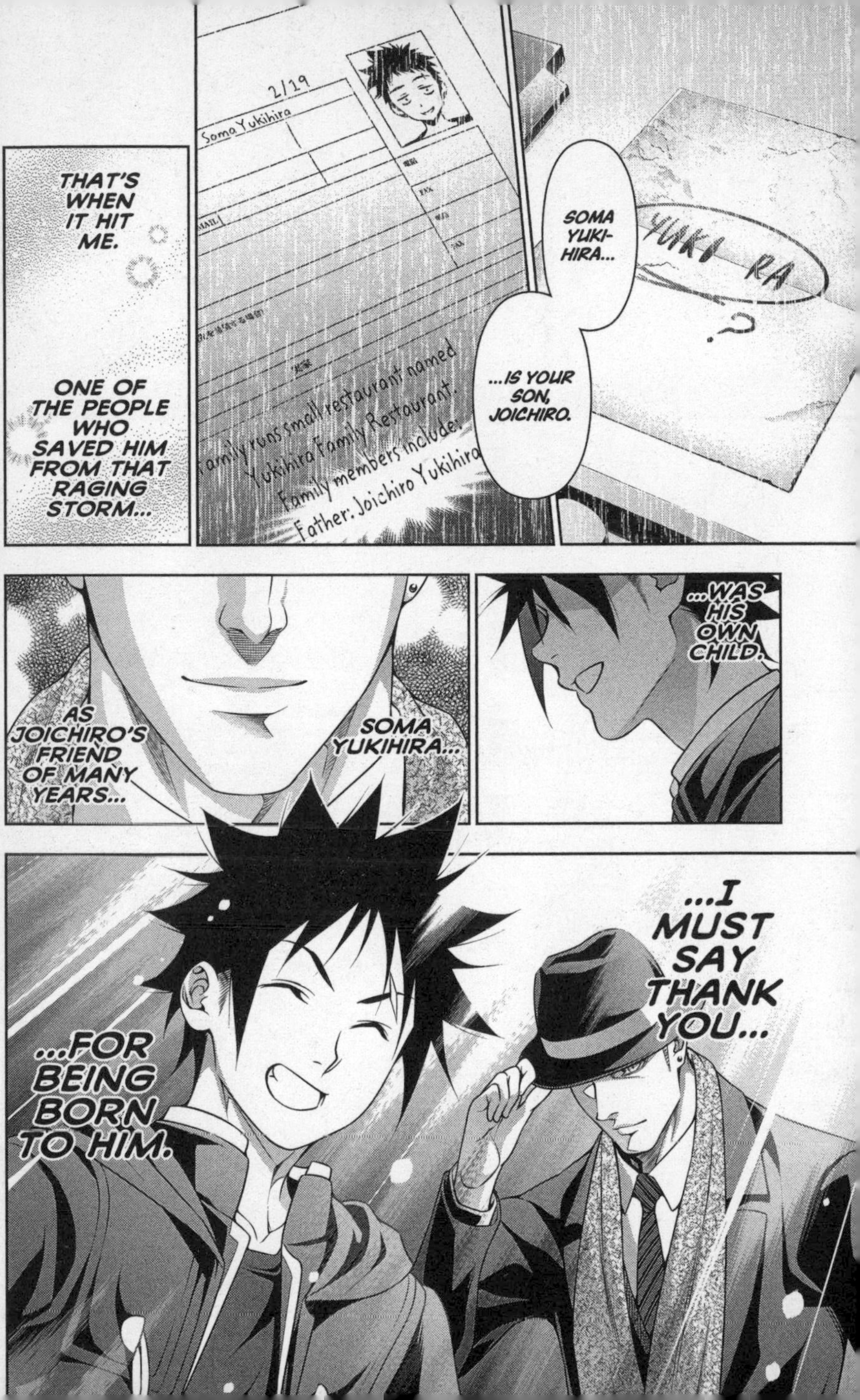
SOMA YUKI-HIRA...
...IS YOUR SON, JOICHIRO.
2/19
Soma Yukihira
amily runs small restaurant named Yukihira Family Restaurant.
Family members include:
Father: Joichiro Yukihira
THAT'S WHEN IT HIT ME.
ONE OF THE PEOPLE WHO SAVED HIM FROM THAT RAGING STORM...
...WAS HIS OWN CHILD.
SOMA YUKIHIRA...
AS JOICHIRO'S FRIEND OF MANY YEARS...
...I MUST SAY THANK YOU...
...FOR BEING BORN TO HIM.

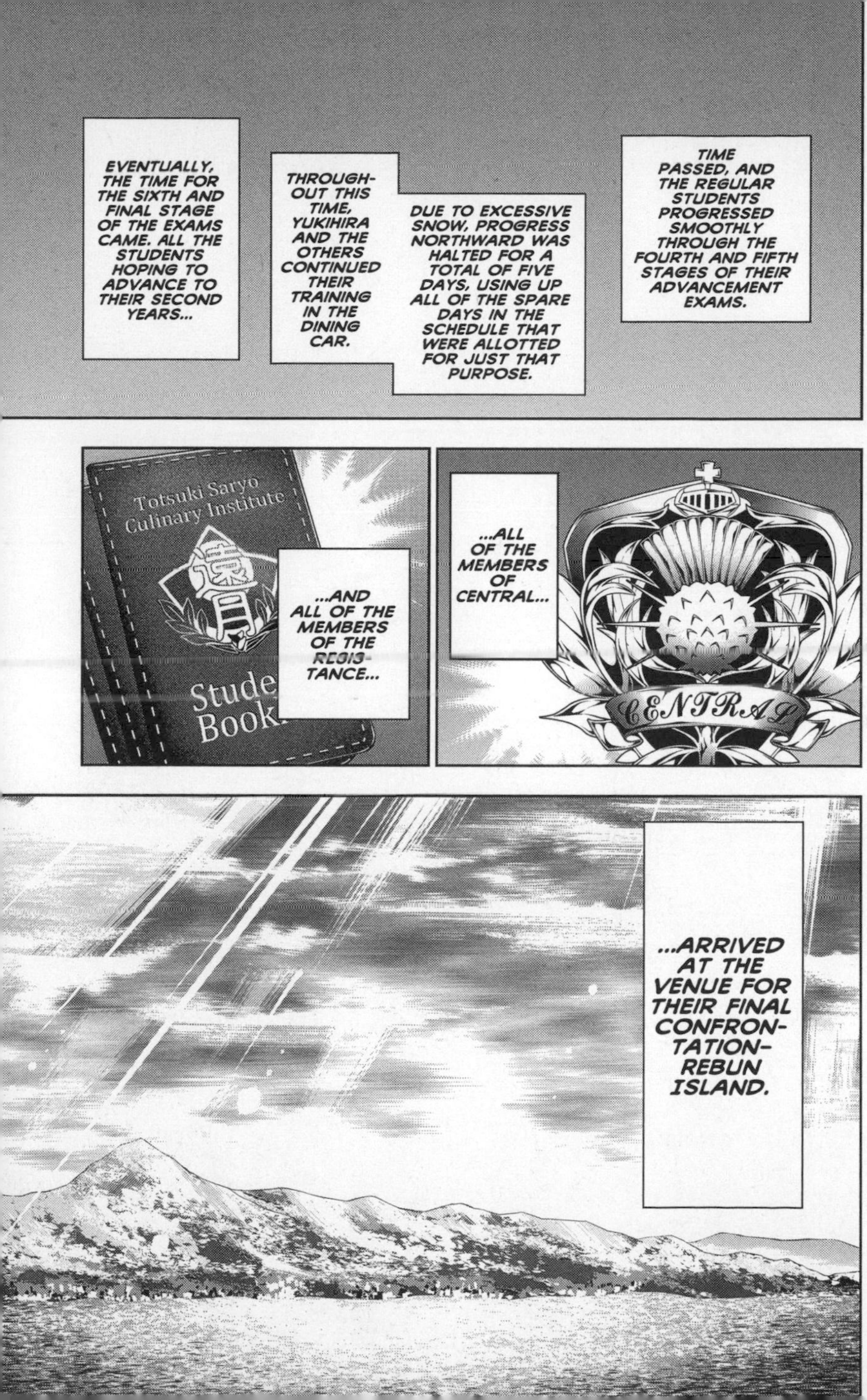
TIME PASSED, AND THE REGULAR STUDENTS PROGRESSED SMOOTHLY THROUGH THE FOURTH AND FIFTH STAGES OF THEIR ADVANCEMENT EXAMS.
DUE TO EXCESSIVE SNOW, PROGRESS NORTHWARD WAS HALTED FOR A TOTAL OF FIVE DAYS, USING UP ALL OF THE SPARE DAYS IN THE SCHEDULE THAT WERE ALLOTTED FOR JUST THAT PURPOSE.
THROUGH-OUT THIS TIME, YUKIHIRA AND THE OTHERS CONTINUED THEIR TRAINING IN THE DINING CAR.
EVENTUALLY, THE TIME FOR THE SIXTH AND FINAL STAGE OF THE EXAMS CAME. ALL THE STUDENTS HOPING TO ADVANCE TO THEIR SECOND YEARS...
...ALL OF THE MEMBERS OF CENTRAL...
CENTRAL
...AND ALL OF THE MEMBERS OF THE RESIS-TANCE...
Totsuki Saryo Culinary Institute
...ARRIVED AT THE VENUE FOR THEIR FINAL CONFRON-TATION—REBUN ISLAND.

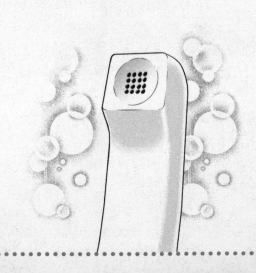

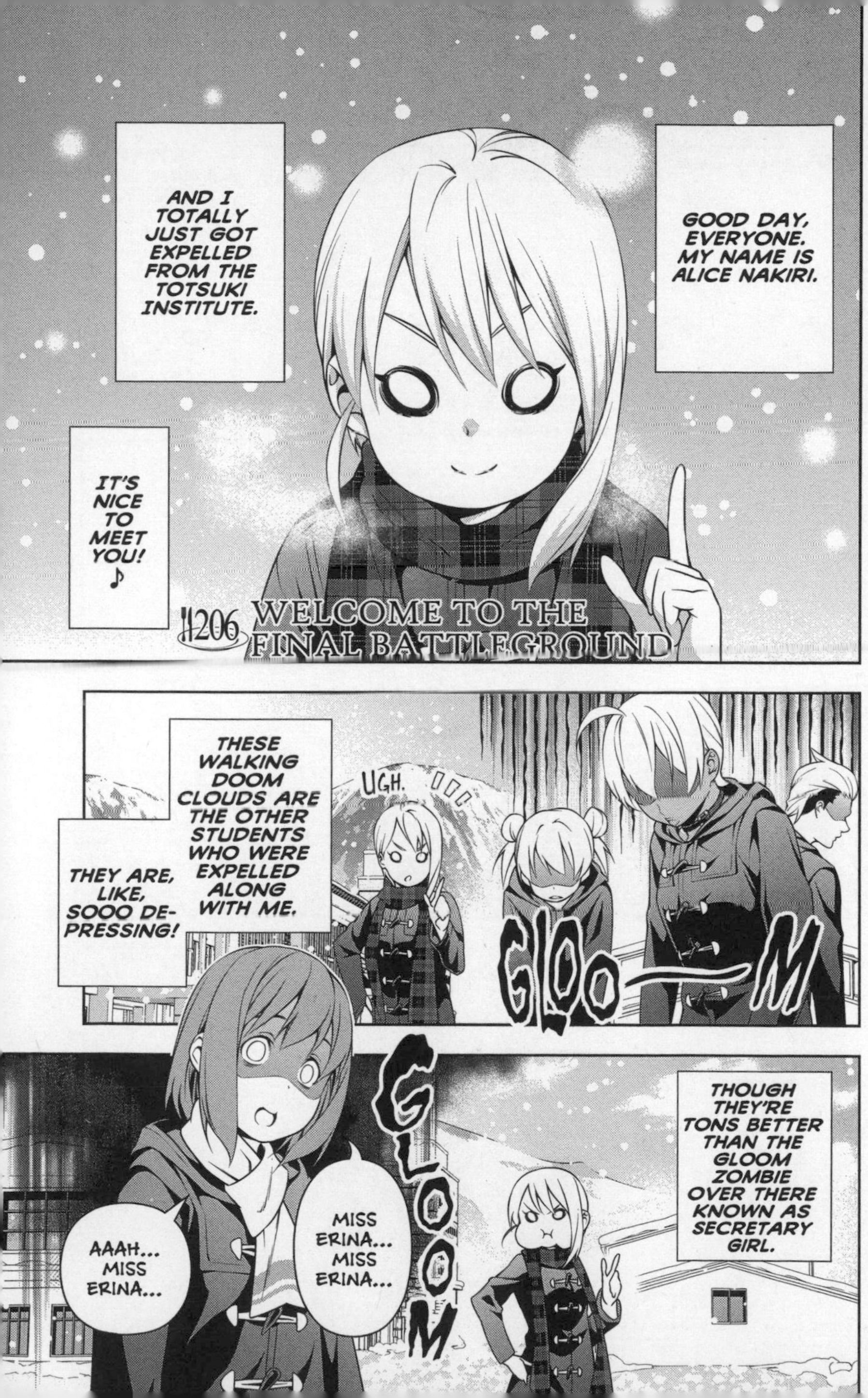
GOOD DAY, EVERYONE. MY NAME IS ALICE NAKIRI.
AND I TOTALLY JUST GOT EXPELLED FROM THE TOTSUKI INSTITUTE.
IT'S NICE TO MEET YOU! ♪
206 WELCOME TO THE FINAL BATTLEGROUND
UGH.
THESE WALKING DOOM CLOUDS ARE THE OTHER STUDENTS WHO WERE EXPELLED ALONG WITH ME.
THEY ARE, LIKE, SOOO DE-PRESSING!
GLOO—M
THOUGH THEY'RE TONS BETTER THAN THE GLOOM ZOMBIE OVER THERE KNOWN AS SECRETARY GIRL.
GLOOM
MISS ERINA... MISS ERINA...
AAAH... MISS ERINA...

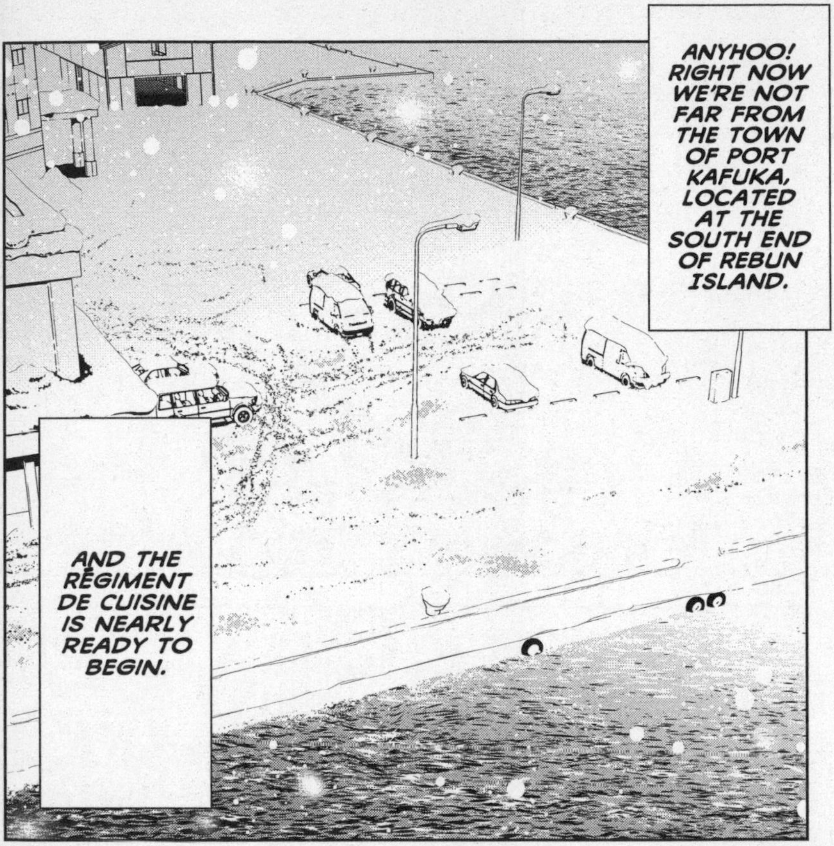
ANYHOO! RIGHT NOW WE'RE NOT FAR FROM THE TOWN OF PORT KAFUKA, LOCATED AT THE SOUTH END OF REBUN ISLAND.
AND THE RÉGIMENT DE CUISINE IS NEARLY READY TO BEGIN.

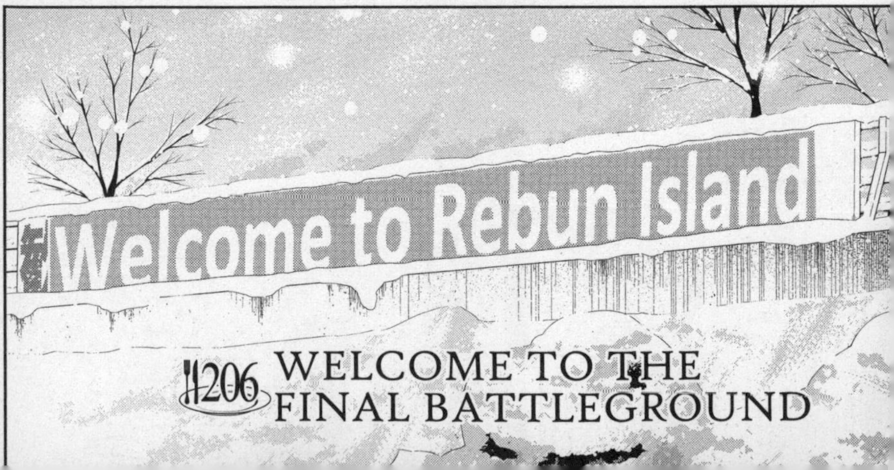
Welcome to Rebun Island

206 WELCOME TO THE FINAL BATTLEGROUND

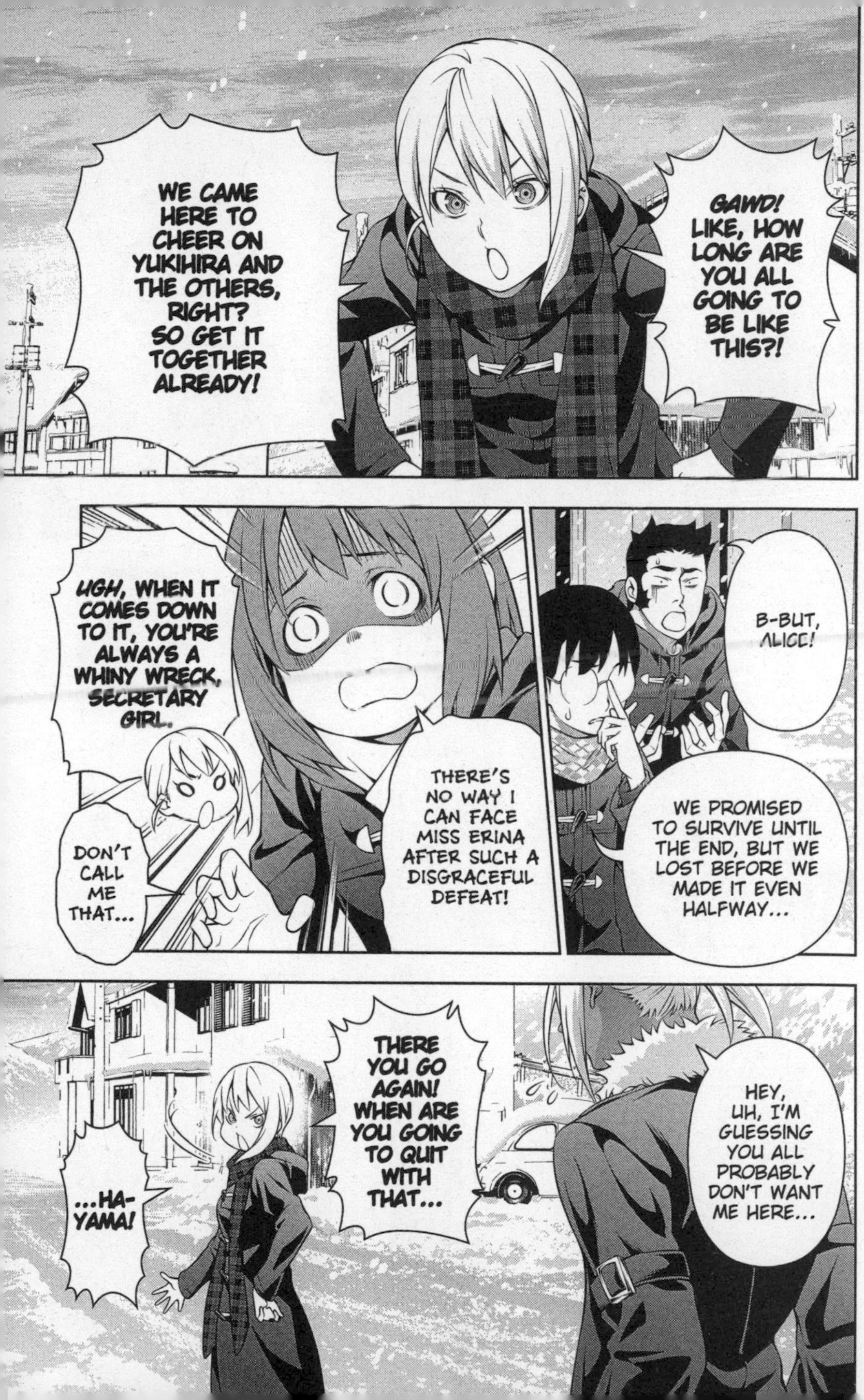
GAWD! LIKE, HOW LONG ARE YOU ALL GOING TO BE LIKE THIS?!
WE CAME HERE TO CHEER ON YUKIHIRA AND THE OTHERS, RIGHT? SO GET IT TOGETHER ALREADY!
B-BUT, ALICE!
WE PROMISED TO SURVIVE UNTIL THE END, BUT WE LOST BEFORE WE MADE IT EVEN HALFWAY...
THERE'S NO WAY I CAN FACE MISS ERINA AFTER SUCH A DISGRACEFUL DEFEAT!
UGH, WHEN IT COMES DOWN TO IT, YOU'RE ALWAYS A WHINY WRECK, SECRETARY GIRL.
DON'T CALL ME THAT...
HEY, UH, I'M GUESSING YOU ALL PROBABLY DON'T WANT ME HERE...
THERE YOU GO AGAIN! WHEN ARE YOU GOING TO QUIT WITH THAT...
...HA-YAMA!

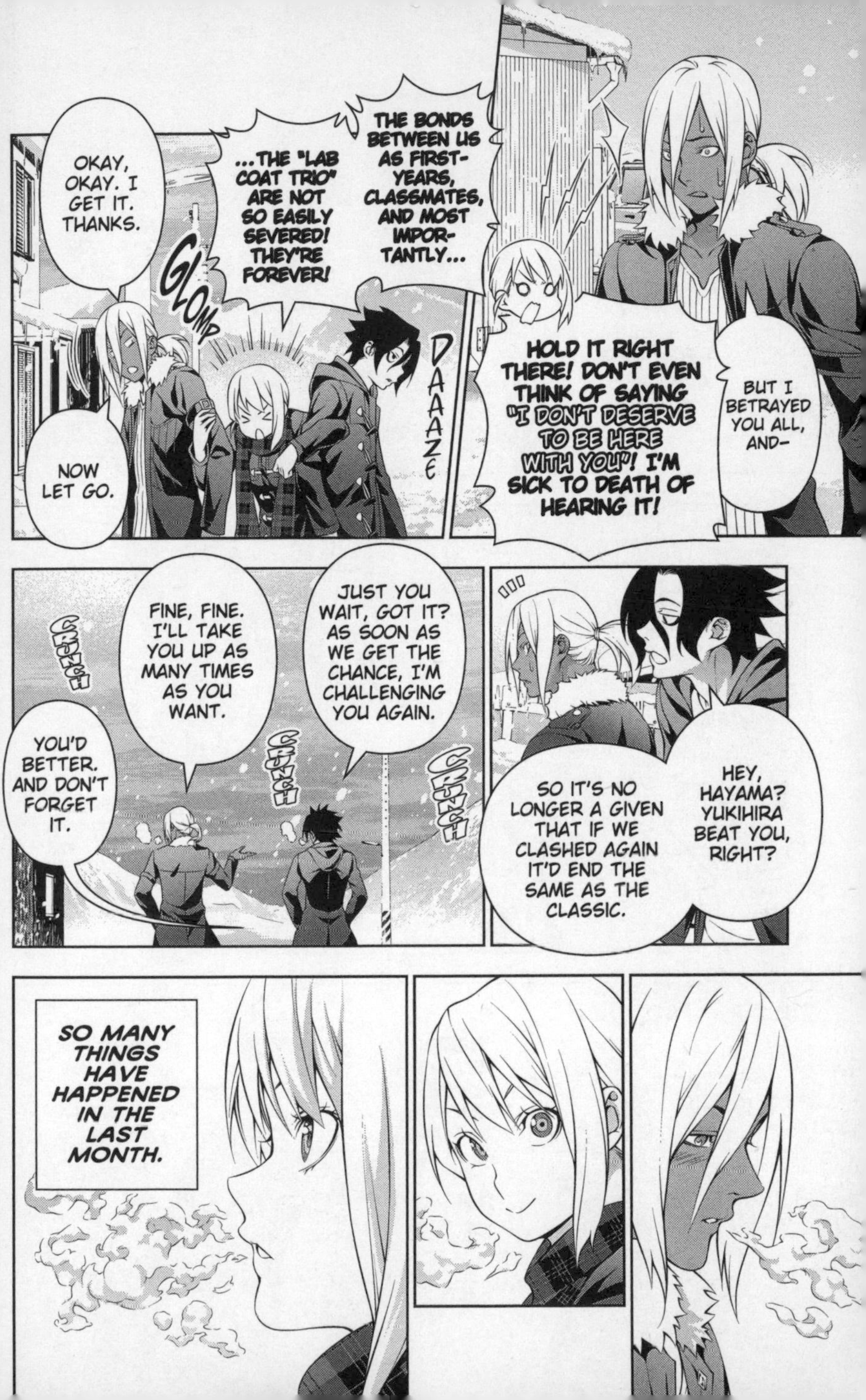

BUT I BETRAYED YOU ALL, AND–
HOLD IT RIGHT THERE! DON'T EVEN THINK OF SAYING "I DON'T DESERVE TO BE HERE WITH YOU"! I'M SICK TO DEATH OF HEARING IT!
THE BONDS BETWEEN US AS FIRST-YEARS, CLASSMATES, AND MOST IMPOR-TANTLY...
...THE "LAB COAT TRIO" ARE NOT SO EASILY SEVERED! THEY'RE FOREVER!
DAAAAZE
GLOMP
OKAY, OKAY. I GET IT. THANKS.
NOW LET GO.
HEY, HAYAMA? YUKIHIRA BEAT YOU, RIGHT?
SO IT'S NO LONGER A GIVEN THAT IF WE CLASHED AGAIN IT'D END THE SAME AS THE CLASSIC.
CRUNCH
JUST YOU WAIT, GOT IT? AS SOON AS WE GET THE CHANCE, I'M CHALLENGING YOU AGAIN.
CRUNCH
FINE, FINE. I'LL TAKE YOU UP AS MANY TIMES AS YOU WANT.
CRUNCH
YOU'D BETTER. AND DON'T FORGET IT.
SO MANY THINGS HAVE HAPPENED IN THE LAST MONTH.

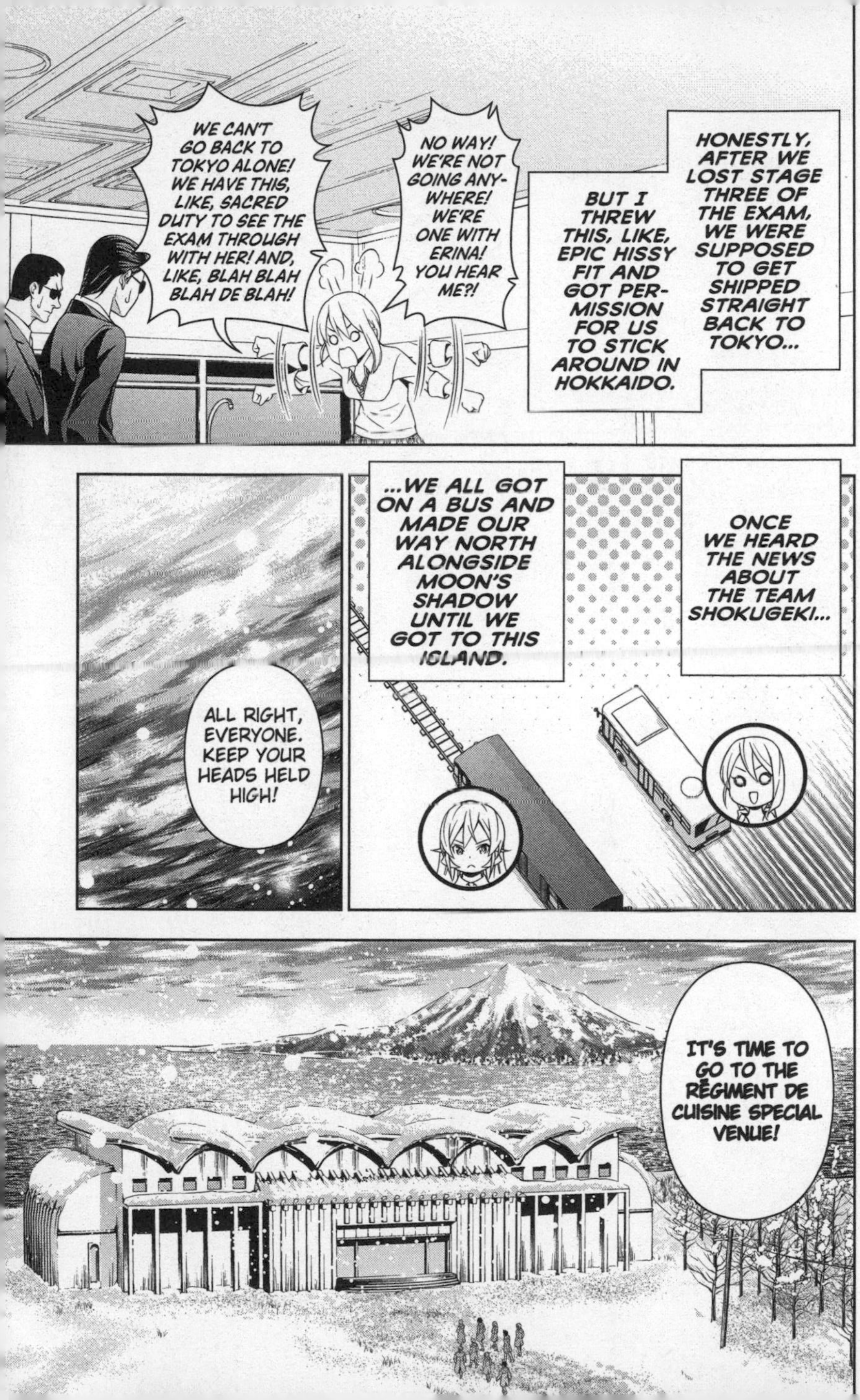
HONESTLY, AFTER WE LOST STAGE THREE OF THE EXAM, WE WERE SUPPOSED TO GET SHIPPED STRAIGHT BACK TO TOKYO...
BUT I THREW THIS, LIKE, EPIC HISSY FIT AND GOT PERMISSION FOR US TO STICK AROUND IN HOKKAIDO.
NO WAY! WE'RE NOT GOING ANYWHERE! WE'RE ONE WITH ERINA! YOU HEAR ME?!
WE CAN'T GO BACK TO TOKYO ALONE! WE HAVE THIS, LIKE, SACRED DUTY TO SEE THE EXAM THROUGH WITH HER! AND, LIKE, BLAH BLAH BLAH DE BLAH!
ONCE WE HEARD THE NEWS ABOUT THE TEAM SHOKUGEKI...
...WE ALL GOT ON A BUS AND MADE OUR WAY NORTH ALONGSIDE MOON'S SHADOW UNTIL WE GOT TO THIS ISLAND.
ALL RIGHT, EVERYONE. KEEP YOUR HEADS HELD HIGH!
IT'S TIME TO GO TO THE RÉGIMENT DE CUISINE SPECIAL VENUE!

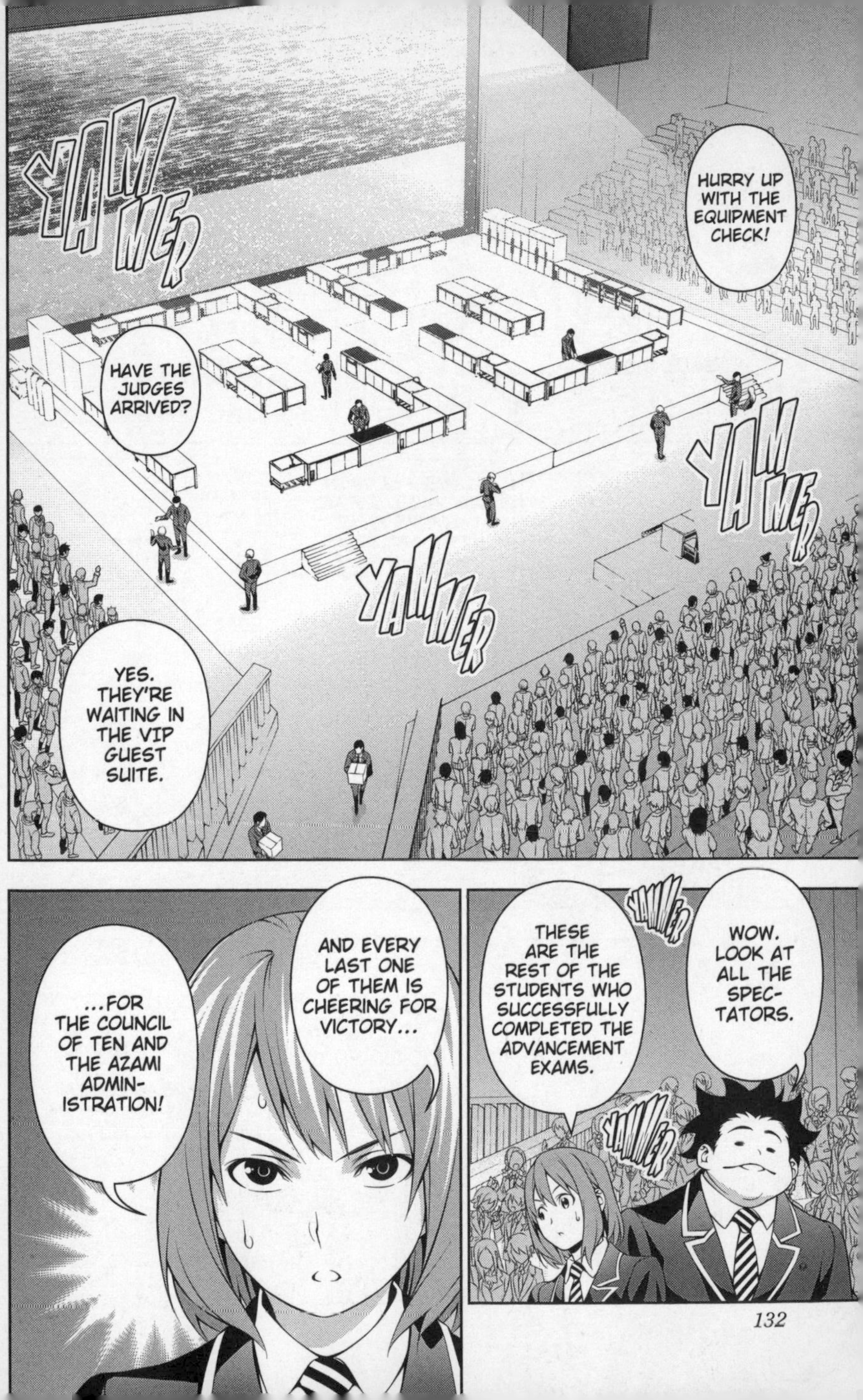
HURRY UP WITH THE EQUIPMENT CHECK!
YAMMER
HAVE THE JUDGES ARRIVED?
YAMMER
YAMMER
YES. THEY'RE WAITING IN THE VIP GUEST SUITE.
WOW. LOOK AT ALL THE SPEC-TATORS.
YAMMER
THESE ARE THE REST OF THE STUDENTS WHO SUCCESSFULLY COMPLETED THE ADVANCEMENT EXAMS.
YAMMER
AND EVERY LAST ONE OF THEM IS CHEERING FOR VICTORY...
...FOR THE COUNCIL OF TEN AND THE AZAMI ADMIN-ISTRATION!

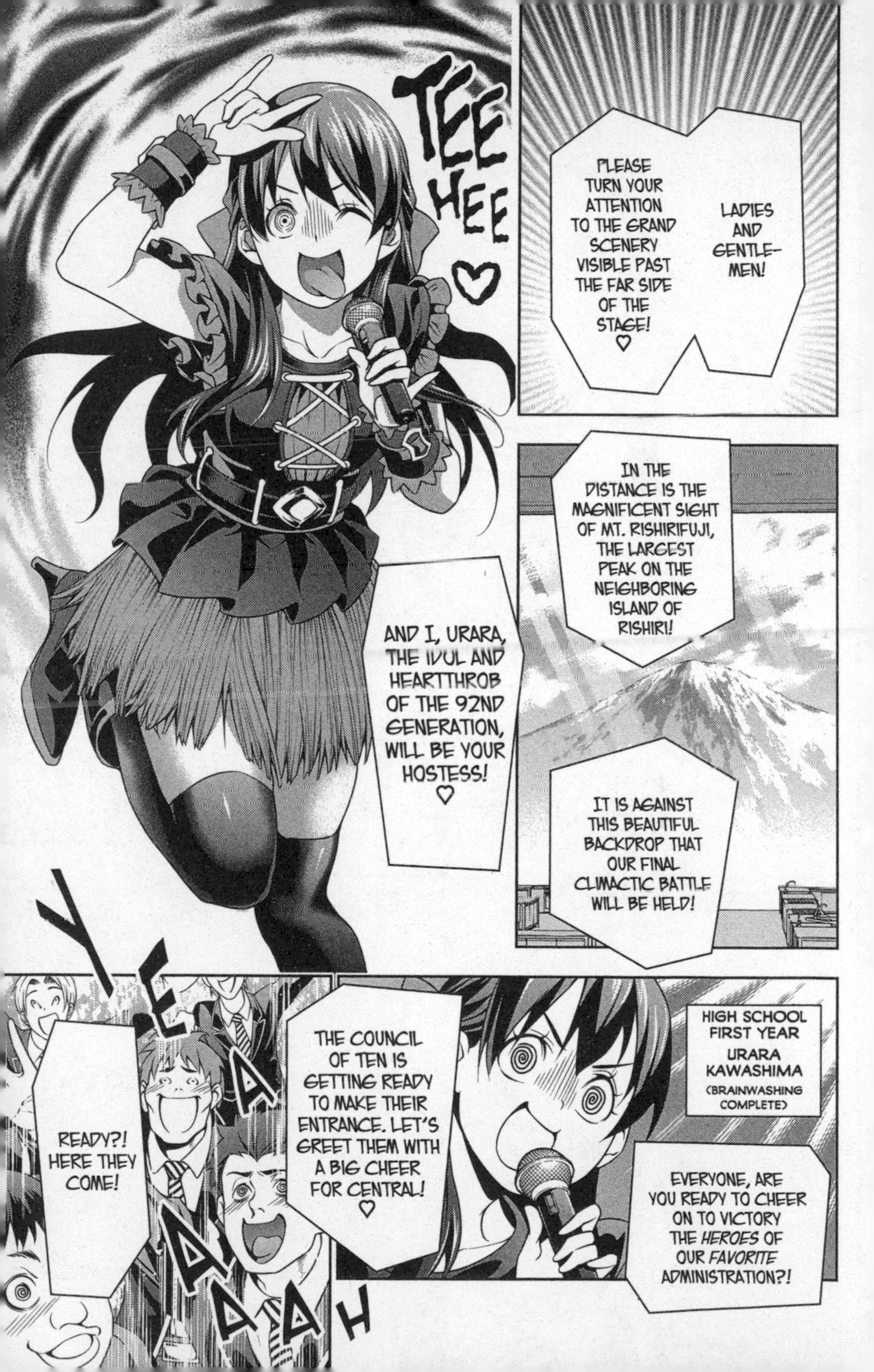
LADIES AND GENTLE-MEN!
PLEASE TURN YOUR ATTENTION TO THE GRAND SCENERY VISIBLE PAST THE FAR SIDE OF THE STAGE! ♡
IN THE DISTANCE IS THE MAGNIFICENT SIGHT OF MT. RISHIRIFUJI, THE LARGEST PEAK ON THE NEIGHBORING ISLAND OF RISHIRI!
IT IS AGAINST THIS BEAUTIFUL BACKDROP THAT OUR FINAL CLIMACTIC BATTLE WILL BE HELD!
TEE HEE ♡
AND I, URARA, THE IDOL AND HEARTTHROB OF THE 92ND GENERATION, WILL BE YOUR HOSTESS! ♡
HIGH SCHOOL FIRST YEAR URARA KAWASHIMA (BRAINWASHING COMPLETE)
EVERYONE, ARE YOU READY TO CHEER ON TO VICTORY THE *HEROES* OF OUR *FAVORITE* ADMINISTRATION?!
THE COUNCIL OF TEN IS GETTING READY TO MAKE THEIR ENTRANCE. LET'S GREET THEM WITH A BIG CHEER FOR CENTRAL! ♡
READY?! HERE THEY COME!
YEAAAAAAH

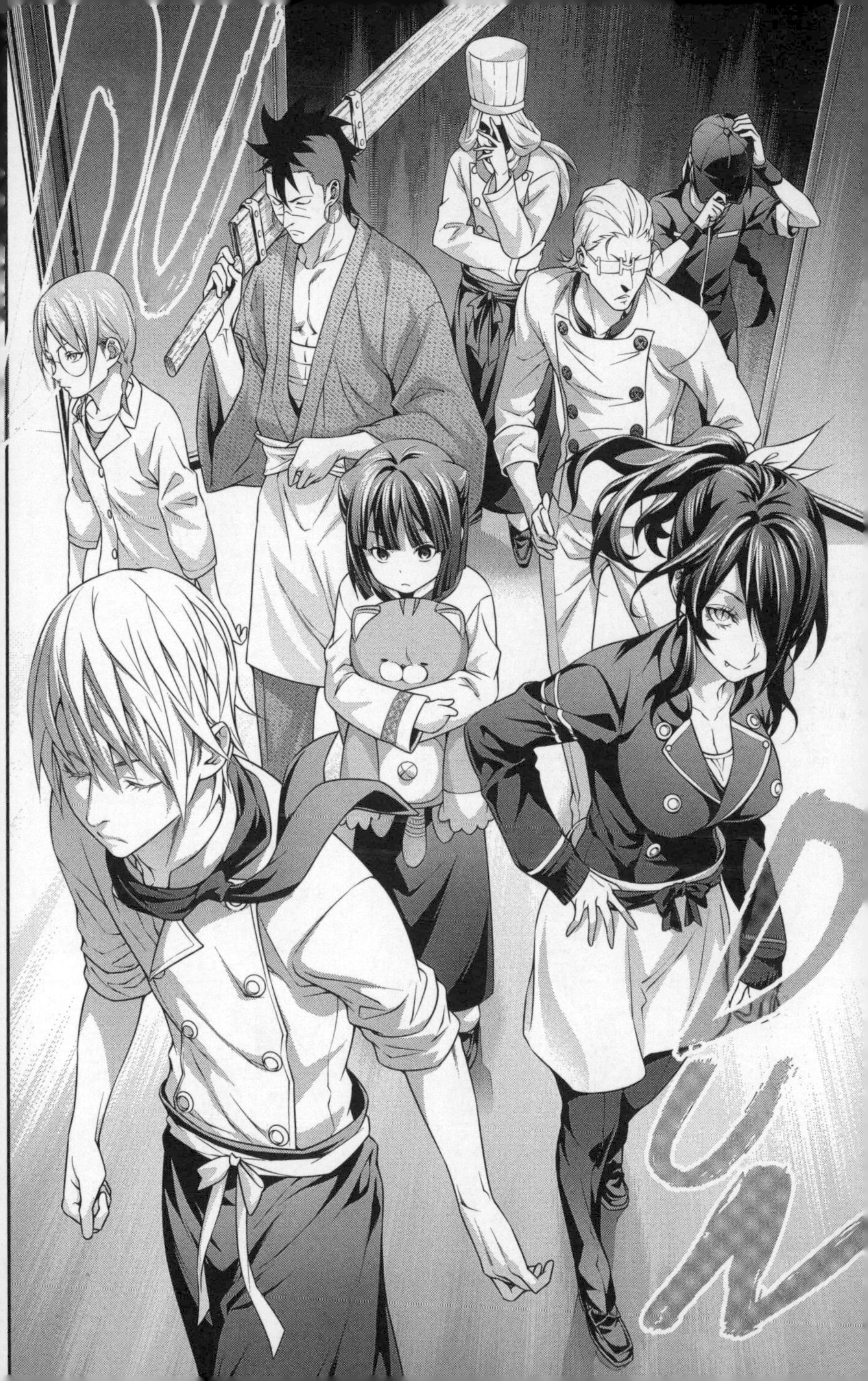

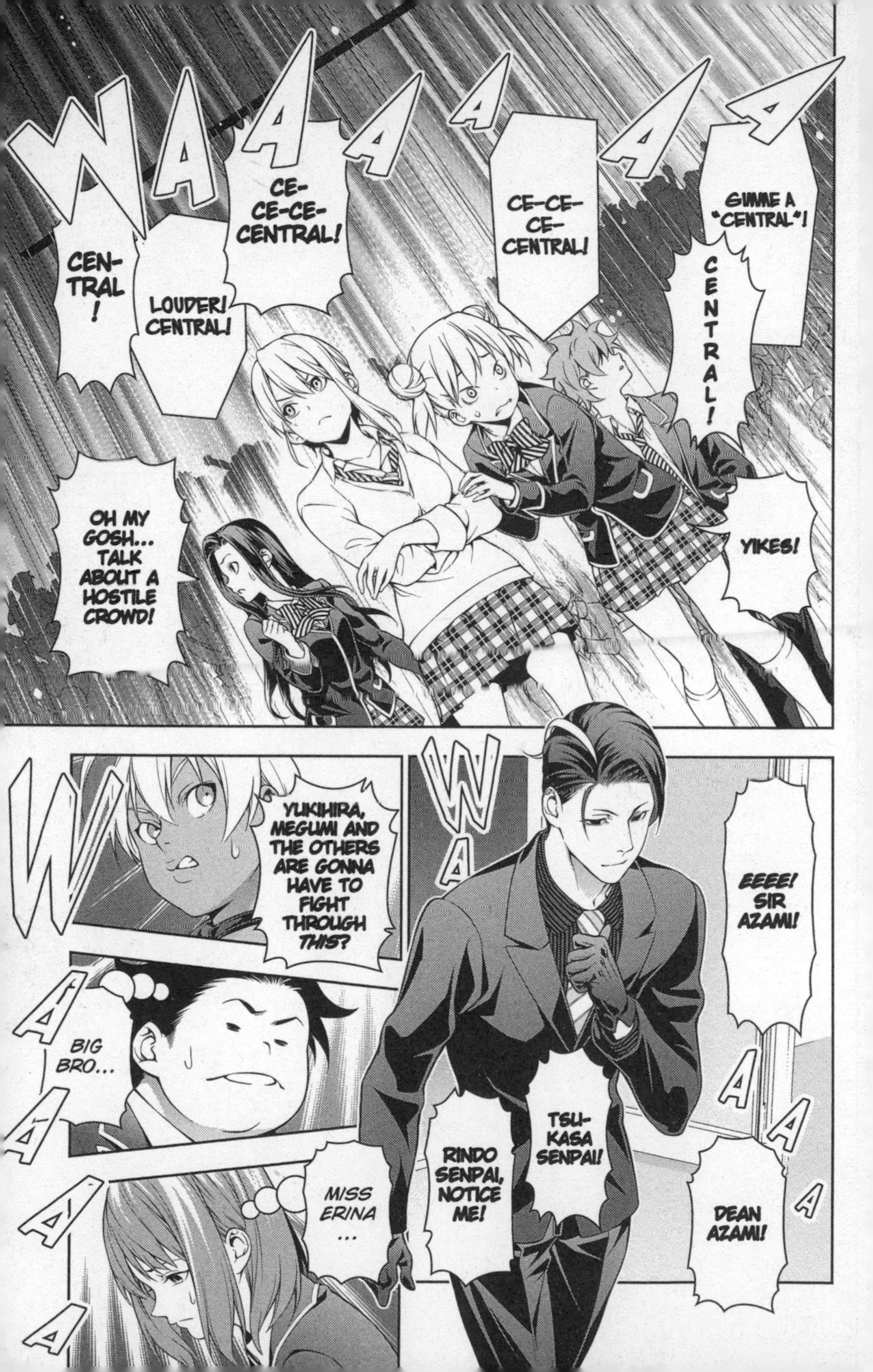
WAAAAAAA
GIMME A "CENTRAL"!
CENTRAL!
CE-CE-CE-CENTRAL!
CE-CE-CE-CENTRAL!
CEN-TRAL!
LOUDER! CENTRAL!
YIKES!
OH MY GOSH... TALK ABOUT A HOSTILE CROWD!
EEEE! SIR AZAMI!
TSU-KASA SENPAI!
DEAN AZAMI!
RINDO SENPAI, NOTICE ME!
WAAAAAA
YUKIHIRA, MEGUMI AND THE OTHERS ARE GONNA HAVE TO FIGHT THROUGH THIS?
BIG BRO...
MISS ERINA...

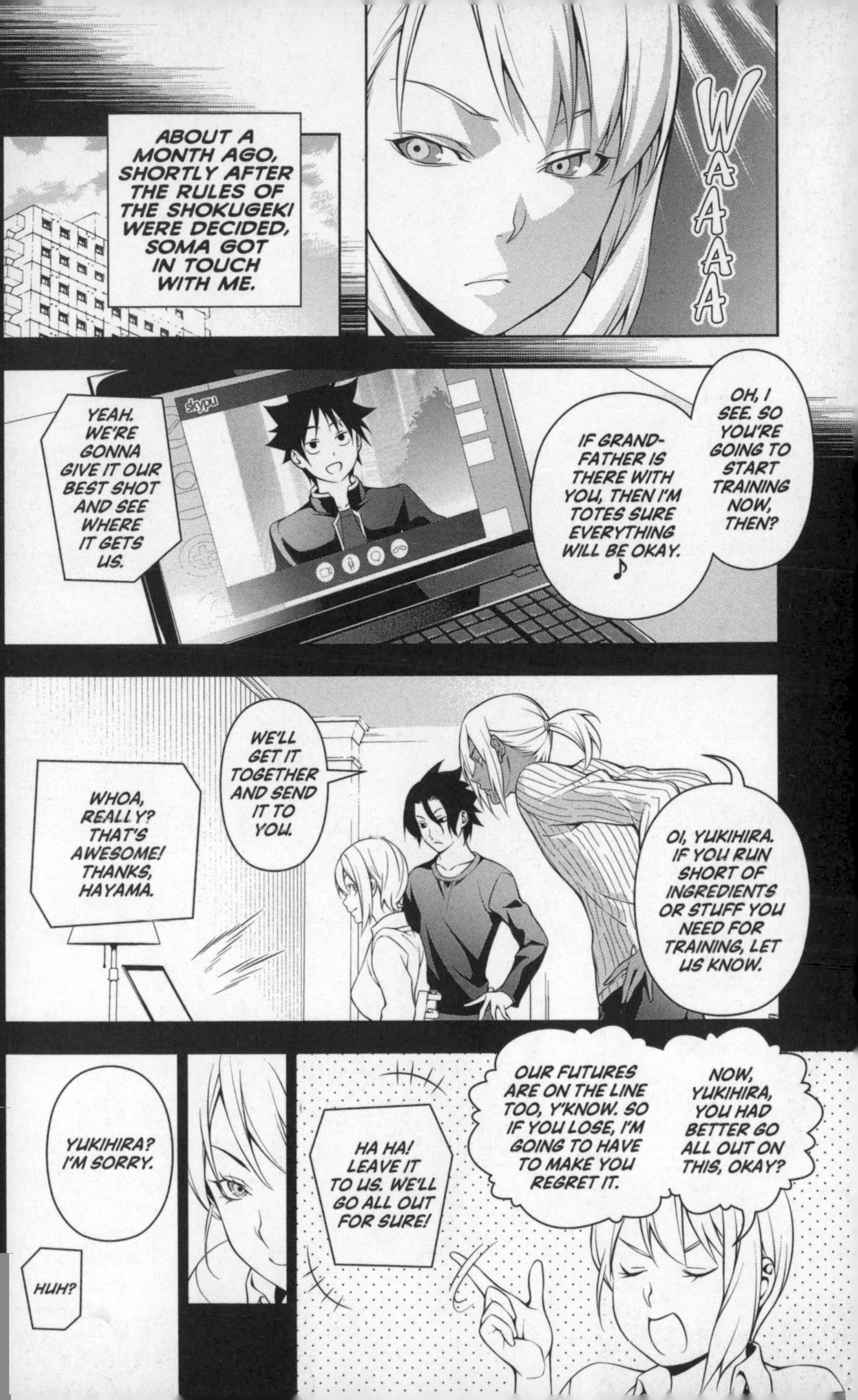
WAAAA
ABOUT A MONTH AGO, SHORTLY AFTER THE RULES OF THE SHOKUGEKI WERE DECIDED, SOMA GOT IN TOUCH WITH ME.
OH, I SEE. SO YOU'RE GOING TO START TRAINING NOW, THEN?
IF GRAND-FATHER IS THERE WITH YOU, THEN I'M TOTES SURE EVERYTHING WILL BE OKAY. ♪
skypu
YEAH. WE'RE GONNA GIVE IT OUR BEST SHOT AND SEE WHERE IT GETS US.
OI, YUKIHIRA. IF YOU RUN SHORT OF INGREDIENTS OR STUFF YOU NEED FOR TRAINING, LET US KNOW.
WE'LL GET IT TOGETHER AND SEND IT TO YOU.
WHOA, REALLY? THAT'S AWESOME! THANKS, HAYAMA.
NOW, YUKIHIRA, YOU HAD BETTER GO ALL OUT ON THIS, OKAY?
OUR FUTURES ARE ON THE LINE TOO, Y'KNOW. SO IF YOU LOSE, I'M GOING TO HAVE TO MAKE YOU REGRET IT.
HA HA! LEAVE IT TO US. WE'LL GO ALL OUT FOR SURE!
YUKIHIRA? I'M SORRY.
HUH?

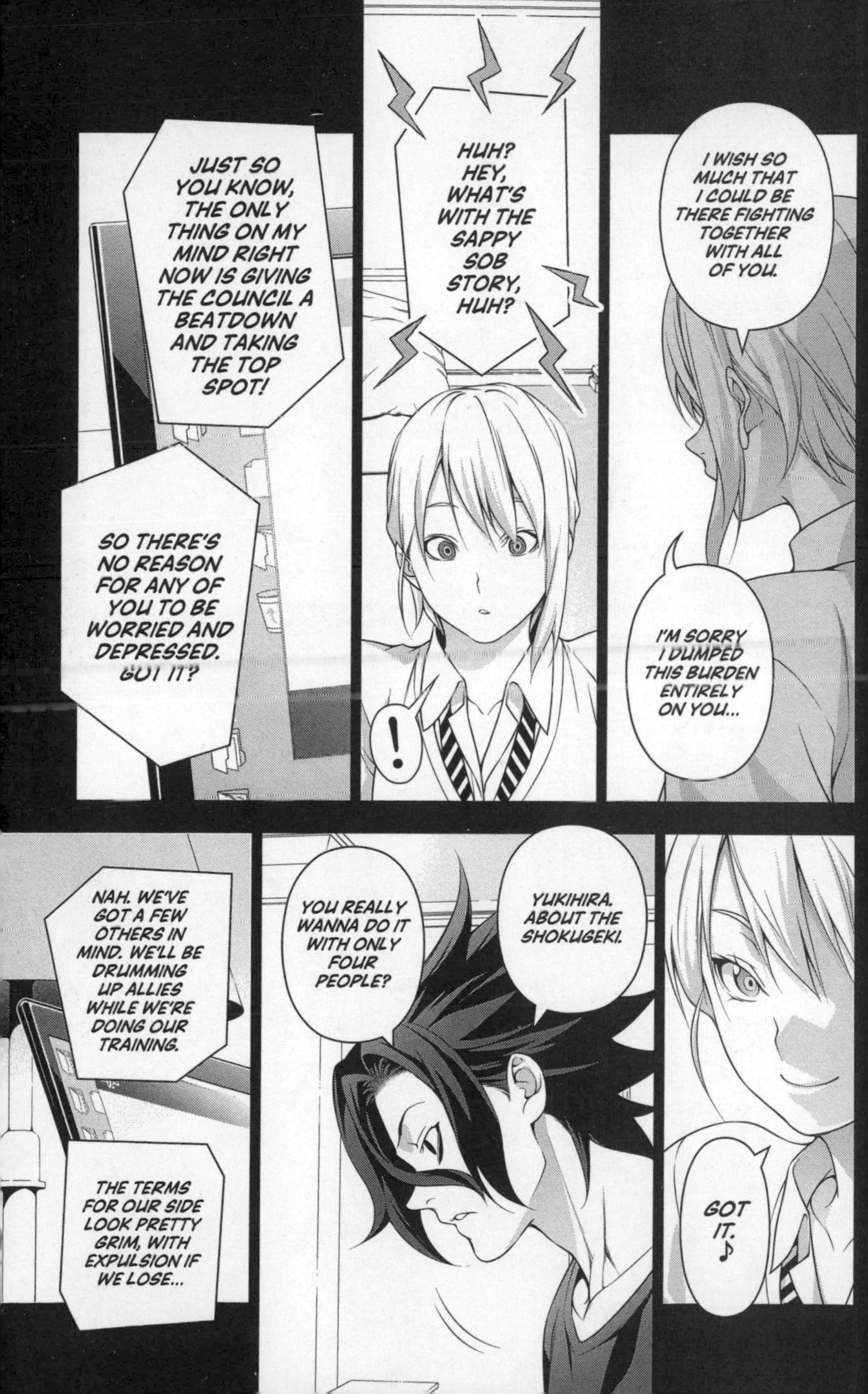
I WISH SO MUCH THAT I COULD BE THERE FIGHTING TOGETHER WITH ALL OF YOU.
I'M SORRY I DUMPED THIS BURDEN ENTIRELY ON YOU...
HUH? HEY, WHAT'S WITH THE SAPPY SOB STORY, HUH?
!
JUST SO YOU KNOW, THE ONLY THING ON MY MIND RIGHT NOW IS GIVING THE COUNCIL A BEATDOWN AND TAKING THE TOP SPOT!
SO THERE'S NO REASON FOR ANY OF YOU TO BE WORRIED AND DEPRESSED. GOT IT?
GOT IT. ♪
YUKIHIRA. ABOUT THE SHOKUGEKI.
YOU REALLY WANNA DO IT WITH ONLY FOUR PEOPLE?
NAH. WE'VE GOT A FEW OTHERS IN MIND. WE'LL BE DRUMMING UP ALLIES WHILE WE'RE DOING OUR TRAINING.
THE TERMS FOR OUR SIDE LOOK PRETTY GRIM, WITH EXPULSION IF WE LOSE...

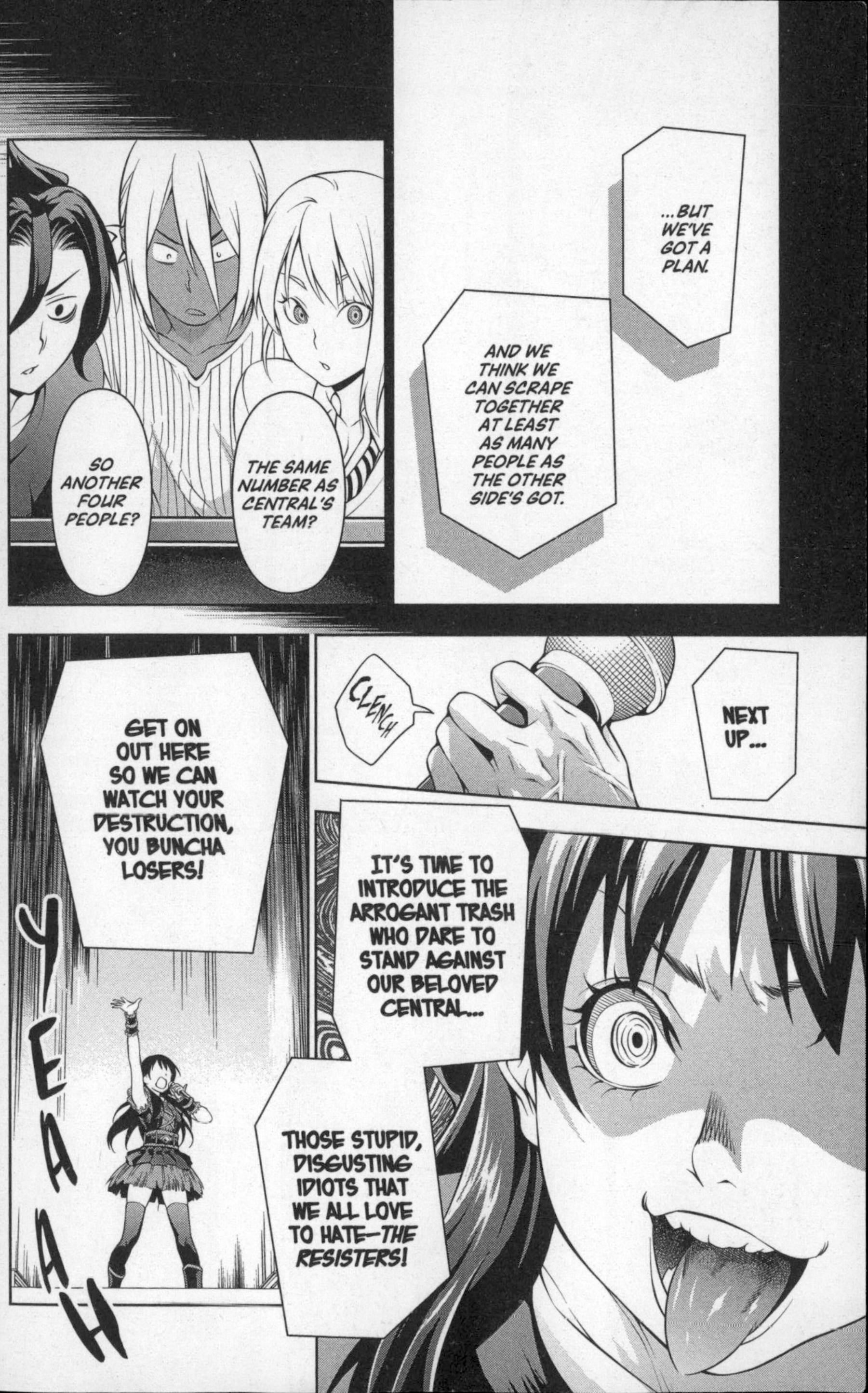
...BUT WE'VE GOT A PLAN.
AND WE THINK WE CAN SCRAPE TOGETHER AT LEAST AS MANY PEOPLE AS THE OTHER SIDE'S GOT.
THE SAME NUMBER AS CENTRAL'S TEAM?
SO ANOTHER FOUR PEOPLE?
NEXT UP...
CLENCH
IT'S TIME TO INTRODUCE THE ARROGANT TRASH WHO DARE TO STAND AGAINST OUR BELOVED CENTRAL...
THOSE STUPID, DISGUSTING IDIOTS THAT WE ALL LOVE TO HATE—THE RESISTERS!
GET ON OUT HERE SO WE CAN WATCH YOUR DESTRUCTION, YOU BUNCHA LOSERS!
YEAAAH

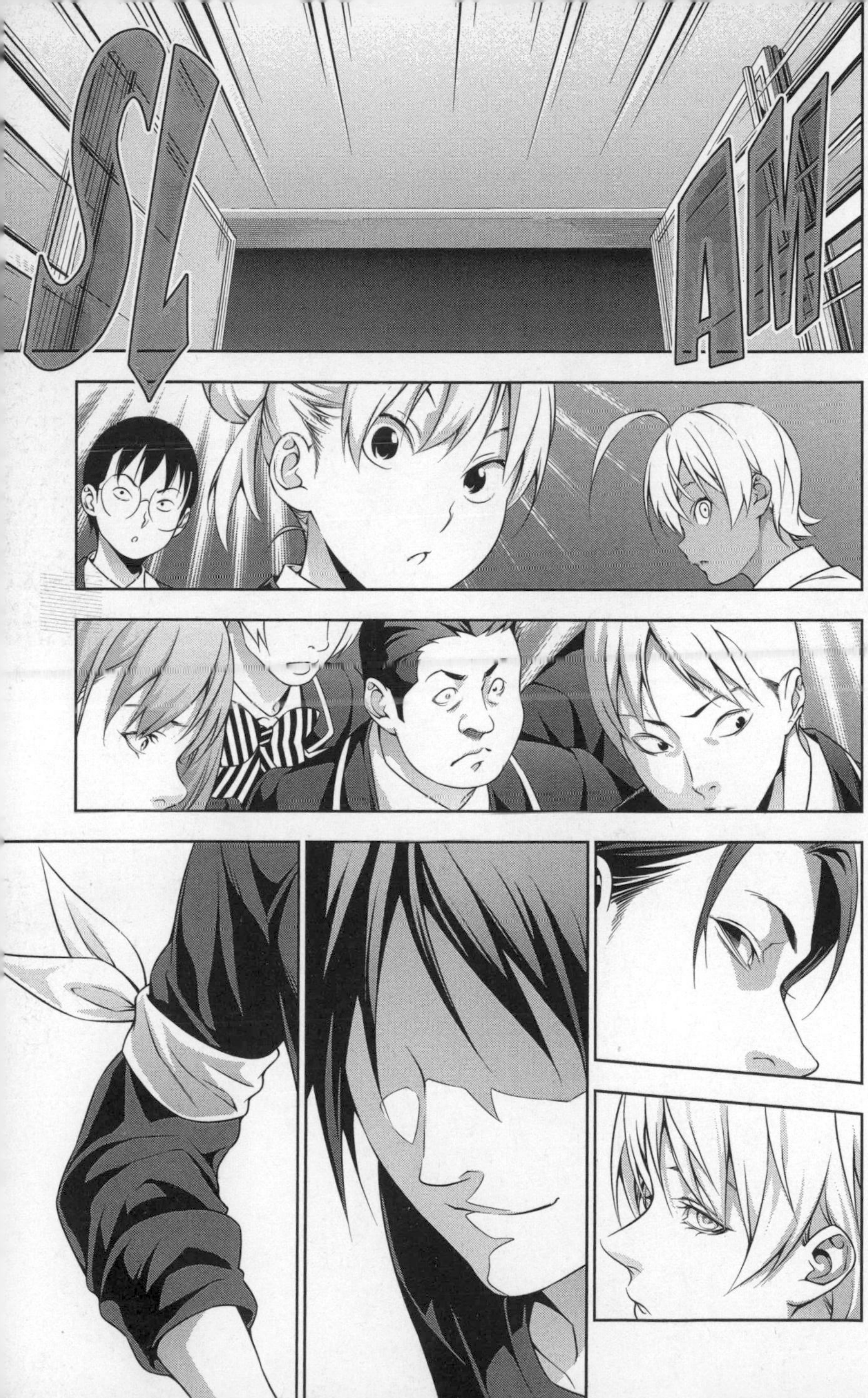
SLAM!

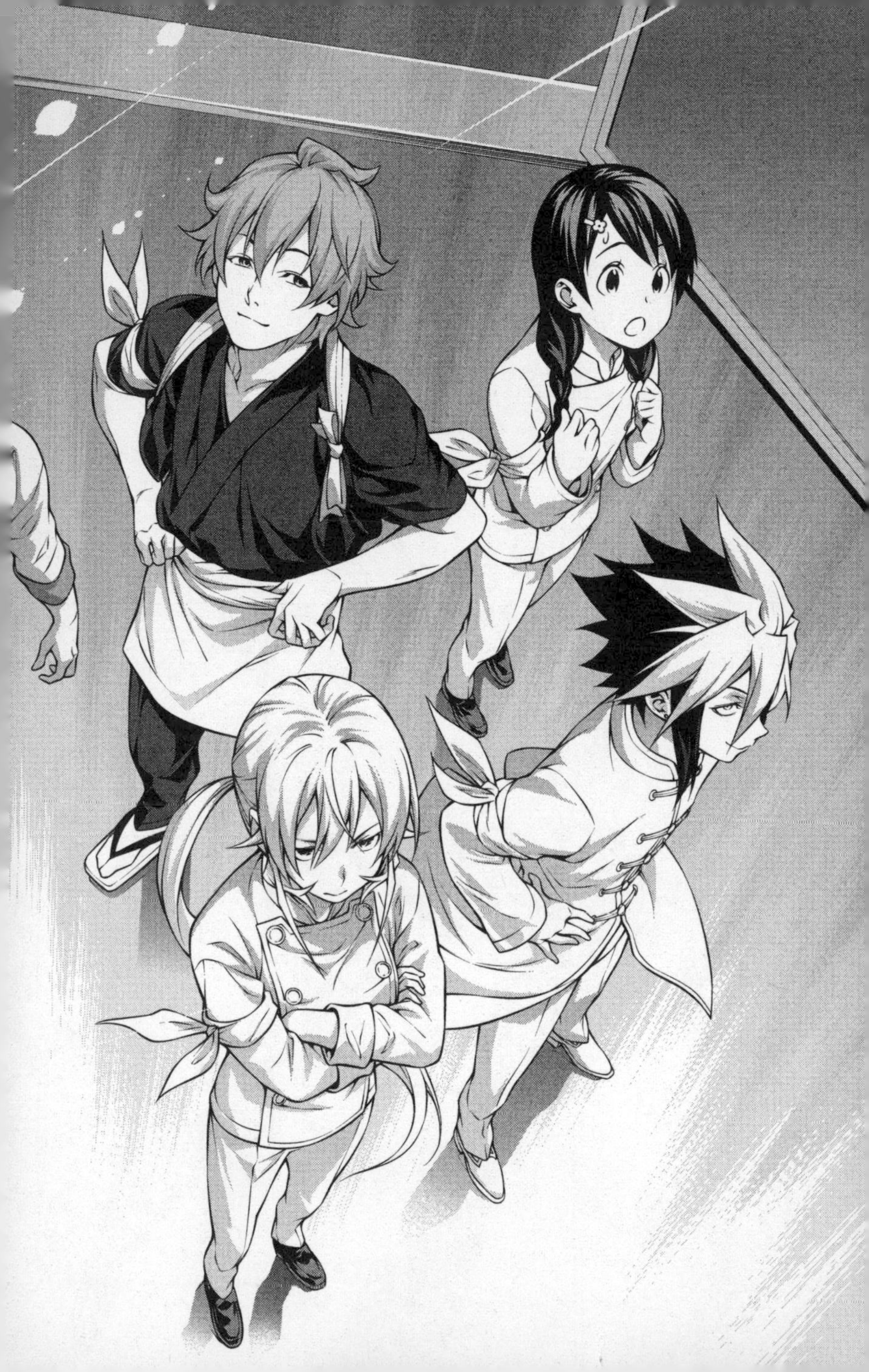

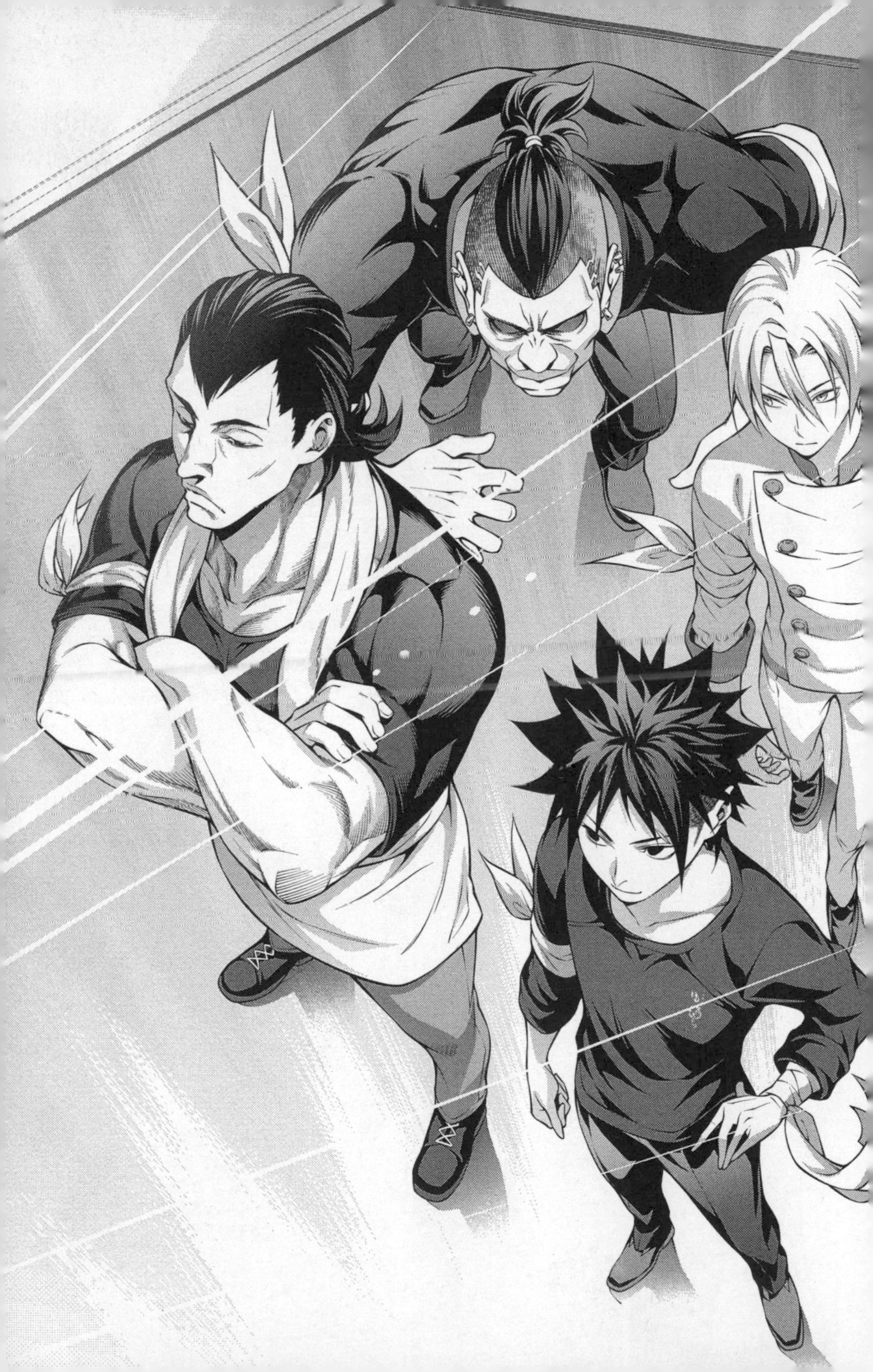

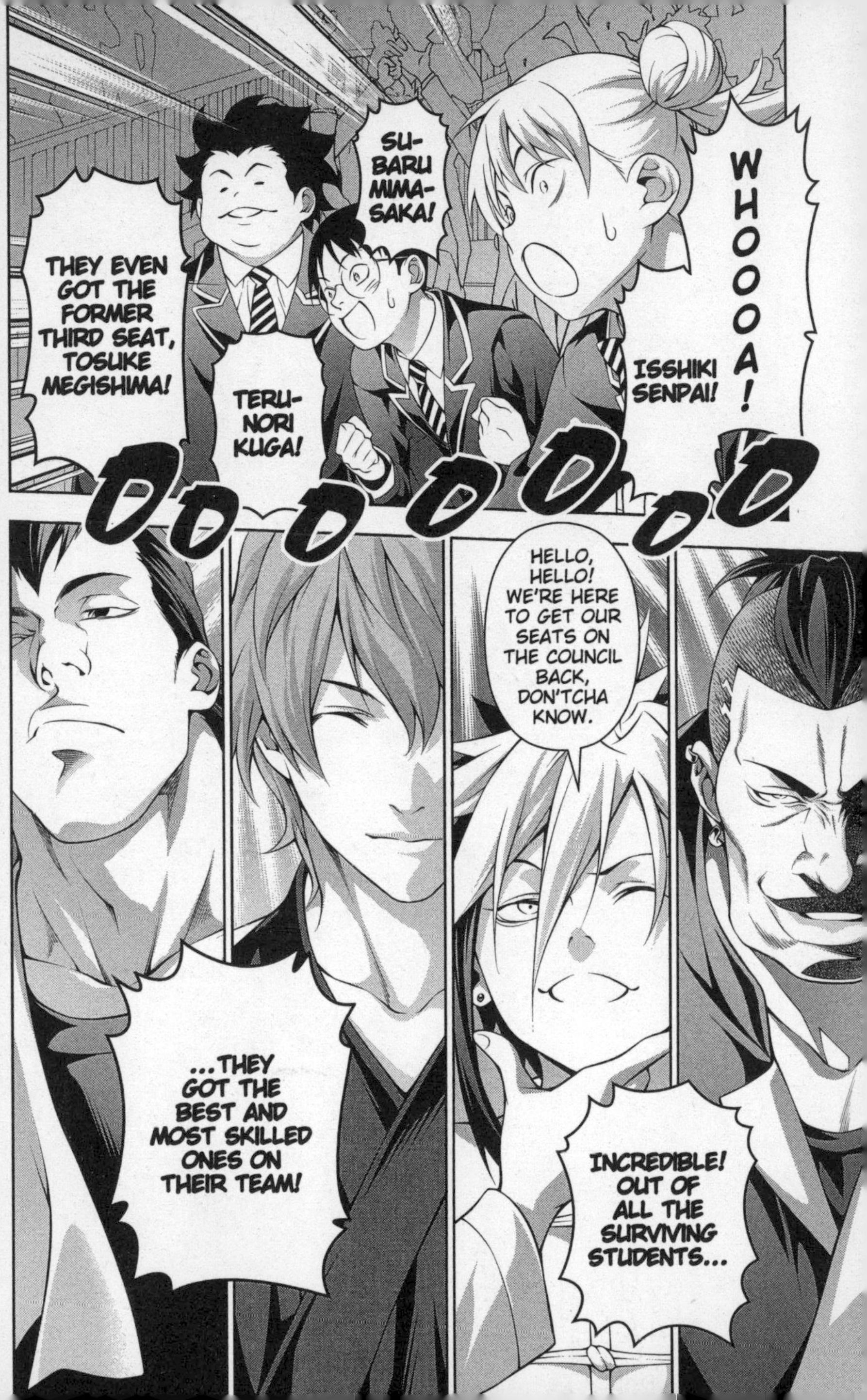
WHOOOOA!
ISSHIKI SENPAI!
SU-BARU MIMA-SAKA!
TERU-NORI KUGA!
THEY EVEN GOT THE FORMER THIRD SEAT, TOSUKE MEGISHIMA!
HELLO, HELLO! WE'RE HERE TO GET OUR SEATS ON THE COUNCIL BACK, DON'TCHA KNOW.
INCREDIBLE! OUT OF ALL THE SURVIVING STUDENTS...
...THEY GOT THE BEST AND MOST SKILLED ONES ON THEIR TEAM!

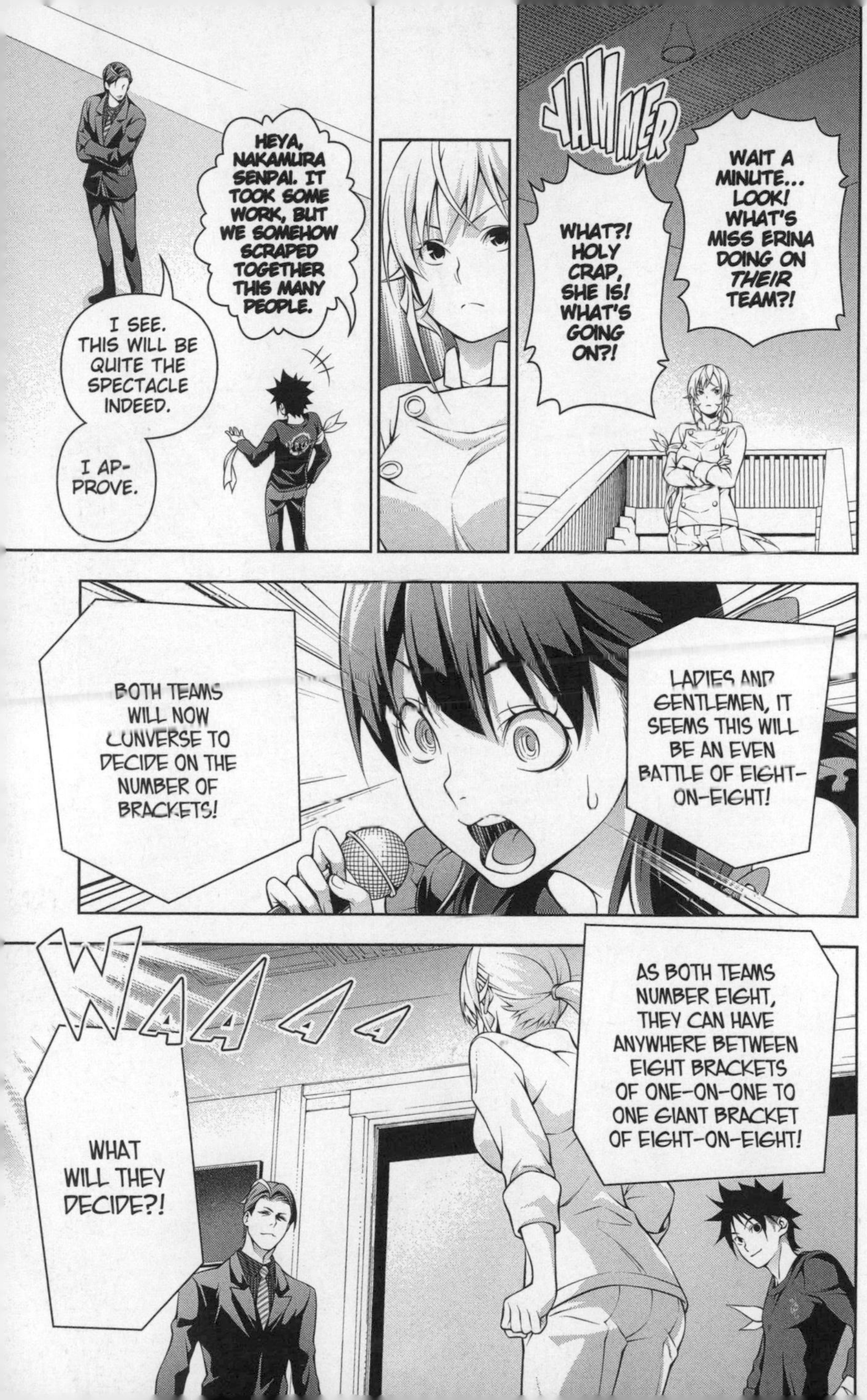
YAMMER
WAIT A MINUTE... LOOK! WHAT'S MISS ERINA DOING ON THEIR TEAM?!
WHAT?! HOLY CRAP, SHE IS! WHAT'S GOING ON?!
HEYA, NAKAMURA SENPAI. IT TOOK SOME WORK, BUT WE SOMEHOW SCRAPED TOGETHER THIS MANY PEOPLE.
I SEE. THIS WILL BE QUITE THE SPECTACLE INDEED.
I AP-PROVE.
LADIES AND GENTLEMEN, IT SEEMS THIS WILL BE AN EVEN BATTLE OF EIGHT-ON-EIGHT!
BOTH TEAMS WILL NOW CONVERSE TO DECIDE ON THE NUMBER OF BRACKETS!
AS BOTH TEAMS NUMBER EIGHT, THEY CAN HAVE ANYWHERE BETWEEN EIGHT BRACKETS OF ONE-ON-ONE TO ONE GIANT BRACKET OF EIGHT-ON-EIGHT!
WAAAAA
WHAT WILL THEY DECIDE?!

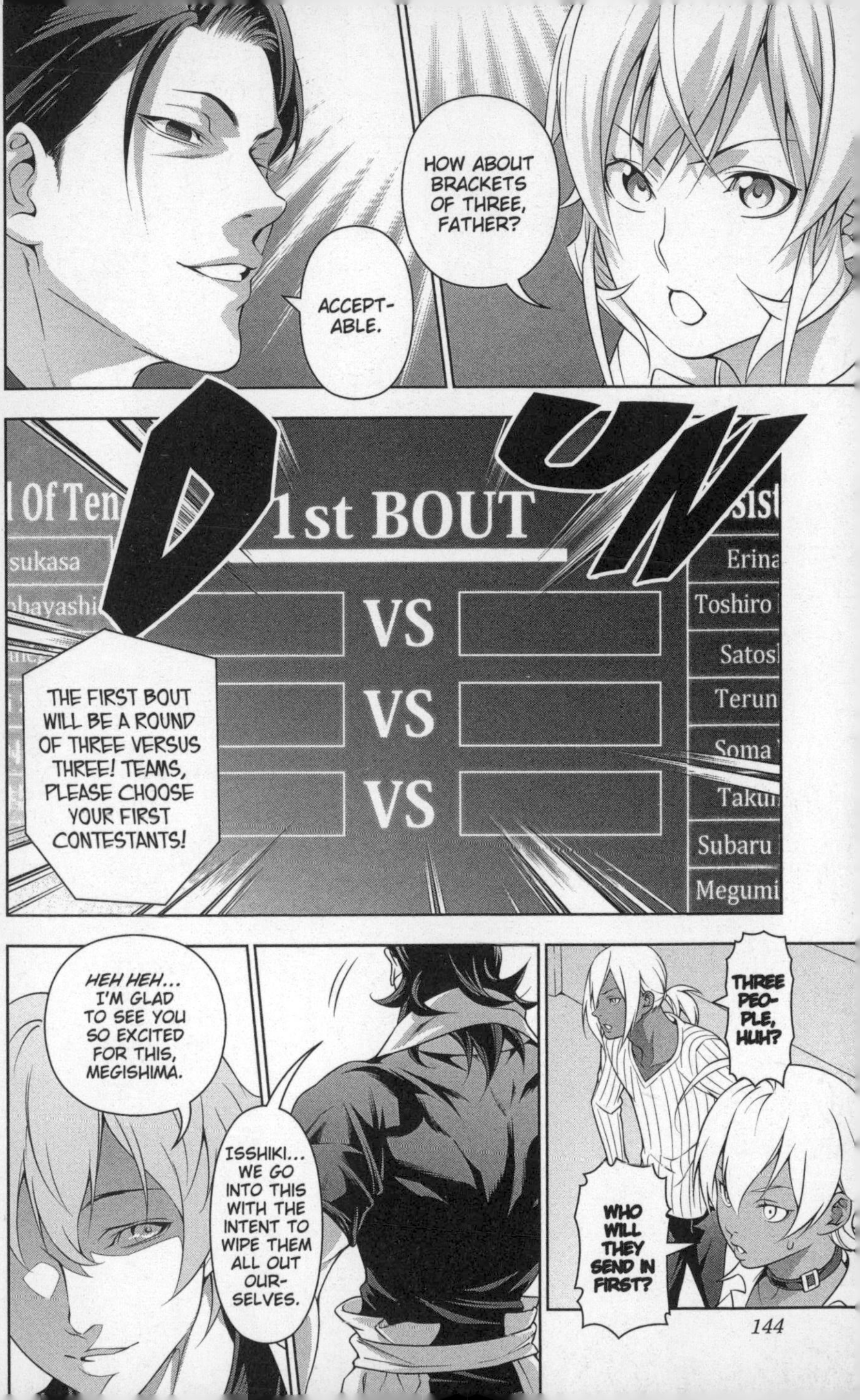
HOW ABOUT BRACKETS OF THREE, FATHER?
ACCEPTABLE.
DUN
sist
Erina
Toshiro
Satosh
Terun
Soma
Takun
Subaru
Megumi
1st BOUT
VS
VS
VS
Of Ten
sukasa
bayashi
THE FIRST BOUT WILL BE A ROUND OF THREE VERSUS THREE! TEAMS, PLEASE CHOOSE YOUR FIRST CONTESTANTS!
THREE PEOPLE, HUH?
WHO WILL THEY SEND IN FIRST?
ISSHIKI... WE GO INTO THIS WITH THE INTENT TO WIPE THEM ALL OUT OURSELVES.
HEH HEH... I'M GLAD TO SEE YOU SO EXCITED FOR THIS, MEGISHIMA.

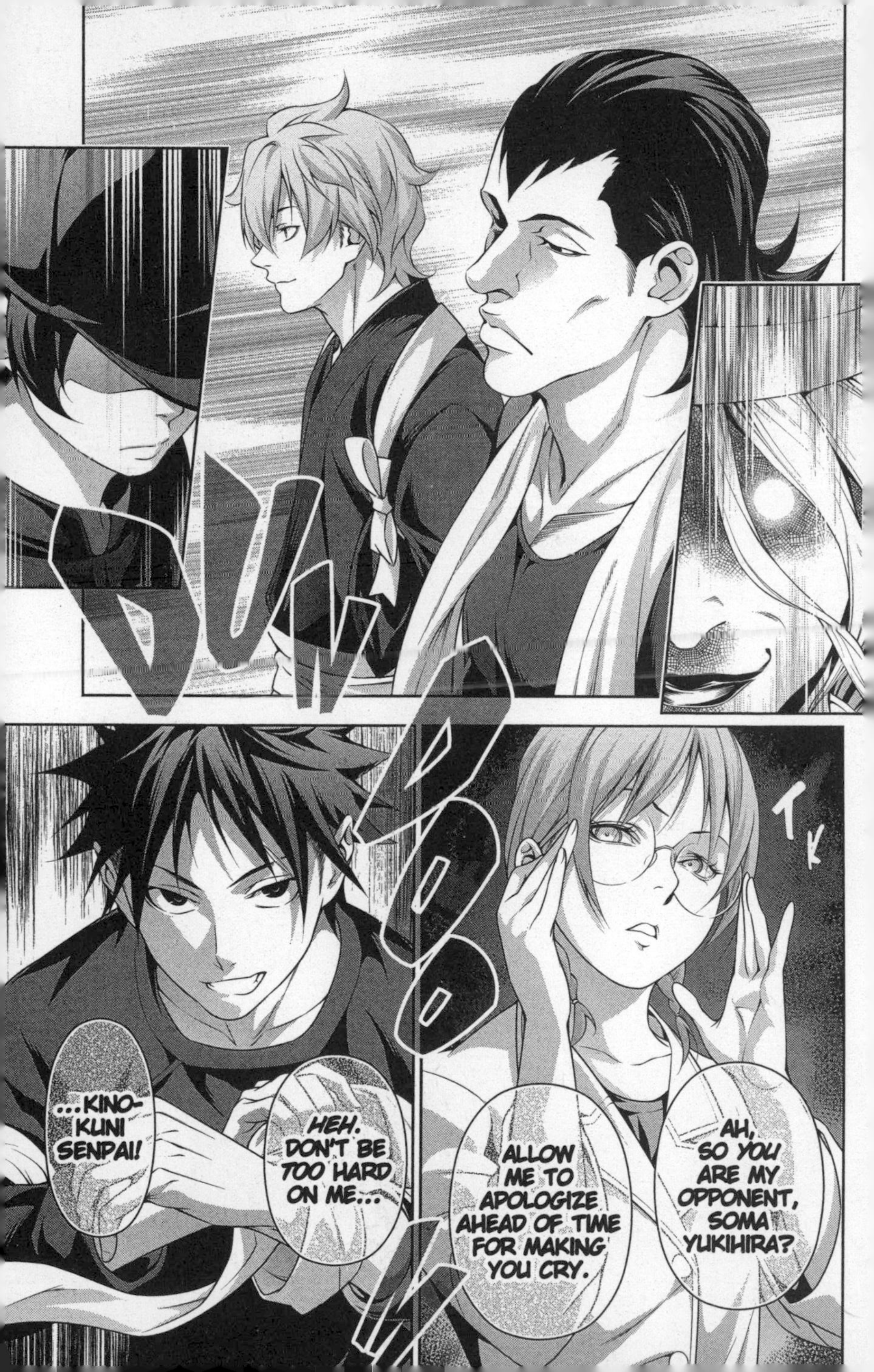
TK
AH, SO YOU ARE MY OPPONENT, SOMA YUKIHIRA?
ALLOW ME TO APOLOGIZE AHEAD OF TIME FOR MAKING YOU CRY.
HEH. DON'T BE TOO HARD ON ME...
...KINO-KUNI SENPAI!

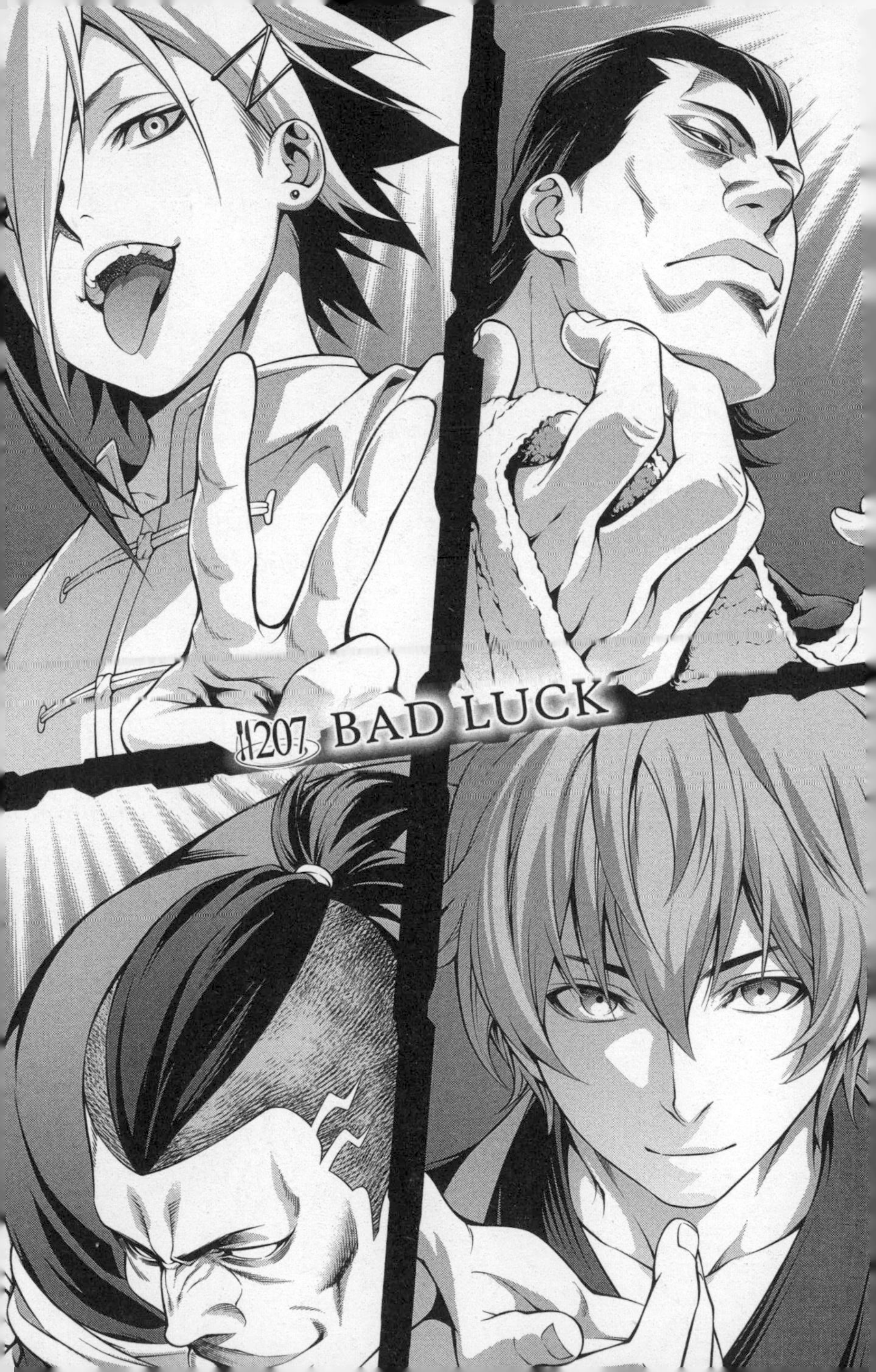
207 BAD LUCK

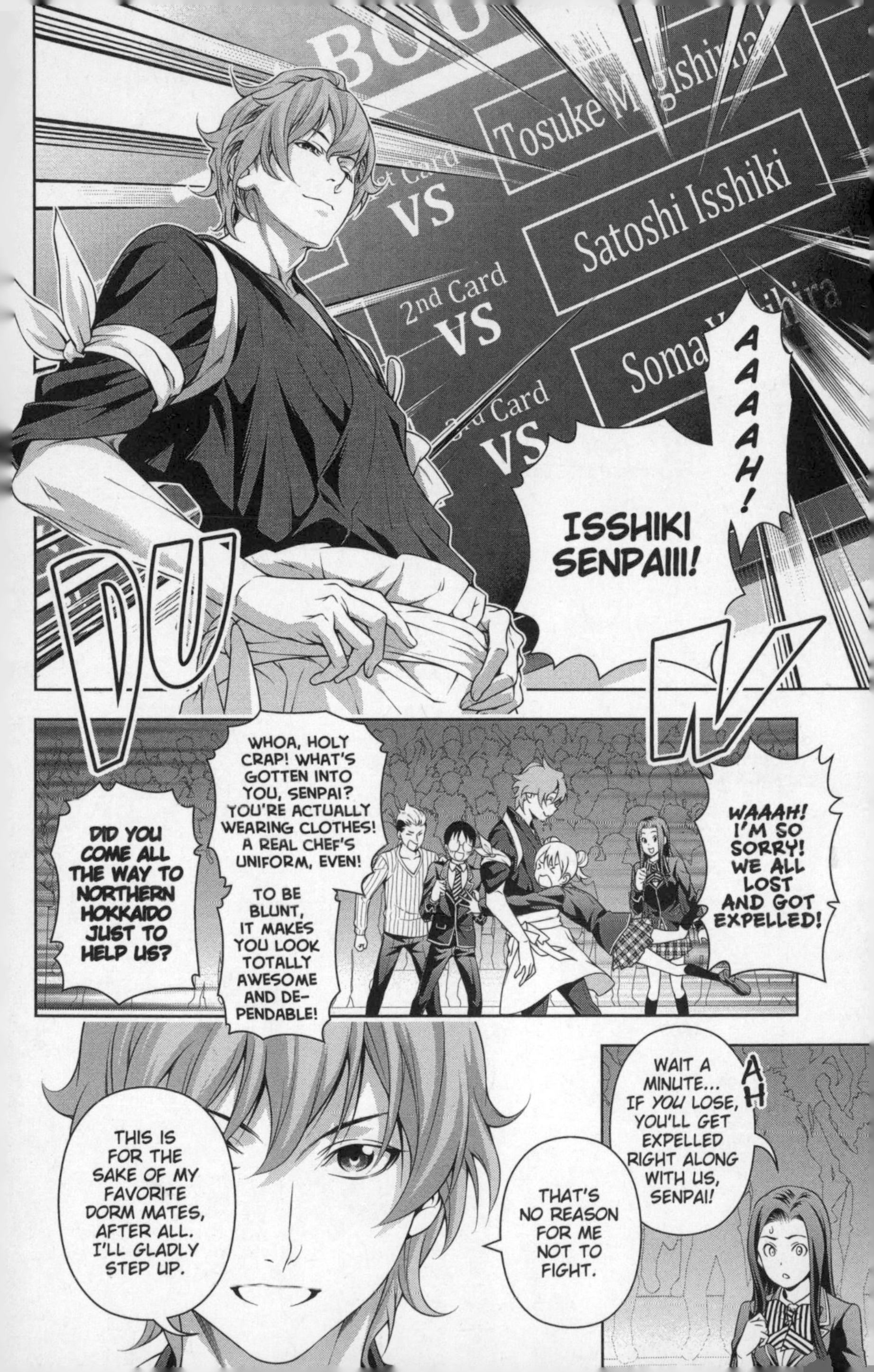

Tosuke
Satoshi Isshiki
2nd Card
VS
VS
VS
AAAAAH!
ISSHIKI SENPAIII!
DU
N
WAAAH! I'M SO SORRY! WE ALL LOST AND GOT EXPELLED!
WHOA, HOLY CRAP! WHAT'S GOTTEN INTO YOU, SENPAI? YOU'RE ACTUALLY WEARING CLOTHES! A REAL CHEF'S UNIFORM, EVEN!
TO BE BLUNT, IT MAKES YOU LOOK TOTALLY AWESOME AND DE-PENDABLE!
DID YOU COME ALL THE WAY TO NORTHERN HOKKAIDO JUST TO HELP US?
AH
WAIT A MINUTE... IF YOU LOSE, YOU'LL GET EXPELLED RIGHT ALONG WITH US, SENPAI!
THAT'S NO REASON FOR ME NOT TO FIGHT.
THIS IS FOR THE SAKE OF MY FAVORITE DORM MATES, AFTER ALL. I'LL GLADLY STEP UP.

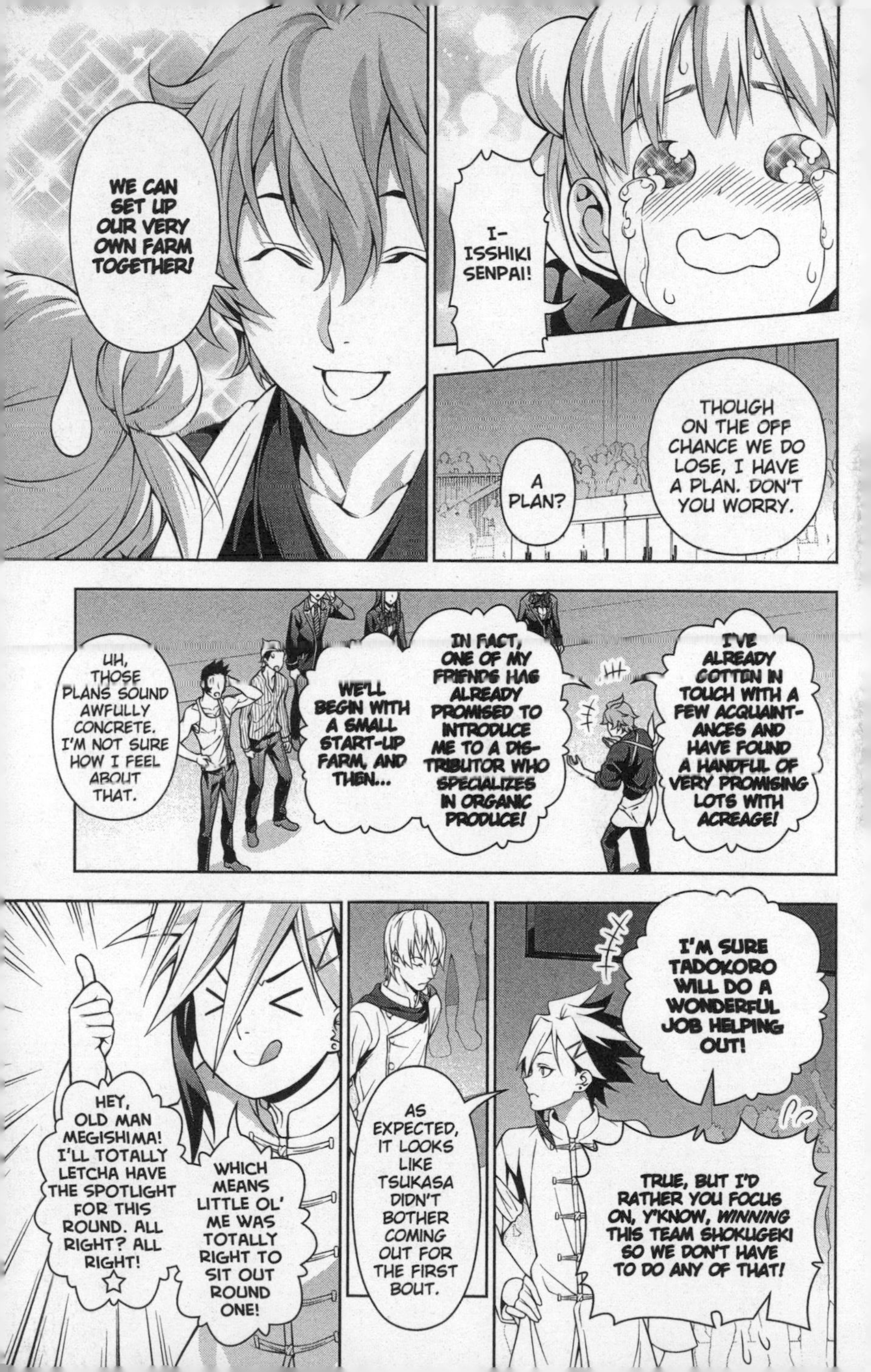
I- ISSHIKI SENPAI!
THOUGH ON THE OFF CHANCE WE DO LOSE, I HAVE A PLAN. DON'T YOU WORRY.
A PLAN?
WE CAN SET UP OUR VERY OWN FARM TOGETHER!
I'VE ALREADY GOTTEN IN TOUCH WITH A FEW ACQUAINT-ANCES AND HAVE FOUND A HANDFUL OF VERY PROMISING LOTS WITH ACREAGE!
IN FACT, ONE OF MY FRIENDS HAS ALREADY PROMISED TO INTRODUCE ME TO A DIS-TRIBUTOR WHO SPECIALIZES IN ORGANIC PRODUCE!
WE'LL BEGIN WITH A SMALL START-UP FARM, AND THEN...
UH, THOSE PLANS SOUND AWFULLY CONCRETE. I'M NOT SURE HOW I FEEL ABOUT THAT.
I'M SURE TADOKORO WILL DO A WONDERFUL JOB HELPING OUT!
TRUE, BUT I'D RATHER YOU FOCUS ON, Y'KNOW, *WINNING* THIS TEAM SHOKUGEKI SO WE DON'T HAVE TO DO ANY OF THAT!
AS EXPECTED, IT LOOKS LIKE TSUKASA DIDN'T BOTHER COMING OUT FOR THE FIRST BOUT.
HEY, OLD MAN MEGISHIMA! I'LL TOTALLY LETCHA HAVE THE SPOTLIGHT FOR THIS ROUND. ALL RIGHT? ALL RIGHT! ☆
WHICH MEANS LITTLE OL' ME WAS TOTALLY RIGHT TO SIT OUT ROUND ONE!

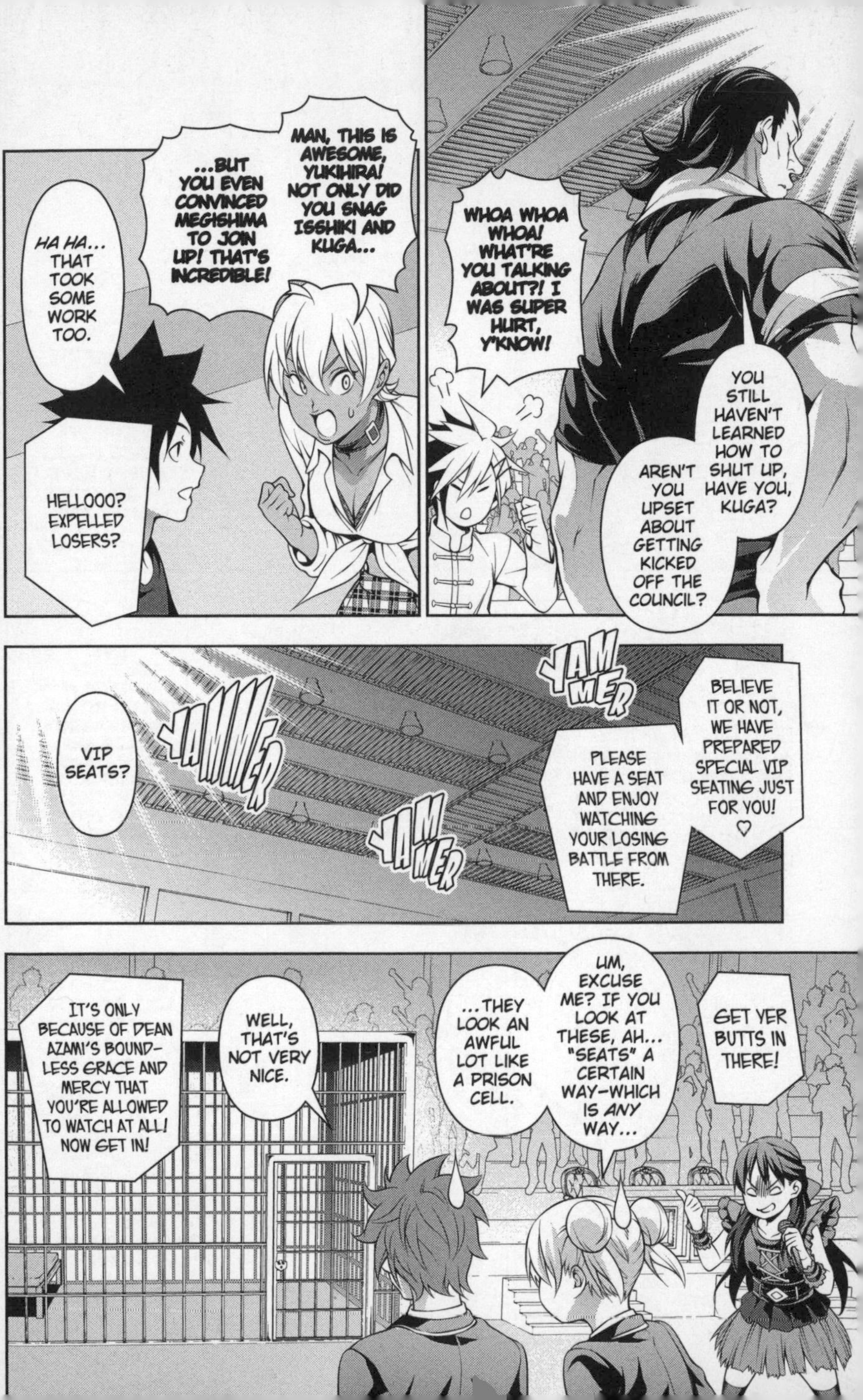
YOU STILL HAVEN'T LEARNED HOW TO SHUT UP, HAVE YOU, KUGA?
AREN'T YOU UPSET ABOUT GETTING KICKED OFF THE COUNCIL?
WHOA WHOA WHOA! WHAT'RE YOU TALKING ABOUT?! I WAS SUPER HURT, Y'KNOW!
MAN, THIS IS AWESOME, YUKIHIRA! NOT ONLY DID YOU SNAG ISSHIKI AND KUGA...
...BUT YOU EVEN CONVINCED MEGISHIMA TO JOIN UP! THAT'S INCREDIBLE!
HA HA... THAT TOOK SOME WORK TOO.
HELLOOO? EXPELLED LOSERS?
YAMMER
BELIEVE IT OR NOT, WE HAVE PREPARED SPECIAL VIP SEATING JUST FOR YOU! ♡
PLEASE HAVE A SEAT AND ENJOY WATCHING YOUR LOSING BATTLE FROM THERE.
YAMMER
YAMMER
VIP SEATS?
GET YER BUTTS IN THERE!
UM, EXCUSE ME? IF YOU LOOK AT THESE, AH... "SEATS" A CERTAIN WAY—WHICH IS ANY WAY...
...THEY LOOK AN AWFUL LOT LIKE A PRISON CELL.
WELL, THAT'S NOT VERY NICE.
IT'S ONLY BECAUSE OF DEAN AZAMI'S BOUNDLESS GRACE AND MERCY THAT YOU'RE ALLOWED TO WATCH AT ALL! NOW GET IN!

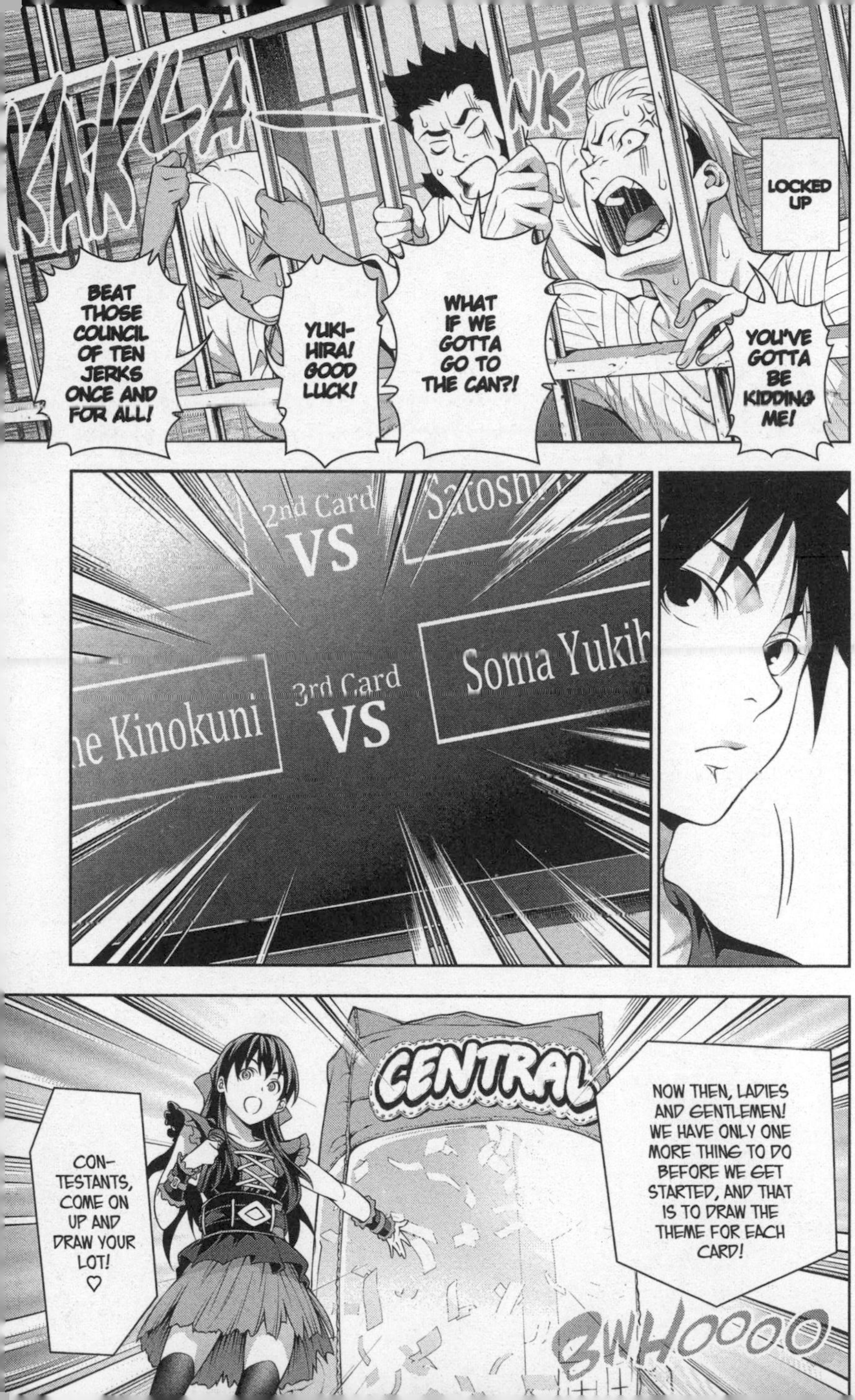
LOCKED UP
YOU'VE GOTTA BE KIDDING ME!
WHAT IF WE GOTTA GO TO THE CAN?!
YUKI-HIRA! GOOD LUCK!
BEAT THOSE COUNCIL OF TEN JERKS ONCE AND FOR ALL!
2nd Card VS
3rd Card VS
Kinokuni
Soma
NOW THEN, LADIES AND GENTLEMEN! WE HAVE ONLY ONE MORE THING TO DO BEFORE WE GET STARTED, AND THAT IS TO DRAW THE THEME FOR EACH CARD!
CENTRAL
CON-TESTANTS, COME ON UP AND DRAW YOUR LOT! ♡
BWHOOOO

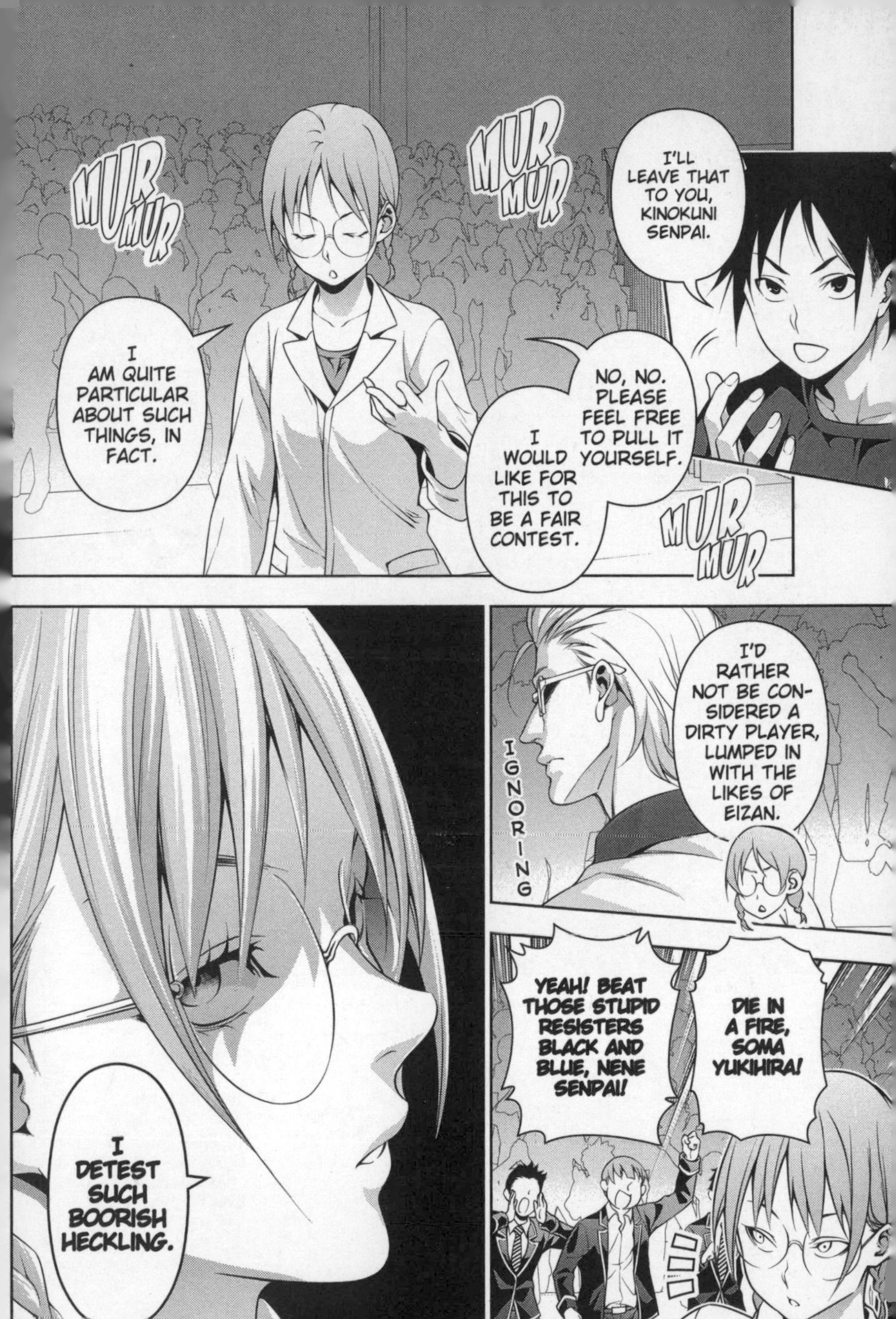
I'LL LEAVE THAT TO YOU, KINOKUNI SENPAI.
MUR MUR
MUR MUR
NO, NO. PLEASE FEEL FREE TO PULL IT YOURSELF.
I WOULD LIKE FOR THIS TO BE A FAIR CONTEST.
I AM QUITE PARTICULAR ABOUT SUCH THINGS, IN FACT.
MUR MUR
I'D RATHER NOT BE CONSIDERED A DIRTY PLAYER, LUMPED IN WITH THE LIKES OF EIZAN.
IGNORING
DIE IN A FIRE, SOMA YUKIHIRA!
YEAH! BEAT THOSE STUPID RESISTERS BLACK AND BLUE, NENE SENPAI!
I DETEST SUCH BOORISH HECKLING.

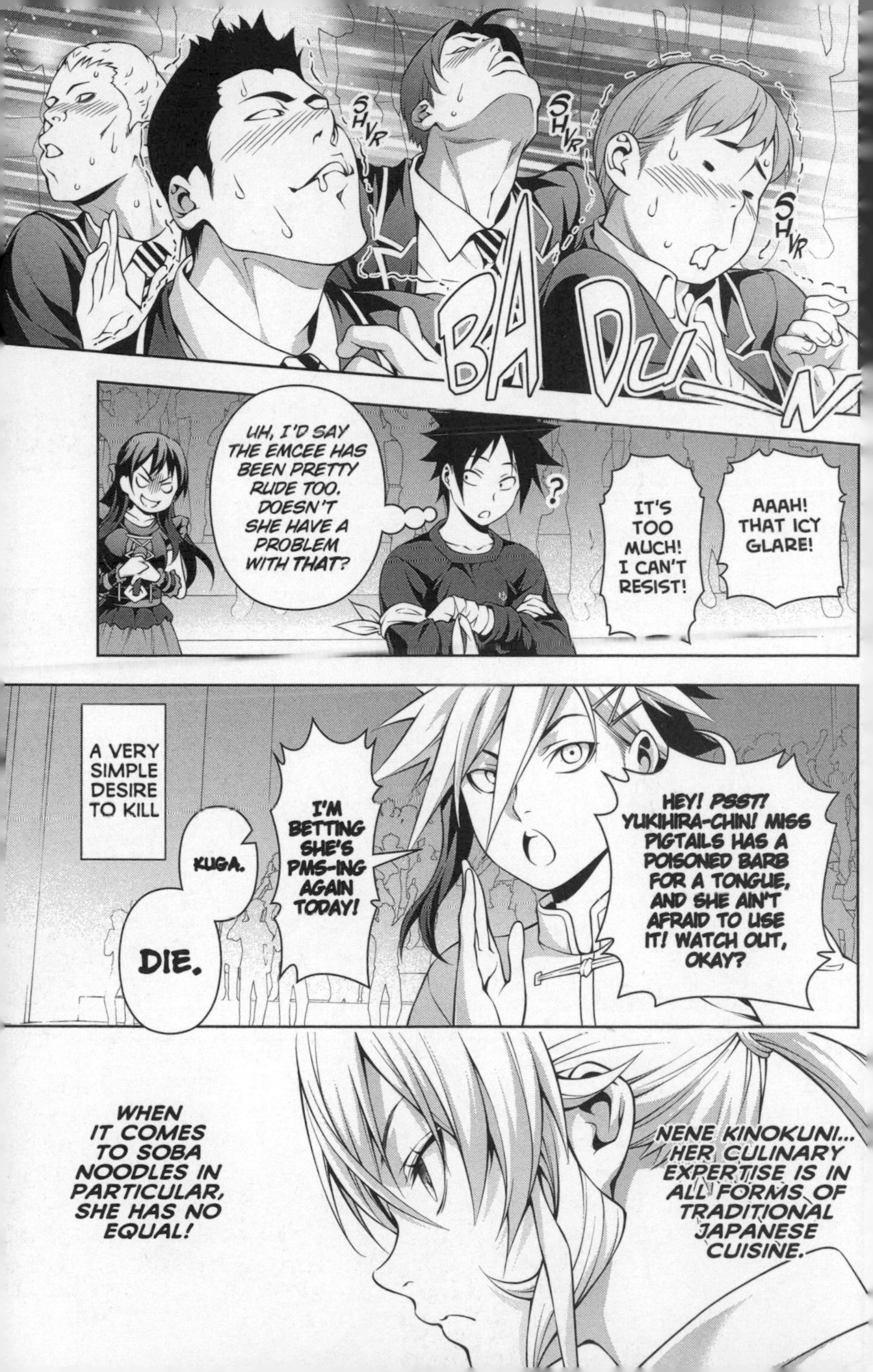
SHVR
SHVR
SHVR
BA DUN
AAAH! THAT ICY GLARE!
IT'S TOO MUCH! I CAN'T RESIST!
?
UH, I'D SAY THE EMCEE HAS BEEN PRETTY RUDE TOO. DOESN'T SHE HAVE A PROBLEM WITH THAT?
HEY! PSST! YUKIHIRA-CHIN! MISS PIGTAILS HAS A POISONED BARB FOR A TONGUE, AND SHE AIN'T AFRAID TO USE IT! WATCH OUT, OKAY?
I'M BETTING SHE'S PMS-ING AGAIN TODAY!
A VERY SIMPLE DESIRE TO KILL
KUGA.
DIE.
NENE KINOKUNI... HER CULINARY EXPERTISE IS IN ALL FORMS OF TRADITIONAL JAPANESE CUISINE.
WHEN IT COMES TO SOBA NOODLES IN PARTICULAR, SHE HAS NO EQUAL!

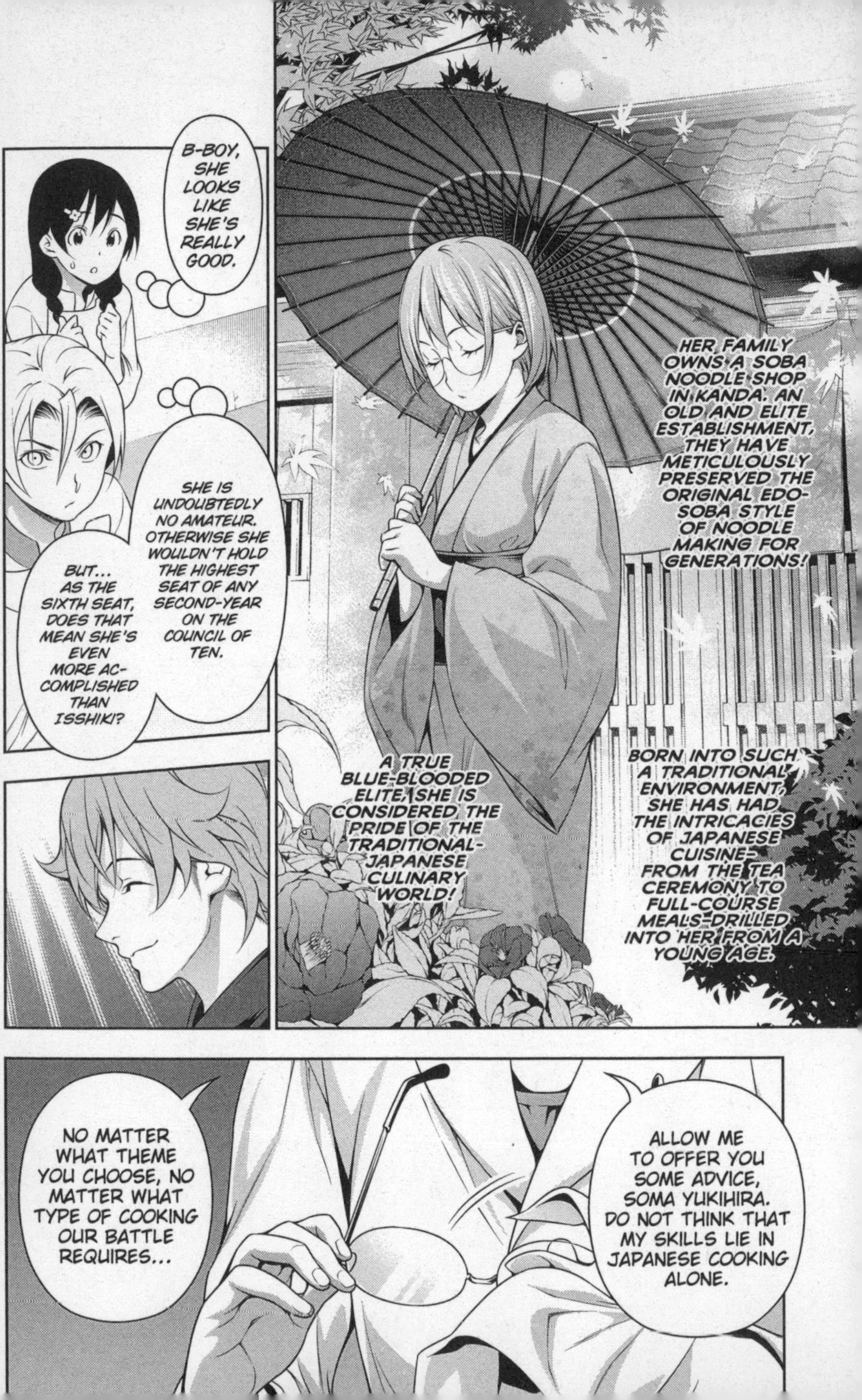
HER FAMILY OWNS A SOBA NOODLE SHOP IN KANDA. AN OLD AND ELITE ESTABLISHMENT, THEY HAVE METICULOUSLY PRESERVED THE ORIGINAL EDO-SOBA STYLE OF NOODLE MAKING FOR GENERATIONS!
BORN INTO SUCH A TRADITIONAL ENVIRONMENT, SHE HAS HAD THE INTRICACIES OF JAPANESE CUISINE—FROM THE TEA CEREMONY TO FULL-COURSE MEALS—DRILLED INTO HER FROM A YOUNG AGE.
A TRUE BLUE-BLOODED ELITE, SHE IS CONSIDERED THE PRIDE OF THE TRADITIONAL-JAPANESE CULINARY WORLD!
B-BOY, SHE LOOKS LIKE SHE'S REALLY GOOD.
SHE IS UNDOUBTEDLY NO AMATEUR. OTHERWISE SHE WOULDN'T HOLD THE HIGHEST SEAT OF ANY SECOND-YEAR ON THE COUNCIL OF TEN.
BUT... AS THE SIXTH SEAT, DOES THAT MEAN SHE'S EVEN MORE AC-COMPLISHED THAN ISSHIKI?
ALLOW ME TO OFFER YOU SOME ADVICE, SOMA YUKIHIRA. DO NOT THINK THAT MY SKILLS LIE IN JAPANESE COOKING ALONE.
NO MATTER WHAT THEME YOU CHOOSE, NO MATTER WHAT TYPE OF COOKING OUR BATTLE REQUIRES...

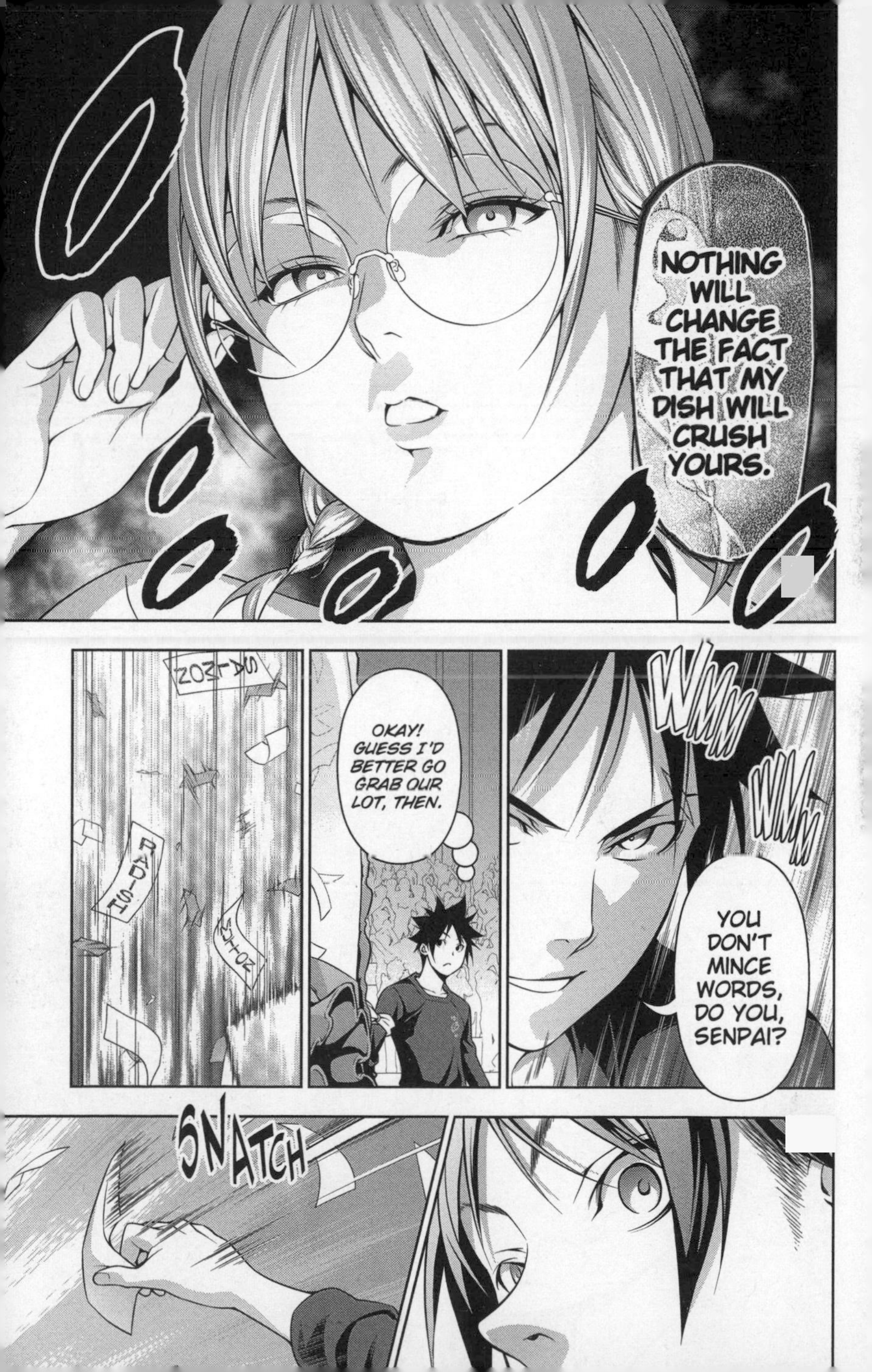
NOTHING WILL CHANGE THE FACT THAT MY DISH WILL CRUSH YOURS.
WMM
WMM
YOU DON'T MINCE WORDS, DO YOU, SENPAI?
OKAY! GUESS I'D BETTER GO GRAB OUR LOT, THEN.
SNATCH

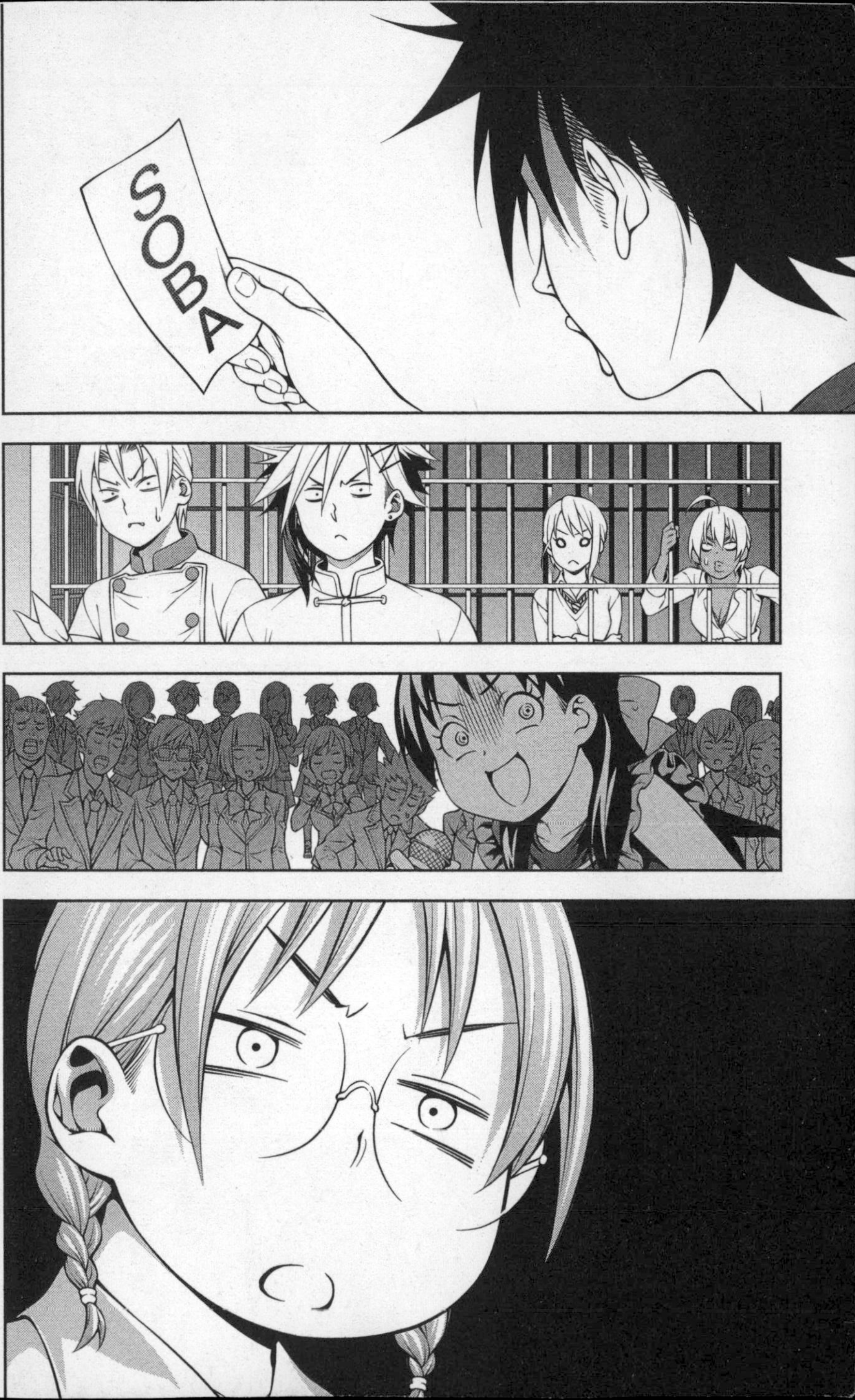
SOBA

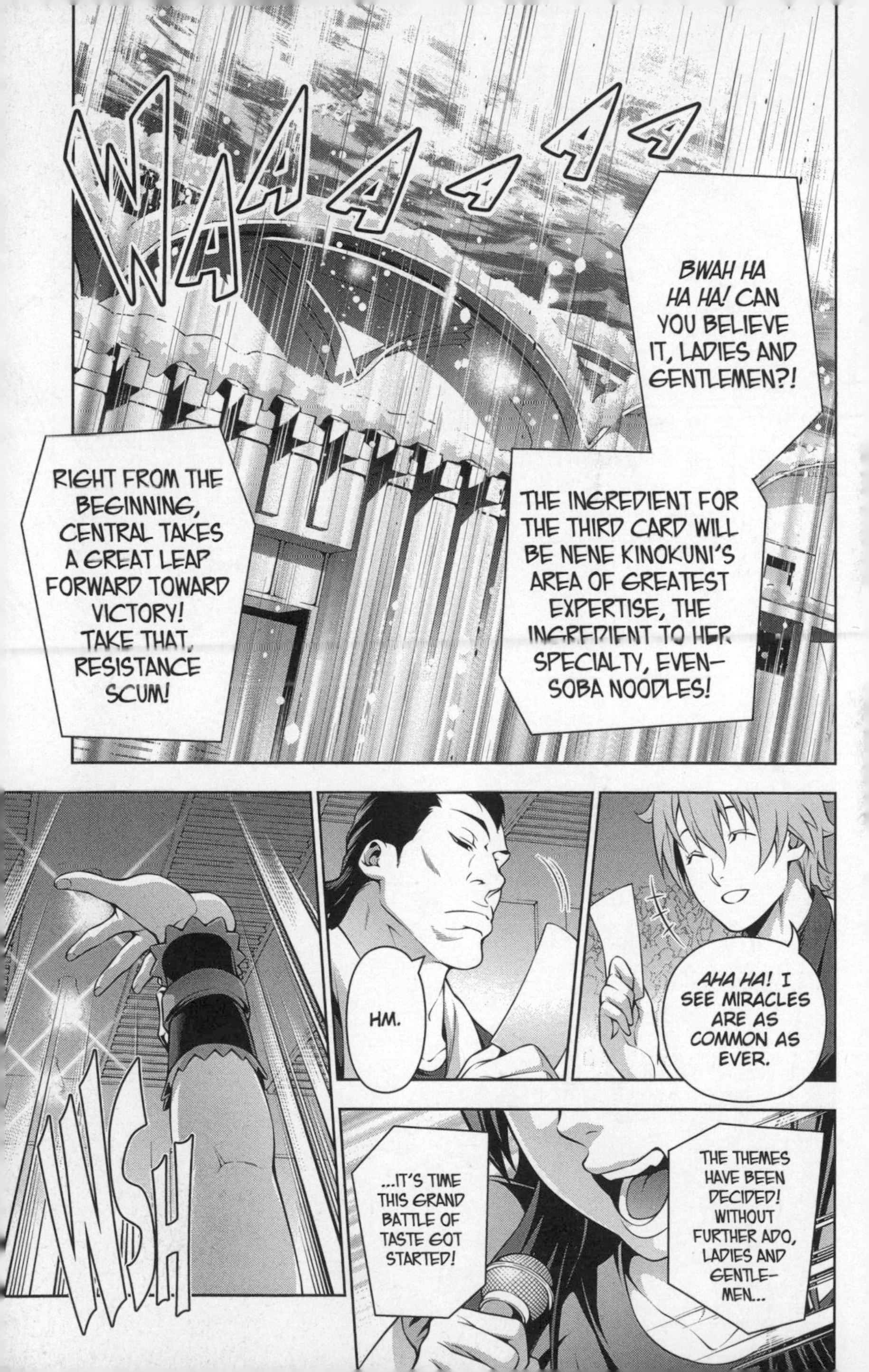
WAAAAAAAA
BWAH HA HA HA! CAN YOU BELIEVE IT, LADIES AND GENTLEMEN?!
THE INGREDIENT FOR THE THIRD CARD WILL BE NENE KINOKUNI'S AREA OF GREATEST EXPERTISE, THE INGREDIENT TO HER SPECIALTY, EVEN—SOBA NOODLES!
RIGHT FROM THE BEGINNING, CENTRAL TAKES A GREAT LEAP FORWARD TOWARD VICTORY! TAKE THAT, RESISTANCE SCUM!
AHA HA! I SEE MIRACLES ARE AS COMMON AS EVER.
HM.
THE THEMES HAVE BEEN DECIDED! WITHOUT FURTHER ADO, LADIES AND GENTLE-MEN...
...IT'S TIME THIS GRAND BATTLE OF TASTE GOT STARTED!
WSH

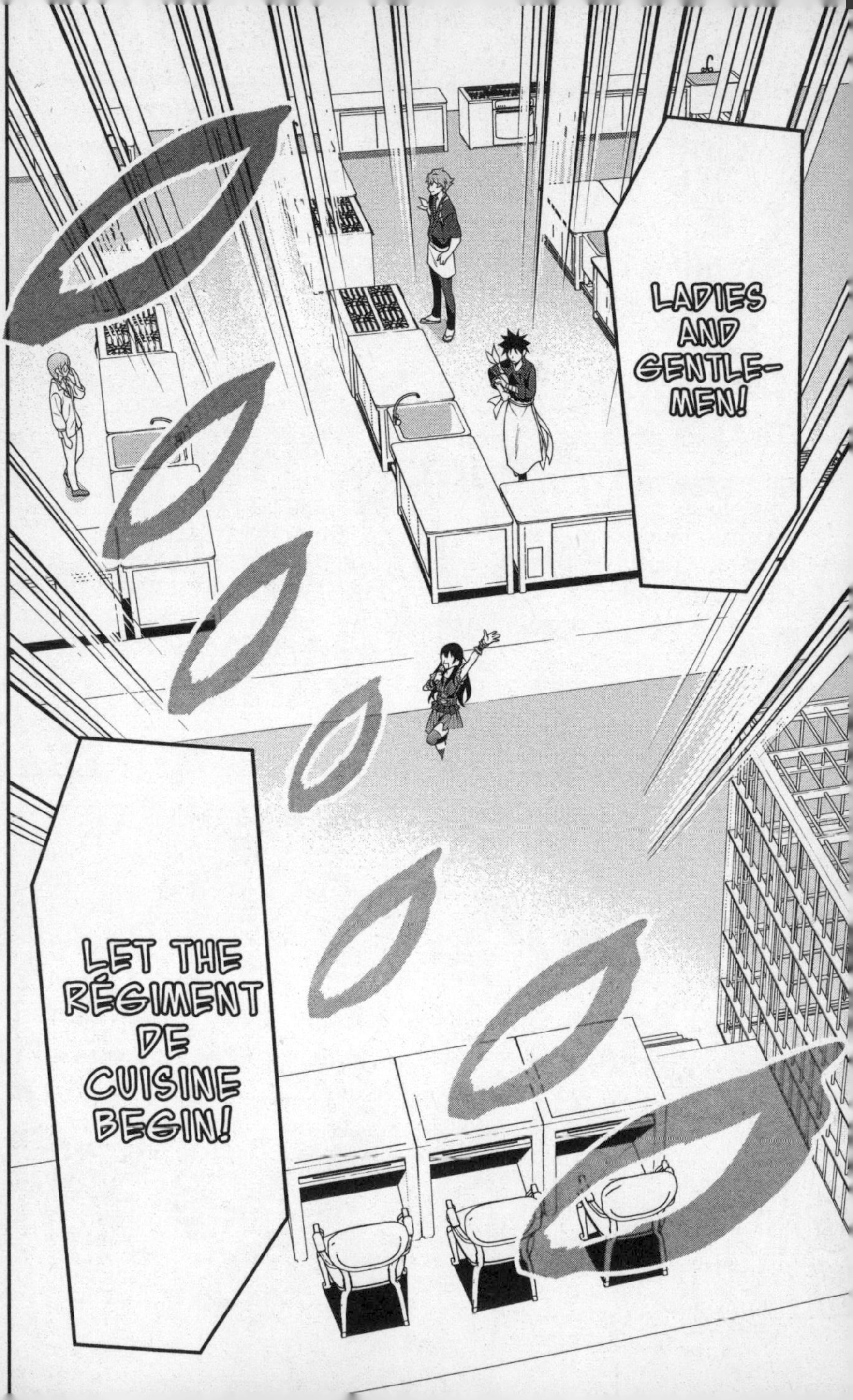
LADIES AND GENTLE-MEN!
LET THE RÉGIMENT DE CUISINE BEGIN!

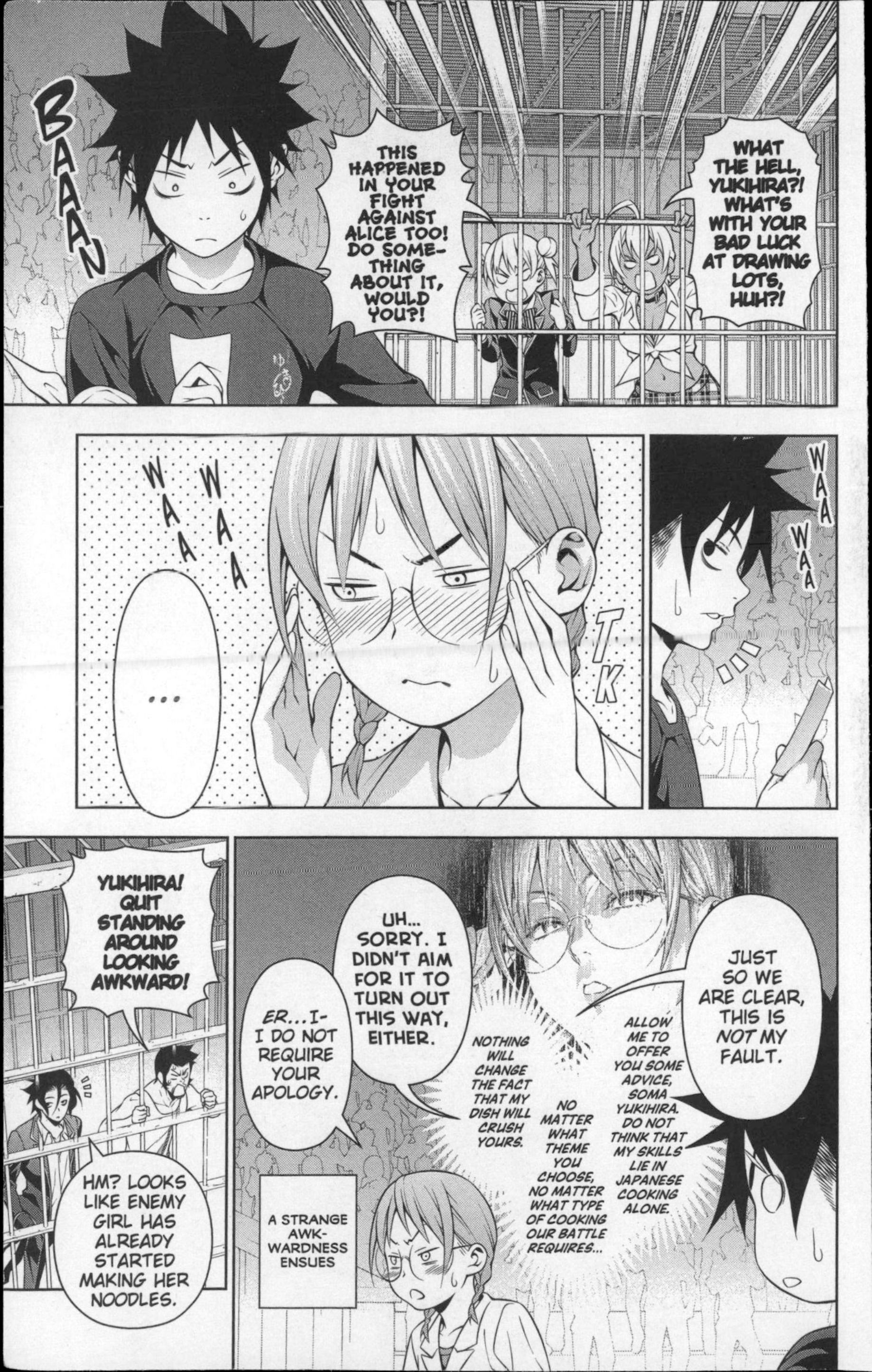
WHAT THE HELL, YUKIHIRA?! WHAT'S WITH YOUR BAD LUCK AT DRAWING LOTS, HUH?!
THIS HAPPENED IN YOUR FIGHT AGAINST ALICE TOO! DO SOME-THING ABOUT IT, WOULD YOU?!
BAAAAN
WAA WAA
...
TK
WAA WAA
...
JUST SO WE ARE CLEAR, THIS IS NOT MY FAULT.
ALLOW ME TO OFFER YOU SOME ADVICE, SOMA YUKIHIRA. DO NOT THINK THAT MY SKILLS LIE IN JAPANESE COOKING ALONE.
NO MATTER WHAT THEME YOU CHOOSE, NO MATTER WHAT TYPE OF COOKING OUR BATTLE REQUIRES...
NOTHING WILL CHANGE THE FACT THAT MY DISH WILL CRUSH YOURS.
UH... SORRY. I DIDN'T AIM FOR IT TO TURN OUT THIS WAY, EITHER.
ER... I- I DO NOT REQUIRE YOUR APOLOGY.
A STRANGE AWK-WARDNESS ENSUES
YUKIHIRA! QUIT STANDING AROUND LOOKING AWKWARD!
HM? LOOKS LIKE ENEMY GIRL HAS ALREADY STARTED MAKING HER NOODLES.

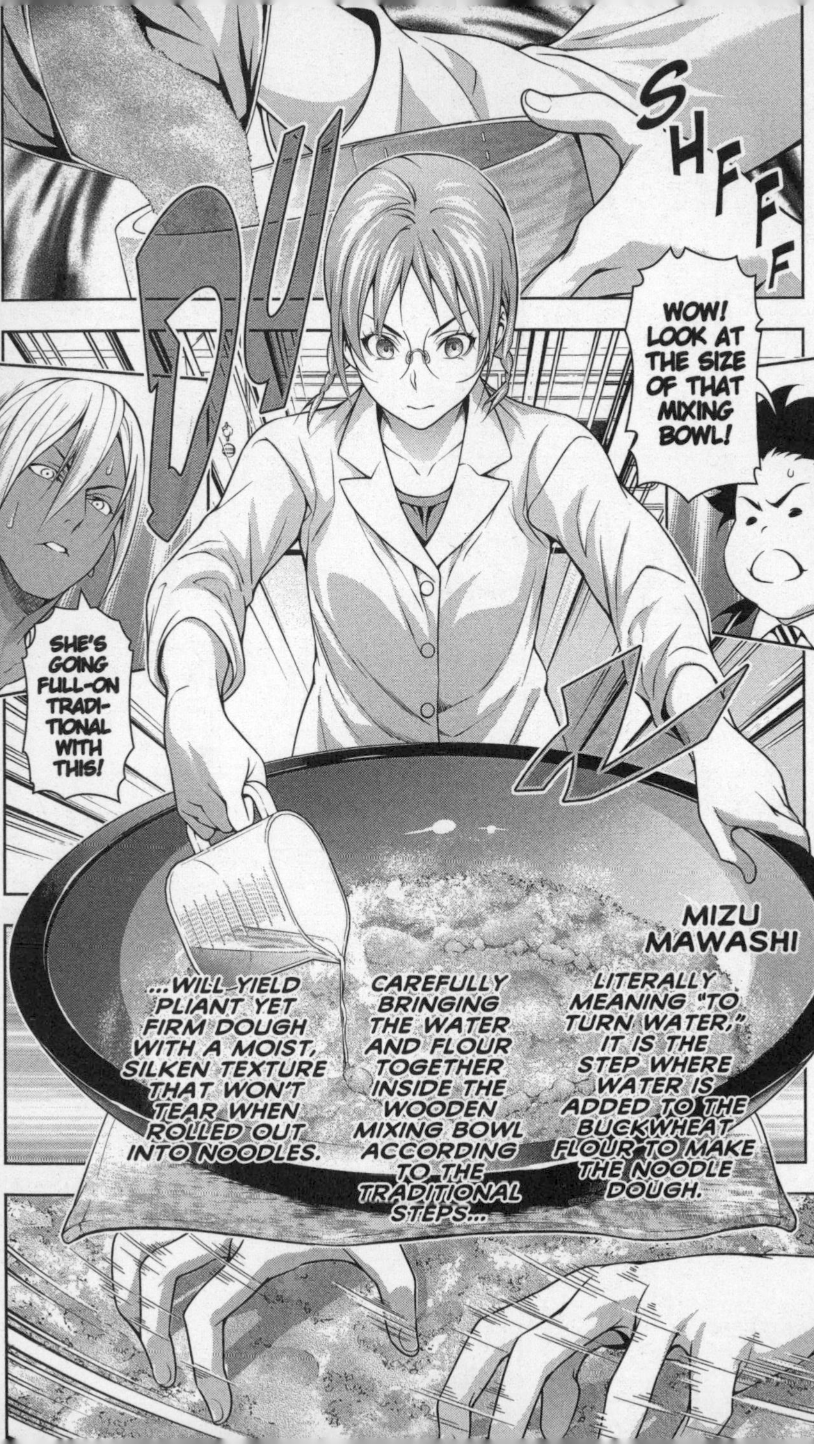
SHFFF
WOW! LOOK AT THE SIZE OF THAT MIXING BOWL!
SHE'S GOING FULL-ON TRADITIONAL WITH THIS!
MIZU MAWASHI
LITERALLY MEANING "TO TURN WATER," IT IS THE STEP WHERE WATER IS ADDED TO THE BUCKWHEAT FLOUR TO MAKE THE NOODLE DOUGH.
CAREFULLY BRINGING THE WATER AND FLOUR TOGETHER INSIDE THE WOODEN MIXING BOWL ACCORDING TO THE TRADITIONAL STEPS...
...WILL YIELD PLIANT YET FIRM DOUGH WITH A MOIST, SILKEN TEXTURE THAT WON'T TEAR WHEN ROLLED OUT INTO NOODLES.

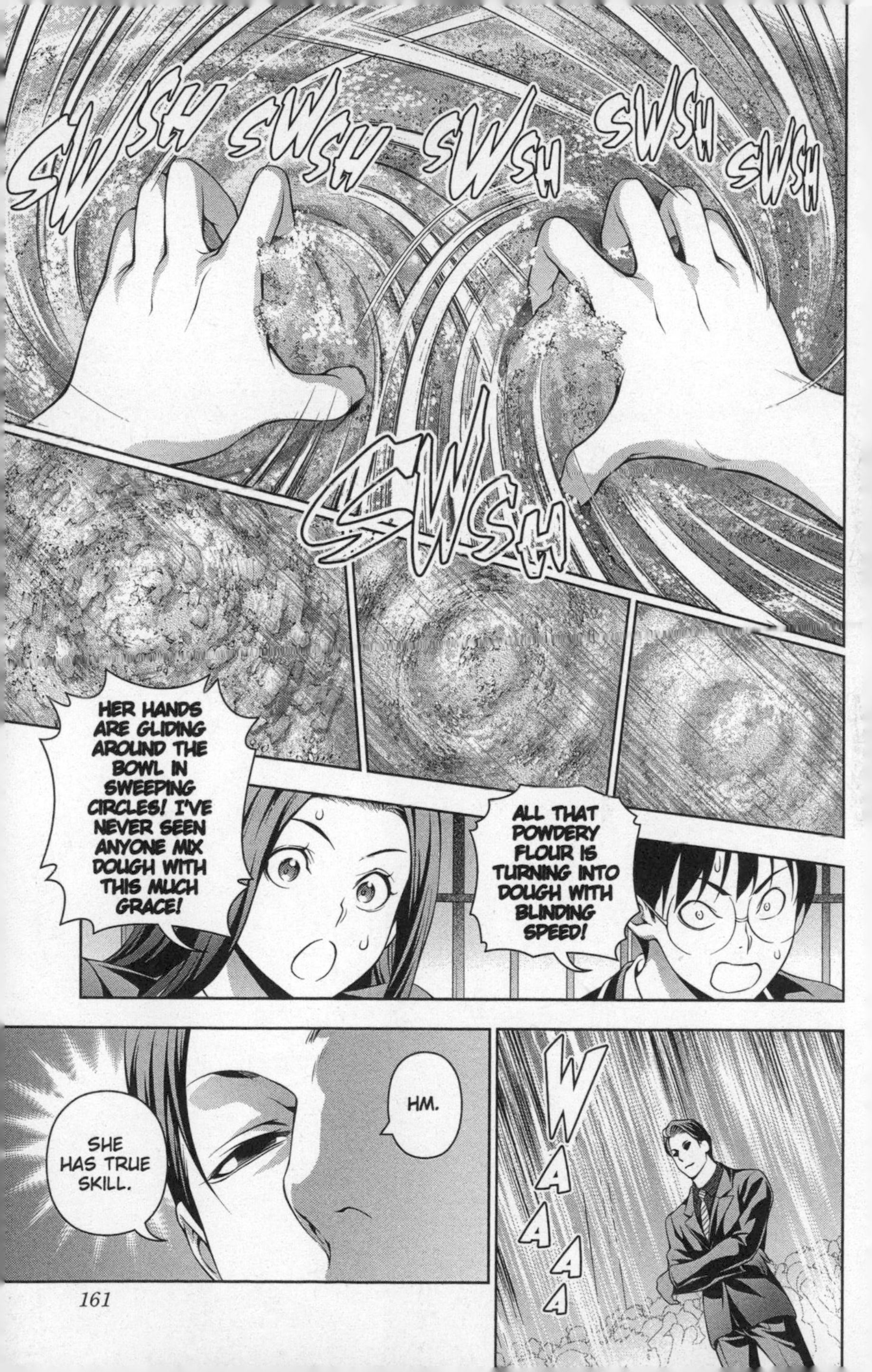
SWSH SWSH SWSH SWSH SWSH
SWSH
ALL THAT POWDERY FLOUR IS TURNING INTO DOUGH WITH BLINDING SPEED!
HER HANDS ARE GLIDING AROUND THE BOWL IN SWEEPING CIRCLES! I'VE NEVER SEEN ANYONE MIX DOUGH WITH THIS MUCH GRACE!
WWAAAAA
HM.
SHE HAS TRUE SKILL.

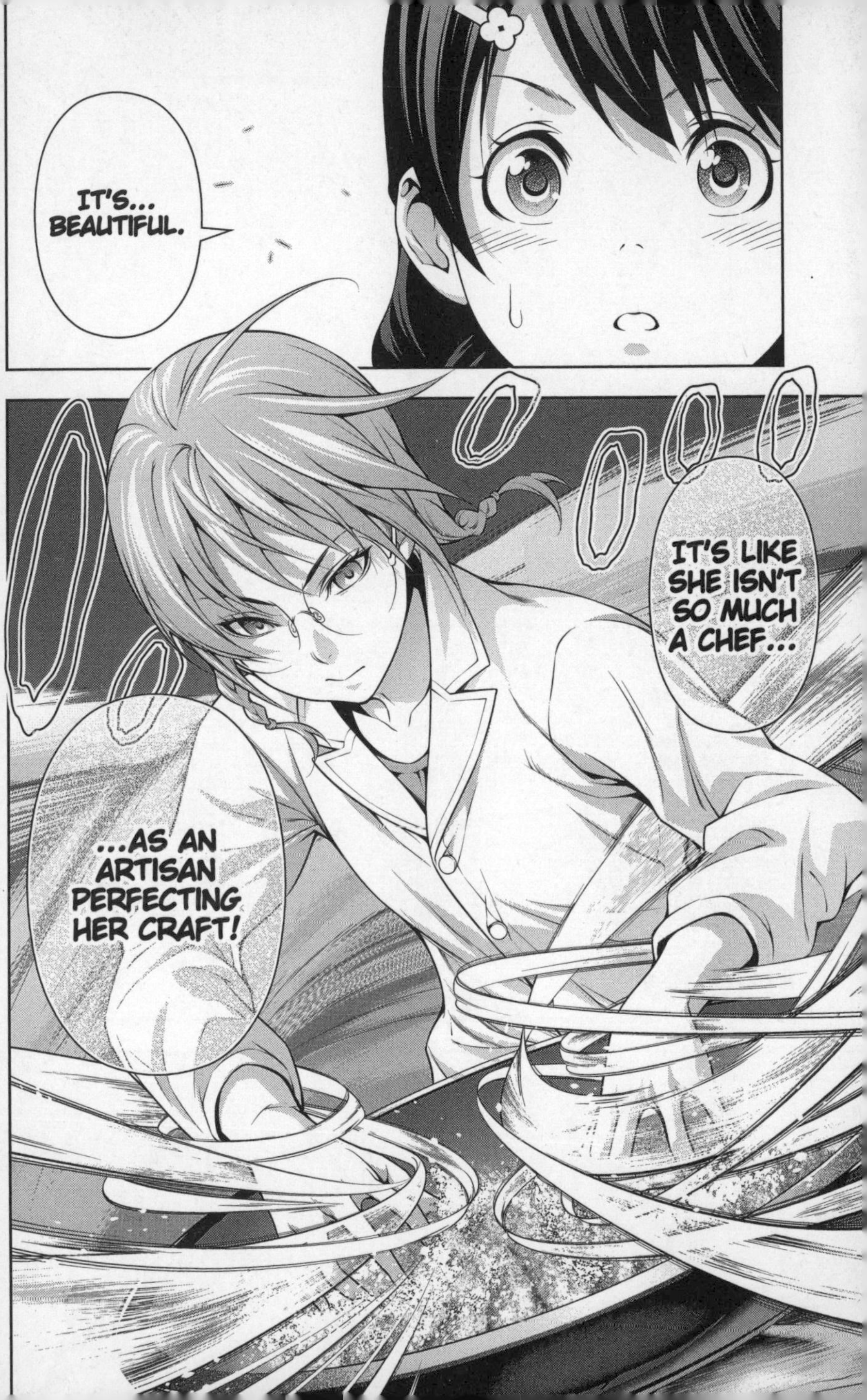
IT'S... BEAUTIFUL.
IT'S LIKE SHE ISN'T SO MUCH A CHEF...
...AS AN ARTISAN PERFECTING HER CRAFT!

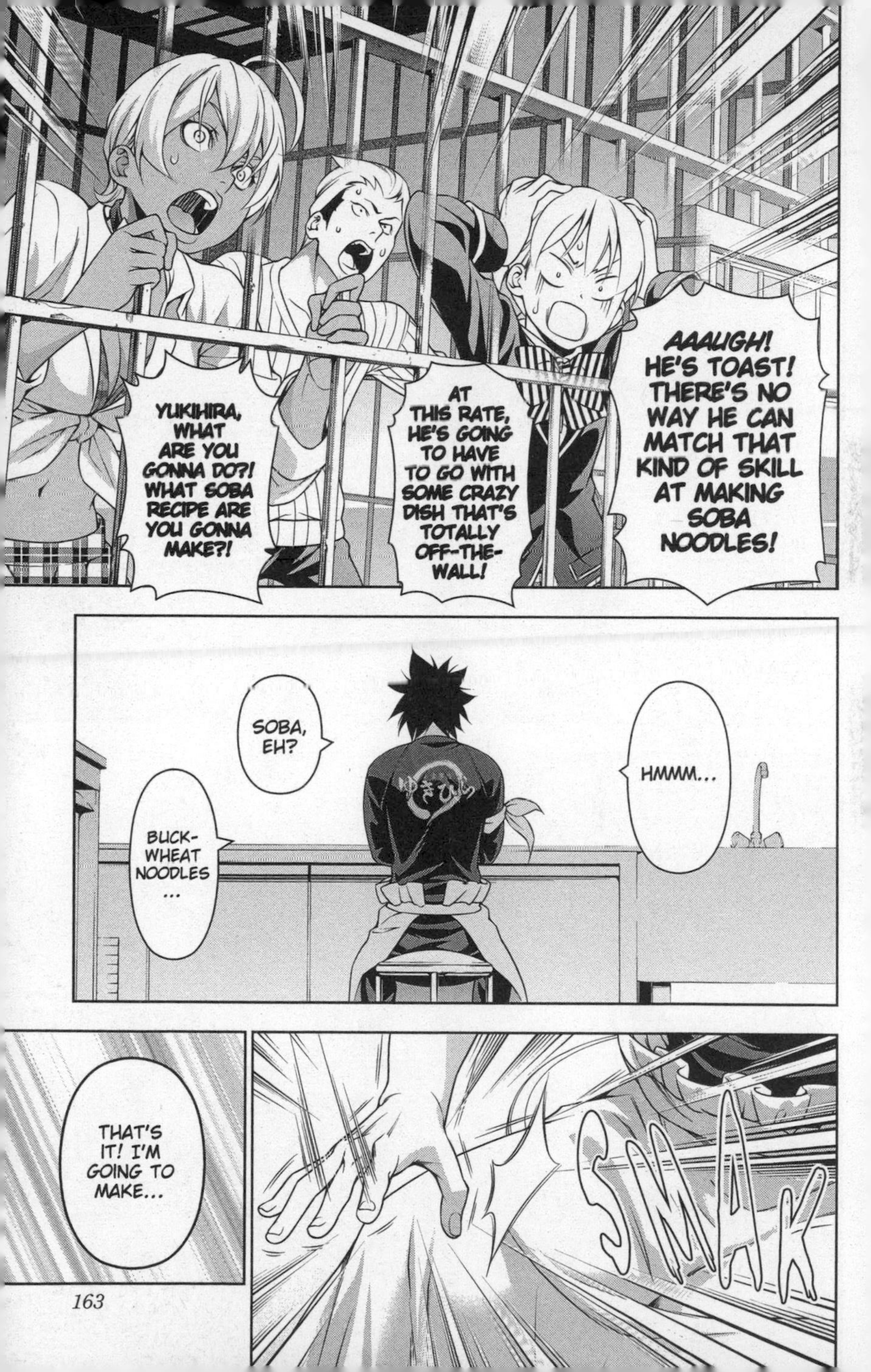
AAAUGH! HE'S TOAST! THERE'S NO WAY HE CAN MATCH THAT KIND OF SKILL AT MAKING SOBA NOODLES!
AT THIS RATE, HE'S GOING TO HAVE TO GO WITH SOME CRAZY DISH THAT'S TOTALLY OFF-THE-WALL!
YUKIHIRA, WHAT ARE YOU GONNA DO?! WHAT SOBA RECIPE ARE YOU GONNA MAKE?!
HMMM...
SOBA, EH?
BUCK-WHEAT NOODLES...
SMAK
THAT'S IT! I'M GOING TO MAKE...

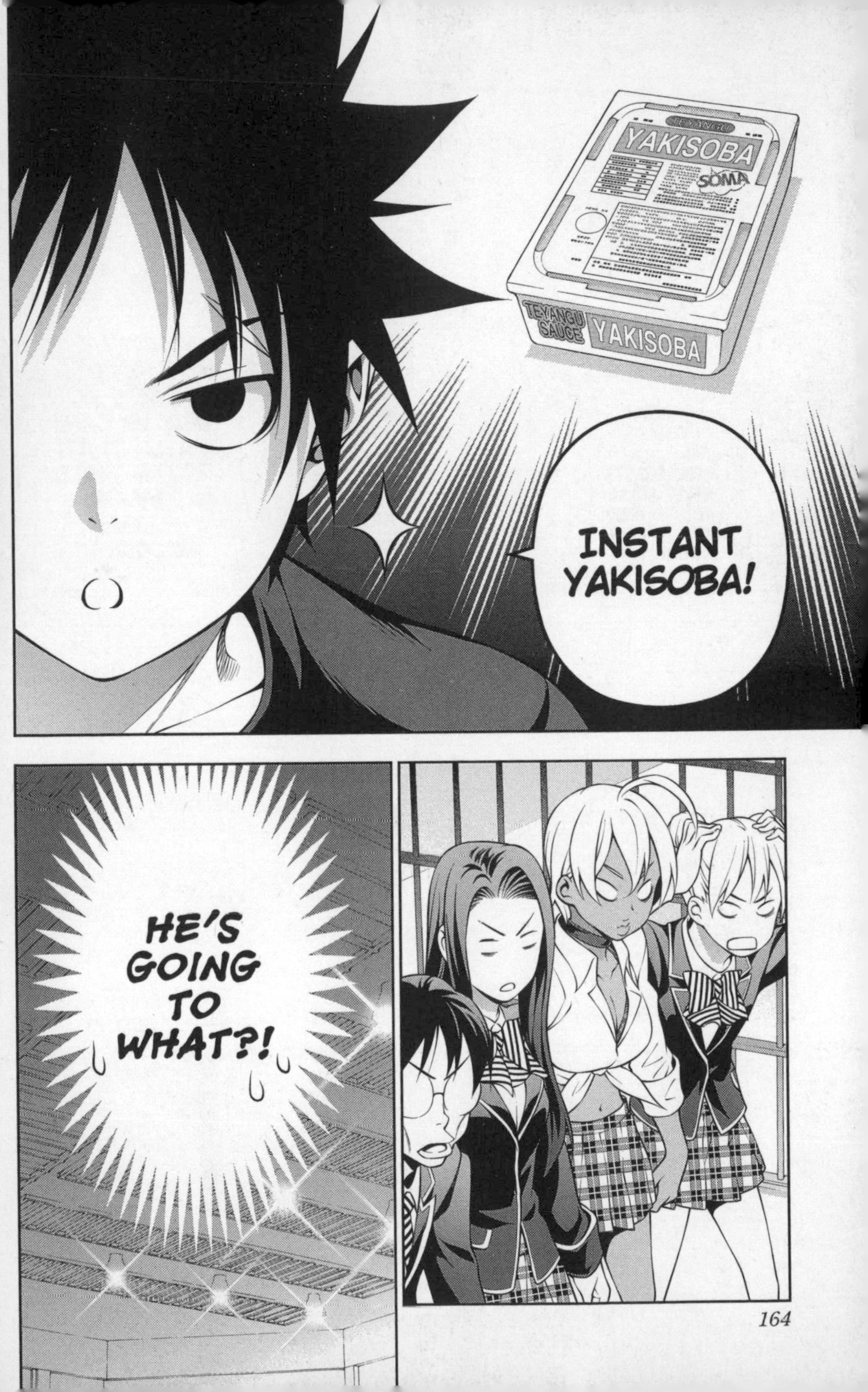
TEYANGU
YAKISOBA
SOMA
TEYANGU SAUCE
YAKISOBA
INSTANT YAKISOBA!
HE'S GOING TO WHAT?!

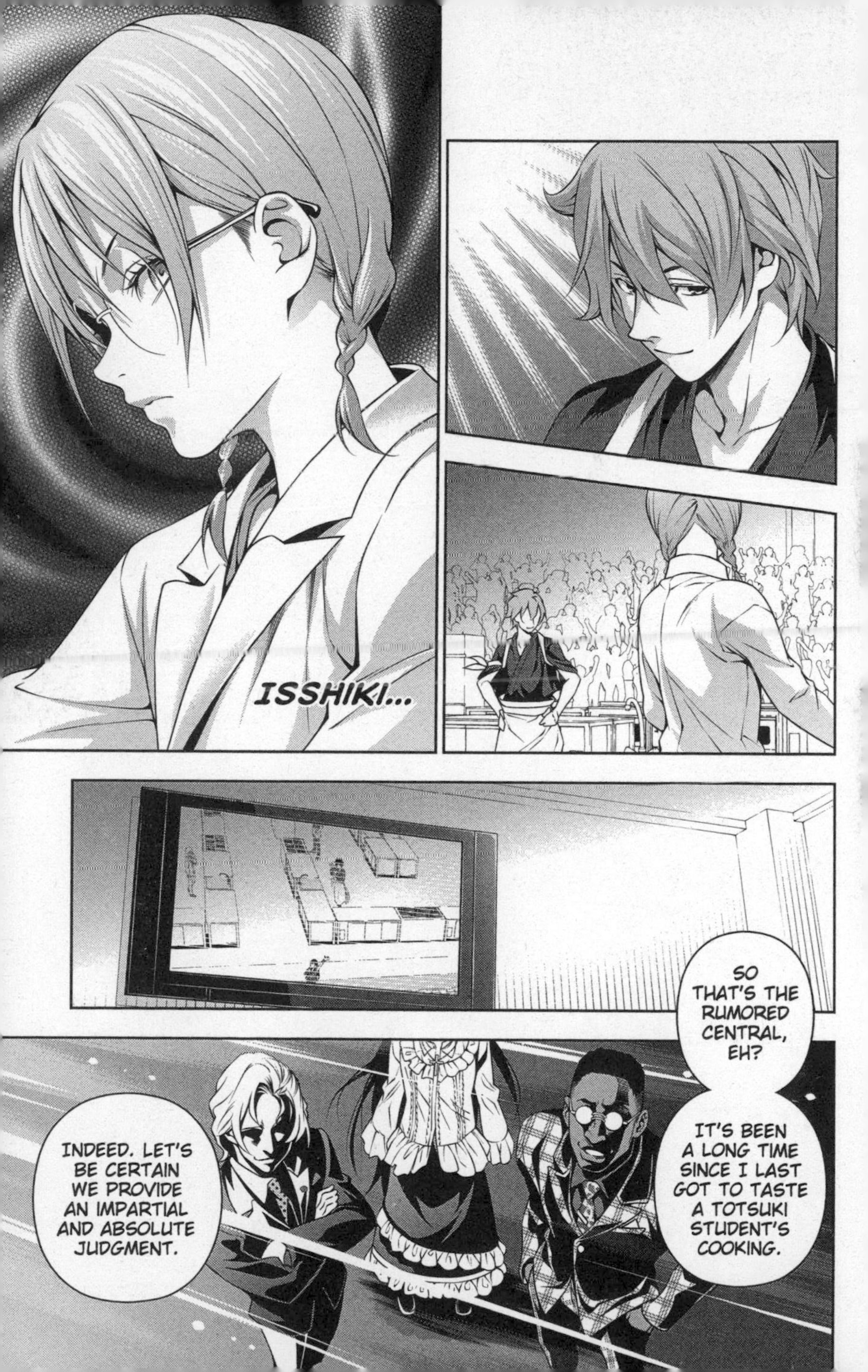
ISSHIKI...
SO THAT'S THE RUMORED CENTRAL, EH?
IT'S BEEN A LONG TIME SINCE I LAST GOT TO TASTE A TOTSUKI STUDENT'S COOKING.
INDEED. LET'S BE CERTAIN WE PROVIDE AN IMPARTIAL AND ABSOLUTE JUDGMENT.

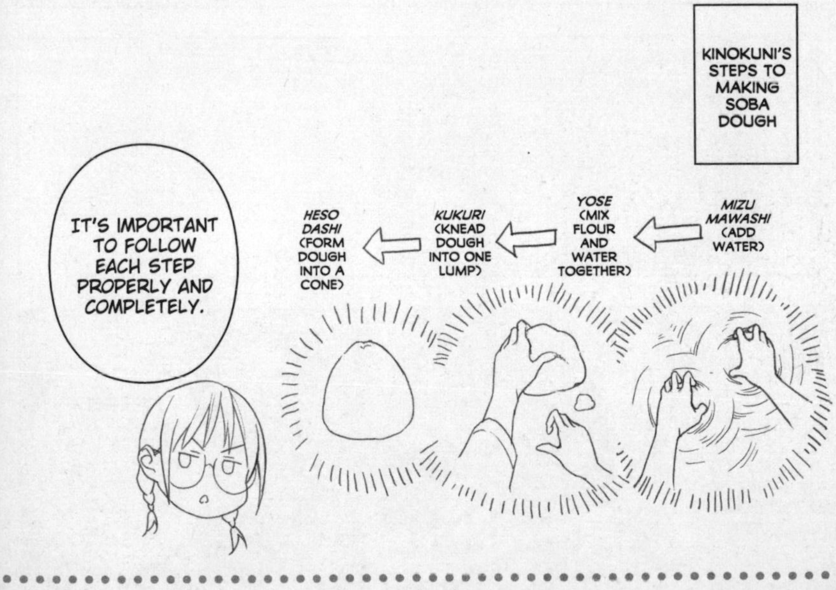
KINOKUNI'S STEPS TO MAKING SOBA DOUGH
MIZU MAWASHI (ADD WATER)
YOSE (MIX FLOUR AND WATER TOGETHER)
KUKURI (KNEAD DOUGH INTO ONE LUMP)
HESO DASHI (FORM DOUGH INTO A CONE)
IT'S IMPORTANT TO FOLLOW EACH STEP PROPERLY AND COMPLETELY.

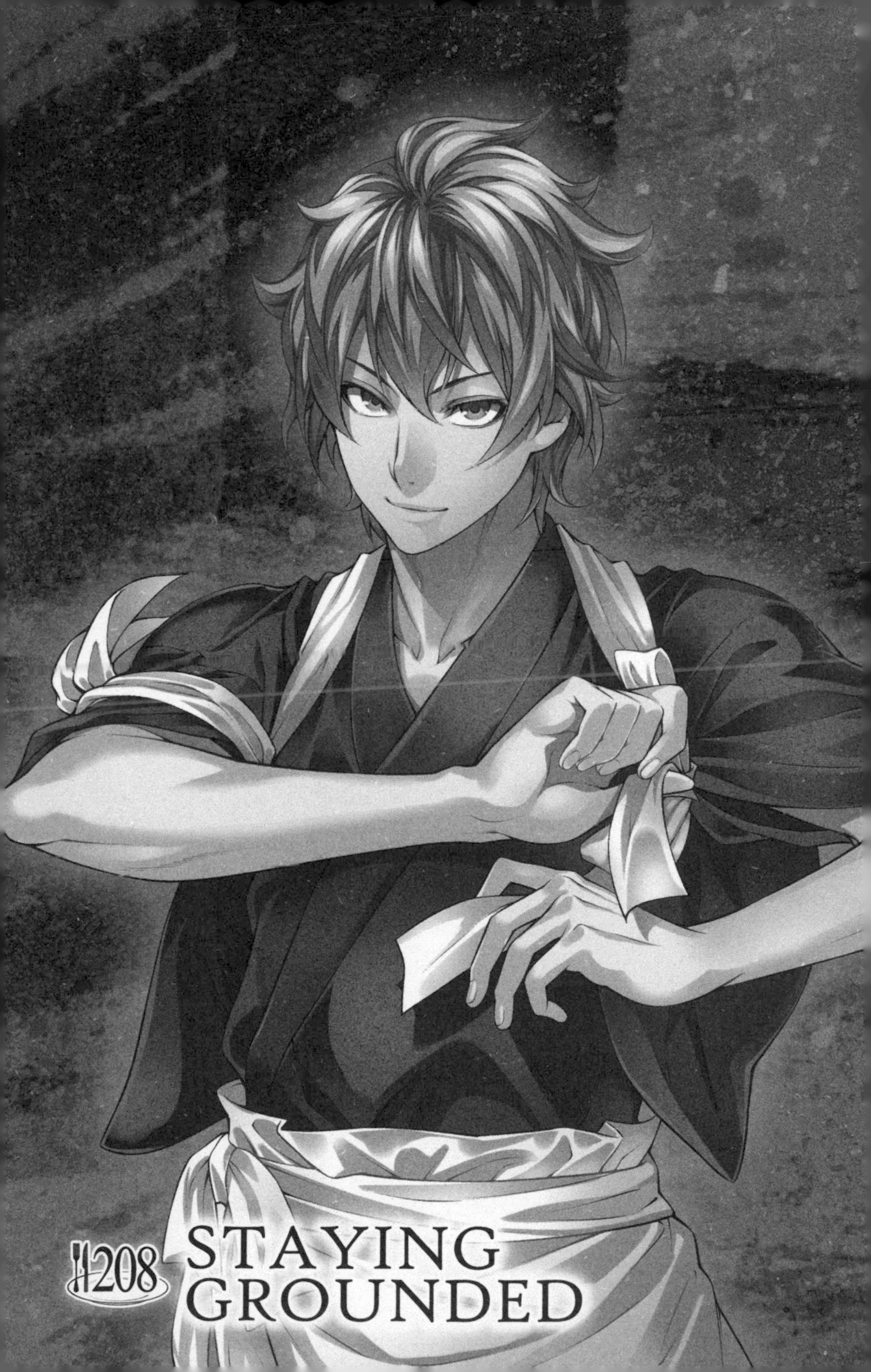
208
STAYING
GROUNDED

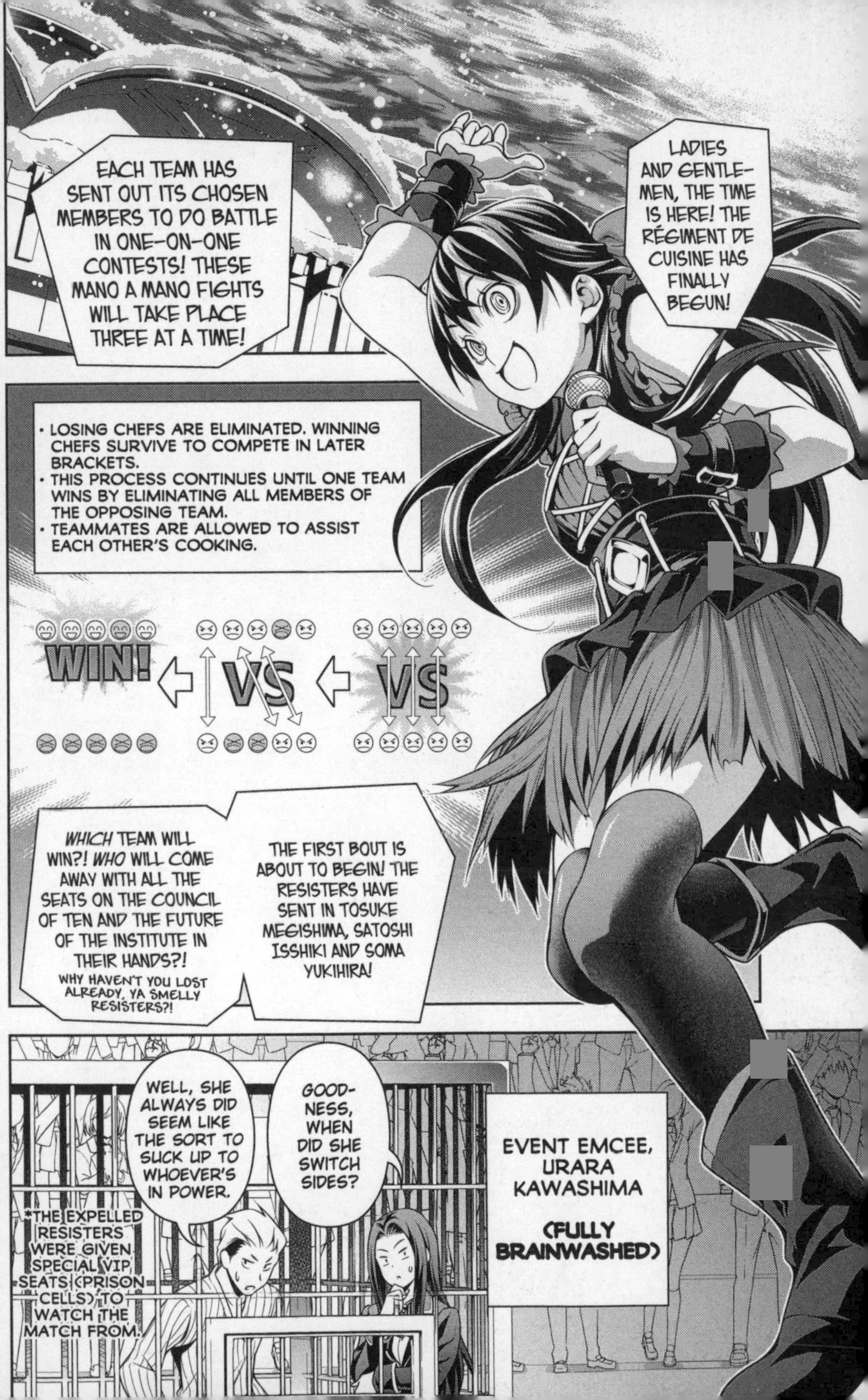
LADIES AND GENTLE-MEN, THE TIME IS HERE! THE RÉGIMENT DE CUISINE HAS FINALLY BEGUN!
EACH TEAM HAS SENT OUT ITS CHOSEN MEMBERS TO DO BATTLE IN ONE-ON-ONE CONTESTS! THESE MANO A MANO FIGHTS WILL TAKE PLACE THREE AT A TIME!
• LOSING CHEFS ARE ELIMINATED. WINNING CHEFS SURVIVE TO COMPETE IN LATER BRACKETS.
• THIS PROCESS CONTINUES UNTIL ONE TEAM WINS BY ELIMINATING ALL MEMBERS OF THE OPPOSING TEAM.
• TEAMMATES ARE ALLOWED TO ASSIST EACH OTHER'S COOKING.
VS
VS
WIN!
THE FIRST BOUT IS ABOUT TO BEGIN! THE RESISTERS HAVE SENT IN TOSUKE MEGISHIMA, SATOSHI ISSHIKI AND SOMA YUKIHIRA!
WHICH TEAM WILL WIN?! *WHO* WILL COME AWAY WITH ALL THE SEATS ON THE COUNCIL OF TEN AND THE FUTURE OF THE INSTITUTE IN THEIR HANDS?!
WHY HAVEN'T YOU LOST ALREADY, YA SMELLY RESISTERS?!
EVENT EMCEE, URARA KAWASHIMA
(FULLY BRAINWASHED)
GOOD-NESS, WHEN DID SHE SWITCH SIDES?
WELL, SHE ALWAYS DID SEEM LIKE THE SORT TO SUCK UP TO WHOEVER'S IN POWER.
*THE EXPELLED RESISTERS WERE GIVEN SPECIAL VIP SEATS (PRISON CELLS) TO WATCH THE MATCH FROM.

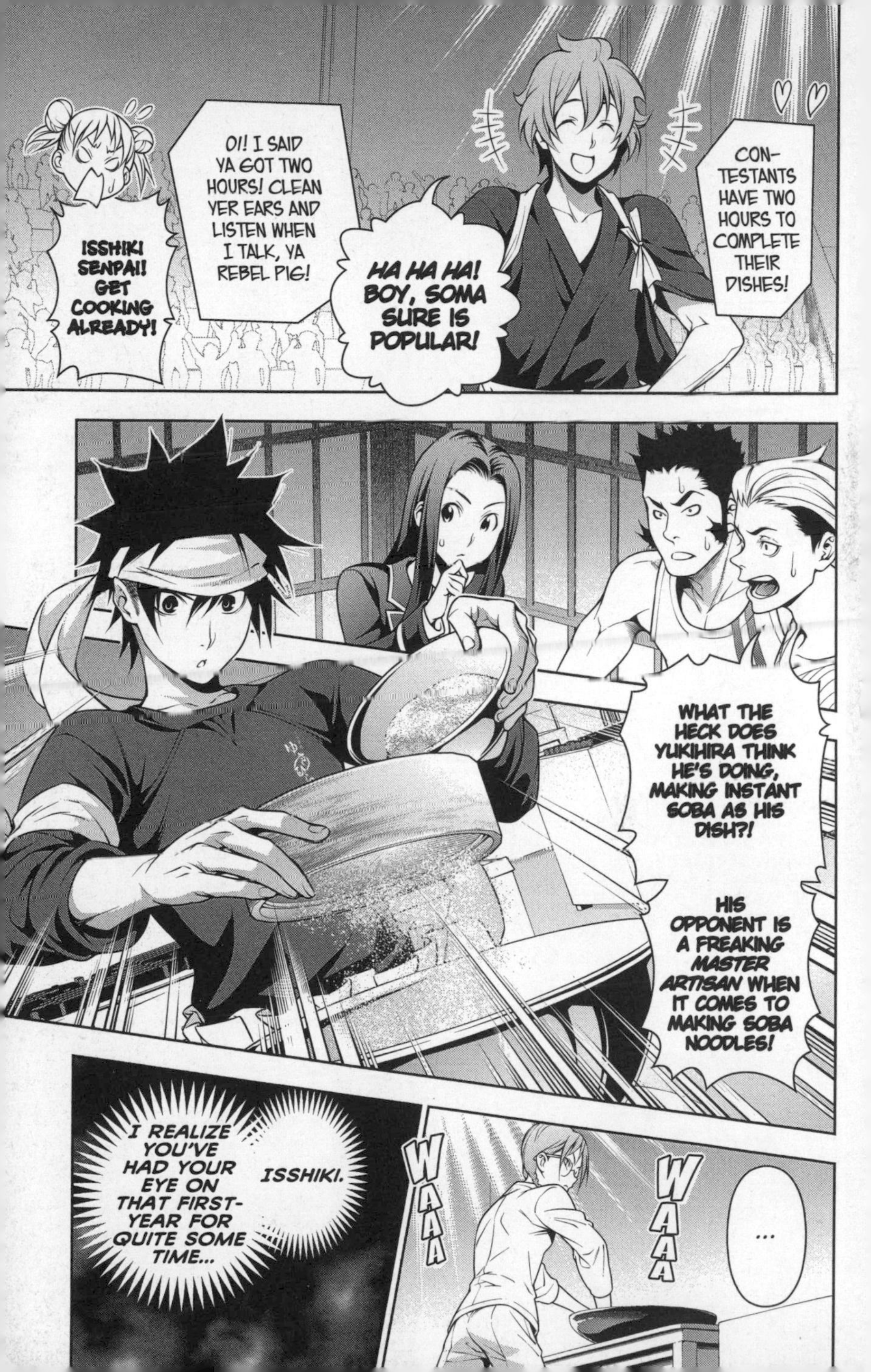
CON-TESTANTS HAVE TWO HOURS TO COMPLETE THEIR DISHES!
HA HA HA! BOY, SOMA SURE IS POPULAR!
OI! I SAID YA GOT TWO HOURS! CLEAN YER EARS AND LISTEN WHEN I TALK, YA REBEL PIG!
ISSHIKI SENPAI! GET COOKING ALREADY!
WHAT THE HECK DOES YUKIHIRA THINK HE'S DOING, MAKING INSTANT SOBA AS HIS DISH?!
HIS OPPONENT IS A FREAKING MASTER ARTISAN WHEN IT COMES TO MAKING SOBA NOODLES!
...
WAAA
WAAA
ISSHIKI.
I REALIZE YOU'VE HAD YOUR EYE ON THAT FIRST-YEAR FOR QUITE SOME TIME...

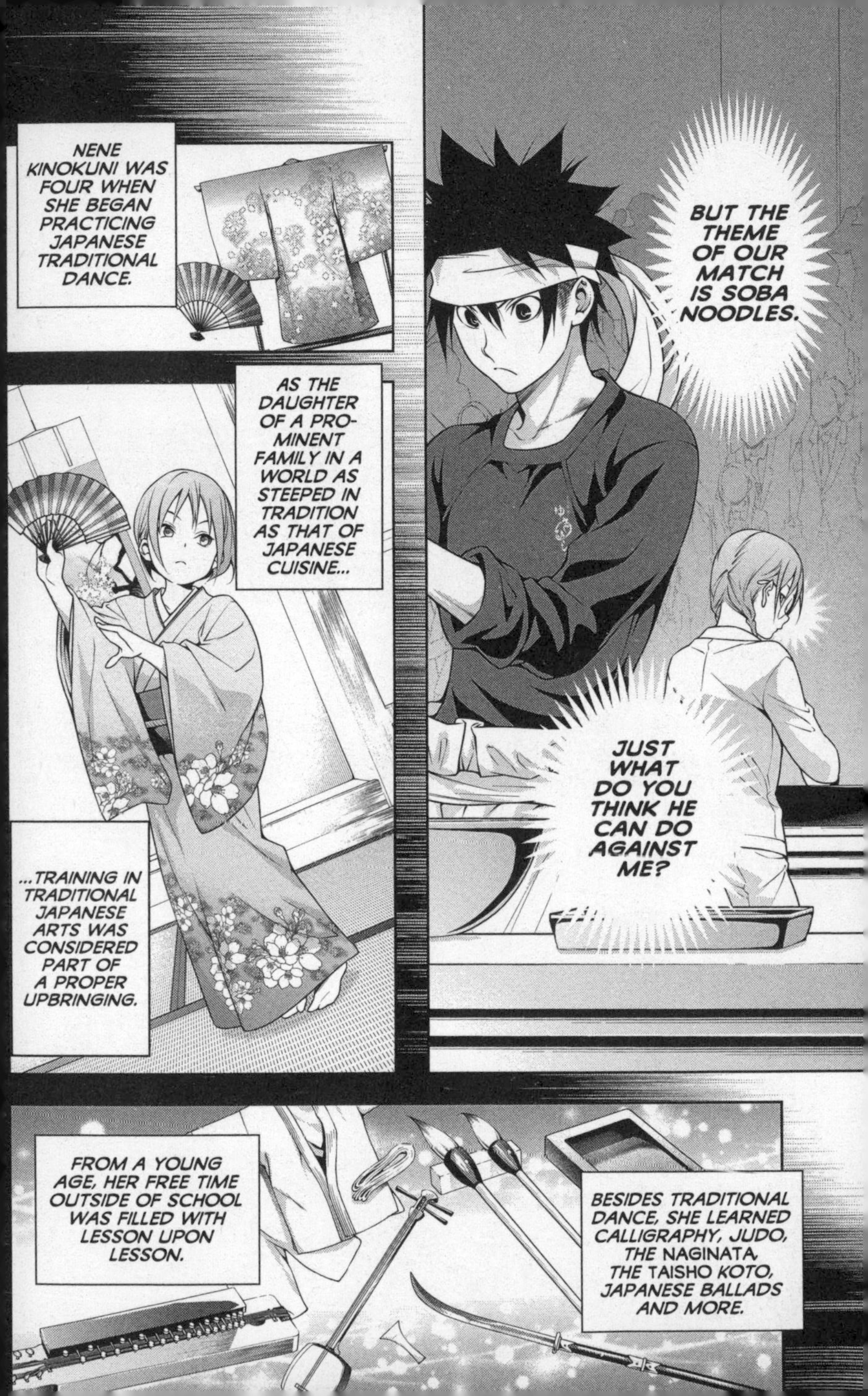
BUT THE THEME OF OUR MATCH IS SOBA NOODLES.
JUST WHAT DO YOU THINK HE CAN DO AGAINST ME?
NENE KINOKUNI WAS FOUR WHEN SHE BEGAN PRACTICING JAPANESE TRADITIONAL DANCE.
AS THE DAUGHTER OF A PRO-MINENT FAMILY IN A WORLD AS STEEPED IN TRADITION AS THAT OF JAPANESE CUISINE...
...TRAINING IN TRADITIONAL JAPANESE ARTS WAS CONSIDERED PART OF A PROPER UPBRINGING.
FROM A YOUNG AGE, HER FREE TIME OUTSIDE OF SCHOOL WAS FILLED WITH LESSON UPON LESSON.
BESIDES TRADITIONAL DANCE, SHE LEARNED CALLIGRAPHY, JUDO, THE NAGINATA, THE TAISHO KOTO, JAPANESE BALLADS AND MORE.

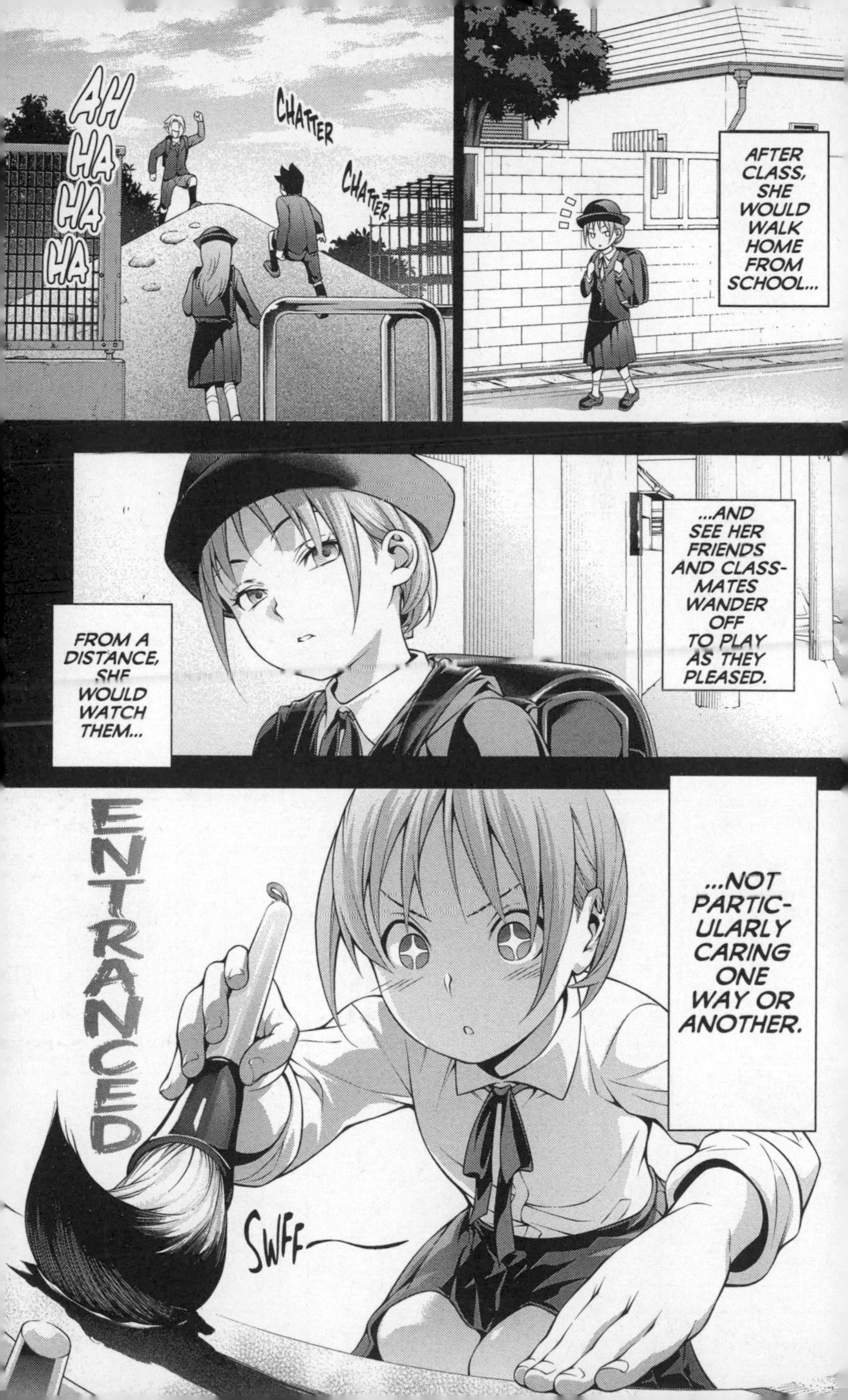
AFTER CLASS, SHE WOULD WALK HOME FROM SCHOOL...
AH HA HA HA HA
CHATTER
CHATTER
...AND SEE HER FRIENDS AND CLASSMATES WANDER OFF TO PLAY AS THEY PLEASED.
FROM A DISTANCE, SHE WOULD WATCH THEM...
...NOT PARTICULARLY CARING ONE WAY OR ANOTHER.
ENTRANCED
SWFF

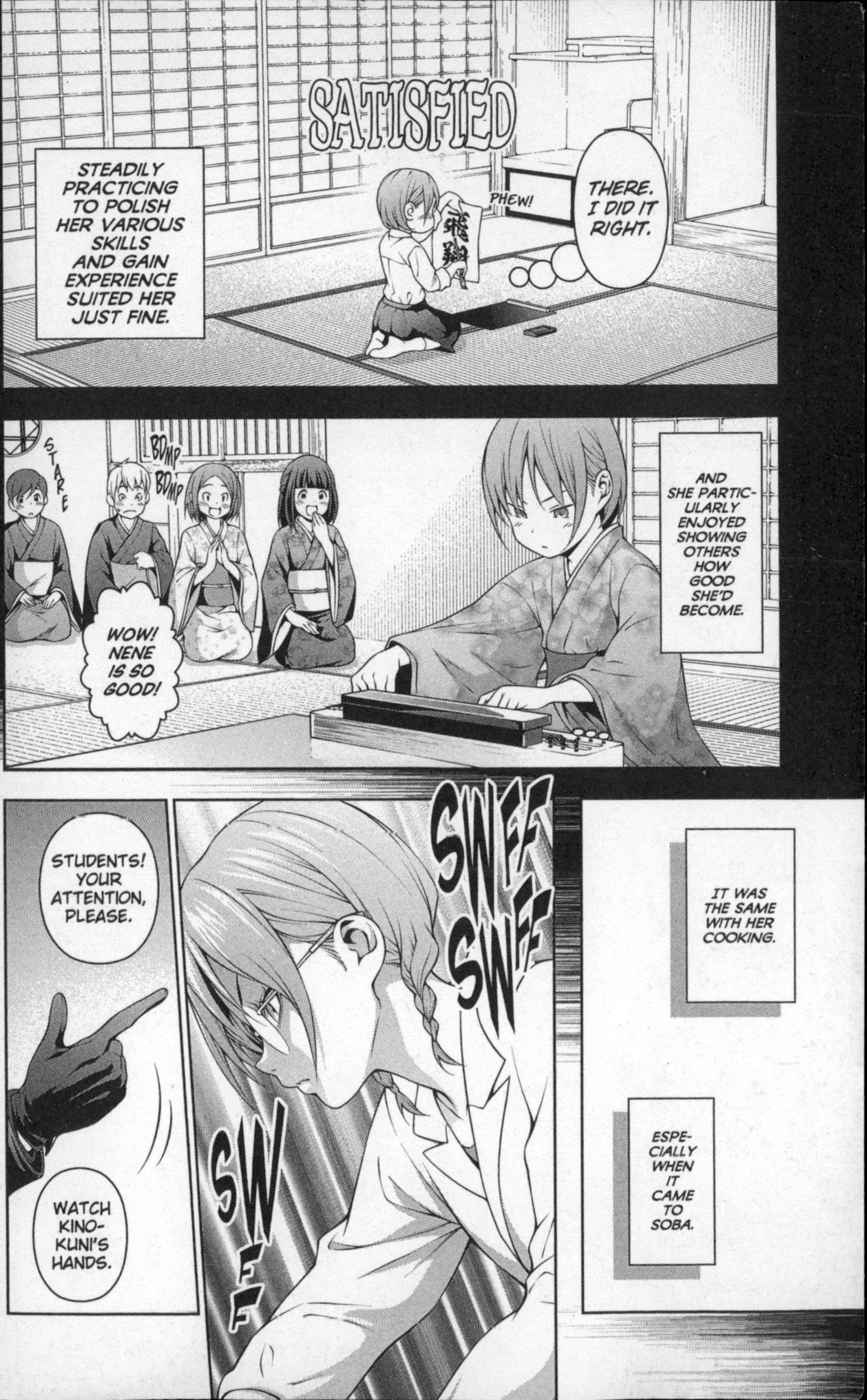
SATISFIED
THERE. I DID IT RIGHT.
PHEW!
STEADILY PRACTICING TO POLISH HER VARIOUS SKILLS AND GAIN EXPERIENCE SUITED HER JUST FINE.
AND SHE PARTICULARLY ENJOYED SHOWING OTHERS HOW GOOD SHE'D BECOME.
BDMP BDMP
STARE
WOW! NENE IS SO GOOD!
IT WAS THE SAME WITH HER COOKING.
ESPECIALLY WHEN IT CAME TO SOBA.
SWFF SWFF
SWFF
STUDENTS! YOUR ATTENTION, PLEASE.
WATCH KINOKUNI'S HANDS.

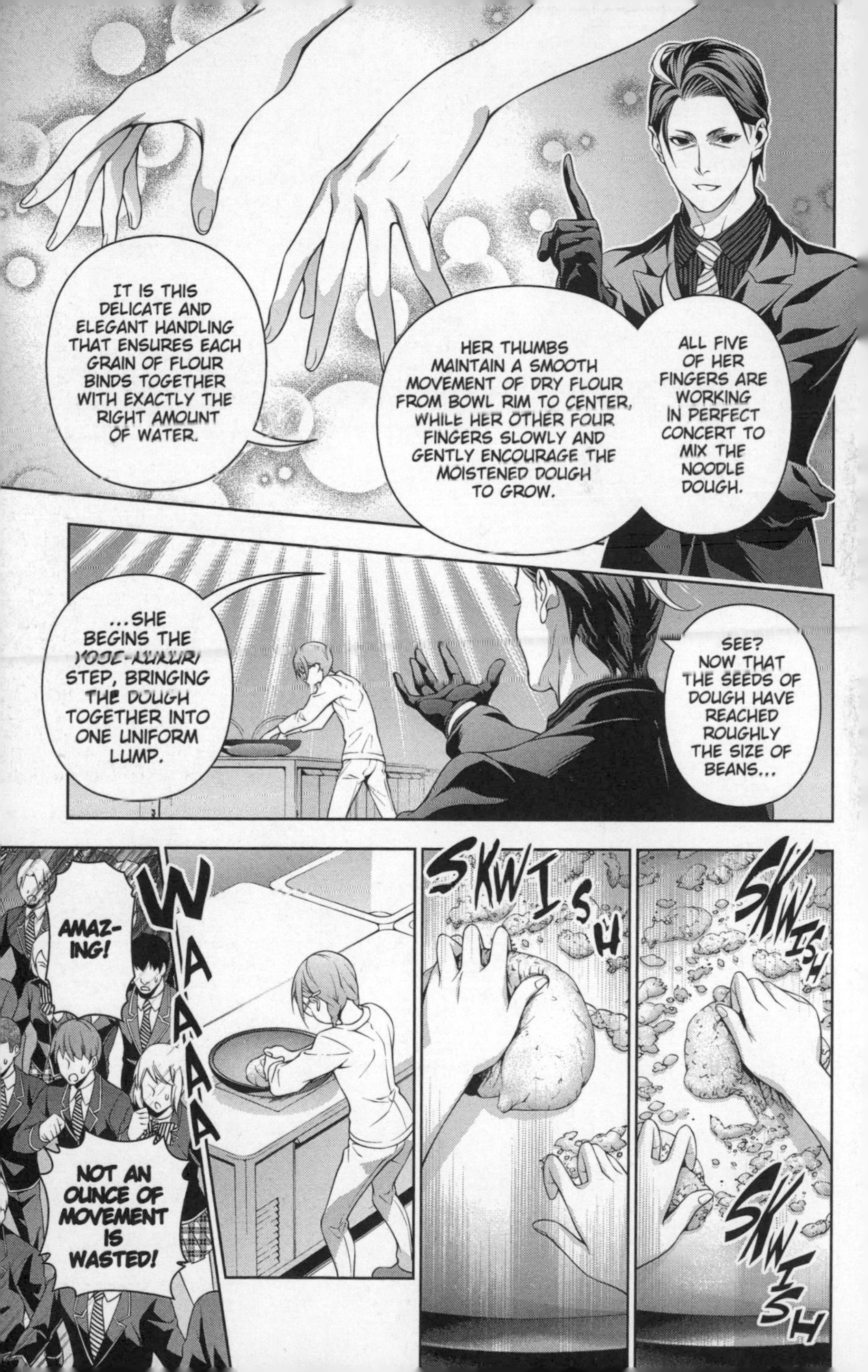
ALL FIVE OF HER FINGERS ARE WORKING IN PERFECT CONCERT TO MIX THE NOODLE DOUGH.
HER THUMBS MAINTAIN A SMOOTH MOVEMENT OF DRY FLOUR FROM BOWL RIM TO CENTER, WHILE HER OTHER FOUR FINGERS SLOWLY AND GENTLY ENCOURAGE THE MOISTENED DOUGH TO GROW.
IT IS THIS DELICATE AND ELEGANT HANDLING THAT ENSURES EACH GRAIN OF FLOUR BINDS TOGETHER WITH EXACTLY THE RIGHT AMOUNT OF WATER.
SEE? NOW THAT THE SEEDS OF DOUGH HAVE REACHED ROUGHLY THE SIZE OF BEANS...
...SHE BEGINS THE YOJE-KUKURI STEP, BRINGING THE DOUGH TOGETHER INTO ONE UNIFORM LUMP.
SKWISH
SKWISH
SKWISH
WAAAAA
AMAZ-ING!
NOT AN OUNCE OF MOVEMENT IS WASTED!

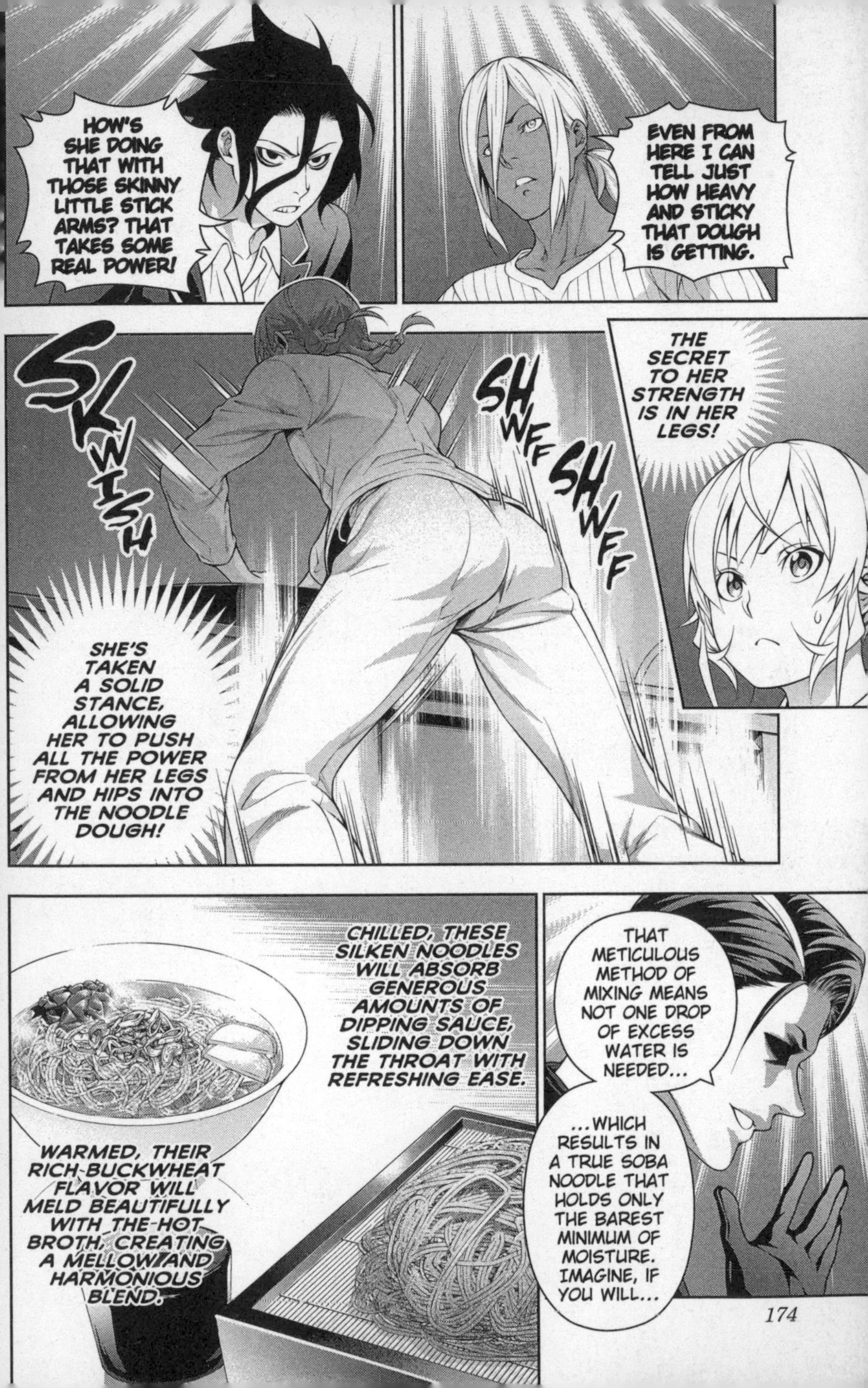
EVEN FROM HERE I CAN TELL JUST HOW HEAVY AND STICKY THAT DOUGH IS GETTING.
HOW'S SHE DOING THAT WITH THOSE SKINNY LITTLE STICK ARMS? THAT TAKES SOME REAL POWER!
THE SECRET TO HER STRENGTH IS IN HER LEGS!
SHWFF SHWFF
SKWISH
SHE'S TAKEN A SOLID STANCE, ALLOWING HER TO PUSH ALL THE POWER FROM HER LEGS AND HIPS INTO THE NOODLE DOUGH!
THAT METICULOUS METHOD OF MIXING MEANS NOT ONE DROP OF EXCESS WATER IS NEEDED...
...WHICH RESULTS IN A TRUE SOBA NOODLE THAT HOLDS ONLY THE BAREST MINIMUM OF MOISTURE. IMAGINE, IF YOU WILL...
CHILLED, THESE SILKEN NOODLES WILL ABSORB GENEROUS AMOUNTS OF DIPPING SAUCE, SLIDING DOWN THE THROAT WITH REFRESHING EASE.
WARMED, THEIR RICH BUCKWHEAT FLAVOR WILL MELD BEAUTIFULLY WITH THE HOT BROTH, CREATING A MELLOW AND HARMONIOUS BLEND.

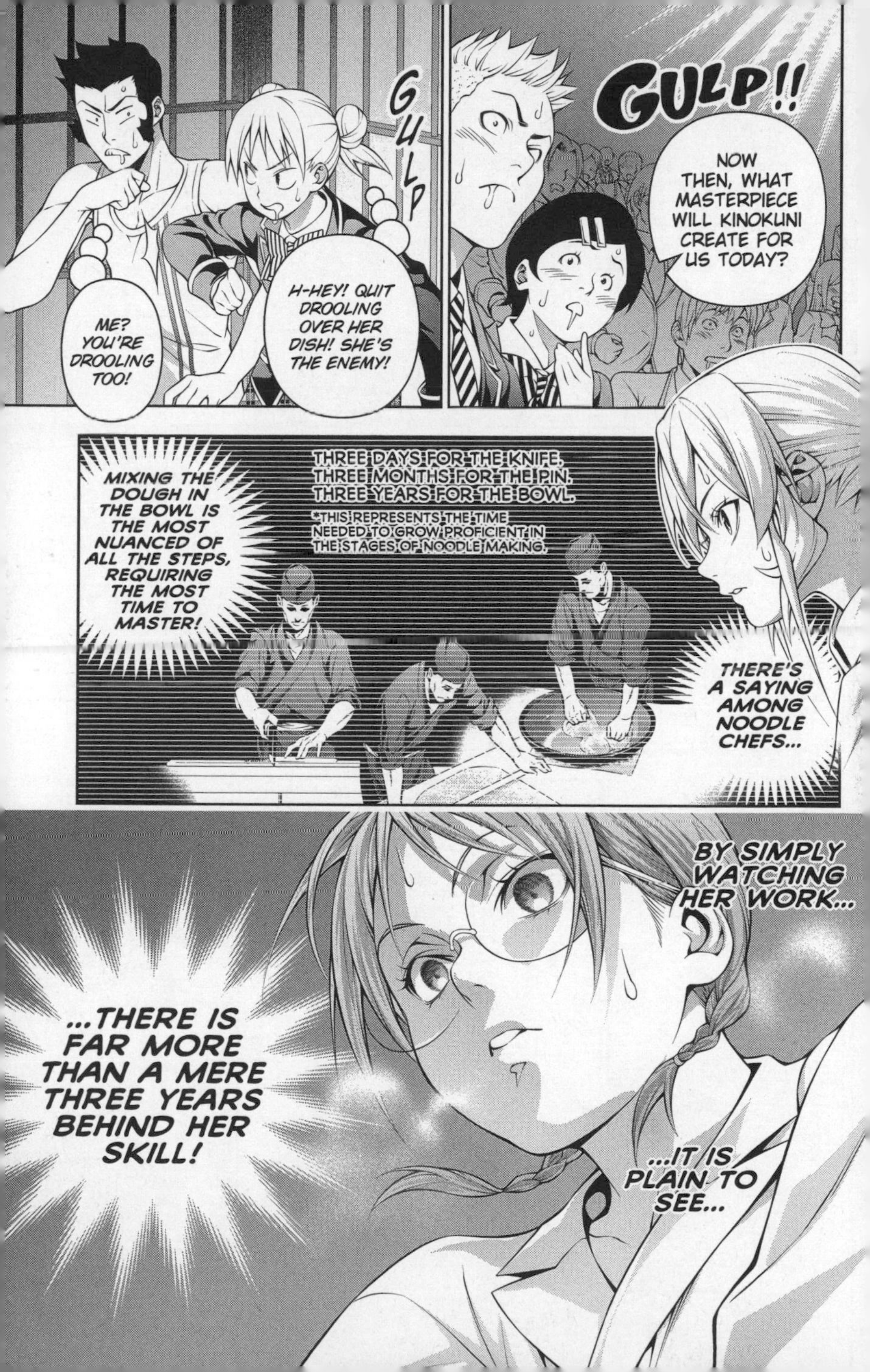
GULP!!
NOW THEN, WHAT MASTERPIECE WILL KINOKUNI CREATE FOR US TODAY?
GULP
H-HEY! QUIT DROOLING OVER HER DISH! SHE'S THE ENEMY!
ME? YOU'RE DROOLING TOO!
THERE'S A SAYING AMONG NOODLE CHEFS...
THREE DAYS FOR THE KNIFE. THREE MONTHS FOR THE PIN. THREE YEARS FOR THE BOWL.
*THIS REPRESENTS THE TIME NEEDED TO GROW PROFICIENT IN THE STAGES OF NOODLE MAKING.
MIXING THE DOUGH IN THE BOWL IS THE MOST NUANCED OF ALL THE STEPS, REQUIRING THE MOST TIME TO MASTER!
BY SIMPLY WATCHING HER WORK...
...IT IS PLAIN TO SEE...
...THERE IS FAR MORE THAN A MERE THREE YEARS BEHIND HER SKILL!

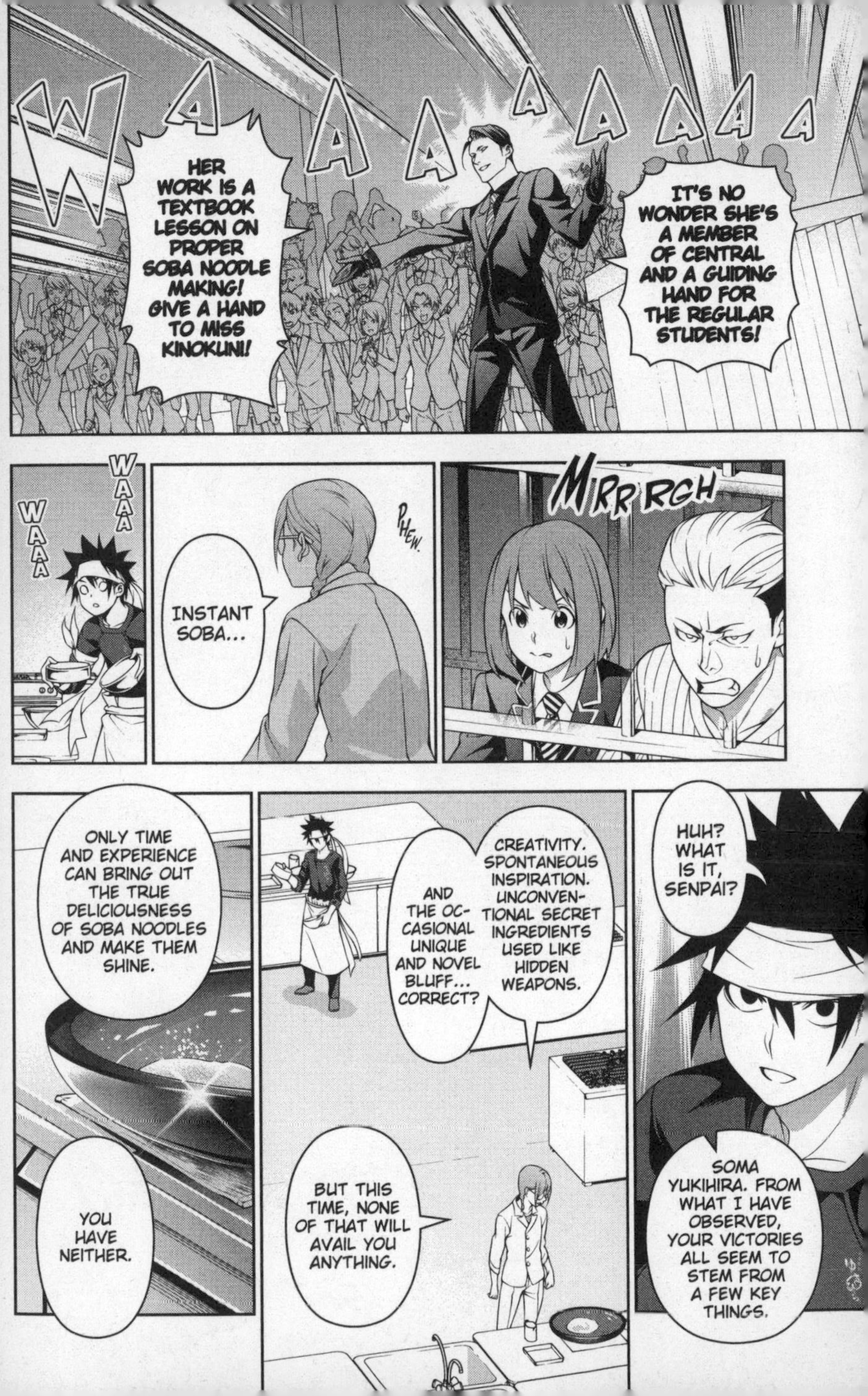
WAAAAAAAAA
IT'S NO WONDER SHE'S A MEMBER OF CENTRAL AND A GUIDING HAND FOR THE REGULAR STUDENTS!
HER WORK IS A TEXTBOOK LESSON ON PROPER SOBA NOODLE MAKING! GIVE A HAND TO MISS KINOKUNI!
MRRRGH
PHEW.
INSTANT SOBA...
WAAA
WAAA
HUH? WHAT IS IT, SENPAI?
SOMA YUKIHIRA. FROM WHAT I HAVE OBSERVED, YOUR VICTORIES ALL SEEM TO STEM FROM A FEW KEY THINGS.
CREATIVITY. SPONTANEOUS INSPIRATION. UNCONVENTIONAL SECRET INGREDIENTS USED LIKE HIDDEN WEAPONS.
AND THE OCCASIONAL UNIQUE AND NOVEL BLUFF... CORRECT?
BUT THIS TIME, NONE OF THAT WILL AVAIL YOU ANYTHING.
ONLY TIME AND EXPERIENCE CAN BRING OUT THE TRUE DELICIOUSNESS OF SOBA NOODLES AND MAKE THEM SHINE.
YOU HAVE NEITHER.

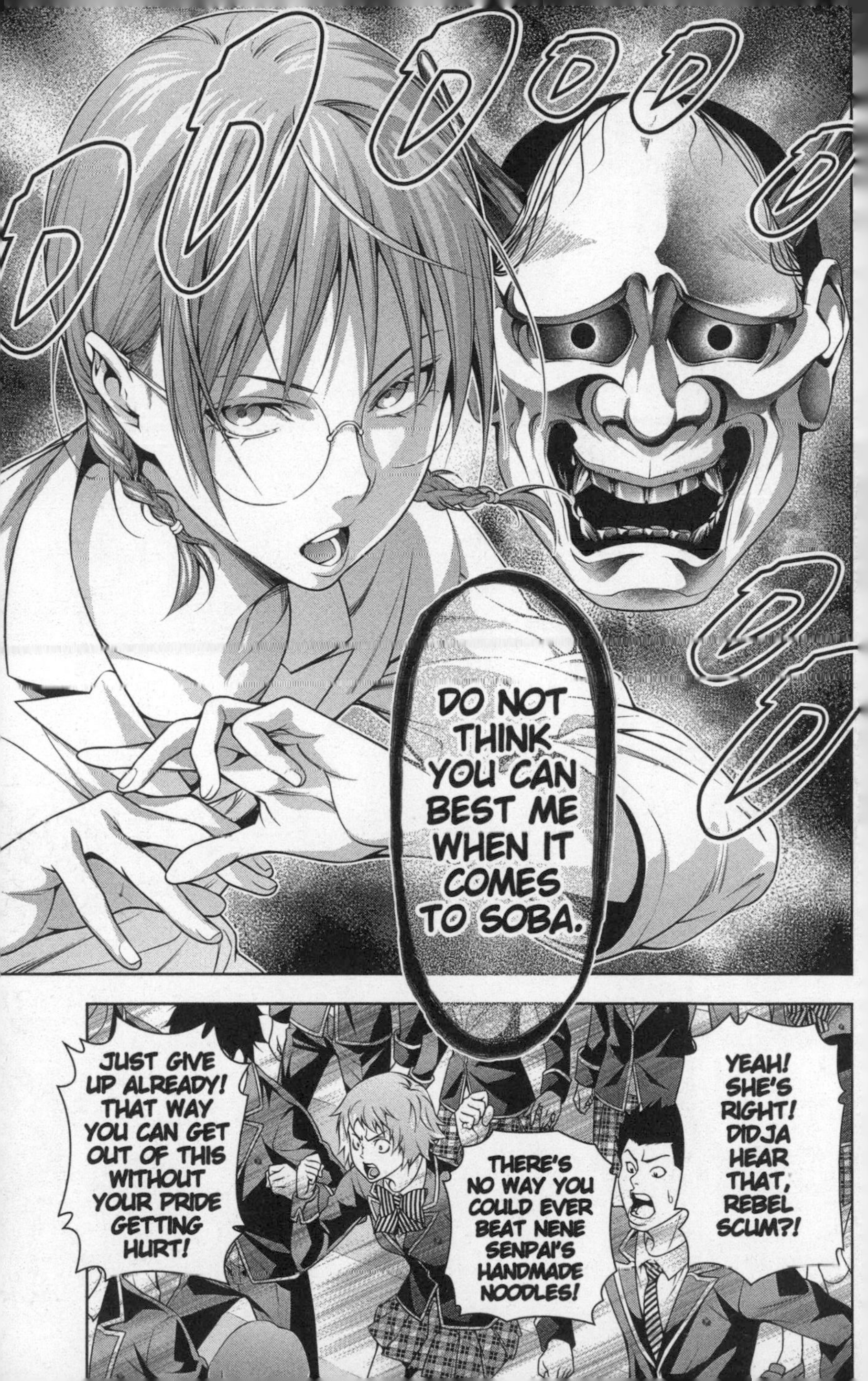
DO NOT THINK YOU CAN BEST ME WHEN IT COMES TO SOBA.
YEAH! SHE'S RIGHT! DIDJA HEAR THAT, REBEL SCUM?!
THERE'S NO WAY YOU COULD EVER BEAT NENE SENPAI'S HANDMADE NOODLES!
JUST GIVE UP ALREADY! THAT WAY YOU CAN GET OUT OF THIS WITHOUT YOUR PRIDE GETTING HURT!

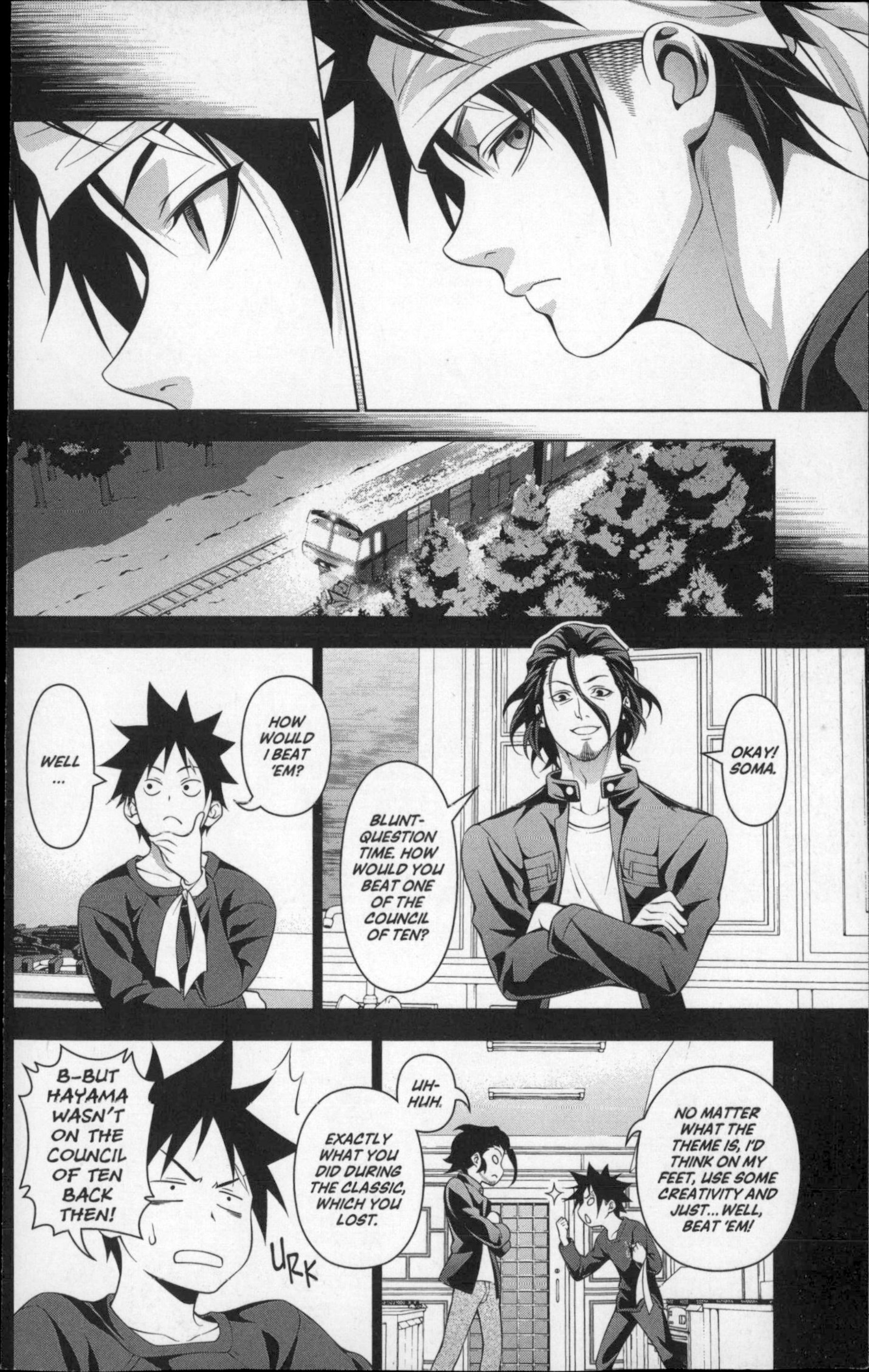
OKAY! SOMA.
BLUNT-QUESTION TIME. HOW WOULD YOU BEAT ONE OF THE COUNCIL OF TEN?
HOW WOULD I BEAT 'EM?
WELL ...
NO MATTER WHAT THE THEME IS, I'D THINK ON MY FEET, USE SOME CREATIVITY AND JUST... WELL, BEAT 'EM!
UH-HUH.
EXACTLY WHAT YOU DID DURING THE CLASSIC, WHICH YOU LOST.
URK
B-BUT HAYAMA WASN'T ON THE COUNCIL OF TEN BACK THEN!

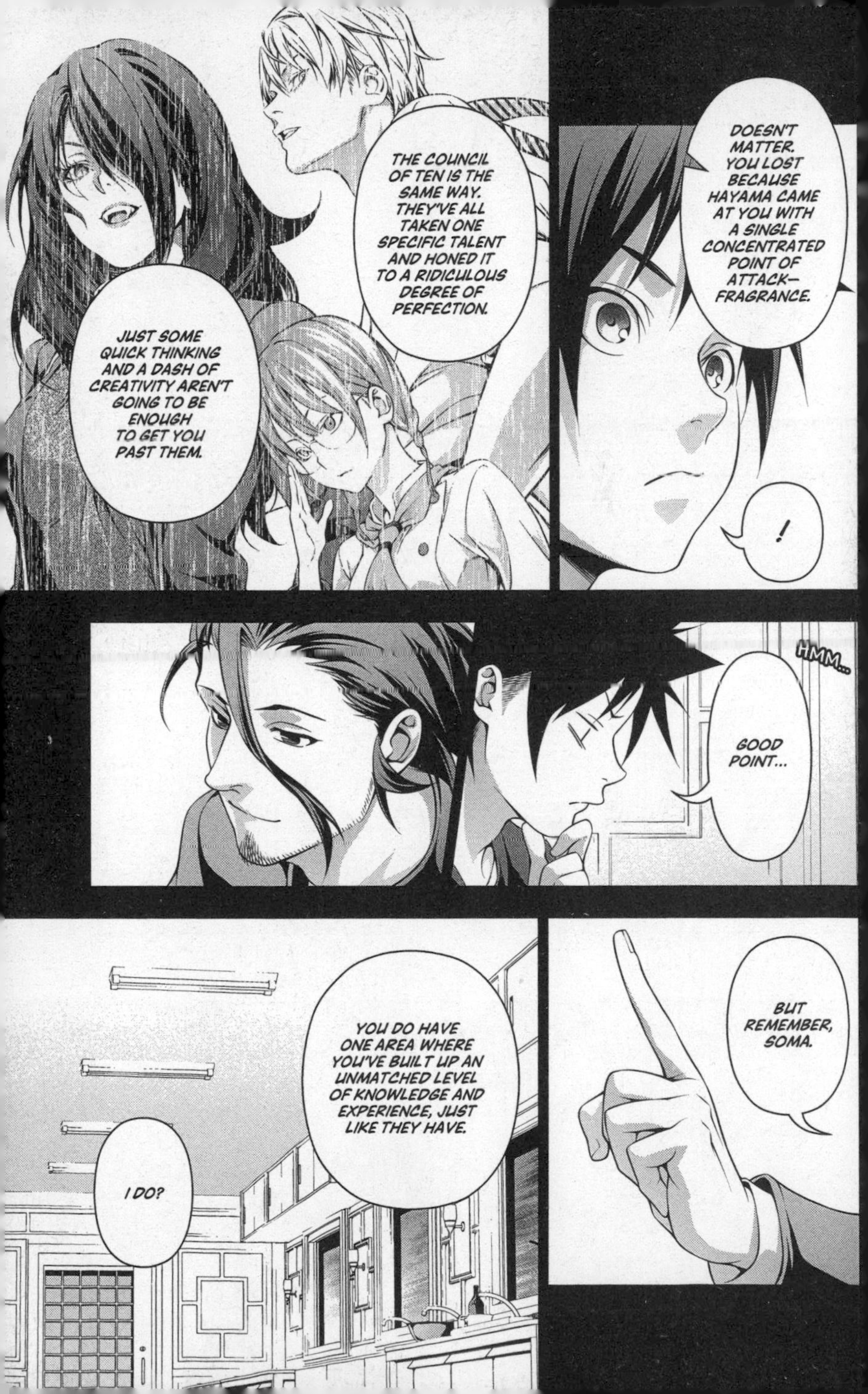
DOESN'T MATTER. YOU LOST BECAUSE HAYAMA CAME AT YOU WITH A SINGLE CONCENTRATED POINT OF ATTACK—FRAGRANCE.
!
THE COUNCIL OF TEN IS THE SAME WAY. THEY'VE ALL TAKEN ONE SPECIFIC TALENT AND HONED IT TO A RIDICULOUS DEGREE OF PERFECTION.
JUST SOME QUICK THINKING AND A DASH OF CREATIVITY AREN'T GOING TO BE ENOUGH TO GET YOU PAST THEM.
HMM...
GOOD POINT...
BUT REMEMBER, SOMA.
YOU DO HAVE ONE AREA WHERE YOU'VE BUILT UP AN UNMATCHED LEVEL OF KNOWLEDGE AND EXPERIENCE, JUST LIKE THEY HAVE.
I DO?

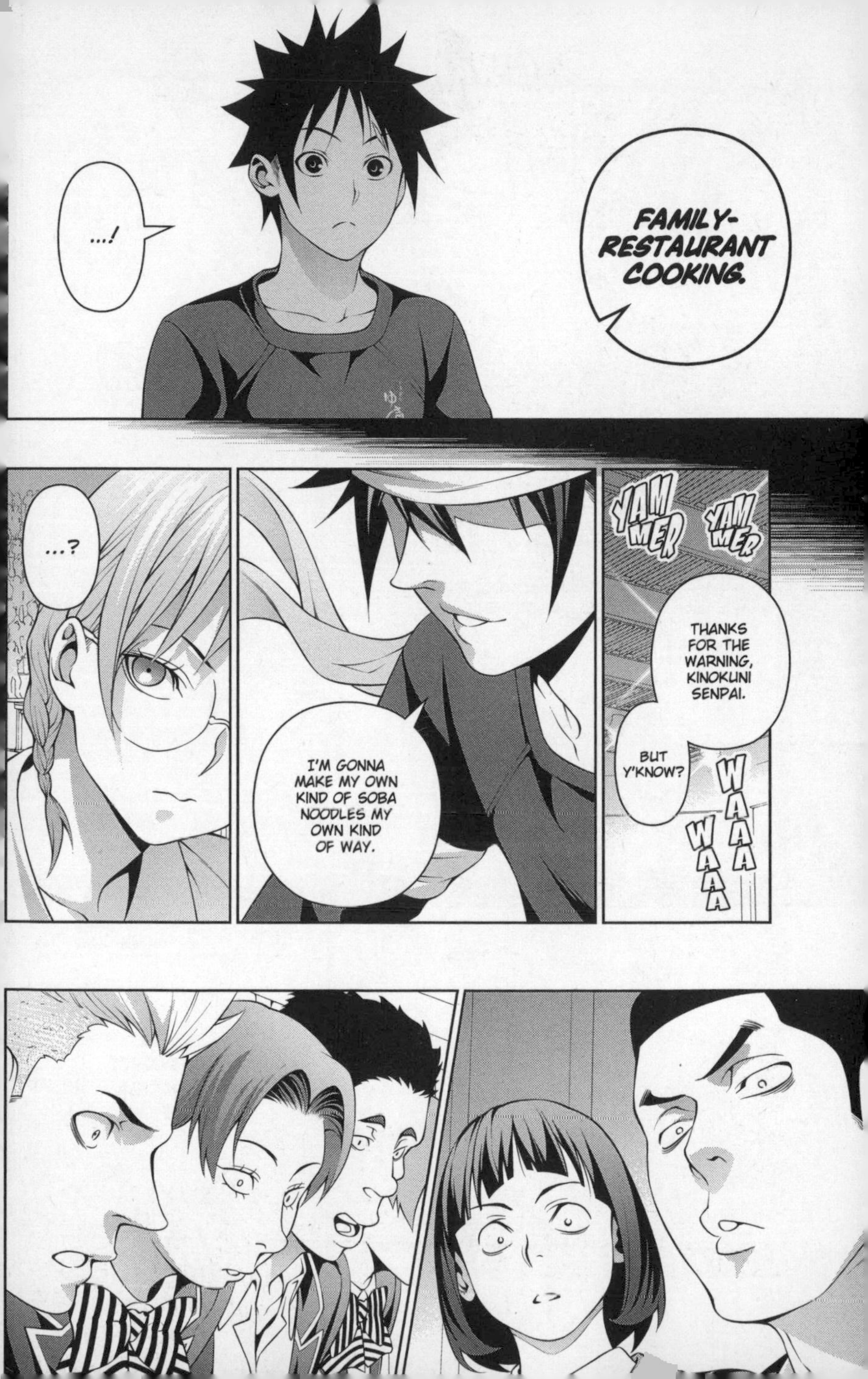
FAMILY-RESTAURANT COOKING.
...!
YAMMER YAMMER
THANKS FOR THE WARNING, KINOKUNI SENPAI.
BUT Y'KNOW?
WAAA WAAA
I'M GONNA MAKE MY OWN KIND OF SOBA NOODLES MY OWN KIND OF WAY.
...?

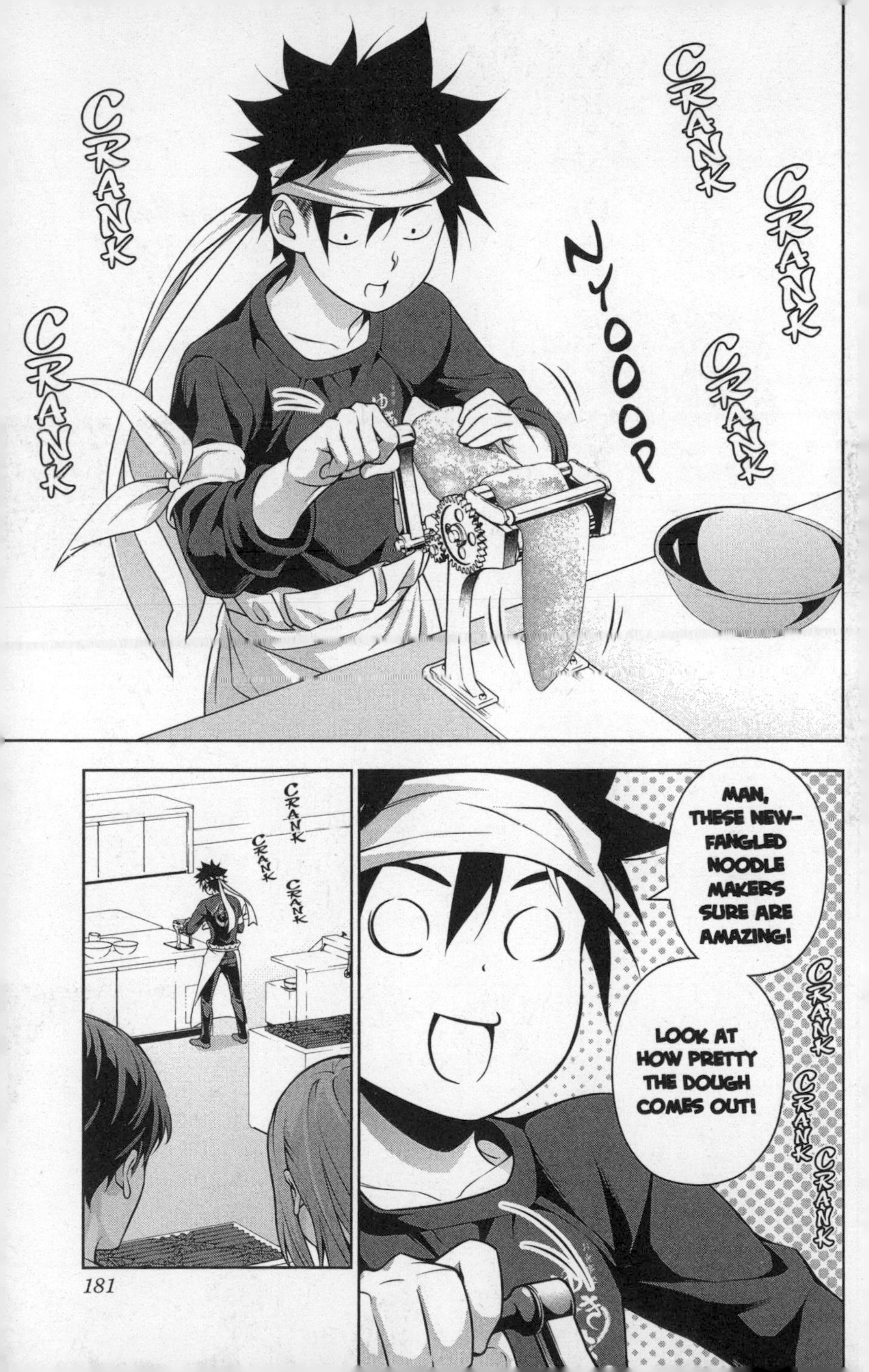
CRANK
CRANK
CRANK
NYOOOP
CRANK
CRANK
MAN, THESE NEW-FANGLED NOODLE MAKERS SURE ARE AMAZING!
LOOK AT HOW PRETTY THE DOUGH COMES OUT!
CRANK
CRANK
CRANK
CRANK
CRANK
CRANK

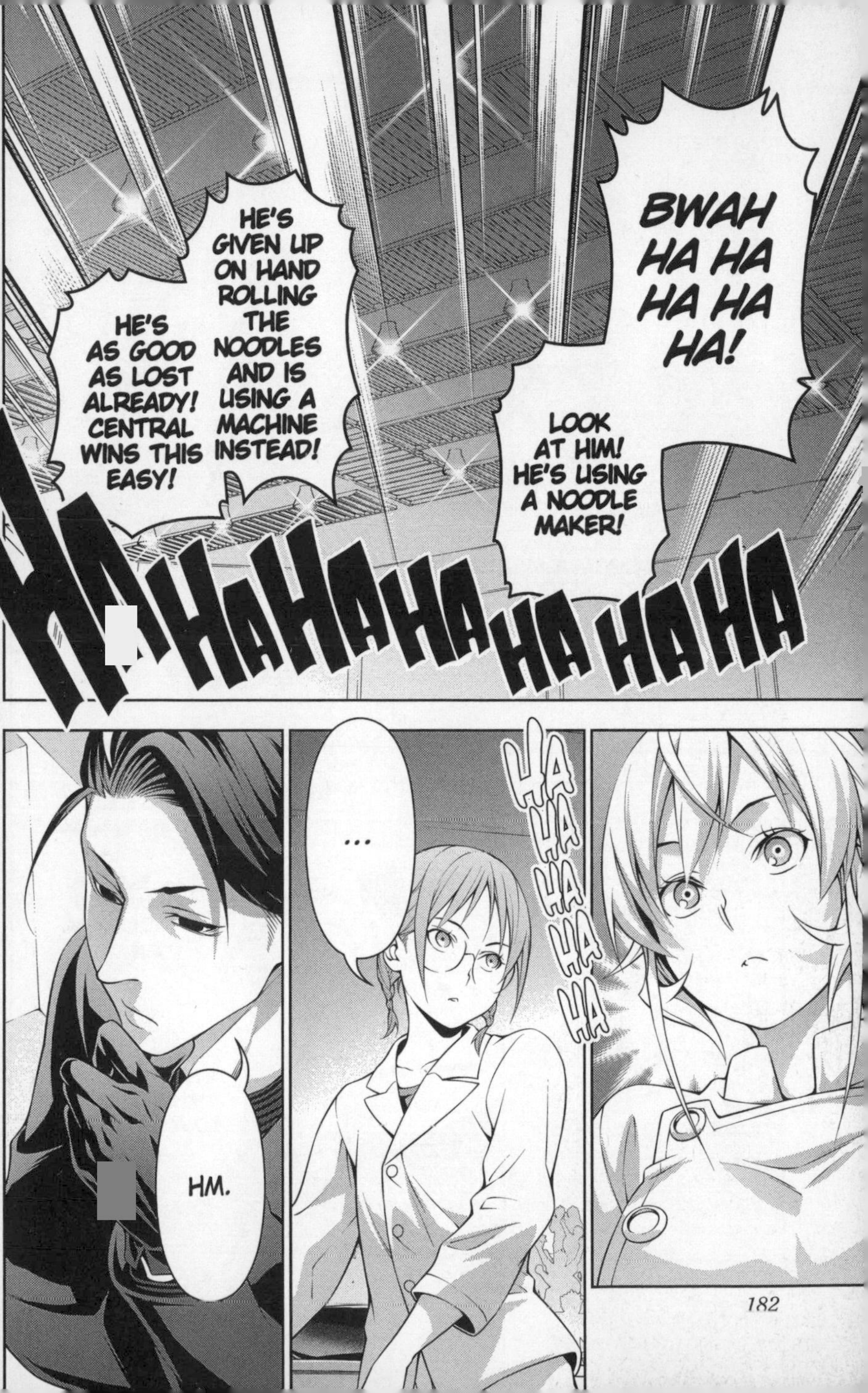

BWAH HA HA HA HA HA!
LOOK AT HIM! HE'S USING A NOODLE MAKER!
HE'S GIVEN UP ON HAND ROLLING THE NOODLES AND IS USING A MACHINE INSTEAD!
HE'S AS GOOD AS LOST ALREADY! CENTRAL WINS THIS EASY!
HA HAHAHAHA HA HAHA
HA HA HA HA HA
...
HM.

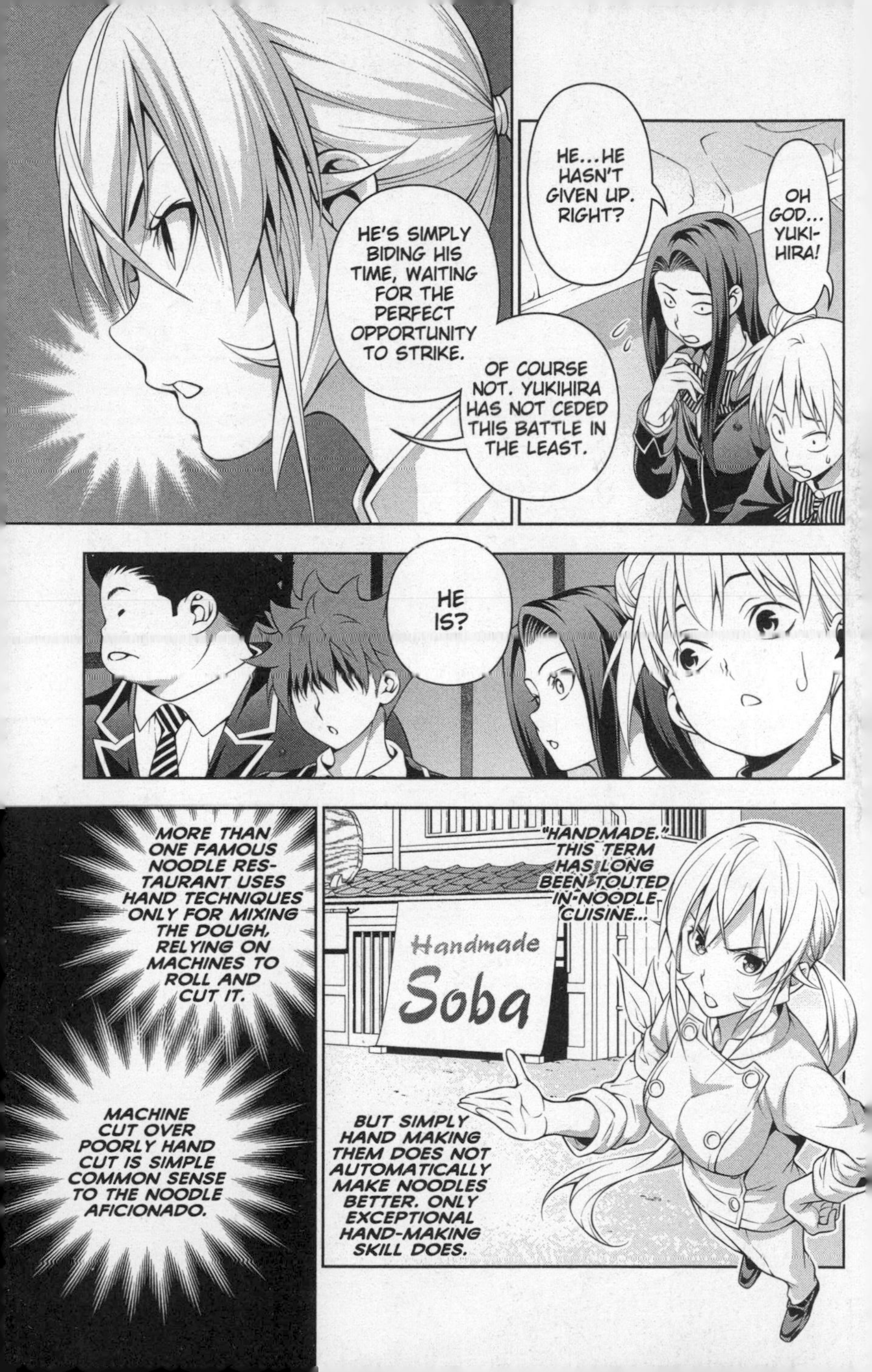

OH GOD... YUKIHIRA!
HE...HE HASN'T GIVEN UP. RIGHT?
OF COURSE NOT. YUKIHIRA HAS NOT CEDED THIS BATTLE IN THE LEAST.
HE'S SIMPLY BIDING HIS TIME, WAITING FOR THE PERFECT OPPORTUNITY TO STRIKE.
HE IS?
"HANDMADE." THIS TERM HAS LONG BEEN TOUTED IN NOODLE CUISINE...
Handmade Soba
BUT SIMPLY HAND MAKING THEM DOES NOT AUTOMATICALLY MAKE NOODLES BETTER. ONLY EXCEPTIONAL HAND-MAKING SKILL DOES.
MORE THAN ONE FAMOUS NOODLE RESTAURANT USES HAND TECHNIQUES ONLY FOR MIXING THE DOUGH, RELYING ON MACHINES TO ROLL AND CUT IT.
MACHINE CUT OVER POORLY HAND CUT IS SIMPLE COMMON SENSE TO THE NOODLE AFICIONADO.

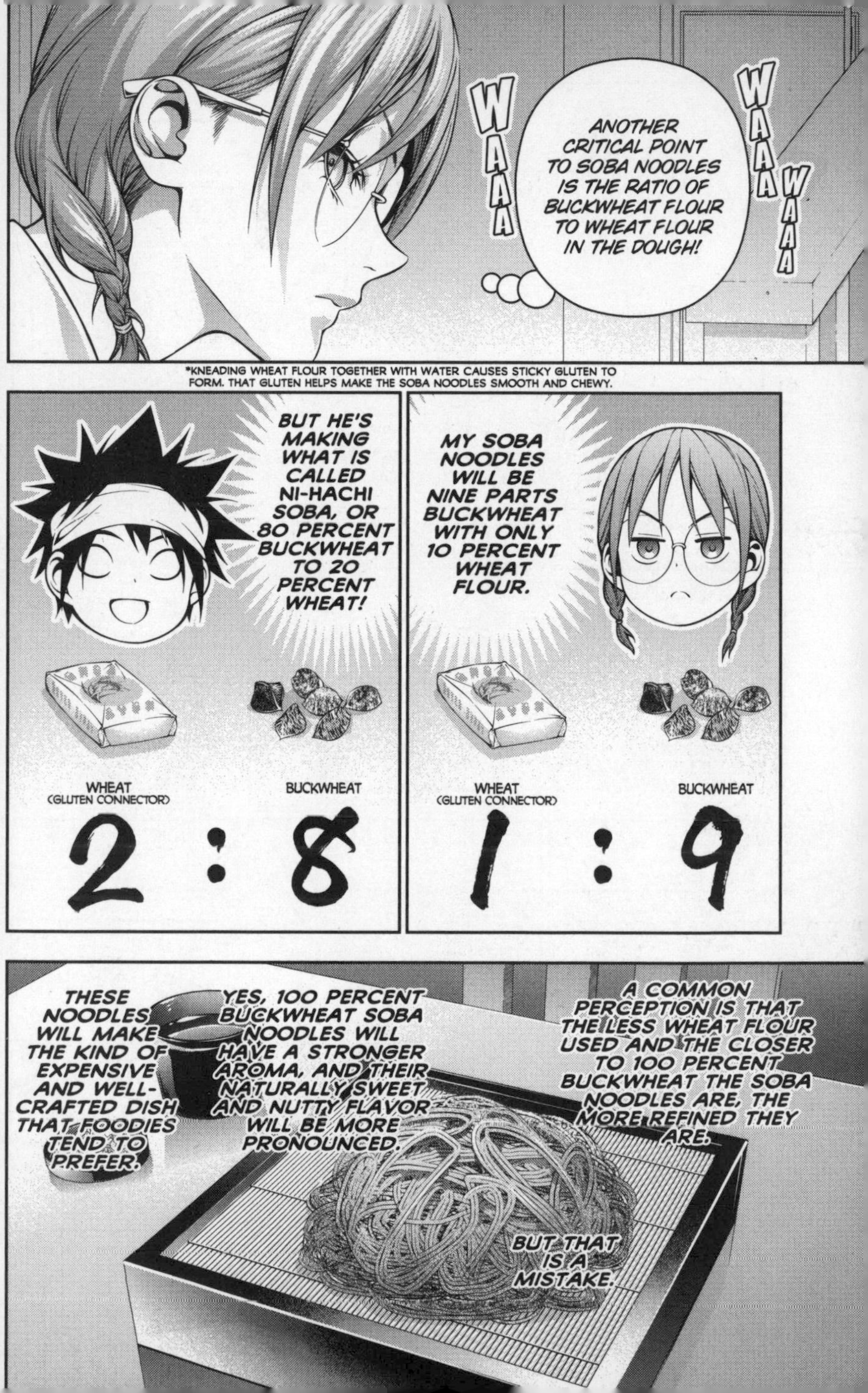
WAAAA
ANOTHER CRITICAL POINT TO SOBA NOODLES IS THE RATIO OF BUCKWHEAT FLOUR TO WHEAT FLOUR IN THE DOUGH!
WAAAA
WAAAA
*KNEADING WHEAT FLOUR TOGETHER WITH WATER CAUSES STICKY GLUTEN TO FORM. THAT GLUTEN HELPS MAKE THE SOBA NOODLES SMOOTH AND CHEWY.
MY SOBA NOODLES WILL BE NINE PARTS BUCKWHEAT WITH ONLY 10 PERCENT WHEAT FLOUR.
WHEAT (GLUTEN CONNECTOR)
BUCKWHEAT
1 : 9
BUT HE'S MAKING WHAT IS CALLED NI-HACHI SOBA, OR 80 PERCENT BUCKWHEAT TO 20 PERCENT WHEAT!
WHEAT (GLUTEN CONNECTOR)
BUCKWHEAT
2 : 8
A COMMON PERCEPTION IS THAT THE LESS WHEAT FLOUR USED AND THE CLOSER TO 100 PERCENT BUCKWHEAT THE SOBA NOODLES ARE, THE MORE REFINED THEY ARE.
YES, 100 PERCENT BUCKWHEAT SOBA NOODLES WILL HAVE A STRONGER AROMA, AND THEIR NATURALLY SWEET AND NUTTY FLAVOR WILL BE MORE PRONOUNCED.
THESE NOODLES WILL MAKE THE KIND OF EXPENSIVE AND WELL-CRAFTED DISH THAT FOODIES TEND TO PREFER.
BUT THAT IS A MISTAKE.

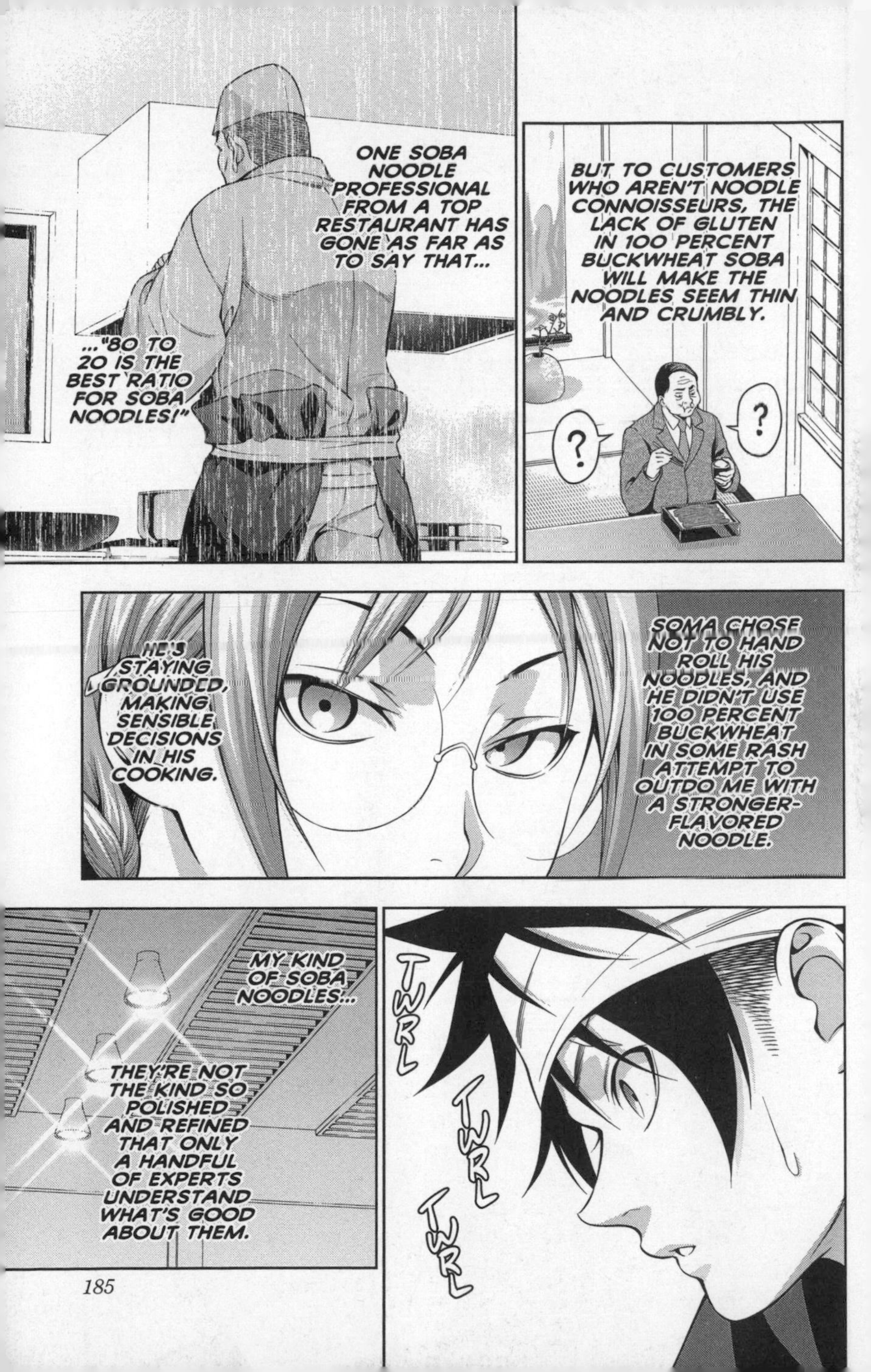
BUT TO CUSTOMERS WHO AREN'T NOODLE CONNOISSEURS, THE LACK OF GLUTEN IN 100 PERCENT BUCKWHEAT SOBA WILL MAKE THE NOODLES SEEM THIN AND CRUMBLY.
?
?
ONE SOBA NOODLE PROFESSIONAL FROM A TOP RESTAURANT HAS GONE AS FAR AS TO SAY THAT...
..."80 TO 20 IS THE BEST RATIO FOR SOBA NOODLES!"
SOMA CHOSE NOT TO HAND ROLL HIS NOODLES, AND HE DIDN'T USE 100 PERCENT BUCKWHEAT IN SOME RASH ATTEMPT TO OUTDO ME WITH A STRONGER-FLAVORED NOODLE.
HE'S STAYING GROUNDED, MAKING SENSIBLE DECISIONS IN HIS COOKING.
TWRL
TWRL
TWRL
MY KIND OF SOBA NOODLES...
THEY'RE NOT THE KIND SO POLISHED AND REFINED THAT ONLY A HANDFUL OF EXPERTS UNDERSTAND WHAT'S GOOD ABOUT THEM.

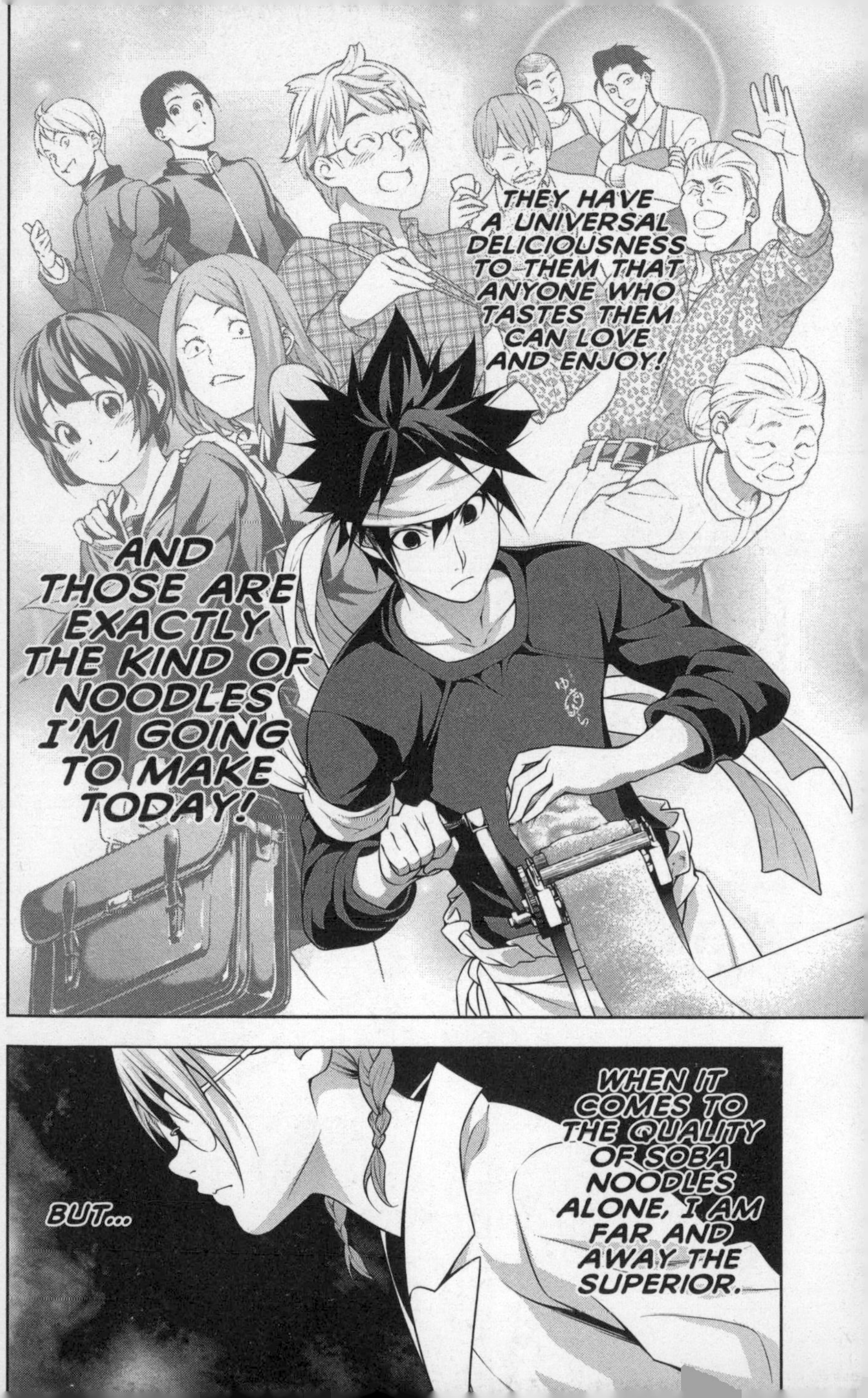
THEY HAVE A UNIVERSAL DELICIOUSNESS TO THEM THAT ANYONE WHO TASTES THEM CAN LOVE AND ENJOY!
AND THOSE ARE EXACTLY THE KIND OF NOODLES I'M GOING TO MAKE TODAY!
WHEN IT COMES TO THE QUALITY OF SOBA NOODLES ALONE, I AM FAR AND AWAY THE SUPERIOR.
BUT...

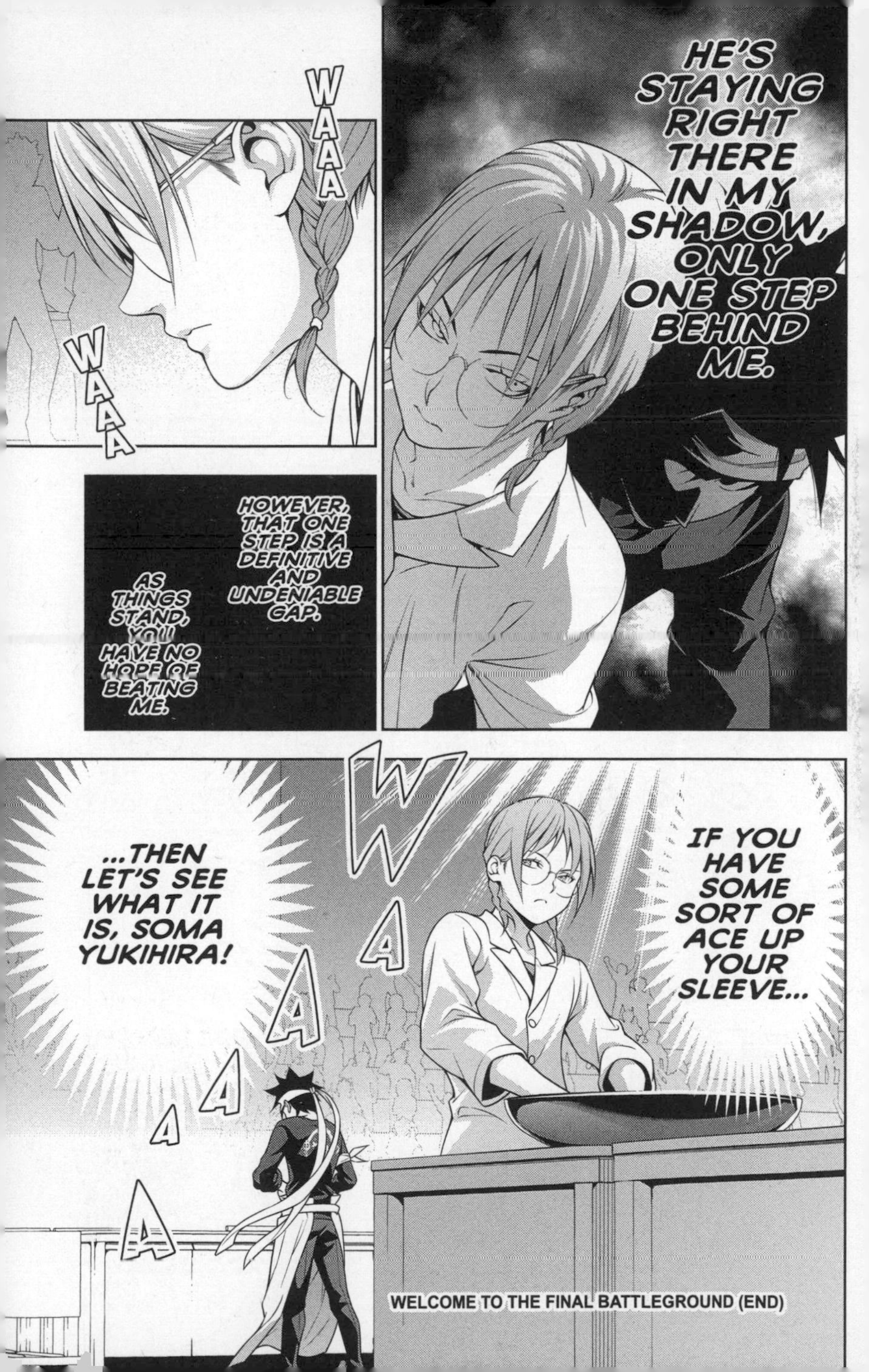
HE'S STAYING RIGHT THERE IN MY SHADOW, ONLY ONE STEP BEHIND ME.
WAAA
WAAA
HOWEVER, THAT ONE STEP IS A DEFINITIVE AND UNDENIABLE GAP.
AS THINGS STAND, YOU HAVE NO HOPE OF BEATING ME.
IF YOU HAVE SOME SORT OF ACE UP YOUR SLEEVE...
WAAAAAA
...THEN LET'S SEE WHAT IT IS, SOMA YUKIHIRA!
WELCOME TO THE FINAL BATTLEGROUND (END)

V24 BONUS STORY 1

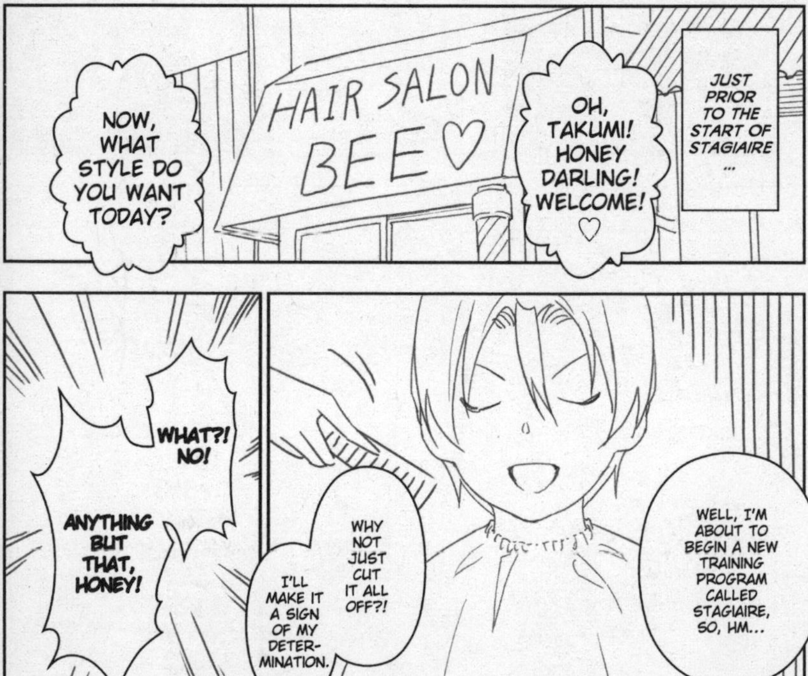
JUST PRIOR TO THE START OF STAGIAIRE ...
OH, TAKUMI! HONEY DARLING! WELCOME! ♡
HAIR SALON BEE ♡
NOW, WHAT STYLE DO YOU WANT TODAY?
WELL, I'M ABOUT TO BEGIN A NEW TRAINING PROGRAM CALLED STAGIAIRE, SO, HM...
WHY NOT JUST CUT IT ALL OFF?!
I'LL MAKE IT A SIGN OF MY DETER-MINATION.
WHAT?! NO!
ANYTHING BUT THAT, HONEY!

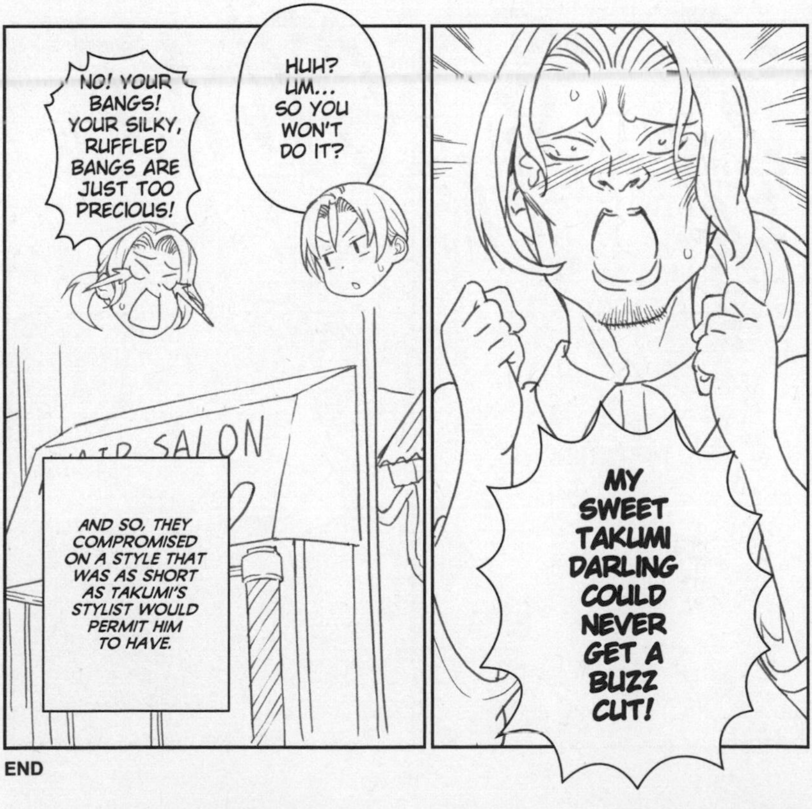
MY SWEET TAKUMI DARLING COULD NEVER GET A BUZZ CUT!
HUH? UM... SO YOU WON'T DO IT?
NO! YOUR BANGS! YOUR SILKY, RUFFLED BANGS ARE JUST TOO PRECIOUS!
SALON
AND SO, THEY COMPROMISED ON A STYLE THAT WAS AS SHORT AS TAKUMI'S STYLIST WOULD PERMIT HIM TO HAVE.

END

V24 BONUS STORY 2

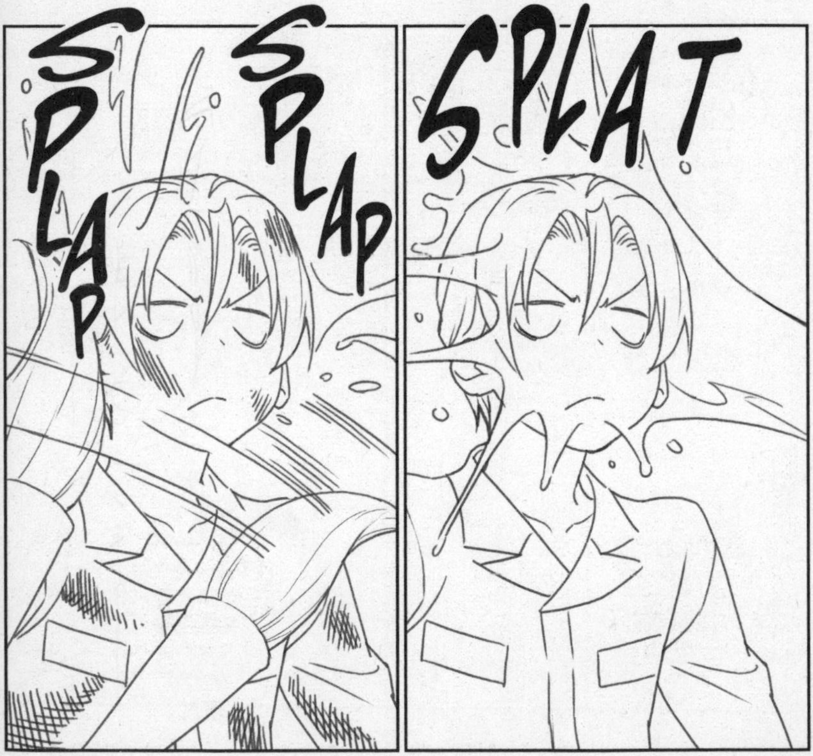
SPLAT
SPLAP
SPLAP

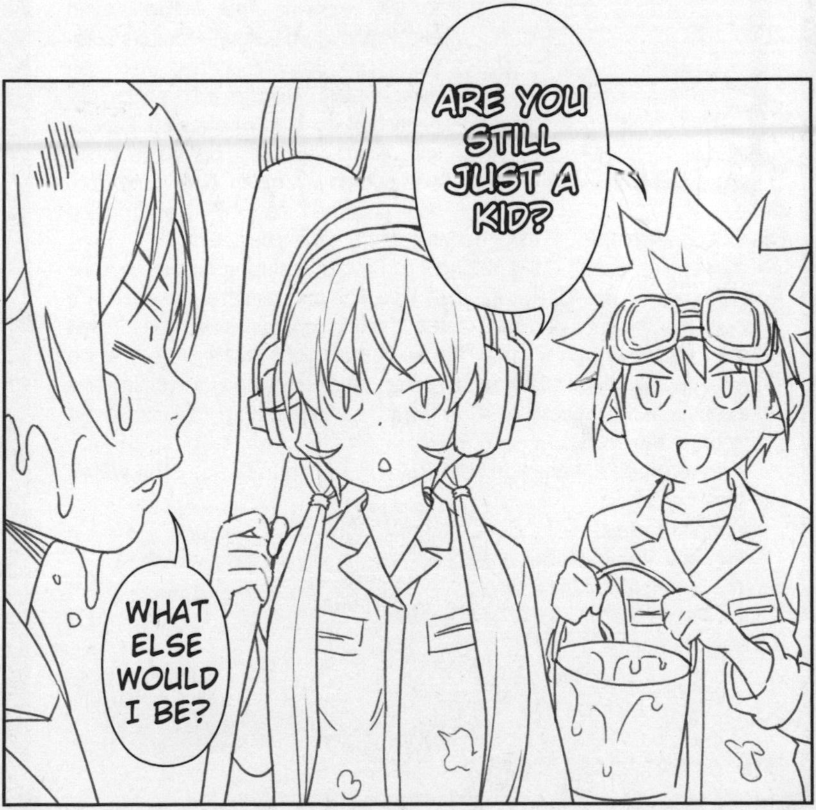
ARE YOU STILL JUST A KID?
WHAT ELSE WOULD I BE?

END

You're R
the Wrong Direction!!

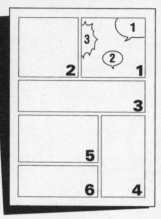

Whoops! Guess what? You're starting at the wrong end of the comic!

...It's true! In keeping with the original Japanese format, **Food Wars!** is meant to be read from right to left, starting in the upper-right corner.

Unlike English, which is read from left to right, Japanese is read from right to left, meaning that action, sound effects and word-balloon order are completely reversed... something which can make readers unfamiliar with Japanese feel pretty backwards themselves. For this reason, manga or Japanese comics published in the U.S. in English have sometimes been published "flopped"—that is, printed in exact reverse order, as though seen from the other side of a mirror.

By flopping pages, U.S. publishers can avoid confusing readers, but the compromise is not without its downside. For one thing, a character in a flopped manga series who once wore in the original Japanese version a T-shirt emblazoned with "M A Y" (as in "the merry month of") now wears one which reads "Y A M"! Additionally, many manga creators in Japan are themselves unhappy with the process, as some feel the mirror-imaging of their art skews their original intentions.

We are proud to bring you Yuto Tsukuda and Shun Saeki's **Food Wars!** in the original unflopped format.

For now, though, turn to the other side of the book and let the adventure begin...!

—Editor